Praise for
A PLACE FOR EVERYTHING

"Fascinating. . . . *A Place for Everything* rewards us with a fresh take on our quest to stockpile knowledge. It feels particularly relevant now that search engines are rendering old ways of organizing information obsolete. . . . That we have acquired so much knowledge is astounding; that we have devised ways to find what we need to know quickly is what merits this original and impressive book."   —*New York Times*

"Fascinating. . . . Truly revelatory."   —*Wall Street Journal*

"One of the many fascinations of Judith Flanders's book is that it reveals what a weird, unlikely creation the alphabet is. . . . An intriguing history not just of alphabetical order but of the human need for both pattern and intellectual efficiency."   —*Guardian*

"A charming repository of idiosyncrasy, a love letter to literacy that rightly delights in alphabetisation's exceptions as much as its rules."   —*Financial Times*

"This is an utterly charming book, packed with engrossing details."   —*Times (UK)*

"For readers who love language or armchair historians interested in the evolution of linguistics, this is catnip. For the mildly curious, it's accessible, narratively adventurous, and surprisingly insightful about how the alphabet marks us all in some way. . . . A rich cultural and linguistic history."   —*Kirkus*

"*A Place for Everything* presents itself as a history of alphabetical order, but in fact it is much more than that. Rather, as the title suggests, it offers something like a general history of the various ways humans have sorted and filed the world around them."   —*Spectator*

"Quirky and compelling. . . . [Flanders] is a meticulous historian with a taste for the offbeat; the story of alphabetical order suits her well."
                        —Dan Jones, *Sunday Times (UK)*

"Surprising and copiously researched."
                        —*Times Literary Supplement*

"Flanders is one of our outstanding popular historians. . . . *A Place for Everything* is an exemplar of the form on which it focuses."
                        —*The Critic*

"Flanders is especially good in discussing when and why alphabetical order was *not* used, or was resisted, even after it was available. . . . The prose is engaging andvthe examples are to the point."
                        —Jack Lynch, *Dictionaries: Journal of the Dictionary Society of North America*

A PLACE
FOR EVERYTHING

A PLACE FOR EVERYTHING

The Curious History of
Alphabetical
Order

JUDITH FLANDERS

BASIC BOOKS
New York

Basic Books
Hachette Book Group
1290 Avenue of the Americas, New York, NY 10104
www.basicbooks.com

Printed in the United States of America

Originally published in 2020 by Picador in the United Kingdom

Published in hardcover and ebook by Basic Books in the US in October 2020
First Trade Paperback Edition: May 2022

Published by Basic Books, an imprint of Perseus Books, LLC, a subsidiary of Hachette
Book Group, Inc. The Basic Books name and logo is a trademark of the Hachette Book
Group.

The Hachette Speakers Bureau provides a wide range of authors for speaking events.
To find out more, go to www.hachettespeakersbureau.com or call (866) 376-6591.

The publisher is not responsible for websites (or their content) that are not owned
by the publisher.

Additional copyright/credits information is on pp. xi–xiii.

Print book interior design by Jeff Williams.

Library of Congress Control Number: 2020943305

ISBNs: 9781541675070 (hardcover); 9781541675063 (ebook);
9781541601161 (trade paperback)

LSC-C

Printing 1, 2022

The aspects of things that are most important for
us are hidden because of their simplicity and
familiarity. . . . We fail to be struck by what,
once seen, is most striking and most powerful.

LUDWIG WITTGENSTEIN
Philosophical Investigations, §129

In memory of my grandmother

DORIS K. MORRISON

who loved a good tidy-up

CONTENTS

List of Illustrations   *xi*
Acknowledgments   *xv*
Preface   *xvii*

Chapter 1

A IS FOR ANTIQUITY

From the Beginning to the Classical World   I

Chapter 2

B IS FOR THE BENEDICTINES

The Monasteries and the Early Middle Ages   27

Chapter 3

C IS FOR CATEGORIES

Authorities and Organization, to the Twelfth Century   43

Chapter 4

D IS FOR DISTINCTIONES

The High Middle Ages and the Search Tool   71

Chapter 5

E IS FOR EXPANSION

The Reference Work in the Thirteenth and Fourteenth Centuries   91

Chapter 6

F IS FOR FIRSTS

From the Birth of Printing to Library Catalogs in the
Fifteenth to Sixteenth Centuries   105

Chapter 7

G IS FOR GOVERNMENT

Bureaucracy and the Office, from the
Sixteenth Century to the French Revolution   131

Chapter 8

H IS FOR HISTORY

Libraries, Research, and Extracting in the
Seventeenth and Eighteenth Centuries   167

Chapter 9

I IS FOR INDEX CARDS

From Copy Clerks to Office Supplies in the
Nineteenth Century   197

Chapter 10

Y IS FOR Y2K

From the Phone Book to Hypertext in the
Twentieth and Twenty-first Centuries   221

Timeline   237
Bibliography   243
Notes   265
Index   301

Photo section appears after page 166

LIST OF ILLUSTRATIONS

IN THE TEXT

1. A round robin letter of 1621, petitioning for the right of Huguenots to settle in the New World. Wikicommons.

2. The first page of a letter in rebus form from Lewis Carroll, the author of *Alice's Adventures in Wonderland* (1865). *The Letters of Lewis Carroll*, ed. Morton N. Cohen, with Roger Lancelyn Green, vol. 1, c. 1837–1885 (London: Macmillan, 1979).

3. Old Babylonian clay tablet, c.1900–1700 BCE. British Museum.

4. A table showing some of Ralph de Diceto's marginal symbols in his *Abbreviationes chronicorum*, Chronicles Précised. British Library Board. Bridgeman Images.

5. The Bakhshali manuscript, third to seventh centuries. Wikicommons.

6. A manuscript copy of the *Decretum Gratiani* dating from the first half of the thirteenth century. Sion/Sitten, Archives du Chapitre/Kapitels-archiv, Ms. 89, f. 223r.

7. Abraham Ortelius, *Thesaurus geographicus*, Geographical Treasure-house. Museum Plantin-Moretus, Antwerp—UNESCO, World Heritage.

8. A writing desk belonging to either Henry VIII or Catherine of Aragon, c. 1525. Victoria and Albert Museum, London.

9. The *Wunderkammer* of Ole Worms. Wikicommons.

10. A piece of specialist furniture for categorizing and displaying a collection, illustrated in Levinus Vincent, *The Wonders of Nature* (1706).

11. A type case housing a printer's metal type. Alamy.

12. Harrison's Ark, as illustrated in Vincentius Placcius, *The Art of Excerpting* (1689).

13. An illustration of the typographical desk from Louis Dumas, *La biblioteque des enfans, ou les premiers elemens des lettres*, The Children's Library, or, First Elements of Writing (1733).

14. A page illustrating Locke's indexing system for commonplace books.

15. A sample page from Bayle's *Dictionaire critique*.

16. A modern solander box. Macmillan Publishers International Limited.

17. The *New York Times* newsroom in the 1920s. Wikicommons.

18. An advertisement for a copy press; an 1890s office.

19. A pigeonhole-style desk in use. Artokoloro Quint Lox Ltd/Alamy.

20. The original Shannon lever-arch file. Hemesh Alles.

IN THE INSERT

21. A fifteenth-century depiction of the *trivium* and the *quadrivium*. Unibibliothek Salzburg, M III 36. Wikicommons.

22. The presentation of an index to the Gospel Commentary of William of Nottingham to the Archbishop of Canterbury. The Bodleian Library, University of Oxford, MS Laud Misc 165, f.5r.

23. Jan Gossart, *Portrait of a Tax-collector* (c. 1530). National Gallery of Art, Washington.

24. A Flemish manuscript of Christine de Pizan's *The City of Women*, 1475. British Library Board. Bridgeman Images.

25. The eighteenth-century library at Admont Abbey. © Jorge Royan / www.royan.com.ar / CC BY-SA 3.0.

26. Bartholomeus van der Helst, *Portrait of Daniël Bernard* (1669). Museum Boijmans van Beuningen, Rotterdam.

27. Detail from Gerrit Berckheyde, *A Notary in His Office* (1672). Wikicommons.

28. Detail from Chardin, *The House of Cards* (1736/7). The National Gallery, London. Bequeathed by Mrs. Edith Cragg, as part of the John Webb Bequest, 1925.

29. A collector's cabinet, 1730. Rijksmuseum, Amsterdam.

30. A Wooton desk, after 1875. Alamy.

31. Gospels of Maél Brigte, or the Armagh Gospels, c. 1138. British Library Board. Bridgeman Images.

32. An early fifteenth-century manuscript of Chaucer's *Canterbury Tales*, known as the Ellesmere Chaucer. EL 26 C 9, Huntington Library, San Marino, California.

ACKNOWLEDGMENTS

As always, my debts far outweigh my ability to thank people and institutions.

I am grateful, first and foremost, to the unknown curators of the Joseph Cornell exhibition at the Royal Academy, London, in 2015, for setting me on a path to look anew at the subject of categories and classification, and to the work of Joseph Cornell himself, for making me realize how very strange the notion of classifying is.

More pragmatically, I am grateful to Dean Antonia Maioni, and to McGill University, Montreal, Canada, where I spent a summer as a Visiting Scholar, and where a great deal of the research for this book was done. My thanks go also to Dr. Richard Cruess, who made the initial contact for me. Christopher Lyons, Head of Rare Books and Special Collections, together with his team, welcomed me, and I am grateful to them, particularly to Melissa Como, who more than once patiently walked me through their systems. My thanks are also due to Associate Dean Nathalie Cooke, Professor Faith Wallis, and Associate Professor Trevor Ponech for many interesting conversations and useful threads.

My debts to other institutions are no less. To the London Library and the British Library, and their extraordinarily helpful staffs. To Herr Wolfgang Mayer of the Staats- und Stadtbibliothek Augsburg, who assisted me with scans and information about that collection's catalog of the library of Jeremias Martius. To Joseph Gerdeman and the Interlibrary Loan Department of the University of Chicago, who graciously bent the rules to get me a PDF of an otherwise unobtainable pamphlet.

Simone Mollea generously took my very basic—and often worse—Latin and rendered it into a polished translation. His help was invaluable, and I thank Professor Matthew Fox, too, for making the introduction. Peter Gilliver, of the *Oxford English Dictionary*, sustained a helpful and most enjoyable email correspondence when I'm sure he had many better things to do. Shaun Whiteside and Tobias Hoheisel were endlessly patient with my queries regarding Dutch and German translations. I am most grateful to them all.

Justice Nicholas Kasirer, Professor Faith Wallis, and Edward Tenner all supplied me with copies of their work when the stalwart efforts of the above libraries failed. Heidi Graf located an image of an early Froschauer broadside and reported on its organizational principles for me. Jean-Jacques Subrenat was enlightening on the subject of Chinese characters, pinyin, and computer technology. Professor Lucy Freeman Sandler guided me to an important essay of hers that I had regrettably overlooked, and supplied me with a scan of an image. Caroline Shenton kindly responded to a late query on *fonds* and archival practice. Again, I owe gratitude to all.

At Picador, my thanks go to Nicholas Blake, Neil Lang, Philippa McEwan, Lindsay Nash, and the inestimable Charlotte Greig, who always exerted calm control. At Basic Books, Claire Potter gave invaluable input, and I am grateful to her, as well as the rest of the team: Jessica Breen, Katie Carruthers-Busser, Lara Heimart, Chin-Yee Lai, Kelsey M. Odorczyk, Melissa Raymond, Bill Warhop, and Jeff Williams. Finally, I must thank my agent, Bill Hamilton, of A. M. Heath, and my editor, Ravi Mirchandani, of Picador Books, neither of whom laughed, or at least not to my face, when I told them I wanted to write a book on the history of alphabetical order.

PREFACE

WRITING, FROM ITS EARLIEST DAYS, HAS BEEN THOUGHT OF as a gift from the gods: in Egypt it was given to humanity by Thoth, the god of culture; in Babylonia, by Nebo, the god of destiny; in Sumeria, it was bestowed by Nabû, the "scribe of the gods." The Greeks sometimes thought writing was granted to mankind by Hermes, the messenger of the gods; at other times they reported that it was given by Zeus to the Muses. Odin bestowed the gift in Norse legend; in India, the elephant-headed god Ganesh used one of his tusks as a pen; while the Mayan Itzamna, a creator-god, first named the objects in the world, and then gave humans the ability to write those names down. The Jews were taught that God had handed the skill to the world through his intermediary, Moses; in the Qur'an, Allah is he who "taught the pen." As late as the fifteenth century, *han'gul*, the newly created script of Korea, was said to have been produced by "the revelation of heaven to the mind of the sage king."[1]

How writing came to be, it appears, is a question that has been explored for almost as long as writing itself. And therefore what writing does—it enables us to read, to gather information, and to pass that information on—seems so obvious that we barely consider the magnitude of this ability. Yet reading and writing, and what we do with those things, are not obvious at all. It might be said that the world broadly divides into two types of writing systems: alphabetic and syllabic, and ideographically based methods. The alphabet, as far as we can tell, was written from its very earliest days in a set order. Why, we don't know, although ease of memorization seems possible, even likely. Nonalphabetic writing systems, by contrast, were organized in a variety of ways—by sound, by meaning, by written structure or shape.

To readers and writers of an alphabetic language such as English, the assumption I just made above—that the elements that make up a writing system, the characters, must be ordered, must be sorted or organized in some way—is automatic, and unquestioned.* Equally, it has become automatic to assume that, once our writing systems evolved, writing was used to give permanence to thoughts and ideas; and then, that methods were devised to enable us to return to those thoughts and ideas, whether ours or someone else's. For writing is a powerful tool—not merely a tool that permits Person A to notify Person B that such-and-such occurred, or will occur, or some other piece of information, but a tool that enables Person B to be notified of these occurrences centuries after Person A has died. (And, it must be noted, it is almost automatic today to label unknown people alphabetically, beginning with Persons A and B; citing anonymous Persons J and D, for example, would be considered bizarre.)

Writing is powerful because it transcends time, and because it creates an artificial memory, or store of knowledge, a memory that can be located physically, be it on clay tablets, on walls, on stone, on bronze, on papyrus, parchment, or paper. And for centuries, that was how it was

---

*I would like to claim that the greater part of this book deals with the ordering systems of Europe because, while the alphabet that originated in the Middle East around two millennia BCE was almost certainly the ancestor of all later alphabetic scripts, many if not most of them developed their alphabetic ordering methods long after its European appearance, often by direct emulation. In reality, however, this book concentrates on Europe and the Anglo-American world because my knowledge of non-European languages is limited, and also because exploring further afield would have meant a book of unmanageable length.

used. Words were written, and they were stored. We can guess from what has survived that it was expected that this stored material would be referred back to. But how, and why, did we learn this art, or science, of reference, of "looking things up"? How did we learn to find what we needed when we needed it, in the mass of written words that have surrounded us daily for a millennium and more?

IT IS HARD TODAY TO IMAGINE not being able to look something up—not to know how to use an index, a dictionary, or a phone book. It is harder still to imagine a world in which there are no indexes, no dictionaries, no phone books. Ordering and sorting, and then returning to the material sorted via reference tools, have become so integral to the modern Western mindset that their significance is both almost incalculable and curiously invisible. For categorizing is what we do every day of our lives, frequently every hour of every day, and not just through paper. We use dozens of products daily without ever considering that they have been specially designed for our perpetual sorting needs, so that we can locate material swiftly and without effort.

Thus, a wallet has a pocket for coins, longer slots for banknotes, shorter ones for credit cards; handbags have small flat pockets for mobile phones, zipped pockets for keys, flaps for bus passes. These of course are personal sorting categories: I might put my phone in a pocket someone else uses for a wallet, and vice versa. Other items need to be sorted in ways that are comprehensible to a wider audience. A newspaper separates articles reporting on internal political events from articles dealing with world news, those on sports from arts reviews or editorials. This is not done for the ease of the newspapers' producers (a single journalist might write articles across several fields), but to assist their readers. The displays in supermarkets, by contrast, are in part dictated by technological constraints—until recently, chilled and frozen foods were almost always found against the shops' walls, where the cabinets could be plugged into electrical outlets—but otherwise they use broad categories: meat, fish, fresh fruit and vegetables, just as furniture stores such as IKEA sort their items by room—bedroom furniture here, kitchen equipment there.

These methods are so obvious to us, we barely think of them as organizing or sorting, and yet of course that is what they are. They allow someone searching for information, or physical objects, to locate what they need. Yet what all these methods rely on is some, even if limited, previous knowledge on the part of the person doing the searching. A reader has to know that an article on the French Open tennis tournament will be categorized by the game being played, rather than by the country in which it takes place, in "sports" rather than "world news." Similarly, supermarket shoppers are expected to look for their tomatoes in the vegetable section, even though they are technically fruit; and that dill, if it is dried, will be found in the herbs and spices section, but if it is fresh, with the vegetables.

Almost all sorting systems similarly require some level of familiarity on the part of their users. To modern eyes, printed lists and alphabetical order are in essence synonymous—we assume alphabetical order has always been humanity's default sorting method for things that are written down. It is an unspoken assumption of alphabetic writing systems that the alphabet is primary. Letters near the beginning of the alphabet are somehow superior to those that follow: alpha males dominate romantic fiction; in the 1950s, B-movies followed or preceded the main feature; in the 1960s the B-side of records carried the songs that were not expected to be hits. The preeminence of ABC over, say, DEF, or LMN, runs unconsciously through every part of the world that uses an alphabet, and some regions that do not: there have been broadcasting companies named ABC in the USA, Australia, Britain, the Philippines, and even in Japan, a nonalphabet country; it is also the title of a Swedish news program, a Spanish newspaper, and several food companies and cinema chains across the globe. As well as an Arab Banking Corporation in alphabetic Bahrain, there is an Agricultural Bank of China in decidedly nonalphabetic China. ABC is a programming language, and a streaming algorithm. English-speakers learning first aid are reminded to check ABCs (airways, breathing, circulation). Mathematics has an abc conjecture, an ABC formula, and Approximate Bayesian Computation. The Admiralty, Baranof, and Chichagof Islands off the coast of Alaska are known as the ABC Islands; their counterparts in the Lesser Antilles are Aruba, Bonaire, and Curaçao.

This alphabetic predominance makes it hard for us to remember today that the phrase "alphabetical order" has two parts, and that they might be of equal weight: "alphabetical," yes, but also "order." And that all order, and ordering, is not of necessity alphabetical—indeed, for centuries the idea of ordering by random chance, by the letters of the alphabet, was considered less useful than a multitude of other sorting methods—geographical, chronological, hierarchical, categorical. Sometimes things had, and continue to have, no visible organizing method, their innate order being so essential that it is simply remembered. For a medieval clergyman, what would have been the point of putting the books of the Bible in alphabetical order? To him, it was obvious that Genesis comes before Exodus, just as, to us, it is obvious that Monday comes before Tuesday, September before October. In fact, it is surprisingly difficult to put the days of the week or the months of the year into alphabetical order, because the days and months have a "natural" order, one that is not alphabetical.[2]

Other types of categorizing and sorting that were natural to generations past today seem as peculiar to us as April heading a list of the months of the year because it begins with A. Yet in a world more stratified than our own, sorting things hierarchically was once a natural impulse. The Domesday Book, that summary of land occupancy in England and parts of Wales produced for William the Conqueror in 1086, assessed the values of 13,418 places, organizing them first by status, then by geography, then by status again, and finally by wealth. The king came first, followed—broken down by region—by the great clergy, the powerful barons, and, lastly, each district's most humble tenants.

But of course, for the information in the Domesday Book to be accessible to later readers, they had to know the regions of England and Wales, and the orders of hierarchy—who outranked whom. For, in all the millennia of reading and writing, only one major sorting system has evolved that requires no previous knowledge from the searcher: alphabetical order. To use it, the only thing searchers need to know is a list of approximately (depending on the language) two dozen characters, in an established order. They do not need to know on what continent a city is located to find it in an atlas, nor if a bishop outranks a cardinal to find him in a list of participants at a clerical summit. Neither do they need to know whether the English Civil War preceded or postdated the American Civil War to locate it in an alphabetical list of "Wars Through History"; nor, indeed, do they need to know whether a pumpkin is considered a vegetable or a fruit to search for it in a seed catalog.

Alphabetical order is in this way entirely neutral. Someone whose name begins with A is at the start of the list not because they are a great landowner, nor because they have more money, nor were born before the others on the list, but simply because of a random chance of the alphabet. This lack of inherent meaning, of preordained value, makes alphabetical order a sorting tool that does not reflect back to its users the values of its creators, nor even an image of the world in which it was created. In 1584, the compiler of the first French bibliography included a dedication to the king apologizing for his use of alphabetical order and acknowledging that his choice had upended hierarchy, allowing the possibility that entries for lesser men might well appear before those of their social superiors, children before their parents, the ruled before their rulers. "Certainly," he wrote, "I have felt the impropriety of having thus observed an alphabetical or A, B, C order," but he had nonetheless persisted with this system not, as we might assume today, to make the entries easier to find, but "to avoid all calumny, and to remain in amity with everyone": that is, to ensure he did not trespass unknowingly against hierarchy by setting a less prominent person ahead of a greater one.[3] In 1584, therefore, alphabetical order was still a fallback to some, a way of avoiding a social faux pas in print.

Two hundred years later, in the late eighteenth century, Harvard and Yale Colleges still used hierarchy and status as their primary sorting filter for their students, with enrollment lists ordered first by the students' families' social position and wealth, then subcategorized by whether or not their fathers had attended the same college. The students' own performance powered their rise or fall in the class lists as the year progressed, but at formal events social status remained the sorting tool for the order in which students entered rooms, and for seating arrangements.[4] Today, it is as unimaginable to contemplate ranking students by their parents' wealth, or by their race or gender, as it is by the color of their hair or their perceived level of attractiveness to their fellow students (at least, not overtly). Nor do we, in our democratic age, group students by their grades, even though "Will the smart people sit at the front, please" was once routine.

The very benefit of alphabetical order, to our eyes, is that it says nothing at all about the people or objects being sorted: "The alphabet can help in finding [or organizing] things, but not in understanding them. It cannot tell you why a whale has more in common with an elephant than a shark."[5] It is value-neutral, simply guiding those using it to the places where they can learn meaning or value for themselves.

And yet, when looked at from this angle, alphabetical order seems oddly useless. That very value—that it is neutral—also means it is devoid of meaning, and therefore it is rarely the sorting system of first resort. Phone books, which appear to a modern eye to be entirely alphabetical, use at least two preliminary sorting filters: first by country, then by region or city (geographical), then by type, residential or business (occupational), before finally getting down to alphabetical. Schools that use alphabetical order to record their students in registers first divide the attending children by classes (age), and only then by the alphabet. Bookshops and libraries, too, rarely, if ever, rely purely on an alphabetical organizing system. My last name begins with F, and so does F. Scott Fitzgerald's. This coincidence would tell readers nothing about our respective books, were they to see them sitting next to each other on a shelf. Which is why in virtually all bookshops, Flanders and Fitzgerald are separated: Fitzgerald in fiction; Flanders in nonfiction (primary sorting level). Then, Flanders is in "history," Fitzgerald in, perhaps, "twentieth-century fiction" (secondary); after that, European history versus short-story writers (tertiary); and only then might the books be sorted Fa, Fe, Fi, Fl . . .

Of course, once these same books are taken home, there is no reason why Fitzgerald and Flanders might not be shelved side by side if their owners decide to use alphabetical order as their primary sorting system. Or if the system is to be used by a single or a limited number of searchers, more idiosyncratic or value-laden systems can work efficiently, based as they are on previous knowledge held by the searchers: all books with a yellow spine together, or books given to us by our mothers, or according to geographical or chronological order by place or date of purchase.

The short-story writer and essayist Jorge Luis Borges gave the most memorable, and picturesque, reminder of the reality that all sorting methods by their very nature are obscure: as the world is random, so too must be the methods that seek to categorize, and thus rationalize, the world. "Obviously," he wrote, "there is no classification of the universe that is not arbitrary and conjectural . . . the impossibility of penetrating the divine scheme of the universe cannot dissuade us from outlining human schemes, even though we are aware that they are provisional." He mocked a natural philosopher of the seventeenth century who had attempted through categorization and classification to invent an artificial world language, highlighting its "ambiguities, redundancies, and deficiencies," and claiming that it reminded him of a (probably imaginary, and invented by Borges) Chinese encyclopedia, which classified all animals by dividing them into the following groups: "(a) those that belong to the Emperor, (b) embalmed ones, (c) those that are trained, (d) suckling pigs, (e) mermaids, (f) fabulous ones, (g) stray dogs, (h) those that are included in this classification, (i) those that tremble as if they were mad, (j) innumerable ones, (k) those drawn with a very fine camel's hair brush, (l) others, (m) those that have just broken a flower vase, (n) those that resemble flies from a distance."[6]

CLASSIFICATION, AND THE SORTING TOOLS we have created to enable it, may never be quite as bizarre and as memorable as Borges's mythical encyclopedia, but the history of how we moved from the arrival of the alphabet around 2000 BCE to the slow unfolding of alphabetical order as a sorting tool some three thousand years later, in the thirteenth century CE, is filled with nearly as many surprises and wonders.* For sorting is, ultimately, magical—indeed, the word "abracadabra," that invocation of magicians from classical times onward, is a word built on the first four letters of the Latin alphabet.[7] This magical tool, the alphabet, bestows the ability to create order out of centuries of thought, of knowledge, of literature, scientific discovery, and history. Sorting, and classification, allow us to locate the information we need, and to disseminate it in turn. Without sorting, all the knowledge in the world would lie in great unsifted stacks of books, themselves unfindable, unread, and unknown.

Despite this, alphabetical order has remained almost unrecorded for most of its history. Its arrival was remarked on as it was laboriously invented and reinvented, explained and reexplained. But once it was assimilated, it swiftly faded into the background, becoming so much part of the scenery that everyone ceased to notice its existence. A historian of the development of the alphabet lamented the lack of study given

---

* To assist the reader in these millennial leaps, there is a very basic timeline on pages 237–241.

to his discipline: there was no academic school of study called "history of writing," he mourned, no museum, nor even a section of a museum, devoted to it. Instead, his field was divided up among anthropology, archaeology, Assyriology, Egyptology, ethnology, Mesoamerican studies, paleography, philology, and Sinology (to list them alphabetically).[8] But at least there are disciplines for all of these things. Historians of Early Modern Europe are now beginning to study archiving and organization as they emerged in the Renaissance, but for most of history, to learn about classification was to be forced to read between the lines, to search out how people sorted by working backward from end results, where those have survived, to our best guesses as to their intentions.

It may be that classification more generally, and alphabetical order in particular, has been rendered invisible in part because of another automatic assumption, one we make about reading: that when we talk about reading, we are talking about narrative prose. Whether it's a romance set in Siberia, a history of the Roman Empire, or a government report on the after effects of a hurricane, our notion of reading presupposes that we are being told some sort of story, where events happen in a careful arc, one after the other, and they have a meaning, or if not, the point is their lack of meaning. Readers are expected to start at the beginning of an essay, a newspaper article, or a book, then continue through the middle to the end. Yet there are so many other types of reading that we do daily: we browse, entering a text randomly until we find something that captures our attention; we search, jumping through a text to isolate a specific point or piece of information we need; we study, reading one text intensively, but breaking off to check the endnotes, to follow up a digression, to source a quote in another book, or to look up a definition or explanation in a reference work; and we revisit, returning to a text to reacquaint ourselves with something we already know.[9]

Even these different kinds of reading, however, make up just a tiny percentage of most people's reading lives. We also read maps and GPS directions; we read the letterhead on office stationery; we read advertising copy in camping-gear catalogs; we read train or bus time-tables; we read highway signs and street signs and signs that tell us when we can park our cars; we read the opening hours of shops, whose signs bear their names, which we also read, to distinguish them from the shops next door; we read the instructions on bottles of prescription pills, and directions on how to turn on the oven's self-cleaner; we read menus and our list of appointments each day. And, of course, we scan many lists in alphabetical order for information: address books and con-tacts lists; indexes to books or maps; or lists of people named "Brown" on Wikipedia. Much of our reading, therefore, is not remotely narrative, not destinational, but instead is directed toward retrieving a single piece of information, which is often found by searching a list that is ordered alphabetically.[10] But this form of reading is never written about in books and magazines, nor studied in universities. Often, it is barely considered even to be reading. And yet at home, at school, and at work, we make notes, which are ordered into shopping lists, reports, articles, letters, budgets, or other office documents; we compile lists—for our insurance companies, to build an address book, to inventory our possessions or a library, or to organize an office filing cabinet.

A Place for Everything is a look at the history of this ordering and classification, at how sorting came to be, in particular via the alpha-bet. Much of our lives is spent creating archives of documents, and then developing ways of finding those documents. The word "archive" itself comes from the Greek *arkheion,* meaning a magistrate's resi-dence, a place that housed not only government documents, but also papers lodged there by private citizens as a place of safe storage. And from there, as one of the earliest alphabetical list–makers, Isidore of Seville, noted, it came to encompass a chest or strongbox (*arca*) and an archive (*archivum*), as well as mystery (*arcanum*).[11] An archive (the room) and an archive (the papers it contains) are both the container and the thing contained, while classification, whether alphabetical order or any other system, is the tool we use to navigate them, our map to guide us through this mysterious and secret world of paper. The chests used to store papers for most of history—the arks—subliminally return us to the Bible, to the Ark of the Covenant and to Noah's Ark, containers of God's word and all of the planet's sentient beings. Arks are mere wooden boxes, and yet as such they symbolize the wisdom of the ages, of God's promise for humanity.[12]

BILL GATES ONCE IDENTIFIED the development of the transistor in 1947 as "a key transitional event in the advent of the information age."[13] Other key moments, according to historians, include the inventions of writing, of double-entry bookkeeping, printing, the telegraph, and the computer. What is notable in this list is that none of these are inventions that created new knowledge themselves, but are instead inventions that created new ways of *accessing* knowledge. It was not the machines—not the telegraph, not the printing press, nor even the computer—that revolutionized the world, but the information those machines transmitted: information that was the software to the hardware of the printing press or the telegraph or the computer. To function, these new types of software required systems of organization, and especially the alphabet—that ABC that was devised so many thousands of years before—to guide them to a new world of order. How that happened is the story that follows.

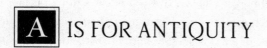 IS FOR ANTIQUITY

From the Beginning to the Classical World

THE EARLIEST "WRITING" WAS NOT WRITING AS WE RECOGNIZE IT today. It was not built on a series of symbols, which we call "letters," that represent sounds, and which when combined make up words. Instead, the earliest writing consisted of images painted on rock, probably representations to be used in the service of ritual beliefs rather than to communicate abstract thoughts or concrete objects. After these came pictographs, where a single standard image became the representation of an object. Pictographs emerged independently around the world, from the Middle East to Australia, and in many parts of the Americas. These were followed by ideographic writing, where pictographs were used to represent not a thing but an idea associated with a thing: a circle might denote "the sun" or "light," "brightness" or "day." This form of writing was also found across the globe, from China to North and Central America, to Africa, Australia, and Siberia.[1]

The world's first complex writing form, Sumerian cuneiform, followed this evolutionary path, moving around 3500 BCE from pictographic to ideographic representations, from the depiction of objects to that of abstract notions. Sumerian cuneiform was a linear writing system, its symbols usually set in columns, read from top to bottom and from left to right. This regimentation was another form of abstraction: the world is not a linear place, and objects do not organize themselves horizontally or vertically in real life. Those early rock paintings, thought to have been created for ritual purposes, were possibly shaped and organized to follow the walls of the cave, or the desires of the painters, who may have organized them symbolically, or artistically, or even randomly. Yet after cuneiform, virtually every form of script that has emerged has been set out in rows with a clear beginning and endpoint.[2] So uniform is this expectation, indeed, that the odd exception is noteworthy, and generally established for a specific purpose, such as those "round robin" letters of complaint to higher authorities, in which the complainants sign in a circular fashion to ensure that no ringleader can be singled out.

Sumerian writing then made another conceptual leap, by originating a method of representing grammatical parts of speech using the symbols for words that already existed and that shared the grammatical element's sound. This sound/sign system is more easily explained to English speakers who are familiar with its use in the rebus, a traditional puzzle game. In a rebus, a picture of an eye, for example, might represent the word "I," a picture of a sheep ("ewe") the word "you" (see page 4).

In Sumeria, writing became a bureaucratic tool during a period of rapid urbanization, as a powerful upper class oversaw large-scale civic construction, as well as the creation and expansion of the complex distribution networks needed to feed the inhabitants of these new cities. Yet while the skill was widely recognized, at the same time it was accessible only to the elite. Learning to write Sumerian cuneiform required both time and intelligence: there were around three hundred basic symbols to memorize, as well as another thousand less frequently used ones. In addition, many were then combined to create further meanings: for example, the symbol for "mountains" also meant "foreign place," and when it was used together with the symbol for "woman," the compound character meant "slave."[3]

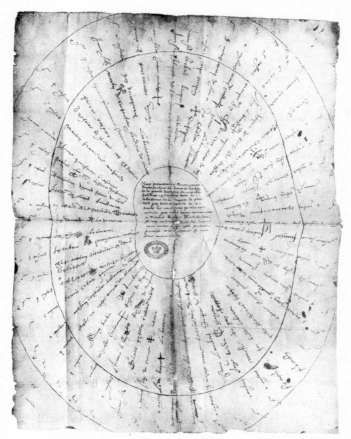

A round robin letter of 1621, petitioning for the right of Huguenots to settle in the New World. The petition is in the center, reading conventionally, top to bottom and left to right, while the signatures deviate from this standard pattern to obscure the petition's originators.

The first page of a letter in rebus form from Lewis Carroll, the author of Alice's Adventures in Wonderland (1865). Note that "and" is represented by a picture of a hand, presumably with the dropped H common in many English dialects.

By around 3000 BCE, trading routes between Mesopotamia and Egypt were well established. Ideas, as well as goods, traveled along these routes in both directions, and one of those ideas was a phonetic writing system. Initially, the new Egyptian hieroglyphics were pictographic, representing objects, but within a century Egyptian writing had made the same conceptual leap as cuneiform, incorporating rebus-like wordplay to convey abstractions. By around 2000 BCE, seven hundred standard hieroglyphic signs were in use in Egypt; two thousand years later, the number had grown to over five thousand. Eventually, Egypt had four types of writing: hieroglyphics themselves; a simplified form of hieroglyphics known as hieratic, or sacred, script; and two cursive scripts, which were written more fluidly. Both the cursives and the hieratic

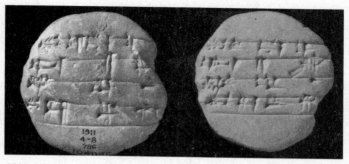

Old Babylonian clay tablet, c. 1900–1700 BCE, *inscribed with a proverb written by a teacher (left), and copied onto the rear of the tablet by a student (right).*

script were quicker and easier to write than the original hieroglyphics, although these latter continued to be used for inscriptions, on monuments, and for civic or religious displays; the cursive scripts were kept for letters, business transactions, and other day-to-day affairs, where speed was more important than appearance.

In many ways, the societies of Egypt and Sumer evolved along parallel tracks. Both developed densely populated urban centers, new ways of irrigating land, and, between them, invented or elaborated on methods of dividing years into weeks and hours into minutes. Sumeria probably also saw the invention of the wheel, of sailing ships, of brick manufacture, and, perhaps most importantly, of the idea of making marks in wet clay that, when the clay dried, preserved the information that the marks conveyed for later reference. By contrast, writing in Egypt began on an entirely different scale: glyphs dealing with matters of religious importance were painted onto walls, or onto large banners designed to hang across the façades of buildings. ("Hieroglyph" means "sacred carving.") Over time, these glyphs were adapted for smaller-scale use, diminishing from building-sized to handheld as they began to be inked onto papyrus scrolls.[4]

The simplest hieroglyphs were ideograms, where a symbol represented a concrete object: a picture of a bull just meant "bull." Then came phonograms, where a symbol stood for a sound that had some connection with that symbol: a glyph representing a female hare did not mean "female hare," but the sounds "w" and "n," which were the consonants that made up the word "female hare." Symbols that are today called determinatives, placed after a word, indicated what class or category that word belonged to: glyphs for plants were followed by a determinative meaning "grass," to show that the glyph that preceded it fell into the plant category; similarly, all symbols followed by a pen symbol fell into the realm of ideas. Egyptian writing could be inscribed in columns, read top to bottom, or in rows, which could be read in either direction: readers knew where to start by looking at the faces in the human and animal pictograms, which always faced the beginning of the text. As with Sumerian cuneiform, Egyptian hieroglyphs and hieratic and cursive scripts were complex and required long periods of study before any skill could be demonstrated by a would-be writer.[5]

Writing was altogether a complex business, and across the world was probably invented at the very most half a dozen times—one historian believes that it might have been independently invented just three times in all of humanity's existence.[6] China was one of the first civilizations to generate a writing form. Early prototypes of inscribed writing had appeared there by the last quarter of the second millennium BCE; by around 1200 BCE, divinations were scored onto the ox bones and turtle shells called oracle bones. (Fragments with incised markings date back to c. 4800 BCE, but these incisions cannot authoritatively be called writing.) The script used in China today is a descendant of a writing form that originated in the Shang or Yin dynasty (c. 1600–1046 BCE). It is logographic, with each word represented by a character. In its early form, some of the characters were representations of concrete objects; some were rebus-like, the logograph standing in for a similar-sounding word; still others were related not by sound, but by meaning. As with Egyptian hieroglyphics, the characters were followed by determinatives to clarify their category.[7] By 100 CE, this system had nearly ten thousand characters.

Then there was the writing system of the Maya of Mesoamerica, whose first surviving glyphs date from around the third century BCE. These, however, are most likely the descendants of an earlier writing system, or systems, about which we know nothing. It is thought today that those earlier glyphs were ideograms, partly pictorial, but no one really knows. Later glyphs were logograms, which represented entire words, used in conjunction with glyphs representing single syllables. These were incised, carved, and painted: into stone, wood, onto walls, and, more portably, onto both pottery and bark paper.[8]

All of these systems were difficult to learn, requiring a great deal of both time and resources. The appearance of a new method of writing, one that had fewer than thirty symbols, was to prove a revelation—and, ultimately, a worldwide revolution. Writing, if not given to humanity by the gods, was nonetheless a skill that was carefully guarded by the priestly and elite classes: control of writing was a component in the control of religion, the control of government, the control, even, of much of business. The new writing system, however, did not emerge from the temples or the princely courts, nor even from an urban center. Instead, we think that it was born in the Western Desert of Upper Egypt, some-where between the cities of Thebes and Abydos, along a route that was frequented by both traders and soldiers, especially mercenaries from across the Middle East. These people shared no mother tongue, nor were they from an educated, literate elite. Of necessity, therefore, they communicated in a creole, a hybrid of their many native languages. And yet these rude, uneducated, disregarded people most likely invented what became the ancestor of all the world's alphabets. For while it is possible that writing was invented fewer than half a dozen times, the very idea of an alphabet was so completely novel in its level of abstraction that it is thought that in all of human history it was invented only once: at this time, in this place. As far as we know, every alphabetic script derives from this single source.

The central innovation of alphabetic writing is that it reduces every word to smaller units by representing each individual sound, without any connection to a word's meaning. This novelty has been compared to the creation of money, which dates from about the sixth century BCE, in the Lydian kingdom in Asia Minor.[9] Both alphabet and money are abstractions: money is a symbol of value, not something of value itself; letters are symbols of sounds, not the sounds themselves. It is difficult for us today to understand how the alphabet changed everything through its extreme abstraction. Yet alphabetic writing altered the way we think. If the word "god" is read backward, it becomes "dog." It isn't simply that this type of inversion is impossible in a writing system without an alphabet. If that were so, it would merely be a game, a charming quirk. But in a writing system without an alphabet there is no backward. Spoken words have an ephemeral, fleeting order as they are uttered, and until words are written down they are not fixed one after the other. But once they are written in an alphabetic writing system, words do have an order, and so do their individual components, letters. The component elements of Chinese graphs, for example, cannot be taken apart and individually reversed and read backward—there is no meaning, even, to that concept.[10]

However radical the alphabet might be understood to be in retrospect, its ease of use in practice—memorizing twenty or thirty symbols instead of thousands—meant that this new system spread rapidly among the desert travelers: many dozens of rock inscriptions have been found in the Western Desert, at Wadi el-Ḥôl, which are thought to date from around 2050–1550 BCE. They have not yet been definitively deciphered, but they bear a close resemblance to the later alphabet of what is known as North Semitic script, which flourished around 1800–1700 BCE. It is likely that the inscriptions were carved by mercenaries who had seen Egyptian hieroglyphics, in particular the symbols the Egyptians used to transcribe foreign words and names phonetically. The Wadi el-Ḥôl carvings are visibly based on these hieroglyphics, although they do not represent the same sounds—further evidence, perhaps, that the people who carved them were familiar with, but not part of, Egyptian society.[11]

The linguistic group that included the Canaanites, the early Hebrews, the Phoenicians, and the Aramaeans used a form of North Semitic script, which had twenty-two letters and was an *abjad*, an alphabet consisting entirely of consonants, with no vowels. We know that Old Hebrew used the same order of letters as North Semitic because an excavation has uncovered a late ninth- or early eighth-century BCE carving—virtually graffiti—of the first five letters of the early Hebrew alphabet, and they are in the same order. The Book of Psalms, too, in the Old Testament, contains psalms in the form of acrostics, in which every line of verse begins with a word that starts with each successive letter of the alphabet, again confirming that the order of the alphabet had been established by the sixth or fifth centuries BCE.

This writing form, which required its users to remember only two dozen symbols, could be learned fairly swiftly, at least in comparison to the lengthy study periods needed for cuneiform and hieroglyphics, and thus ensured that it was readily adopted by merchants and traders. And so the alphabet made its way from hierarchical Egypt to the relatively egalitarian land of Israel. (It was not egalitarian in our modern sense, yet was a place where lower-caste prophets, at least according to the books of the prophets in the Old Testament, railed publicly and without retribution at the upper echelons of society, who regulated both religion and law.)[12] It then moved on to Greece via Phoenician traders, to the civilization that was to turn skeptical thinking and inquiry into a philosophical value.[13] The alphabet may have appeared in Europe as early as the eleventh century BCE, although it would be at least a couple more centuries before it was widely used.

Another descendant of this early alphabet developed independently: surviving inscriptions show that by the sixth century BCE a forerunner to Arabic script was in use in a trading colony in the southwest of the Arabian peninsula, where languages that are collectively referred to as Old South Arabic, an offshoot of Canaanite, were spoken. The direct ancestor of the modern Arabic script, however, was to emerge in Petra, the center of the Nabataean kingdom, in the second century BCE, a place where a dialect of Aramaic was spoken.[14]

Greek and Arabic alphabets both adopted, and adapted, the Semitic names for each of the alphabet's letters, the European versions of the alphabet in addition acquiring vowels, while the Arabic alphabet remained an abjad. It is presumed that early nonalphabetical writing systems used the word or idea each pictograph stood for as its name: the pictograph of an ox was probably called "ox." With an alphabet, that no longer worked. Early on, the name of each individual letter had been based phonetically on the word the letter represented, as children's books today explain that "A is for Apple," but by the time of their wider dissemination they no longer meant anything at all, and the Romans reduced them even further.* Early Greek retained the Semitic outlines of the alphabet: it was arranged in mostly the same order, apart from some letters that had been added to accommodate the different sounds of the Greek language; the letters were almost the same; and initially the reading direction was the same. After 800 BCE the Etruscans then adopted, and adapted, the Greek alphabet, making their own changes to suit their language and pronunciation; and from there came the Latin alphabet, as the Etruscans were assimilated into the early Roman republic sometime after the fourth century BCE. The Latin alphabet

---

* A few letters have retained meanings, or vestiges of meanings, even after millennia. In Greek, for example, omicron is *ò mikrón*—short, or little, "o"—to make clear the distinction between that letter and omega, ō *méga*—long, or big, "o"; epsilon, *è psilón*, or naked "e," clarifies that that letter is not the same as *êta*, which, owing to its accent, is not naked, but dressed. In French, the name of the letter "y" is pronounced "ee-grek," that is, "Greek 'i'," while in English "w" is pronounced "double u," a reminder that the written letter is made up of two u's joined together.

appropriated twenty-one of the Greek letters, dropping *zeta* (deemed unnecessary) and adding g, then later reincorporating z as well as y, in order to be able to transliterate Greek names.

But all this time, no one had as yet used the word "alphabet," which made a surprisingly late appearance. The Romans said *"literae,"* letter, or *"elementa,"* element, a direct translation from the Greek. It was around 200 CE that the theologian Hippolytus of Rome wrote the phrase *"ex graecorum alphabeto,"* meaning "from the Greek alphabet"— the first surviving use of the word. By the fourth century St. Jerome was using the word as though it were well known: his aim was *"alphabetum hebraicum discerem,"* "to learn the Hebrew alphabet."[5]

LEARNING THE ALPHABET, HOWEVER, even learning it in a set order, is not the same as using alphabetical order. The alphabet was—give or take the odd letter—established in a fairly fixed order from the start. But it took some time before anyone thought that order might be useful for anything other than memorizing the names of the letters to help students learn to read—up to three thousand years, in fact.

In 2350 BCE, Sumeria was conquered by the Akkadians who, as conquerors often do, adopted many of the elements of the civilization they had defeated. To continue to maintain the very fine Sumerian bureaucracy that they had commandeered, the Akkadians therefore needed clerks who could read Sumerian. Sumerian, however, was a non-Semitic language, while Akkadian was a Semitic one. Faced with two entirely unrelated languages, the Akkadians drew up numerous word lists, early precursors to dictionaries, with Akkadian vocabulary facing its Sumerian equivalent. The earliest surviving example of one of these word lists is the Urra=hubullu, a set of twenty-four vocabulary tablets dating from the second millennium BCE. The words they contain were grouped by subject: words relating to the law, to government administration, and to objects—everything from different types of naval and land transport, to domestic, farm, and wild animals. Within these categories, items were ordered by the material they were made of: for instance, there were tablets covering the vocabulary for trees, and therefore anything made of wood, such as ships and carts; another listed items made of clay.

This sort of word list, an early version of the topically ordered vocabulary lists in modern phrasebooks, became a standard tool, especially among traders and merchants, who regularly dealt with people from other parts of the world. These lists, however, might be organized by any number of different principles. Around Phoenicia, in Ebla (near modern-day Aleppo), for example, word lists have been found that sorted entries by the sound of the first syllable of each word.[16]

A more general form of organizing and categorization can be seen in the discoveries at Kanish (the modern Kültepe, in central Anatolia), where around twenty thousand cuneiform tablets have been excavated. There, tablets bearing different kinds of information were carefully stored in different places, organized by type or subject. Some still carry small clay labels on which were inscribed descriptions of their contents: "messages of A," "tablets of the city," "tablets which are copies of . . . ," "tablets of the will of PM," "testimony of PN," and so on.[*17]

In other locations, the letters of the alphabet were used as reference marks in construction and carpentry. In Nimrud in the ninth century BCE, ivory pieces that were to be inlaid as decorative motifs in furniture each had a letter of the alphabet on the reverse side, to signal the order in which they were to be fixed, indicating that even workmen knew the alphabet in order. Similarly, six centuries later, letters were incised into the wooden beams of a ship to guide the carpenters, just as we see

---

*Of course, clay is durable. We have scant but tantalizing glimpses of other writing materials, and thus of other organizing systems, that existed. A single set of hinged, wax-covered boards, dating from the late second millennium BCE, has been found in Turkey, suggesting that a temporary, memo-pad form of writing tool was in use in the first millennium BCE, although only one other find, in Nimrud, has produced a similar ivory writing board, as well as fragments of both ivory and wood boards.[18] (For later temporary writing systems, see pages 132–134.)

on the instruction sheets for modern flat-pack furniture. And at Petra in the first century CE, great blocks of hewn stone also carried letters, again, presumably, to show the order in which they were to be erected in a temple.[19] Thus the alphabet was being used as an organizing tool, although not yet as a sorting tool. It indicated a process (beam A was to be erected before beam B), but not that all items beginning with the letter A should go *here*, while all those beginning with the letter B should go *there*. At this point in history, it appears that there was no need.

IN CLASSICAL GREECE, THE WRITING was literally on the walls, inscribed into stone. After c. 650 BCE, laws were sometimes also written down in more portable form: the Prytaneion, the place of the executive, had tables where oral decrees were recorded in more permanent form.[20] Yet how these decrees were stored afterward, and if they were sorted, is unknown. We have only a handful of examples from these centuries that might tell us something about how the classical world looked at sorting, and at categorization. The two earliest surviving long lists in Greek literature both appear in Book II of the *Iliad*, dating from the eighth or seventh century BCE: one is a catalog of 1,186 Greek ships, and the other a list of those who fought for Troy. Both are (mostly) divided by geographical origin. Four centuries later, a geographical division was also the choice for an official list of Athenian citizens, which was organized by *deme*, or district.[21] In the sixth century BCE (probably—the date is uncertain) *The Catalogue of Women*, often ascribed to Hesiod, instead used genealogy as its primary sorting system.

By subject, material, geography, genealogy: compilers of the ancient world, it is clear, saw sorting as a complex business, with a range of possibilities to select from as they were faced with ever larger amounts of information. Yet before looking more closely at the systems they chose, a technological digression is necessary.

Papyrus was commonly used as a writing surface in Egypt in the fourth millennium BCE. The reeds from which it was made were widely available, and could be produced with different finishes and in different qualities, it was inexpensive, and thus it spread around the Mediterranean. Its main drawback was one that showed itself only over time: papyrus begins to deteriorate after a century, and it disintegrates completely within two. By contrast, parchment, made from animal skins, has a much longer life. Manufactured initially in the fourth century BCE in Pergamum, from which the word "parchment" ultimately derives, by the second century BCE the skins were widely used, and becoming more so over the next couple of centuries owing to this very longevity. For works originally written on papyrus to survive into modern times, they had to have been important or popular enough to have been copied several times over several centuries at a minimum in order to reach the period when they could finally be copied onto a more durable writing surface such as parchment.[22] It is therefore important to remember that surviving writings from the preclassical period have with few exceptions been copied and recopied, and thus later hands may well have intervened in the organization and meaning of the texts.

From our vantage point, it appears unremarkable that in the fourth century BCE Aristotle arranged his *Constitutions* and *Politics* in some measure of alphabetical order. But now we must consider what those works were written on, how many times they would have been copied, and, possibly, amended, adapted, and reordered. For there is no evidence at all that permits us to know when the order of these texts was established—no evidence that the order and organization that we know today were set down by Aristotle himself, or even if any reordering occurred in the earliest centuries when his work was disseminated. The first mention of the *Politics* being organized in alphabetical order comes from a text written several centuries later, by an author active in Alexandria, in Egypt—a fact that may not be coincidental. Because it was Ptolemaic Egypt, that dynasty founded in 323 BCE and ending with the death of Cleopatra in 30 BCE, that was the sole place, and time, when alphabetical order was in use in the Mediterranean world in any sustained way before the High Middle Ages.[23]

In the late fourth or early third century BCE, the scholar and poet Philitas of Cos produced a glossary, of which only tiny fragments have survived. Its title has been translated as *Rare Words in No Particular Order*, which suggests, first, that the entries were random; and that, as a corollary, the author thought that words do have a set order, which he chose to disregard. However, other possible translations of this title include *Miscellaneous Glosses* and *Disorderly Glosses*—that is, it was the words themselves that were "disorderly," the glossary covering dialect words, not that their arrangement was poor.[24] Yet the possibly crucial detail that gives weight to one meaning over the others is the knowledge that Philitas lived in Alexandria, where he was tutor to the boy who was to become king of Egypt, Ptolemy II Philadelphus (308/9–246 BCE). Philitas's glossary may have been disorderly, or miscellaneous, or dialectical; or it may have been called "disorderly" because it was not organized in alphabetical order. For it is possible, even likely, that Philitas may have known about alphabetical order. One of his later pupils, the grammarian Zenodotus, who around 285 BCE became the first librarian of the Great, or Royal, Library of Alexandria, certainly did.

The Library of Alexandria was founded around 300 BCE, and it thrived under Ptolemy I (c. 367–283/2 BCE), the father of Philitas's pupil Ptolemy II. Ptolemy I was a rabid collector: he not only requested books from foreign rulers, but he also demanded that every traveler arriving in Alexandria by land or sea hand over all their books temporarily, so that copies could be made for his library. Such was his passion that many suspected that it was the copies that were returned, while the originals were kept for the library. Whether the library housed originals or copies, no one knows how many scrolls it ultimately contained, but estimates range up to nearly half a million. (Scrolls, it should be noted, are not compact, and it took many scrolls to encompass the material that would now fill a single printed volume.)

This unprecedented quantity of scrolls in one location created a need for an ordering principle. Scientists today suggest that experts in any one field can routinely remember up to a few hundred items devoted to their own specialty. Once the numbers rise above that, however, memory prompts become necessary. The arrangement of scrolls in the Library of Alexandria is a subject that has been much examined, but perhaps the most important thing to say about it is that we simply don't know anything for sure. We have some information, and more has been put forward as supposition to fill in the gaps, but ultimately it is all speculation built out of fragments and hints.

Many histories name the poet and scholar Callimachus (c. 310–240 BCE), who worked at the library, as the author of a catalog of its holdings entitled the *Pinakes*, or Tables, which has been called the world's first library catalog.* But this misunderstands several important elements. Callimachus did not work at the library in the sense that he was employed there; he was a member of the Mouseion, followers of the Muses, an institution that housed notable scholars who by virtue of their eminence had access to the scrolls. And he may, or may not, have been the actual author of the *Pinakes*: his name might simply have become associated with it because of his renown. It was Zenodotus, pupil of Philitas, who was the actual librarian. He too may, or may not, have had something to do with the *Pinakes*, or the ordering of the scrolls on the library shelves.[25] The *Pinakes* themselves have not survived; our knowledge of their content, and its arrangement, is based on later reports, and

---

*The word "tables" was used for many types of précis or synopses of information, arranged in a variety of ways, well into the eighteenth century, and sometimes even later. Today many of these synopses are given more specialized terms, including table of contents, times tables (for multiplication), the periodic table, as well as the more generic "table" to cover summaries of statistical material drawn up into columns. However, for the early periods covered in this book, tables might encompass any of the above, as well as indexes, concordances, catalogs or inventories, diagrams, or a combination of several of these elements.

its full title, *Tables of Men Illustrious in Every Field of Learning and of Their Writing*, hints that the work might not have been a library catalog at all, but a bibliography. (A library inventory lists what a library owns; a library catalog, both what it owns and where those items can be located. A bibliography is a compilation of all works on a single subject, or by a single author, or from a specific place or, later, printer.)

Whatever the *Pinakes* contained, whether it was a list of works owned by the Library of Alexandria or of works that its author thought were important, it is likely that the entries were grouped first by genre: verse, divided into the subcategories of epic, lyric, tragic, and comic poetry; history; philosophy, which also included natural philosophy, or what today we call science; medicine; law; and then a miscellaneous grouping. After this primary classification, it seems possible, based on an extract from the *Pinakes* that survives from the third century, that the scrolls in each genre were shelved in first-letter alphabetical order: authors whose names began with A in one section, those whose names began with B in the next. For while today we do not think of alphabetical order as something that can be partial—to us, entries are either in alphabetical order, or they are not—historically, alphabetical order developed incrementally.

The Library of Alexandria probably used, at most, first-letter alphabetical order, where all the letters after the initial letter are disregarded. It was in the Middle Ages that second- and then third-letter alphabetical order appeared. No longer might Aristotle, for example, be listed before Alcestis, or Demosthenes after Dionysus. From the ninth and tenth centuries, entries were alphabetized by ordering words using the first two letters: Cato, Calpurnia, Catullus was perfectly acceptable. As alphabetical order moved on to third-letter ordering, this list would have been adjusted to read Calpurnia, Catullus, Cato, or Calpurnia, Cato, Catullus: either would have been correct. It was to be several more centuries before absolute alphabetical order, where *all* the letters of a word are taken into account, became the norm, and the order

Calpurnia, Cato, Catullus was the only possible one for a list to be described as alphabetical.

And even so, alphabetical ordering would fail to account for up to three-quarters of the Library of Alexandria's scrolls, which were likely to have been compilations, with each scroll containing the works of several authors. How these were ordered remains unknown. For, as we saw in Greece, alphabetical order, when it was used at all, was just one system among many. Zenodotus and Callimachus both compiled glossaries, or word lists. Callimachus's *Local Terms* was probably ordered by subject categories; Zenodotus's *Rare Words* was said to be alphabetical. And a glossary of post-Homeric Greek produced by a pupil of both men was almost certainly organized by subject.[26]

While the evidence we have for the organizing principles of the Library of Alexandria is both minimal and inconclusive, there are surviving documents from this period and region that show alphabetical order was known, which adds to the possibility that the *Pinakes*, and the Library of Alexandria, used some form of first-letter alphabetical order. Several examples can be drawn from the collection known today as the Oxyrhynchus Papyri, a cache of some half a million papyri dating from the third century BCE to the seventh century CE, which were preserved by chance and uncovered in the late nineteenth century a hundred miles southwest of modern-day Cairo. Most are government documents such as tax and court records, or business items—notices of sales, invoices, and accounts—but there is also private correspondence and some literature. The texts were written in various Egyptian scripts, as well as Hebrew, Aramaic, Greek, Latin, and Arabic, and they include a tax register that has a partial list of the plays of Euripides in first-letter alphabetical order on its reverse side. There is also a list of merchants, one for each letter of the alphabet, in order; and a potsherd from the second century BCE from Karnak, with a Greek or Roman name for each letter of the alphabet, again in alphabetical order. Some surviving tax and census records and poll-tax payment receipts also contain sections in first-letter alphabetical order.[27]

Yet for every one of these alphabetically ordered lists there are hundreds more where alphabetical order could have been used, but was not. Three book lists from this period have survived, only one of which is alphabetical.[28] Similarly, the word lists, or glosses, that have survived from ancient Egypt were most commonly organized by subject, gathering words into groups in order to present a picture of an orderly universe: first the sky, sea, and land; then people, divided into court and occupations, classes and tribes, and so on. Other lists were ordered by sound—that is, using a system similar to, if not the same as, alphabetical order.[29]

Knowledge of, and consequent use of, alphabetical order was not entirely confined to Egypt. Examples have been found as far as the Greek islands of Cos, Kalymnos, and Rhodes, and, on the mainland, around Boeotia, near Thebes, where it was used in the same intermittent fashion as in Ptolemaic Egypt: one list of the names of the participants in the cult of the Delian Apollo grouped them first by tribe, then gender, then age, then location, but gathered the entries within each category into first-letter alphabetical order. A list of saltwater fish, possibly a merchant's price list, was also laid out alphabetically. And a century afterward, a stone carving on Rhodes included a fragment of a list of books in first-letter alphabetical order.[30]

These are worth noting individually simply because they were so rare. The Greeks, and more particularly the Greeks of Ptolemaic Egypt, knew how to organize material into alphabetical order, but they evidently found it to be not terribly useful, and generally overlooked it. The Romans turned to this method even less frequently, the government organizing material primarily into geographical categories. And, like Greek public inscriptions, Roman inscriptions rarely used alphabetical order. Of the several thousand surviving inscriptions from the seventh century BCE to the fifth century CE found across the Roman Empire, just four are alphabetical.[31]

Instead, it seems that the alphabet was often less a tool, more something to be treated symbolically, or playfully. Nine of the Psalms in the Old Testament are acrostic poems, where each line or series of lines or each verse begins with a subsequent letter of the alphabet. The first two lines of Psalm 9, for example, both begin with *aleph*, or A, the next two with *beth*, or B, and so on: here the completeness and order of the alphabet symbolized the completeness and order of God's creation, the universe. In the secular classical world, the alphabet was more of a game. In one work, the second-century BCE poet Nicander spelled out his own name via an acrostic. The Roman playwright Plautus (254–184 BCE) used acrostics in his comedies, and elsewhere incorporated alphabetical order for comedic effect: in one play, a wife finds her husband with another woman, and says, "Well! So that's why he's always going out to dinner. He tells me he's going to see Archimedus, Chæreas, Chærestratus, Clinias, Chremes, Cratinus, Dinias, Demosthenes . . . "[32]

Other Roman writers actively rejected alphabetical order. The grammarian and antiquarian Varro (116–27 BCE), a Hellenist, did use alphabetical order—which, as we have seen, appeared far more commonly in Greece and Greek Egypt—when organizing a list of writers in his *Res rusticae*, On Farming [or Agriculture]. But when another Roman author copied his list, he reordered the writers geographically, either because he didn't know what alphabetical order was, and so Varro's order made no sense to him, or simply because he thought it pointless. A few other Roman writers were more appreciative of Varro's systems of organization. Pliny the Elder's *Natural History* (77–79 CE) drew on Varro for its list of those who were to receive meat from a sacrifice: thirty-one names, all in first-letter alphabetical order. Elsewhere in Pliny, what is or is not listed alphabetically can seem random, and it could be that Pliny followed whatever style his sources used: if they used alphabetical order, that was the way he reproduced it; if they did not, neither did he. In literature, Virgil (70–19 BCE) used alphabetical order for his list of heroes in the *Aeneid* (with one analphabetic intrusion in the middle): Aventinus, Catillus, Coras, Caeculus, Messapus, Clausus, Halaesus, Oebalus, Ufens, Umbro, and Virbius.[33]

By the second century CE, alphabetical order had established itself in two distinct fields: medicine and lexicography. Galen (129–200/216 CE), a physician whose profound influence on medical thought remained paramount for more than a thousand years, right up to, and sometimes beyond, the Renaissance, may have used alphabetical order in his *Interpretation of Hippocratic Glosses*, where the text promises that "the arrangement of [this] work shall be according to the order of letters with which the glosses begin." This implies both that Galen ordered his work in first-letter, or at most second-letter, alphabetical order, and, from the awkwardness of the phrasing, that he did not expect his readers to have much, or possibly any, experience of that type of ordering.

But we cannot be certain that Galen knew of it either. The *Interpretation* has survived only in later copies, which are in almost absolute alphabetical order, where all the letters of the word are taken into account when ordering, a level of alphabetization that was barely known until the ninth and tenth centuries.[34] It may well be, then, that Galen set his glosses in rudimentary first-letter order, describing them in that cumbersome manner, and the entries were reordered by a scribe centuries later. Or it may all be a later addition, for other works by Galen show a range of categorizing methods. In *On the Properties of Food* the material is divided topically, with a section for cereals and pulses, another for plants, others for fish and for meat. Then within these sections Galen used a subjective order, beginning with foods he considered to be "the most useful" or "the most nourishing," such as wheat, which he thought was important for giving the most nutrition in the smallest unit.[35]

It is difficult, so many centuries into the age of print, to keep in mind how fluid manuscripts were, how easily they could be transformed from copy to copy, from scribe to scribe, intentionally or by accident. So many works that are today described as being alphabetically organized we know only from later copies, which might well have been rearranged into ordering systems substantially different from the originals'. While retrospectively we say that dictionaries and word lists were among the earliest examples of routine alphabetical order, in reality we know little about how pervasive the use of that system was. One example is the first Latin dictionary that we know of, *De verborum significatu*, On the Meaning of Words, by the Roman grammarian Marcus Verrius Flaccus (55 BCE–20 CE), which has survived only insofar as extracts were copied by Festus (Sextus Pompeius Festus, late second century CE) into a work of his own. That work, in turn, also survived only in fragments, copied this time by an eighth-century Benedictine scribe, Paul the Deacon. He may have copied them directly, or he may have reordered the text at this stage, as it appears in part alphabetized to the third letter, in part to the first.[36] When the history of such a work is laid out like this, it becomes clear that we can know nothing at all about the arrangement of the original.

Thus we are forced to acknowledge that in Europe at this point we have little hard information about then-current systems of classification. And yet, nevertheless, alphabetical order continued to make its shadowy presence felt, often quite literally in the margins of manuscripts. A glossary from the end of the second century CE, another Oxyrhynchus fragment, lists about twenty words beginning with the syllable *mu* in Persian, Lydian, and Chaldaean: they appear in absolute alphabetical order, possibly the first time this was ever done.[37]

On the other side of the globe and in an entirely nonalphabetic writing system, in China during the Han dynasty (206 BCE–221 CE), organizing principles were well in advance of the West's as far as government administration was concerned. Emperor Cheng (51–7 BCE) commissioned an inventory and catalog of all documents in the imperial archives. Three imperial libraries were built and catalogs were drawn up, organized into subject categories: general summaries, the Confucian classics, philosophy, poetry, warfare, divination, and medicine.[38] Dictionaries were also compiled. *The Cangjie Primer* (c. 220 BCE) was intended as a textbook to teach children their Chinese characters. It has not survived, but was said to have categorized the characters by meaning and by their structure. So "madness," "blemish," "sore head," and "burn" were grouped together, all being related to the character for "illness."

This was followed by the *Erya* (c. 200 BCE), which has been called the first Chinese dictionary. It too was divided topically, by subject, with linked words grouped together within each category, although the connections are not necessarily ones we recognize today: roads and bridges were considered to originate from the court of the emperor, and thus they appear under the heading "Interpreting the Court"; warfare too was the province of the ruler, who was divinely ordained, and thus it fell into the section dedicated to "Interpreting the Heavens." In around 100 CE the *Shuō wén jiĕ zì* dictionary, containing some 9,500 characters, originated a sorting system based not on meaning but on the manner in which a character was written. Each was defined as either a single unit or a compound character, and then categorized by 540 elements, called radicals, which might be semantic elements of the character or might be graphic ones—the direction of a stroke, for example. Each character was then listed under a single radical, which came to define it for lexicographical purposes.[39]

In Europe, nothing of this level of sophistication had been attempted. And where alphabetical order was used, in many cases it was considered not as a tool of reference but as one of recall, a way of imprinting a series of items onto the memory in a culture that continued to rely heavily on oral transmission. It may be for this reason that the second-century *Sentences* of Sextus, 123 maxims on how to live a philosophically good life, were arranged in alphabetical order. Or it may not have been: once again, all we have are later copies, which might well have been reordered. (And, in addition, the named author, Sextus the Pythagorean, is unlikely to be the actual author of the work.)[40] We know this type of reordering was routine. Fables by an author named Babrius, some of which are today collected under a generic authorship as *Aesop's Fables*, survive in copies that were organized by the first letter of the opening word of each fable. Yet an Oxyrhynchus fragment of the same fables, dating from the second century, shows that at least one earlier version was not in this order. The purpose of the reordering may well have been to help listeners remember the stories so that they, in turn, could retell them. For memory was a recurring component of alphabetization: the Greek grammarian Athenaeus listed eighty-one species of fish in first-letter alphabetical order, "in order that what is said may be easier for you to remember."[41]

Even so, it must be said that most types of ordering remained unusual. The most common form of organizing in the second century is one seen in the rhetorician Julius Pollux's *Onomasticon*, a thesaurus of terms in Attic Greek, the Greek spoken in earlier centuries, which by this date was partly incomprehensible to the author's contemporaries. Here the reader is told: "I shall take my beginning from exactly where the pious should, from the gods; as for the rest, I shall arrange matters as they occur," ordering his work first hierarchically, from greater to lesser as defined by religion and society, and then by subcategories that were arranged along a lifespan. The vocabulary for women followed the vocabulary for men, because men were considered to be more important than women; in the section for women, words used for all women head the list, followed chronologically by those for young women, then mature women, and finally old women.[42] (At least, once again, we think so: what we know of the *Onomasticon* comes from manuscripts produced from an early tenth-century epitome, or abridgement.)[43]

Even as copies vanished, were destroyed, or disintegrated, reading technology itself was changing. Scrolls were well suited to continuous reading, but they actively impeded the practice of looking things up. To read a scroll, the user rolled it open to the unread portion, rolling up the finished sections behind as they went along. By the first century CE, therefore, scrolls were gradually being replaced by codices, which were initially wooden tablets bound together with leather ties, then parchment sheets tied together. This new format gave readers of antiquity the flexibility that we expect from books today: codices are designed to be opened at any point, and readers can move backward and forward with ease. No longer locked into the rolling and unrolling of scrolls, they could now begin in the middle, or break off and check something earlier in the codex or toward the end. It makes sense, therefore, that some of the earliest texts to be transferred to codices were technical works and the Bible, which reward nonlinear reading.[44]

Reading technologies were changing elsewhere too, of course. The first common Chinese writing surface had been bamboo tablets; from around 200 BCE these were sometimes replaced by sheets made of silk waste, bamboo fibers, or linen, on which rubbings could be made from stone inscriptions. According to legend, it was in 105 CE that Cai Lun, a Han court official, came up with a new material that had a surface that took ink and was made from mulberry fibers, fishing nets, hemp waste, and rags: paper. In reality, paper appears to have been known for several centuries before this peculiarly specific date of 105, and may have been in use from the second century BCE, although probably not for writing. By the third century, knowledge of paper had spread to Korea, and by the fourth century from there to Japan.[45]

Simultaneously with the appearance of these new scrolls came a raft of glosses and materials designed to assist comprehension of other works, materials that today we call reference works. These works are not designed for continuous reading, but primarily as aids in looking things up. In the fourth century, Eusebius, a historian and biblical scholar, produced his *Onomasticon*, On the Place Names in the Holy Scriptures, a survey of all the places mentioned in the Bible. In his preface he explained: "I shall collect the entries from the whole of the divinely inspired Scriptures, and I shall set them out grouped by their initial letters, so that one may easily perceive what lies scattered throughout the text."[46] Thus Eusebius used first-letter alphabetical order, and after that, under each letter, he returned to the then more common method, arranging his list in the order the place names appear in the Bible.

In the next century, St. Jerome (347–420) translated Eusebius's work and produced his own *Liber interpretationis hebraicorum nominum*, The Book of Interpretation of Hebrew Names. Here too the names were arranged in first-letter alphabetical order, and then by their order of appearance in the Bible. For both these theological writers, and for their readers, the Bible's order was more ingrained than that of the alphabet: they knew many biblical passages by heart, and seeing the names in order was a memory prompt, enabling them to recall each passage as they moved from one to the next.[47]

This reliance on memory may be why alphabetical order, although known, was frequently passed over in favor of other types of ordering: it was simply not particularly useful to a primarily oral culture where large quantities of text were routinely memorized, or where people read through texts from beginning to end rather than searching out salient points—looking things up.

CHAPTER 2

B IS FOR THE BENEDICTINES

The Monasteries and the Early Middle Ages

THE FALL OF THE WESTERN ROMAN EMPIRE IN 476 CE CAUSED A fissure with the classical tradition in Western Europe. Literacy, both for those who taught and for those they were teaching, now fell almost entirely under the aegis of the Church, while public literary life outside the religious institutions dwindled precipitously. The last public library in Rome was founded by the Emperor Alexander Severus (r. 222–235), after which civic libraries of the classical world were no more.

This did not mean that there were no libraries, just that they were now to be found located in the religious world, in monasteries and convents. Eusebius reported using a Jerusalem library under the authority of Bishop Alexander (d. 250); there are records of a church library in the very early fourth century at Cirta, in modern-day Algeria, and another of the same date at a monastery at Tabennisis, near Dendera in Egypt. The first monastery library that we know of in Western Europe dates from the sixth century, at Vivarium, in what is now Calabria, and was founded by Cassiodorus (c. 485–c. 585), a high official in the Ostrogothic kingdom, in his retirement.[1]

Libraries like these were not established to display the riches of the monasteries to the world, but as functional collections for the purpose of supplying their community members with religious sustenance. At Tabennisi, the monastic rule dictated that every evening the monks were to return the books they had been reading that day to a designated brother, who counted them to ensure no losses had occurred before locking them in the *fenestra*, often a barred niche in a stone wall.[2] (In Latin, *fenestra* most commonly translates as "window," but it can also mean a breach or opening in a wall.)

And so began a millennium of monastic learning. St. Benedict (480–543/7) drew up a series of precepts known as the Rule of St. Benedict to ensure a harmonious religious communal life, the chief of which was *ora et labora*, pray and work. Reading was a spiritual occupation, and the brothers were required to spend set hours at their books. At Lent, Benedict decreed, each brother was to "receive a book apiece from the library, and read it straight through," which strongly suggests that Benedictine monasteries expected to hold a sufficient quantity of books to supply all the members of the order simultaneously. By 831, the library of the Benedictine Abbey of St. Riquier in northern France contained 250 volumes, which were listed by category: divinity, grammar, history, geography, sermons, and service books; the library of the Benedictine Abbey of St. Gallen, founded in 720 in what is now Switzerland, used similar categories.[3]

Many other libraries also organized their book lists, and most likely the books themselves, in a hierarchical order. The first, and most important, group consisted of copies of the Bible; then came the writings of the Church Fathers;* then theology more generally; followed by

---

*The term "Church Fathers" encompasses a fluid number of influential theologians who lived and wrote before the seventh and eighth centuries. In the Western canon

homilies or sermons; the lives of the saints; and finally secular works, a category that was sometimes further subdivided into works by Christian authors, which were given precedence over works by pagan writers.

One notable exception to the religious dominance of libraries was the palace library in Aachen, at the court of Charlemagne, although even this princely library was overseen by a member of the clergy. In 782, Alcuin (735–804), an English cleric, writer, and teacher who had been educated in York by students of the Venerable Bede, was installed as master of the palace school, and there he oversaw an expansion of the court library, turning it into a renowned center from which learning, and manuscripts, were disseminated widely. Under Alcuin the palace library appears to have included not just the standard theological texts, but secular works, and even books in German as well as Latin.[4] Despite the literary riches found here, Alcuin remained nostalgic for the York library of his student days, producing what amounts to a dream catalog—not a real one, for we know that York did not at that date hold all the books he listed—which he organized much as a monastery library would have been, in hierarchical order of importance:

> *Here shines what Jerome, Ambrose, Hilary, thought*
> *Or Athanasius and Augustine wrought.*
> *Orosius, Leo, Gregory the Great,*
> *Near Basil and Fulgentius coruscate.*
> *Grave Cassiodorus and John Chrysostom*
> *Next Master Bede and learned Aldhelm come,*
> *While Victorinus and Boethius stand*
> *With Pliny and Pompeius close at hand.*
> *Wise Aristotle looks on Tully near.*

---

there were four Great Fathers of the Church—Ambrose, Jerome, Augustine of Hippo, and Gregory the Great—with a larger number of Apostolic, Latin, and Greek Church Fathers, including Clement of Rome, Clement of Alexandria, Gregory Nazianzus, Isidore of Seville, John Chrysostom, John of Damascus, Justin Martyr, Origen, and Tertullian.

Sedulius and Juvencus next appear.
Then come Albinus, Clement, Prosper too,
Paulinus and Arator. Next we view
Laetantius, Fortunatus. Ranged in line
Virgilius Maro, Statius, Lucan, shine.
Donatus, Priscian, Probus, Phocas start
The roll of masters in grammatic art.
Eutychius, Servius, Pompey, each extend
The list. Comminian brings it to an end.
There shalt thou find, O reader, many more
Famed for their style, the masters of old lore,
Whose many volumes singly to rehearse
Were far too tedious for our present verse.[5]

This sort of idealized catalog had at least one predecessor. A century and a half before, an equally imaginative cataloging method had been used by Isidore of Seville (c. 560–636), one of the Church Fathers, for his own personal library.* Few had as impressive a private collection as Isidore, whose volumes filled fourteen bookcases and were organized by author, but in neither alphabetical nor hierarchical order. Instead, the archbishop dedicated individual shelves to seven theologians, four Christian poets, two ecclesiastical historians, Gregory the Great, Isidore's brother St. Leander, three jurists, and two medical writers. One historian has noted that the works of several of these writers were too slight to fill the spaces allocated to them, and he suggests that Isidore might have named each bookcase after a representative author as a mnemonic device, filling the shelves with works on related subjects.[7]

---

*As a side note, Isidore, Archbishop of Seville, had three siblings, all of whom were venerated as saints: St. Leander of Seville (himself predecessor to Isidore as that city's archbishop), St. Fulgentius of Cartagena, and St. Florentina. This saintly siblinghood was outmatched, however, by that of the fourth-century St. Gregory of Nyssa, whose four siblings—Basil the Great, Macrina the Younger, Naucratius, and Peter of Sebaste—were also all canonized, as was their grandmother, Macrina the Elder.[6]

That Isidore might have kept his books in a way that reveals a deep interest in ordering and arranging diverse materials is not unexpected, for in his writings he pioneered what was to become one of the supreme forms of organizing knowledge: the encyclopedia. The stated aim of his *Etymologiae*, Etymologies (begun 600 CE), could not have been more ambitious: a summary of everything that could be known in the universe, not only based on Christian theology but drawing also on classical literature. Isidore divided his work into twenty books, the first five following the *trivium* and *quadrivium*, the seven liberal arts of classical education. The *trivium*, or threefold path, taught the basics: grammar, rhetoric, and logic; the *quadrivium*, or fourfold way, covered mathematics, geometry, music, and astronomy. The two combined were considered to be the foundation from which a student could then progress to the greater fields of philosophy and theology.

From there Isidore continued to other areas of knowledge: theology, of course, and medicine and jurisprudence, both of which were considered to be mechanical rather than liberal arts, as well as geography and the study of the natural world. Isidore's work, novel in itself, was prefaced by another novelty: a list of the topics explored, in the order they appeared in the book—what we call a table of contents. The *Etymologies* became a standard work; copies circulated extensively, so much so that in the following two hundred years virtually no major center of learning was without one. More than a thousand manuscript copies survive today, indicating just how many were once in existence.[8] Thus, what were then innovative information and organizational tools—the encyclopedia itself and the table of contents—became familiar to many.

These were not the only original contributions made by Isidore. Book 9 of the *Etymologies* dealt with people and kingdoms, and Book 11 with mankind and "portents," both structured in a traditional subject-based manner. But in between, Book 10, where Isidore covered "Vocabulary," is suddenly different, its contents sorted first into first-letter alphabetical order; then, within that order, by the words' etymology; and, finally, by a third organizing principle, Isidore's own subjective judgment, with words having benign or positive meanings being given precedence over those that held negative associations.[9]

For Isidore was a man facing in two directions. With his table of contents and his first-letter alphabetization, he was looking ahead to a system of organizing texts that would not flourish until the end of the twelfth and into the thirteenth centuries. At the same time his encyclopedia, which aimed to hold up a mirror to a world that was, as he saw it, designed as a part of God's plan for mankind, made him very much of his own day.

In the twenty-first century, we consider many things to be neutral that to the medieval European mind had symbolic meaning; things that we regard as entirely fixed in meaning were, in the Middle Ages, just as entirely fluid. Then as now, a day and a night spanned twenty-four hours, but how those hours were divided then is radically different from our own twenty-four equal units. There were, according to medieval understanding, twelve hours of daytime and twelve of night, and therefore a daytime hour in summer was substantially longer than one in winter in southern Europe, and in northern Europe summer's twelve-hour nights passed by in a flash. And time itself was not purely a measure, but had meaning: the symbolic value of the numbers, as a reminder of God's eternal being, was often given precedence over their expression as the time of day. Numbers more generally also represented more than mere quantity. Three was a key number, representing as it did the holy Trinity; six was perfect, because God created the universe in six days; the number seven was important too, for God rested on the seventh day; ten stood for the number of the commandments; forty, for the days Christ spent on earth after the Resurrection.*[10]

---

* Not that we have any right to the condescension of posterity regarding the supposed superstition of earlier times. Doctors in the West today routinely prescribe drugs for three or seven days—those numbers of the Trinity, and of the Sabbath—even though evidence from clinical trials suggests that two or eight days works every bit as well.[11]

Medieval encyclopedists naturally partook of this worldview, and utilized it when organizing information. We think of an encyclopedia as a reference tool to be dipped into, to enable us to locate a single piece of information. To the great encyclopedists of the Middle Ages, and to their readers, this format, which thrived from Isidore's day to the thirteenth century, was instead, as Augustine put it, "an instrument of education, whose aim was [to build] a life happy through the knowledge of God." Happiness and knowledge through religion were inextricably entwined: you could not have one without the other. Furthermore, it was impossible to understand the world without understanding God's plan for it, and any well-constructed encyclopedia had to explain the world by reflecting God's plan in its organizational structure, as well as in the information it contained. In the thirteenth century, *De proprietatibus rerum*, On the Nature of Things, by Bartholomew the Englishman (before 1203–1272, and who, despite his name, lived and wrote in Paris, and whose country of origin is unknown), set out the order of the great chain of being: from God, to man, to animals, to inanimate objects.[12] God had created a hierarchical world, and those who followed him reflected that hierarchy in their work. Alphabetical order looked like resistance, even rebellion, against the order of divine creation. Or possibly ignorance: an author who placed *angeli*, angels, before *deus*, God, simply because A comes before D, was an author who had failed to comprehend the order of the universe. It was only when dealing with matters such as vocabulary, where one word had no inherent superiority or inferiority to another, that an author like Isidore might adopt a neutral organizing principle.

This theologically based structure was not too dissimilar to the shaping of encyclopedias in other parts of the world. In China, *leishu*, books of categories or of classification, in effect embryonic dictionaries and encyclopedias, had flourished long before the genre developed in Europe, from as early as the third century. These works emerged in a period of political upheaval—the earliest surviving complete work dates to the beginning of the seventh century, under the Tang dynasty—and consisted of citations from texts arranged first in subject categories, then according to the level of authority attributed to each author.[13] Like their later Western counterparts, these works were for an educated readership: here, candidates studying for the civil service exams that led to court positions.

In Europe, Isidore's innovative use of alphabetical order to organize his work on vocabulary was instead proving influential in a parallel genre: glosses. Glosses had originally appeared in the manuscripts they were glossing, where they explained the meanings of difficult words in Latin or translated foreign words. In both cases, the gloss was written either above the relevant word or beside it, in the margin. Later, sometimes for clarity, sometimes to preserve a valuable manuscript, glosses began to be written out as a separate document, initially continuing to list the words in the order in which they appeared in the primary text, so tying a gloss to a single work, or even, because of the reshaping and reordering that we have seen in copied manuscripts, to one particular copy of a work. Gradually, however, the utility of a gloss that included vocabulary from more than one work became apparent, even if it meant it was no longer practicable to list the words in order of appearance.

And so experiments began with different ordering systems. One possibility was alphabetical order. Another was subject categories, particularly for glosses of technical vocabulary, grouping together words relating to hunting, for example, or words for military fortifications or for parts of the body. Other glosses relied on organizing principles that are far more foreign to us today. The *Læcboc, or Medicinale anglicum*, The Leech Book, or English Remedies, written in Old English around 950, was arranged, as were many medical texts of the period, with diseases and cures situated along the human body *a capite ad calcem*, from head to heel.[14] In the Byzantine Empire, texts were generally organized by subject, sometimes geographically, or by name. Only the *Suda*, a Byzantine encyclopedic dictionary dating from the late tenth century, was an alphabetical compilation, magisterially ordering thirty-one thousand historical, biographical, and lexicographical entries into a single alphabetical order. But it was an outlier, both in Byzantium and in Western Europe too at that date.[15]

Glosses, owing their existence to readers' difficulties with Latin, were more common in countries where the local language had no etymological connection with Latin. Native English, or German, or Flemish readers had greater need of assistance with Latin vocabulary than did French or Italian or Spanish readers, and so it follows that some of the earliest glosses we know of, from the seventh and eighth centuries, were produced by English and Irish speakers. The *Leiden Glossary* was probably compiled in St. Gallen, but by someone who, judging from the English translations, probably came from what is now Kent, in England. He translated the Latin vocabulary into either Old English or Old High German, and arranged the entries, at least in part, in first-letter alphabetical order.*[16] By the eighth century one glossary, which defined nearly five thousand Latin words, ordered just under two thousand of them into fairly consistent first-letter alphabetical order. One extraordinary copy of another glossary, the *Liber glossarum*, The Book of Glosses, which may have been produced at a convent at Soissons and was based in part on Isidore's *Etymologies*, was in almost absolute order, one of the very earliest examples.[17]

For the most part, however, we must once again remind ourselves how little information we have on the original arrangement of these

---

* I am writing of this author as though he were a man because the manuscript was almost certainly written in a monastery. Elsewhere, I make the same assumption about gender simply through weight of mathematical probability. There were educated women, and women scribes, and some convents were known for their erudition—for an example of which, look no further than the end of this paragraph. The vast majority of manuscripts and books, however, were written by men and for men, right up through much of the nineteenth century. It is the same for the education of boys: some girls received an education, but far fewer, and far less systematically, and the books that were written on or for the education of children virtually always assumed those children were boys. My choice of pronoun throughout is a description, not an endorsement.

glossaries, for they were copied and recopied, and it is those later manuscripts that have survived. Whether the originals were in alphabetical order or their contents were rearranged later is unknown.[18] Moreover, when scholars state that the Such-and-Such Glossary was in alphabetical order, what they generally mean is that some copies are in alphabetical order, or perhaps even just one. For example, a glossary known as the *Glossarium affatim*, The Sufficient [or Ample] Glossary, probably dating to around 760–780, which survives in a manuscript in St. Gallen, is in second-letter alphabetical order; another copy, probably created a little later, in the late eighth or early ninth century, and now in Amiens, is in first-letter order.[19] For even when alphabetical order was used, it was not a simple progression, with early manuscripts using first-letter, then later copies second-letter, and so on until a pinnacle of absolute alphabetical order was achieved.

In the non-Christian world in the Middle East and Europe, in the same period, the sixth and seventh centuries, Hebrew scholars were also producing glosses, typically as interlinear or marginal explanations, like their Christian coevals. Some also produced separate word lists in alphabetical order, although their purpose is uncertain. One comprised all the two-letter words in the Bible, yet supplied no references to enable a reader to locate those words: it was seemingly drawn up for information only. By the ninth century, however, many Hebrew codices appended lists of words at the end of a manuscript: early versions of the index.[20]

The Rav Saadiah Gaon (882–942), who headed a rabbinic school in Babylonia, compiled the first Hebrew dictionary that we know of, entitled the *Kitāb usūl al-shi'r al'Ibrāni*, Book of the Elements of Hebrew Poetics, fragments of which were discovered in the nineteenth century. By the third century, Hebrew had died out as the spoken language of the Jews of the Middle East, most commonly replaced with Aramaic or Persian; by the tenth century these had been replaced in turn by Arabic, and the written language of Hebrew scholars had become Judeo-Arabic—Arabic in language, but written in Hebrew characters. This was what the Rav Saadiah Gaon used, dividing his work in two parts, both alphabetical: one by the first letter and one the final letter, to enable novice poets to find appropriate rhymes—possibly the world's first rhyming dictionary. In the tenth century in Córdoba, Menahem Ibn Saruq, a doctor at the court of 'Abd el-Rahman III, was the author of a dictionary of biblical Hebrew, *Mahberet Menahem*, Menahem's Notebook, which alphabetically glossed 1,600 words in the Tanach, the Hebrew Bible.[21]

But alphabetical order continued to be one system among many. Aelfric (c. 950–c. 1010), abbot of the Benedictine Abbey of Eynsham, in what is today Oxfordshire, produced his *Nomina multarum rerum anglice*, The Names of Many Things in English. He divided those many English things into eighteen categories, beginning with God, followed by the heavens, angels, the sun and moon, the earth and the sea; then men, women, parts of the body, family relationships, professions, trades, diseases, seasons, and times of day; then colors, animals (themselves divided by whether they lived on land or sea, walked or flew), plants, household goods, weapons, cities, metals, and gems; and concluding with a roundup of general terms, divided into abstract and concrete.[22] After the Norman invasion of England in 1066, an Anglo-Norman glossary, *Nominale sive Verbale in Gallicis cum expositione eiusdem in Anglicis*, French Vocabulary, Translated into English, explained words and their meanings to the mutually uncomprehending conquerors and conquered. The work was divided topically—weather and storms, names of trees and fruits, and even *"La noyse de ditz Bestes,"* the noises that animals make.[23]

The shift in organizing principles from subject categories to alphabetical order was more than a move from an unwieldy to a more convenient system (our perception, of course, not theirs). It required an altered perspective, from seeing words primarily in terms of their meanings, to seeing that in addition to words having meaning they were also composed of individual letters of the alphabet that in and of themselves were meaningless. To modern eyes, *deus* means God; it is also a Latin word, and it is in addition made up of four letters, d-e-u-s, which are a linguistic construct, created by humans, that hold no inherent meaning or value. To Isidore of Seville, however, the word *deus*, even spelled out on a page in his *Etymologies*, was indissoluble with the abstract idea the word represented. It took a shift in perception for medieval thinkers before locating d-e-u-s under D, rather than at the head of the text, caused no profound sense of transgression.

That shift began slowly, and little obviously changed until 1053, when Papias the Lombard completed his *Elementarium doctrinae rudimentum*, Teaching the Basic Elements. Papias today can fairly be described as the first Western lexicographer, for his dictionary was a revolution: the first Latin dictionary of any substantial length, arranged in third- and sometimes fourth-letter alphabetical order. In his preface, Papias explained the ordering system he had chosen—or, rather, from the painfully elaborate way he phrased it, the ordering system he believed he had invented: "Anyone who wishes to find anything quickly must also notice that this whole book is composed according to the alphabet not only in the first letters of the parts but also in the second, third and sometimes even in the further determinative arrangement of the letters." His manuscript marked the first word of each letter with a large A, B, C, etc.; each change of second-letter order (from Ab to Ac, for example), with a medium-sized B and C, etc.; third-letter shifts (from Aba to Abb) with a small a and b, and so on.

And even with all this care, Papias felt obliged to warn his readers, "Even in these first, second and third steps the relationship will sometimes vary because of the writing of different letters. For example, hyena is written by some with an i, by others with a y, or with an aspiration [that is, an h]. And the plant that some call verbena others call berbena."*[24] For, lacking standardized spelling, which in almost all parts of Europe was another half millennium in the future, dictionaries could only gesture toward an absolute order. And while Papias worked hard to explain his method, many of the scribes who copied his work either failed to understand it, or thought it was unnecessary: surviving copies show that, until the twelfth and thirteenth centuries, when alphabetical order began to be used more widely, they frequently disregarded his layout and marginal orderings.[26]

While there was yet a dearth of tools to help people "look things up," the Latin Middle Ages had inherited from the classical world a system of epitomizing, of summarizing and extracting to provide the essence of a book, or a theological argument, or other core material of a specific text. (See, for example, page 24, for the survival of Julius Pollux's *Onomasticon* through an epitome.) Much of Isidore of Seville's encyclopedia consisted of summaries and précis of his classical reading, although at first he was the exception; by the late eighth and the ninth centuries, however, references and citations from classical authors were increasingly appearing in works presented by churchmen. Aristotle, in

---

* It is worth reminding ourselves that it was not merely spelling that was not standardized in a Western Europe where for the educated Latin predominated over the vernaculars, and the nation–state had yet to supersede the courts of small princelings and other aristocracy. A scant decade after Papias's dictionary began to be copied, England was invaded by the Normans, and by the twelfth and thirteenth centuries English, French, and Latin all coexisted in the British Isles, the choice of language depending on whether those involved were speaking, reading, or writing, or to whom they were speaking or writing. Even the documents that have survived provide no guarantee of the original language of the transactions or events they record. One scholar has noted that the king might make a pronouncement in French, which could be read aloud to the people in English, before being written down in Latin. In 1029, John Balliol, King of the Scots, swore fealty to Edward I "with his own mouth in the French language," yet his oath was recorded "literally"—that is, in the language of literacy, Latin.[25]

the fourth century BCE, had outlined his preferred method: "We should select from the written handbooks of arguments, and draw up sketch-lists of . . . several kinds of subject, putting them down under separate headings, e.g., 'On Good,' or 'On Life.'"

This concept of headings was to become more influential than Aristotle could ever have imagined. The headings, or, as he called them, *topoi*, or topics (literally, places), were to become one of the primary units of sorting and reference for adult readers as well as for schoolchildren in Europe for nearly two millennia. The Roman states-man Cicero (106–43 BCE), famed for his oratory, had advised those who wanted to copy him to have "in readiness sundry commonplaces which will instantly present themselves for setting forth [your] case."* Many classical writers became famous among their contemporaries and for centuries afterward for their collections of commonplace extracts: Quintilian's *Institutio Oratoria*, On the Education of the Orator (c. 95 CE), was quoted by Isidore of Seville as early as the seventh century, and it continued to be considered of such significance that it was cited by Alexander Pope more than a thousand years later; in the fourteenth century, Chaucer knew the third- or fourth-century writer Dionysius Cato's *Disticha de moribus*, Musings on Death, as did Benjamin Franklin four hundred years after him, who found it so profound that in 1735 he reworked it into rhyming couplets.[27]

As the world of authorship moved from the classical to the medi-eval, from secular to religious, Christian anthologies of commonplace extracts, known as florilegia—literally, gatherings of flowers, in the sense

---

* Cicero used "commonplace" in its original meaning of an extract or thought forming the basis of an argument or debate. The word thereafter began to mean any idea that was important, or well expressed, or worthy of being written down. It was the sheer omnipresence of these commonplaces, noted in what soon became known as common-place books, that in the Renaissance transformed the definition of a commonplace from something notable into something banal: so ordinary, it was *not* worth writing down.

that the compiler had plucked, or extracted, the choicest blossoms of thought—became popular.* These generally included extracts from the Bible and, especially, the Church Fathers. One of the earliest medieval florilegia was the *Liber scintillarum*, The Book of Sparks. Dating to the second half of the seventh or the early eighth century, it was organized by subject, with headings based on the virtues and vices, or aspects of Christian life such as confession and marriage. Within each topic, the extracts were ordered hierarchically, always beginning with the Gospels, followed by the writings of St. Paul and the Apostles, then the remainder of the Bible; after that came the Church Fathers, with lesser authorities trailing behind.

The *Sacra parallela*, Sacred Parallels, said to have been compiled by John of Damascus (c. 675–749), a Syrian monk, was another such florilegium, of which three manuscript copies have survived, the earliest dating from the mid-850s. From these and a few fragments of other copies, scholars have concluded that the original work fell into three parts, dealing with God, mankind, and the virtues and vices. Each part was divided into twenty-four chapters, one for each letter of the Greek alphabet, and each with a subhead beginning with that letter. Again, within each heading a hierarchical system was used: first came biblical citations, then the Church Fathers, and finally two secular commentators: Philo of Alexandria (c. 20 BCE–c. 50 CE), a Jewish philosopher (and, indeed, based in Alexandria), and Flavius Josephus (37 CE–c. 100), a Roman-Jewish historian from Jerusalem. The scriptural extracts were presented in the order in which they appeared in the Bible, but the rest were sometimes in alphabetical order.[28] This even partial alphabetical organization was unusual. A few florilegia ordered their extracts by, say,

---

*Our modern version of the florilegium (the singular of florilegia) is the anthology, and that word, too, derives from the notion of a bouquet, from the Hellenistic Greek for "gathering of flowers."

the first letter of the names of the Church Fathers, but most utilized subject categorization, the *topoi* of Aristotle.

For it was Aristotle, who had been dead for more than a millennium, who was ultimately to do more for alphabetical order than any living person in the Middle Ages.

CHAPTER 3

 IS FOR CATEGORIES

Authorities and Organization, to the Twelfth Century

THE RULE OF ST. BENEDICT SET OUT A PATTERN OF DAILY STUDY FOR the members of the Benedictine order, study that was ultimately to occupy three and a half hours daily. Reading was encouraged further outside those hours, the Rule denominating it a "work of God." As all monastic inhabitants had taken vows of poverty, renouncing earthly possessions, institutional libraries were both necessary and valued.[1]

St. Boniface (c. 675–754), Archbishop of Mainz, a key figure in the shaping of Christianity in Germany, was educated at a Benedictine monastery, probably in his likely birthplace in Devon, in England, and his longstanding promotion of education in monasteries was directly derived from Benedict's Rule. From the late 710s, he was the pope's missionary bishop in Germany. No longer a member of a monastic community and thus not bound by a vow of poverty, Boniface could give his love of books free rein; he was thought ultimately to have owned as many as fifty volumes, giving him a personal library as large as that of many monasteries of the day. Even later German institutional libraries, which were generally substantially larger than their English counterparts, often held little more.[2] It was the ninth century before half a dozen Benedictine monastery libraries in the German-speaking world contained more than a couple of hundred volumes: the Abbey of Lorsch, under the patronage of Charlemagne, possessed nearly six hundred manuscripts; St. Gallen, founded under Irish influence, had over four hundred, as did Reichenau, near Lake Constance, but there were few others.[3]

By the tenth century, these and other Benedictine monasteries had become the centers of education in Western Europe, followed in the coming century by hundreds of other monasteries, many of them Benedictine houses, others established by orders such as the Carthusians (founded 1084) and the Cistercians (1098) that were springing up as part of a new wave of religious and missionary fervor. By the end of the Middle Ages, there were approximately 350 Benedictine monasteries in the German-speaking lands alone.[4] The spread and plenitude of monasteries meant that education was more readily accessible to many working men and boys; by joining these orders, they could now learn to read and write.

For reading and writing were becoming more important in the world outside the Church, in turn driving an increased demand for the education available within it. The secular world—the world of government, of jurisprudence, and of trade—was beginning to privilege the written over the spoken word. The *Pandects*, or digests of Roman law, which had been compiled under the Eastern Roman Emperor Justinian (r. 527–565), were a model of the same extracting and précising system that had produced florilegia. To create the *Pandects*, more than three dozen scholars had gathered the many sources of the law, compared them, resolved their contradictions while removing repetitions, and so produced a final version that would become, for the Eastern Empire, *the* law. In the ninth century, the code was revised and updated into sixty volumes as the *Basilika*, or Royal Laws, under the Emperor Basil I

(r. 867–886) and his successor, Leo VI (r. 886–912); in the mid-tenth century the *Synopsis basilicorum maior* condensed these into just twenty-four sections, organized not thematically, but in absolute alphabetical order.[5] This law code became widely known over the next centuries, surviving today in more than fifty manuscript copies.

In Western Europe, beginning as early as the sixth and seventh centuries, the Merovingian rulers of Gaul were similarly focused on codification and systematization. Increasingly, legal transactions were being confirmed by written documents rather than by spoken oaths, as had been the case for centuries in Gaul, and continued to be practiced even longer elsewhere. Thus, the upper echelons of society now required men who could read and write to do their legal work and, as a corollary, they also required systems that allowed those literate men to locate a single document from among hundreds, if not thousands, of similar documents. Such ordering systems had yet to be imagined, much less established, and thus it became necessary to devise legal procedures for the not uncommon situations where deeds or charters no longer existed or could not be found.[6]

Over the following centuries, therefore, individual clerical or governmental offices were obliged to create their own organizational systems. In Italy, the Benedictine Cardinal Deusdedit (d. before 1100), a canon lawyer, compiled a list of some eight hundred subject headings, in effect what we think of as a subject index, to help him search his more than one thousand texts. He might well have known Papias's alphabetical Latin dictionary, but he seems not to have considered that the same system of organization, by letter of the alphabet, might be adapted to his own needs. Instead he used a "rational" order—that is, an order that made sense to him, based on his own interests, rather than an order that might be grasped by anyone reading his notes at a later date.[7] Although the cardinal's method could not be universally applied, his list can retrospectively be seen as a precursor to the index, indicating the need for a more universal sorting system created by increasing secular and religious bureaucracy.

While the cardinal was renowned for his use of archives in his legal writings, we have no firm information as to when papal records began. Documents before the ninth century had frequently been written on papyrus, and thus many of those papal registers were in reality later copies. We do know, from a few surviving fragments, that most papal records were sorted and stored in bound ledgers compiled in chronological order, often with a *capitulum*, an early version of a table of contents, at the front, listing all the items in order of appearance.[8] The only exception is a single ledger containing papal bulls, or decrees, promulgated by Gregory VII, who happened to be a friend and patron of Cardinal Deusdedit. This ledger ends with an index headed *Tabula notabilium gestorum quae in hoc libro continentur per alphabetum reducta*, Table of the Notable Deeds in this Book, in Alphabetical Order. Disappointingly, the connection between Gregory and Deusdedit is probably a red herring: the handwriting of the table can be dated to the fourteenth century, and therefore the document was most likely appended later to a much earlier ledger.[9] Because from 1000 CE onward across Europe, society was changing radically, and with it, so was the use of documents and their function, which in some cases also involved a retrospective reorganization of earlier material.

Between 1000 and 1340, the population of Western Europe more than doubled, much of the increase occurring in what were becoming major urban centers: by the early fourteenth century, Venice and London both had populations nearing one hundred thousand. New industries, such as textile weaving and ceramic production—as well as the burgeoning trading markets in which they participated, powered as they were by bookkeepers, merchants, traders, shipowners, shopkeepers, and lawyers—were all increasingly kept in motion by paperwork. (I use the word "paperwork" in a nonliteral sense here, to encompass all documents, on any writing surface.) Meanwhile, both the Church and secular rulers were funding civic growth via taxation, which necessitated a legion of tax collectors and clerks, all of whom produced their own paperwork.[10] Documents, in other words, were coming to permeate society at almost every level, and to an unprecedented degree.

Just as we saw the creation of money at the time that alphabetic writing began to appear, so too, with society's increasing reliance on the written word, now cash became far more widely used, rapidly replacing barter and trade. At the beginning of the tenth century ten mints were sufficient to supply coinage for all of England; a hundred years later, such was the spread of the use of currency that seventy were needed to fulfill the same function. By the thirteenth century a variety of new European currencies were in circulation, among them the genois, the florin, the ducat, and the zecchino, or sequin. The genois was minted in Genoa, the florin in Florence, while the ducat and zecchino were Venetian, although all these coins were in use across Europe, regardless of their place of origin. They, and many other less important currencies, were theoretically worth the value of their metal; in reality, they were worth whatever their governments valued them at: money had become abstract.[11]

In a similar way, from the eleventh to the thirteenth centuries, documents that in England had served as commemorative markers of ceremonial occasions were becoming legal necessities. Until 1250, "to record" had meant, in legal terms, to bear witness in court, the spoken affirmation itself being the record. Soon, however, such affirmations were to be replaced by documents, which were no longer symbols marking the fact that an event had occurred. Now the courts gave preference to written over spoken oaths, a reversal of centuries of precedent. In 1256, the Domesday Book was cited in parliament as evidence that a particular town in Surrey had not historically belonged to the Crown. Previously, an assertion of this nature would have been made by a dozen knights who would have had to be physically present to swear aloud an oath that this was their accurate remembrance. Now, chronicles of historical events, deeds, charters, and surveys were all becoming essential evidence in their own right.

Until this period in England, memory had had a fixed legal span. Up to the reign of Edward I (1272–1307), a witness could legally swear to events that had occurred at any time in the previous hundred years, while anything before that was considered to be beyond the remit of the courts. The form had been for a witness to prove precedent by swearing that he remembered that such-and-such had been done by so-and-so's father, who had told him that he in turn remembered his own father had done or said the same. In 1275, and again in 1293, statutes reinforced the hundred-year rule by laying down that the coronation of Richard I (September 3, 1193) was the "legal limit of memory." But as written documents began to replace memory and its associated sworn testimony, that date of 1193 was never superseded. Now the law relied instead on what might be called artificial memory—paperwork—rather than the testimony of men who recalled events recounted by their fathers and grandfathers.[12] This new dependence on documentation was becoming more common at every level of society: by 1300, even English "serfs or villeins" were presenting documents to the courts to prove points in legal matters.[13]

This change in use, and in expectation, can be seen in the way the documents were written. In the twelfth century there was no standard format for the charters issued by great lords. Instead, these documents tended to be drawn up in any number of hands, indicating that they were written by the nearest available person who had the requisite literacy skills, in whatever format he was familiar with. Less than a hundred years later, however, it was possible to discern a regularization of handwriting, as well as of style and form, as great landowners began to find it worthwhile to employ people with specific training to perform their now overwhelming levels of clerical work: what one scholar has described as "invisible technicians," the secretaries and scribes who would become the engines powering the actions of their lords and masters.[14]

This development occurred across Europe. In the papal archives, fewer than thirty letters a year have survived from the reign of Pope Alexander II (1061–1073); a century later, the archive of Alexander III contains on average 180 surviving letters annually. Philip II of France (r. 1179–1223), or his apparatus of state, left fewer than ten letters a year; that of Philip III, a century later, nearly sixty. In England, William the Conqueror (r. 1066–1087) averaged ten, Henry II (1154–1189), just under 120. By the thirteenth century Pope Boniface was sending fifty thousand letters a year, and Philippe le Beau of France fifteen thousand that we know of.*[15] Similarly, it is estimated that thirty thousand charters were drawn up in England in the twelfth century; between 1250 and 1350 that rose to several million, even in a population that had nearly halved, falling from 4.25 million to 2.6 million after the arrival of the Black Death.**[16]

Documents' change in use produced a change in quantity; the change in quantity, in turn, produced a change in how they were perceived, and thus how they were stored. In 1194, at the Battle of Fréteval, England's Richard the Lionheart was said to have seized the treasury of Philip II of France. A treasury at that time held the ruler's gold and silver and jewels; the great seal of the kingdom; and charters, proclamations, and other documents, including those that facilitated its administration, such as tax ledgers and deeds of land ownership. A legend recounted how for more than half a decade after that battle, one of Philip's loyal courtiers traveled across the country to reconstruct those lost documents of state, his notes themselves temporarily becoming France's administrative core.[17]

While this story was, if not an entire fabrication, at best an embroidery of actual events, it is telling that it emerged at this time: no legends

---

*Survival, of course, does not necessarily correlate with the number of letters that were actually written, but the recurrence of the sharp rise across so many countries suggests that survival in this case is a good, if not complete, indication of historical reality.

**The population of England and Wales is estimated to have been 4.23 million in 1250; it had risen to 4.75 million by 1290, and dropped back to 2.6 million in 1351, falling to 1.9 million a century later. It did not reach 1250 levels again until 1600, when the population is estimated to have been around 4.11 million.

had grown up around paperwork in previous centuries. Just fifty years later, in 1240, legend became reality, as the Sicilian court of Frederick II Hohenstaufen established what might be considered to be the first European chancellery, a physical space with a dedicated staff to oversee a complex system of administration, one that was carried out in written form, and with those documents carefully preserved.

One of the things that made Sicily the perfect location for this innovation was the appearance there of a new writing material that had arrived from the Islamic world: paper. In China, paper had been known as a substance for wrapping goods, possibly from the second century BCE, although it was another couple of hundred years before it replaced silk or bamboo strips as a writing surface. And just as China was far in advance of Europe in its use of writing material, so too it was in its reliance on—and therefore organization of—documents. From the mid-third century the Mi Shu Sheng, the Imperial Palace Library, was both a place to keep books and the central archiving system for all documents pertaining to the emperor and his court. In the twelfth century Cheng Ju, the library's deputy director, wrote *A Tale of the National Library*, which categorized the collection into "Jihn, Shi, Zi, and Ji," Confucian ideas, history, schools, and miscellaneous literature. Other possibilities he discussed were for archives to organize their contents according to the type of documents they stored, or how often they were accessed.

Zheng Quia's *Jiao Chou Luo*, The Theory of Library Science and Bibliography, also concentrated on classification: "If the books are classified," he wrote, "then all schools of thought and all knowledge are well organized and clearly systematized." It was not the quantity of works to be cataloged that was daunting, he continued: what was daunting was to lack a method of classifying them. (He preferred a topical ordering system.)[18] Later, in the Yuan dynasty established under the Mongol leader Kublai Khan (who reigned as Yuan emperor from 1271 to 1294), instructions for administration became more detailed: officers were to stamp each document with the date it was received, separately noting its receipt and then any subsequent actions taken, including the details of outgoing documents sent in response. By 1298, all documents were ordered chronologically, with outgoing and incoming items differentiated by the color of the ink used.[19]

Nothing like this had yet been seen in Europe. Paper had been exported to the Arab world from China by 750. In the nineteenth century a treasure trove of more than a quarter of a million documents dating from the ninth century onward was found stored in a Cairo synagogue. Many of those from the tenth century and later were already written on paper.[20] By 1200, paper had appeared in Islamic Spain, and then, naturally enough, in Sicily, owing to its connections with the Arab world, as well as Sicily's precocious appreciation for governmental documentation. It then spread swiftly: by the end of the fourteenth century there were thirty mills manufacturing this new commodity in Italy alone; half a century later, paper was available across Europe.[21] Paper was not initially considered to be a substitute for parchment in the production of books, but rather as a utilitarian tool for clerical work. As such, it was quickly acclaimed. By 1285 paper account books for bookkeepers, as well as paper notebooks for tax collectors, were in use far from Sicily, in the Low Countries.[22] Half a century later, paper had hopped across the Channel: an English clergyman bequeathed to his heirs "the great quire or book which I was wont to carry about with me, written partly on parchment and partly on paper, wherein I have noted and arranged the [contents] under headings, as it were alphabetically."[23]

Paper transformed everything—not least, organizing systems. Paper was less expensive than parchment, and so it could be used for rough drafts, for calculations, and for ordering diverse content, as well as to record completed processes. Because paper could be used at less cost than the equivalent amount of parchment, it was no longer necessary to cram as much information as possible into as few pages as possible. Instead, in a notebook or ledger kept in chronological order, a new week, or month, or year could be indicated by beginning a new page; when the ledger was complete, more pages could be added to list its contents. Page layouts, too, could be reconfigured and expanded to aid retrieval and to give readers useful prompts, with the document's date or keywords written in margins that might now be inexpensively widened to accommodate them.[24]

The use of documents as primary, rather than supplementary, resources led to further changes. Throughout the twelfth century, few English charters had included dates. Those that did often used fluid dating methods based on local knowledge or information: a document might be dated as having been written so many years after a great storm, or the death of a local alderman, or the laying of a foundation stone for a church. But as time passed and events multiplied, even if the date referred to a national leader or event it might still be difficult to pin down: "after the king's great council at London" was no real guide a decade or more after one of possibly several great councils held by the king, without even taking into consideration which king was meant. In Lincoln, the earliest guild rolls to have survived, from the end of the twelfth century, were dated by an inscription that noted they had been written in the year the earl of Leicester was released from captivity.[*25] The use of this type of relative dating was in part due to localism, but more generally owed its prevalence to the fact that, just as hours were a relative timespan depending on the season, so many, if not most, people at that period did not know what year it was. Relational dates were often the only ones possible.

In England, Ralph de Diceto (d. c. 1200), a dean of St. Paul's Cathedral in London, was one of the earliest to attempt to date material so that it could be understood more widely, and for longer. His survey of

---

*Using modern tools to "look things up," it seems likely that the reference was to Robert de Breteuil, third Earl of Leicester (c. 1130–1190). However, even modern tools are no help upon discovering that the earl was imprisoned twice, once in 1173 and again in 1183. It is logical to think that it was the first captivity that was being referred to, because otherwise the scribe would have written that it was in the year of the earl's *second* release from captivity, but logic is insufficient if the scribe was unaware of either event.[26]

the manors owned by his cathedral was dated precisely: "The 1181st year AD, the 21st year of Pope Alexander III, the 27th regnal year of King Henry II of the English, the 11th regnal year of King Henry the son of the king, the 18th year that time had passed since the translation of Bishop Gilbert Foliot from Hereford to London."[27] While the dates were now in a form we consider modern, it is notable that he presented them hierarchically: first came the ruler of the Christian world, then his own secular ruler, followed by that ruler's heir, then the religious leader to whom the dean himself owed fealty—mirroring exactly the manner in which encyclopedias of the day put *deus* before *angeli*.

Just as, gradually, the need for dates that could be universally comprehended began to be served, so too did the need for organizing principles that could be used to locate documents. In around 1130, the records belonging to a Benedictine monastery north of Rome were reorganized and an alphabetical list of all the community's lands was drawn up, making it easier to locate original titles and leases, and to see at a glance what taxes were owed—as well as making it possible to prove it.[28]

On a more exalted level, in 1291 Edward I of England laid claim to the overlordship of Scotland. To support this, he ordered a search of the chronicles and registers in monasteries across the country, as well as the Chancery rolls, for any historical mentions that would validate his position. These searches were unsuccessful, but the failure was not considered to be owing to the absence of evidence, but to the absence, or at least inadequacy, of what today we call search tools. That very decade, therefore, the government undertook a reorganization of the plea-roll archive, which held details of court cases, and by 1302 other royal archives were also being sifted and sorted, "so that we can be advised of all things at all times that we want," in the words of the royal statement.[29] Over the following twenty years or so, documents were reordered and listed by subject, or by category, or by rationale: charters that conveyed land to the Crown were no longer stored with grants of land from the Crown to others, or with private charters;

legal statutes and papal bulls were each categorized separately, and stored accordingly.

The idea of subject categories was becoming firmly established. From 1285 the Wardrobe accounts, which itemized the expenses of the king's household, were recorded in ledgers with small projecting slips of parchment pasted onto some of the pages where the *titulus*, or subject, was written: an ancestor of the type of tabbed notebooks used in the twentieth century as address books.[30] In London, a list of those named in some deeds that had been kept in chronological order between 1252 and 1312 was reorganized sometime after 1332 into first-letter alphabetical order; after 1377 it was reorganized again, maintaining that first-letter alphabetical order and then, within that, setting the documents into chronological order of probate.[31]

It was not only in England that the benefits of sorting documents for later access were being recognized; different methods were being explored across Western Europe. In one district of Poitiers, in France, the records of payments from vassals to their feudal ruler were reorganized between 1259 and 1261, and many were even retranscribed so that they could be classified by district.[32] In Rome (probably), the *Tabula Martiniana* or *Margarita decretalium*, Martin's Tables, or The Pearls of the Decretals, produced by Martin of Poland (d. 1278), a Benedictine confessor to seven popes, was an important early legal reference work, using alphabetical order to organize a series of legal decrees and other legislation. This work was widely known and long admired: two hundred years later, twelve editions of the *Tabula* were printed in just twenty-five years.[33]

As well as expecting to be able to find the appropriate record with increasing frequency, those in charge of document caches were now also thinking of ways to locate material *within* each document. Marginal abbreviations, especially symbols, had previously been used intermittently to help readers locate information. Ralph de Diceto, Dean of St. Paul's, went further, creating an elaborate private classification system in order "to jog the memory more easily." Some of his symbols were pictorial—for instance, he used a sword to indicate references to Normandy, a cross and crozier for references to the Archbishop of Canterbury, while others took the form of abbreviations, such as "PS" being set next to text references to persecutions of the clergy.[34] Another English Benedictine, Matthew Paris (c. 1200–1259), may have copied the dean directly for his marginal notations, including a reversed shield next to

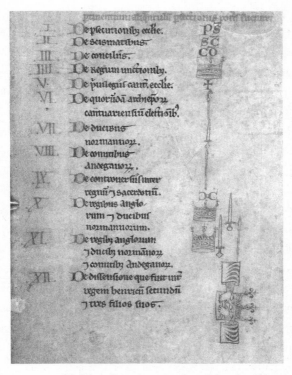

A table showing some of Ralph de Diceto's marginal symbols in his Abbreviationes chronicorum, Chronicles Précised (before 1147). At the top right, "PS" stands for persecutions, "SC" for schisms, "CO" for councils, and the crown for coronations, while lower down, the "C" backed by a reversed "C" stands for Church-state controversies. The swords highlight mentions of the Dukes of Normandy, the spear the Dukes of Anjou; where crowns, spears, and swords appear together, it is because the King of England being referred to also held the titles of Duke of Normandy or Anjou. The most literal symbol is the final one, two hands grabbing a crown, which makes reference to the struggle between Henry II and his heirs.

text referring to the death of a knight, and a reversed miter for the death of a bishop.[35]

Those outside clerical and governmental circles were also finding a way through their increasing paperwork with the assistance of marginals. Richard Hotot, a member of the minor English gentry, kept an estate book that included a list of his tenants, how much rent each owed, and when it fell due. He used marginal symbols to indicate which rental property was under discussion and, in a remarkable innovation, wrote a key to these symbols at the bottom of each page—Hotot had devised something akin to what we today call footnotes.[36]

Marginal symbols were especially useful since it was still a novelty to group together documents based on their contents. More commonly, many different documents were bound together, to our eye indiscriminately. Thus a manuscript of treatises on best management and accounting practices for an estate was bound together with a number of recipes, summaries of parliamentary legislation, and a treatise on gemstones.[37] Even after print arrived, the owner of one early seventeenth-century poetry book added other poems on the blank pages, as well as household accounts, some recipes to cure fits, and a method of perfuming a doublet. Such compilations were in no way out of the ordinary.

Whatever the method of organization, the period's increased reliance on paperwork drove demand for an educated pool of people to produce documents to organize, store, and administer them. Monasteries had long taken on the role of teaching not merely their own brethren but also lay people, sometimes to very high standards of literacy, although more frequently to merely functional ones. Cathedral schools, however, frequently produced exceptional teachers, and students. In the tenth century, the cathedral school of Laon became a renowned center of study, overtaken only in the eleventh century by the cathedral school of Chartres under Bishop Fulbert (d. 1028).

The great scholastic and theologian Peter Abelard (1079–1142) studied in three important cathedral schools: at Laon, at Chartres, and especially in Paris, where the masters—those teachers who were increasingly to be found at these cathedrals—had gathered together to form a *universitas*, a corporation or guild, in this case a guild of study focused around the cathedral of Notre-Dame. The first university in Europe was founded in Bologna in 1088; the university of Salamanca was founded in 1134 (or possibly not until 1218); while Paris was given a royal patent as a university in the year 1200. (Abelard himself had returned to become a master there around 1115.) In 1231, Gregory IX placed it under papal protection, and the Sorbonne, its theological college, was founded twenty-six years later. Oxford was developing from 1167, Cambridge from 1209 (or, by some accounts, 1231; the dates for neither are certain). Two hundred years after the foundation at Bologna, there were twenty-three universities in Western Europe; a hundred years after that, the number had doubled, to forty-five.[38] The separation between religion and secular education was in no way clear-cut: the ranks of university masters were drawn from the clergy, their job being primarily to train the next generation of clerics, although some universities quickly became known for specialties: Paris for theology, Bologna for law.

Paris in particular became a center for new methods of reading, and of searching or consulting, books. University faculties were organized along the lines of the seven liberal arts of the classical age—the *trivium* and *quadrivium*—with further faculties for civil and canon law and medicine, for those who wanted to study for the professions. The teaching method of the "scholastics," or "schoolmen," was for a master to give a lecture in which he set out a thesis, then presented arguments for and against it (the antithesis), using citations from authorities to give weight to his assertions, before drawing a conclusion. Thus, being able to locate a single paragraph, or even a single sentence, in an ever-expanding range of sources was increasingly important as the universities proliferated. Prime among the sources relied on were the Bible and the Church Fathers, alongside the classical texts that were beginning to emerge from centuries of oblivion in the Latin West.

Peter Abelard's *Sic et non*, Yes and No, written in the 1130s, partook of this approach—to a point. It laid out 158 questions on dogma, with, appended to them, conflicting citations from the Bible, the Church Fathers, and other authorities. (Of course, the number of questions depended on the manuscript. One critical edition that has collated eleven twelfth- and early thirteenth-century manuscripts of this work, plus one sixteenth-century transcript, notes that two contain 158 questions, one 154, and one 152; the remainder all have fewer.)[39] No matter the number, this early scholastic text with its many extracts aimed to foster critical thinking. At first glance, *Sic et non* could be confused with the many widely circulated florilegia. But florilegia descended from the tradition and teaching of classical rhetoric, while a *summa*, or compendium of theological texts like Abelard's, was drawn from the teaching of philosophy and dialectical reasoning.* The shocking element for Abelard's contemporaries was that, unlike the lectures given at the university, his book contained neither summations nor solutions from Abelard himself. Instead, in the early pages he laid down an outline of how the contradictions his work highlighted could be reconciled, but he made no attempt to reconcile them, nor did he include any conclusions he had drawn. To many, this placed him in opposition to the central tenet of Church thinking: authority was handed down from God to the Church, and thence to its clergy, who could be relied on to expound it as necessary to the lay population. Bernard of Clairvaux (1090–1153), the reformer who led the Cistercian order, was appalled by the open-ended nature of Abelard's book, and possibly even more appalled by its success: copies of it "fly abroad," he lamented.[40] He was not alone. Abelard was forced out of his mastership at Notre-Dame by many who felt the

---

Summa means more than a single-word translation into English can convey. Many books with this title were in part compendia comprising many extracts, but, as the *Oxford Latin Dictionary* notes, the word means "that which an activity amounts to": a *summa* considered a subject in overview, and also in terms of the subject's most important principles, as in Aquinas's *Summa theologica* (see facing page).

same. But there were a number of other great teachers, such as Albertus Magnus (c. 1200–1280). He had studied at Bologna before teaching theology at the Université de Paris in the 1240s, having one special pupil in particular, the not-yet-sainted Thomas Aquinas, who in turn himself became master in Paris in the 1250s and 1260s.

Around 1150, two decades after Abelard's *Sic et non*, Peter Lombard, Bishop of Paris (c. 1096–1160), produced his *Libri quattuor sententiarum*, The Four Books of Sentences (*sententiae* here meaning citations from the authorities, not our modern grammatical meaning). The *Sentences*, as it is generally known, was a compendium designed to be authoritative, including thousands of citations from the Bible, St. Augustine, and other Church Fathers, and threading together a formulation of standard theology carefully laid out thematically and divided into the Trinity and God, the creation and the angels, salvation, and the sacraments. It followed the style of *Sic et non*, setting out the pros and cons of each argument, but unlike Abelard's work, it firmly established the conclusions that the faithful were expected to assimilate and learn from. Altogether, the book was designed to help eager students reach those answers and, every bit as importantly, to locate the authorities with which to support them. Among the vast array of Christian teachings he selected, Lombard included just three citations from non-Christian sources. A century later, Aquinas's *Summa theologica* (1265–1274) posed questions as Abelard had done, although Aquinas's numbered 631, and, like Lombard, he also drew conclusions. Unlike Lombard, however, Aquinas's *Summa* included 3,500 citations from Aristotle alone. And of those 3,500, nearly half had been entirely unknown in Western Europe when Abelard and Lombard had been writing.[41]

This rediscovery of the classical world, the reintroduction of Greek, and the introduction of Arabic writings to Western Europe brought with them a new way of thinking about, and seeing, the world, in turn driving new attitudes to authority and to textual references. From the eighth century, the Abbasid caliphate centered around Baghdad had overseen a multicultural renaissance; after paper arrived from China in 750, a predominantly oral culture became a predominantly written one. The sciences, and science teaching, developed alongside an increasing focus on the Qur'an, and how to read it correctly; and with the establishment of four new schools of Islamic jurisprudence, education flourished.

So too did libraries. Mosque libraries were common, as were the private libraries of great men: the Fatimid caliph al-Aziz Billah (955–996) was said to have owned eighteen thousand theological manuscripts alone; a library founded in Córdoba by the Umayyad caliph al-Hakam II (915–976) was said to have contained six hundred thousand volumes.[42] The School of Wisdom, a library and center for manuscript-copying as well as teaching, founded in Basra under Harun al-Rashid (r. 786–809) and enlarged by his son al-Mamun (r. 813–833), was until the thirteenth century a meeting point for Muslim, Jewish, and Christian scholars, where works were translated from Greek as well as Persian.[43] In many of these libraries, it has been suggested, the manuscripts were arranged by subject, and then by their order of acquisition.[44]

The Arab scholarly world also valued encyclopedias, which were typically ordered by a variety of systems to demonstrate, as in the West, the perfection of God's universe. In the tenth century in Basra, a sect known as the Brethren of Purity produced a four-part encyclopedia, possibly the first collective encyclopedia outside China, which was organized according to a schema that moved from the concrete to the abstract, drawing on current thought in Greek, Persian, Indian, Jewish, and Christian writings.[45] Persian encyclopedias were sometimes organized by subject, and sometimes divided the world they described into "new" and "ancient" sciences.[46] The *Kitāb iḥsa al-ulûm*, The Book of the Enumeration of the Sciences, a powerful influence on classification and the sciences in the Middle Ages, was compiled by al-Fārābi (d. 950/1), one of the period's greatest scholars and the earliest as well as one of the most important Muslim commentators on Aristotle. He organized his *Kitāb* into eight sections: linguistic, logical, mathematical, physical, metaphysical, political, juridical, and theological.[47]

Other less commonly encountered organizing principles were also to be seen, with categories such as religion, location, and even received opinion used as bases for classification. One of the first biographical dictionaries, the *Kitāb al-abaqāt al-kabīr*, The Book of the Main Classes, by Ibn Sa'd (d. c. 845), began with a biography of the Prophet and then of each of his Companions, their entries organized chronologically by the date they converted to Islam, after which they were subcategorized by tribe and then by geography. Cross-referencing was as yet unknown, as in the West, and so entries were repeated in full whenever they fell into more than one category. Another ninth-century work divided its subjects into pre-Islamic and Islamic poets, and then into ten groups, organized first chronologically, then subjectively, by their reputation.[48] In the eleventh century, one history of Baghdad told through biographical entries was a notable exception. Its author, al-Khatīb al-Baghdādī, began with everyone named Muhammad, in honor of the Prophet, after which he switched to alphabetical order, to ensure the widest possible readership, he wrote.[49]

Alphabetical order was thus known in at least parts of the Muslim world at this date, and was apparently considered attractive to readers. At the same time, what has survived makes clear that it was not frequently used. It appeared occasionally, to index the *Hadith*, the narrative of the sayings of the Prophet, but the received view was that a good scholar knew his material by heart and therefore had no need of artificial ordering systems.[50] Unlike their contemporaries in the West who, as we have seen, responded to the increase in books and the availability and cheapness of paper by an increased reliance on the written word, and consequently by finding or creating the tools to navigate them, the Arab world continued to regard memory as a primary tool of scholarship. For this reason, page layouts in Arabic literature became increasingly elaborate, their decoration, marginals, and intricate scripts demarcating sections of text into books, chapters, and subsections—sometimes as many as a dozen—interspersed with underscoring, different-sized letters to make the divisions clear, and sections or words written in red (rubrication), or in a bolder, darker script—all ultimately serving as memory prompts.[51]

Arabic dictionaries also used nonalphabetical methods of organizing. The *Mukhaṣṣaṣ*, or The Categorized, by Ibn Sīda (d. 1066), was divided, as its title states, by subject or topic, beginning with human nature and continuing on to physiology, psychology, women, clothes, food, and weapons. Al-Khalīl Ibn Aḥmad (d. 791), in his *Kitāb al-'ain*, The Book of [the Letter] 'Ain, used sounds to organize his work: he listed entries in an order of his own, where each sound group was followed by sub-categories based on how many consonants a word contained.* Later on, a similar system—which may, as with the *Kitāb al-'ain*, have drawn on Sanskrit models—was used in the *Lisān al-Arab*, The Language of the Arabs, by Ibn Manẓūr (1233–1311), who categorized the roots of words first by their final consonant, then subcategorized them by the initial consonant, and finally by the middle one. In the Middle Ages, this work was long regarded as the authoritative Arabic-language dictionary, and thus its system of organization was influential.[52]

These mainly nonalphabetical developments contrasted with the works of Hebrew scholars, who tended toward alphabetical order simultaneously with (and occasionally a little ahead of) their Christian contemporaries. At the end of the eleventh century, Nathan ben Jehiel

---

*Verbs and nouns in Semitic languages can be reduced to (most commonly) three-letter root words, made up entirely of consonants. Words related in meaning are created by adding vowels or consonants to the root. In modern Hebrew, for example, s-f-r is the three-letter root for the word book, *sefer*; as well as for *sofer*, scribe; *safra*, scholar; *sifrut*, literature; *sifriyah*, library; *safran*, librarian; *yispor*, to count or to number; *sifrah*, numeral; and *l'saper*, to say or to tell (as in English, telling means both speaking and counting). This root structure makes Semitic-language dictionaries organized in this fashion much easier to navigate than Romance- or Germanic-language ones would be.

(c. 1035–c. 1110) produced his *Sefer ha'Arukh*, The Set Book. Ben Jehiel, who had been born in Rome, spoke Arabic, Aramaic, Greek, Hebrew, Italian, Latin, Persian, and Syriac, and he drew on his knowledge of these languages to produce an alphabetically ordered book of root words occurring in rabbinic literature. It became one of the best-known dictionaries of its type—more than fifty copies survive—as well as being one of the first Hebrew books to be printed, in Rome sometime before 1472.[53]

Many of these works, both in Arabic and Hebrew, and the scholarship that had produced them, became accessible to scholars in Western Europe for the first time as these languages began to be more widely translated into Latin. In the eleventh century, at Monte Cassino in Italy, a Benedictine monk and physician named Constantine the African translated many medical texts, the knowledge of which had spread to northern Europe by the early twelfth century, while in Palermo at about the same date parts of Aristotle, Euclid, and Ptolemy were all being translated. In Spain, under the Benedictine Archbishop Raymond of Toledo (d. 1152), what was virtually a translation factory produced quantities of Latin manuscripts of mainly Arabic works, alongside Greek works that had been translated into Arabic between the ninth and the early twelfth centuries: Ibn Gabirol, al-Ghazali, and al-Fārābi on jurisprudence and ethics; Galen, Hippocrates, Avicenna, al-Razi, and al-Kindi on medicine and the sciences; as well as the works of Aristotle. Further texts by Aristotle were translated in Constantinople, along with others by Galen.[54] That so many of these works returned to the West via Arabic was significant, for earlier Arab scholars had frequently added substantially to the originals, including details of their own work, which was far in advance of much of Western thought at the time.

The Western rediscovery of the classics had two results, one somewhat abstract, one concrete. More generally, the awareness of how many great works had been entirely unknown before the lifetimes of these new readers, and of how many more had been permanently lost, produced a sense that the current generation needed to ensure that this recaptured knowledge, as well as all the works produced under its influence, were preserved for future generations.[55] Further, it created a drive to ensure that the details contained in all these new works could be found easily—in other words, readers wanted not merely to read the books, but to refer to them: they wanted search tools.

These recently translated manuscripts also brought to the West other elements that are crucial for our story. Educated European readers now became increasingly familiar with foreign alphabets. In Italy and France in particular, Hebrew had routinely been transliterated into the roman alphabet when manuscripts were copied; in the rest of Europe, the Greek alphabet had sometimes been used, but less and less as time went on. In Europe, apart from Spain, where Arabic was in common use, Arabic too had been almost always transliterated into the roman alphabet. By contrast, some in the British Isles were familiar with Old English runes, known as *futhorc*, or with the Irish writing system known as Ogham.* Many more would have recognized, and used in conjunction with the roman alphabet, the Old English runic letters such as thorn (Þ, þ) and wynn (Ƿ, ƿ). For these reasons, "foreign"-looking letters were more familiar and less unnerving in the British Isles, and so Latin and Hebrew letters were both used, as they were from the ninth century in Germany, a regular destination for highly educated monks from Ireland and Britain.

---

*Futhark emerged in the first century CE in present-day Denmark and Schleswig-Holstein, and then spread to the rest of Scandinavia, Iceland, Greenland, and the British Isles. It was named after the first six runes, or characters, in the German sequence; the British Isles' variant, spelled *futhorc*, represented a difference in pronunciation rather than ordering. Ogham was an early writing system used in Ireland and in parts of the British Isles where there were Irish settlements. It was originally based on the Latin alphabet, but used notched symbols ordered in groups of five, and is therefore difficult to read: distinguishing, for example, four notches and one notch (C and H) from five notches (Q) relies heavily on context.[56]

This openness to other alphabets meant that by the eleventh century some manuscripts that originated in these regions contained approximations of what would soon become the figures we refer to as Arabic numerals (the numbers 1, 2, 3, 4, 5, 6, 7, 8, 9, and 0, which are more accurately Hindu-Arabic in origin). These first appeared in manuscripts linked to, or copied by, scribes who had knowledge of works from Baghdad, or those created by Persian scholars. By the late twelfth century, scribes in southern England were using numerals that were fairly close in appearance to their modern descendants, and it was English scribes who also pioneered the Western use of Arabic numerals in chapter headings, column numbers, and page numbers—all novelties of the new scholastic movement, encouraged by the need to identify and locate precise text citations.[57]

The Bakhshali manuscript, found in what is today Pakistan, dating to between the third and seventh centuries, shows the numbers then in use, including the first known example of a zero.

In the late twelfth century, the Jewish philosopher and physician Maimonides (c. 1135–1204), born and educated in Córdoba, had set out in his *Book of Commandments* the 613—he counted them—commandments in the Torah, the first five books of the Old Testament, which he organized into fourteen categories, or "principles," as he called them. In the second section of his *Guide for the Perplexed* he likewise began with a list of twenty-five premises, which he used to construct philosophical proof for the existence of God. Through these lists Maimonides established hierarchies and structures of thought, just as Abelard and Aquinas were to do, allowing him to synthesize disparate pieces of information for his readers, shaping them into a method of learning, as well as the learning itself.[58]

With Aquinas and the burgeoning of scholasticism, too, how the texts were laid out became as important as the content itself. Scholasticism, as it manifested in the universities and especially at the Université de Paris, was not a set of philosophical or theological beliefs but a method of teaching relying on dialectic, as explored by Aristotle: a question would be laid out, arguments for and against presented, and a conclusion drawn. Thus while Aquinas's *Summa theologica* has long been recognized as a masterpiece of thought, it was, every bit as importantly, a masterpiece of organization and structure. As Henri-Jean Martin, one of Europe's leading scholars of the history of writing, books, and printing, has noted:

> [In the *Summa*] every part, every treatise, and every question is preceded by a summary. Each article, the basic unit in this hierarchical structure, has a title beginning *utrum* (whether). Alternative possibilities are followed by series of objections, the first of which is introduced by the formula *videtur quot non* (it would seem not) and each of the following by *praeterea* (furthermore). Then, after the formula *sed contra* (but to the contrary), an argument (usually only one) against the point originally raised gives an answer to the question. In the body of the article, introduced by *respondeo dicendum* (I answer [by] saying), each objection is refuted in order, preceded each time by *ad primam*, *ad secundam* [firstly, secondly], and so forth.[59]

Aquinas's magisterial ordering of knowledge drew on the earlier medieval encyclopedists' fascination with summarizing the world they saw around them, as well as the other worlds they hoped, or feared, were to come. And it flourished in an equally golden age for encyclopedists. Isidore's *Etymologies* continued to be widely used for grammar, along with two other works: Alexander Neckam's *De naturis rerum*, On the Nature of Things (c. 1200–1204), one of the earliest encyclopedias to be used by preachers as a resource when preparing their sermons; and the Franciscan Bartholomew the Englishman's *De proprietatibus rerum*, On the Properties of Things (c. 1240). The latter work was considered so essential to students at the Université de Paris that its price was established by statute.[60] In 1398/9 it was translated into English, when it was rearranged into alphabetically ordered summaries to facilitate its use in constructing sermons. Later copies contained alphabetical lists of books and chapters, while two-thirds of the surviving Latin copies include marginal glosses with moral and symbolic explanations for these "properties of things"—the natural world—glosses that swiftly began to be used as search tools to locate relevant sections.[61]

The most notable, and renowned, encyclopedia of the day was the *Speculum maius*, The Great Mirror, compiled by the Dominican Vincent of Beauvais (c. 1184/94–c. 1264), which ran to some 4.5 million words, divided into 9,885 chapters.* This was written between 1244 and 1255, in four sections: the *Speculum naturale*, which dealt with God, angels, devils, and humanity, the story of the creation, and the natural history of the world; the *Speculum doctrinale*, covering grammar, logic, ethics, medicine, and trades; the *Speculum historiale*, a summation of the first two sections, as well as a history of the world; and (largely compiled after Vincent's death), the *Speculum morale*, using Aquinas's *Summa* as its basis.

The *Speculum naturale* used hierarchical organizing principles, beginning with God, then angels, then, dealing with subjects that arose as it followed the order of the six days of creation, from the world being

---

*For comparison purposes, the seven volumes of Proust's *Remembrance of Things Past* put together are less than two-thirds the length of Vincent's work; Tolstoy's *War and Peace* is a tenth of the length. The original eighteenth-century *Encyclopaedia Britannica* (see pages 193–194) consisted of just three volumes; its final print edition, in 2010, was thirty-two volumes but, unlike the work of Vincent of Beauvais, it was produced by a hundred editors and four thousand contributors.

formless matter to the creation of the material world, before returning to a hierarchical arc with man, the soul, the body, and the natural world. The *Speculum doctrinale* put man, not God, at its center, basing its structure on the *trivium* and the *quadrivium* and Aristotle's three fields—theoretical, practical, and logical—supplemented by the mechanical, to cover areas he had omitted. The *Speculum historiale* used chronological order, from the creation of the world to the Last Judgment. Where subjects had neither a natural hierarchical nor a chronological order, Vincent of Beauvais defaulted, as Isidore had done in his *Etymologies*, to putting animals, plants, and minerals in absolute alphabetical order, a very early appearance. Yet this choice of alphabetical order was of an organizing system of last resort. Subjects that to us seem neutral, to Vincent and his readers had more important, and obvious, principles: metals were organized first by their physical qualities, then their alchemical ones, and finally by their medicinal purposes; agriculture was ordered to follow the seasons; in literature, philosophy, as the senior faculty, was given precedence; and so on.

This hierarchical ordering contrasted with the almost contemporaneous, but much less successful, *Fabularius* of Konrad of Mure. Konrad was a teacher at the Grossmünster (Great Minster) in Zurich who, only two decades after Vincent, in 1273, wrote what might well be the first entirely alphabetically ordered encyclopedia in the West. This he ordered up to the second syllable of each word, and then by the number of syllables. "Once the reader understands this method," Konrad wrote hopefully in his preface, "he will easily be able to find whatever he is searching for."[62]

Easy or not, Vincent of Beauvais's *Speculum maius* circulated far more extensively than Konrad's encyclopedia, remaining popular for many centuries afterward, although, given the enormous size of the original, rarely in complete copies. Instead, sections, especially of the *Speculum historiale*, were copied by scribes and then recopied and shared. However partial, these extracts made Vincent's work one of the preeminent resources for preachers, and the finding tools he built into the work may well have encouraged this.

As well as the intermittent use of alphabetical ordering, Vincent drew up a list of chapter titles at the beginning of each book—as with his adoption of absolute alphabetical order, these were among the earliest tables of contents—and later versions of the *Speculum historiale* included early examples of alphabetically ordered indexes, although we don't know if Vincent himself made them, if they were made by others following his instructions, or if they were made independently and added later. But by 1320–1323, one dedicated reader at the papal court in Avignon had organized some twelve thousand keywords to the *Speculum historiale* into alphabetical order to create his very own index.[63] In England half a century later, James le Palmer, a senior Exchequer clerk, copied a Gospel commentary and included with it a *kalendarium*, or table of subject headings, of his own devising, to assist the reader. After his death in 1375, the manuscript came into the ownership of Thomas Arundel, Archbishop of Canterbury, whose clerk produced an index for it—"out of pity for students whose overwork leads to sickness and death"—using James le Palmer's marginal notes for the subject categories.[64]

The notion that the world was a circle of perfection, created by an omnipotent and perfect God, increasingly came into conflict with the need for search tools and the consequent desire to break manuscripts—even manuscripts that described that perfect world—into smaller elements that could be manipulated to make it easier to locate specific sections, or passages, or even single words. Just as it is difficult for us today to remember that before print, every copy of a single work might be different, so too it is difficult to comprehend that before print, readers saw manuscripts as things that could be endlessly revised and renewed. It was only with the arrival of printed books that the concept of a work that was finished, fixed, came to be. Manuscripts from antiquity onward commonly contained wide margins, sometimes to allow for

the inclusion of expensive illuminations and decoration, but more frequently for the addition of annotations and amendments. Between the
late eleventh and the early thirteenth centuries it was standard for the
text on any given page to cover less than half the space, leaving the rest
almost blank; for manuscripts created specifically for students, the margins might occupy 70 percent of a page, sometimes even more, to leave
space for commentary and annotations. (See, for example, page 78.)[65]

Other manipulations of text were also expected. Around 1180, in the
Benedictine monastery of St. Albans, in Hertfordshire, in England, the
Bible was for the first time divided into chapters.[66] (The further division of chapters into verses did not occur until the sixteenth century.)
Only three decades later, these chapter breaks were already being used
regularly in manuscripts, for glosses or marginal notes. Yet while their
convenience made them popular, to many it nevertheless felt wrong that
the unified, sacred word of God should be rent asunder for the sake of
mere convenience, even when in the service of such holy activities as
sermon-writing. This went for any system that privileged ordering over
the divinely ordained.

Albertus Magnus spoke for many when he at one and the same time
condemned alphabetical order as "not proper," while admitting that he
was nevertheless resigned to its use, owing to its importance to the less
educated.[67] For now, the needs of the general population were beginning
to overtake the work of the educated. And in catering to those needs,
the educated were given the impetus to produce new tools, tools that
they previously had no idea they needed.

CHAPTER 4

 IS FOR DISTINCTIONES

The High Middle Ages and the Search Tool

CONTRARY TO OUR MODERN EXPECTATIONS, IN THE TWELFTH CENTURY sermons were not a weekly event in most parish churches. Sermons had two audiences: one of specialists, who listened to technical theological arguments in monasteries, the other made up of would-be converts. Sermons were also preached by bishops in their episcopal sees, but with increasing urbanization, many of these sees were no longer situated in the largest population centers; in such locations there might well be no bishop. Not that this was a concern: regular churchgoers were expected to know how to live good Christian lives without the reinforcement of weekly sermons.

It was only at the end of the century that a radical alteration in how the masses engaged with religion appeared, represented by the arrival of hundreds, possibly even thousands, of mendicant preachers who criss-crossed Europe to speak directly to the common people in public squares,

on village greens, and in taverns. The times were rife with views promoted by those the Church saw as heretical, groups such as the Waldensians and the Cathars, which respectively promoted an ideal of absolute
clerical poverty and rejected the standard theological understanding of
the Trinity, both of which were impossible to reconcile with the existing
tenets of the Church. The Church decided that the most efficient way
to control these preachers was not to outlaw them, but to embrace them.
The result was the foundation of new mendicant preaching orders that
emphasized vows of poverty as well as a life of constant travel, especially
to the new cities and towns, instead of the older pattern of monastic communities typically situated in rural, more sparsely populated districts. Of
these new orders, the Franciscan order was founded in 1209, as was the
Capuchin; the Dominican and the Carmelite in 1215. The Augustinian
order appeared slightly later, in 1244, but its aims were similar to these
other fraternities, which were the major mendicant orders. They joined
the longer-established Cistercian order in the belief that it was not just
non-Christians, or the next generation of priests being educated in the
monasteries, who needed to have the glory of the Gospels explained
to them. Every Christian, they thought, was in need of enlightenment
via preaching.

Unlike the erudite Benedictines, whose rule had ensured that all
in their communities were allocated books and time for study, many
of the members of the new preaching orders were drawn from among
the relatively uneducated—those who might, perhaps, have a very basic
grasp of doctrinal questions, and who might know even less of the many
commentaries and explications of the Church Fathers that had been
produced in the preceding centuries. Works such as Peter Lombard's
Sentences, therefore, were designed to fill in the gaps. For example, the
Dominicans created a formula for sermon-writing using the *Sentences* as
their guide, one that relied on a complex parsing of each individual element and sentence: the meanings would be explicated and also justified

using citations (in descending order of importance) from the Bible, the Church Fathers, and other patristic writings.

As the preaching orders grew in importance, and as more and more preachers ventured into the field, the *Sentences* were reordered to make them easier to use. This precipitated an entirely new genre of preachers' handbooks called *distinctiones*, meaning "distinctions," or divisions, because they "distinguished," or parsed, the figurative and metaphorical uses of biblical words and phrases. These books laid out keywords by type—action words, abstract or concrete nouns, and so on—followed by explanations of their metaphoric or symbolic meanings. One instructed its users: "When one wishes to make a sermon, one should lay as one's foundation some scriptural passage . . . then consider how many keywords are contained in the passage." By looking up each keyword, the would-be sermonizer could construct a sermon based on the information the author of the *distinctio* (the singular of *distinctiones*) had pre-digested for his readers.[1]

One *distinctio*, for example, analyzed the biblical metaphors and symbols for the word "horse." If a sermon was to be about preaching itself, the preacher was guided to a citation from Job, "Wilt thou give strength to the horse, or clothe his neck with neighing?" which was explicated by Gregory the Great's commentary comparing a horse to a preacher who had the strength to master his own vices before he preached ("neighed") to others. If the sermon's theme was the vanity of the world, the preacher was guided to Ecclesiastes: "I have seen servants upon horses"; or he might warn of the risks of wanton and foolish luxury by quoting Psalm 32, "Do not become like the horse and the mule, who have no understanding," while "Let Dan be a serpent in the path, that biteth the horse's heels that his rider may fall backward," from Genesis, was available for a sermon on the follies of the modern world.[2]

Lombard claimed that his work was designed to help preachers "avoid having to search through many volumes, the brevity [of his work] giving the reader what he searches for without effort."[3] Previously, reading, and comprehending what one had read, had been a slow, laborious task, with value vested in the labor as much as in the end result. Now Lombard promised an effort-free search, the goal of all reference works to this day. His book was, as two modern scholars have noted, the first ever written not for its own value, but to enable those who used it to find material of value elsewhere: the modern definition of a reference book.[4]

The genre flourished. Between the late 1180s and about 1200 at least five major collections of *distinctiones* were compiled, each one gathering up to 1,500 biblical terms, with at least half a dozen meanings attributed to each, although some merited more than a dozen.[5] Initially, most *distinctiones* organized their terms by their order of appearance in the Bible, with a few in "rational" order, that is, grouped by themes or topics. These systems, though, were soon overtaken by those *distinctiones* that set their keywords into alphabetical order. So natural had this become to both authors and their readers that new, alphabetically ordered lists swiftly began to be appended to earlier examples of the genre, to enable readers, as one preface said, "to find quite easily what is sought, according to a new method, alphabetical order."[6] By 1214, alphabetical order was so closely associated with *distinctiones* that one volume was entitled *Alphabetum in artem sermoncinandi*, The Alphabet in the Art of Sermons.

Vincent of Beauvais had not organized his great encyclopedia in alphabetical order, even though he had understood the importance of, and been concerned with, the search tools that might be appended to it. In 1244, as he was drawing near the end of his labor, he wrote to Louis IX, King of France, who was also the founder of the monastery of Royaumont, where Vincent was in orders: "I will have the rest of the work copied for you," he promised, "after having carefully corrected the text and clarified it and completed it with concordances."[7] Vincent was here offering the king a novelty: a concordance, or index, to the Bible.

To produce any type of index, each textual mention first has to be noted, then a method devised to identify the location of each of these mentions. Arabic numerals by now appeared in manuscripts with relative frequency, but they were not yet being used to number the pages. And of course, as we have seen, in the age of manuscripts no two copies were ever identical. Without numbered pages or standard texts, only two sorts of index were possible: those drawn up for a specific copy of a manuscript, or those that created a system whereby a single index could be used for all manuscript copies of any one work.[*]

The first solution was the marginal notation. In the early days of indexing, it was rarely the originator of the manuscript—the author, or the scribe who produced the copy—who compiled the index; almost always, it was the manuscript's owner who did so, for his own use and focused on his own interests. We have seen how some compilers or authors such as Ralph de Diceto added marginal symbols to help them locate material. A few decades after that, the device of the marginal symbol was extended by the Franciscan Robert Grosseteste, Bishop of Lincoln (c. 1175/9–1253), who had studied at the Université de Paris and then taught theology at Oxford. With his protégé and fellow Franciscan Adam Marsh, Grosseteste drew up a table with nine parts, or *distinctiones*, encompassing 440 topics, grouped in subject order, by categories, and each represented by a single symbol. These symbols included letters of the Greek and roman alphabets, mathematical symbols, signs of the zodiac, and more, although their purpose is not clear to us today. Some scholars have suggested that Grosseteste jotted down the appropriate symbols in the margins, creating a personal subject index as he went along, the symbols helping him locate material at a later date and also serving as an explication of what he had read, a sort of shorthand way of making notes on the subject. Yet we know that his table was

---

[*]The problem of the single-copy index can be seen in a fifteenth-century manuscript of a Gospel Commentary of William of Nottingham. It contained an index made for a different, fourteenth-century copy of the commentary, with keywords and subject entries that referred to marginal annotations and folio references that were entirely absent from the manuscript it was attached to.[8]

not intended to be only a private, personal tool: either he or Marsh disseminated it to others to use in their own reading (and a number of works with Grosseteste's symbols in the margins have survived).[9] A more recent suggestion has been that they and their followers intentionally read widely, marking up the margins as they went, to produce what was, in effect, a proto-subject index, enabling any later readers with access to the table to locate specific pieces of information rapidly.[10] Nor was this Grosseteste's sole contribution to scholarly innovations that enabled texts to be referenced rather than simply read: he also added running heads to some manuscripts in his possession, as well as chapter numbers and section headings, all means of breaking the material down for easier reference.* (It is worth noting in passing that as far as we are aware, while Grosseteste did not use alphabetical order as a sorting tool, he did know of the *Suda*, that late tenth-century Byzantine encyclopedia with its tens of thousands of alphabetically ordered entries.)[11]

In Paris, meanwhile, the Englishman Alexander of Hales (c. 1185–1245), whose commentary on Lombard's *Sentences* had helped make that work a standard text at the university, may also have created the system of subcategories, or he may simply have disseminated that knowledge. Today, it seems natural to break up a long dense text into sections I, II, III, etc., before subdividing those sections into smaller subcategories and calling them something like A, B, C, then numbering the next level 1, 2, 3, followed by, perhaps, a, b, c, and so on. Alexander of Hales saw such categorization as an expression of God's meaning:

---

*In printed books, running heads are the single lines of text at the top of each page—the most common convention from the twentieth century onward has been to have the book title as the left-hand running head, the chapter title as the right-hand one, or *A Place for Everything* on the left, "D is for Distinctiones" on the right, as this book itself does. In the eighteenth and nineteenth centuries, the right-hand running head was often a précis of the page's contents—"Magellan circumnavigates the globe"—or, in fiction, a plot element: "Jane flees Thornfield Hall."

"[T]he perception of truth," he wrote, " . . . is explained by divisions, definitions and methods."[12]

The elaboration of new ways to enable students, scholars, and other readers to search a text rapidly shuttled back and forth across the Channel. After Paris's contribution of subcategories, Oxford produced a solution to the problem of linking the words in a text with an index entry: each column of text was given a letter of the alphabet, say, from A to D. Then, using the new Arabic numerals, every fifth line of text was numbered.[13]

The Dominican Robert Kilwardby (1215–1279), regent at Oxford University from 1261 (and later Archbishop of Canterbury), used a different system, one that likewise became highly influential in the making of indexes. He divided the text of his manuscripts into numbered sections, then subdivided each section into smaller numbered sections, which could be linked to an index entry, and the numbers replicated in the margins of any manuscript copies of that text, making them searchable too. Using this method he indexed not just Lombard's *Sentences*, but fifty-one works by Augustine and several of the other Church Fathers.[14] The *Decretum Gratiani*, an outline of canon law compiled in the twelfth century in the same style as Abelard's *Sic et non*—principles were outlined, opposition points raised, and then (unlike *Sic et non*) conclusions were drawn—was in the following century glossed and indexed at the University of Bologna so that it could be accessed and utilized rather than read from start to finish, turning it from a historical document into a textbook.[15]

Florilegia from two Cistercian monasteries—at Clairvaux in France and Villers-en-Brabant in what is now Belgium—were indexed much as Kilwardby had suggested, with the texts divided into numbered sections and lettered subsections, the index then referring readers to the relevant entry via the section number, the subsection letter, and the headword of the extract. One surviving manuscript of this type very efficiently indexed more than two thousand keywords. Other Cistercian houses explored different methods. In the Low Countries, two monasteries developed a system using a series of letters and dots inscribed on a parchment strip that permitted the division of a text into sections without damaging valuable manuscripts. Any index could be unlocked when the guideline parchment key was held against the page.[16]

A manuscript copy of the Decretum Gratiani *dating from the first half of the thirteenth century. The text in the center has interlinear and marginal glosses, as well as being surrounded by a double layer of commentary in a number of different hands dating from the thirteenth and fourteenth centuries.*

However clumsy these systems appear to us today, they were a revelation at the time, and their utility can be appreciated by the speed with which they were embraced by students at both Oxford and Paris. Those students, in turn, disseminated the knowledge of indexes and indexing systems after they graduated and returned to their homes to teach or preach. By the end of the thirteenth century, the Dominican John of Freiburg included an index in his *Summa confessorum*, making him possibly the first author to produce his own index as an integral part of his work at the time he wrote it, rather than someone else adding it later.[17]

And all of these possibilities were establishing themselves in parallel with the biblical concordance, which indexed every word of any importance in the Bible (and was therefore sometimes called a "verbal concordance"). Between the fifth and seventh centuries, the Masoretes, Hebrew biblical scholars working in the Middle East, had compiled lists of biblical vocabulary that, it has been suggested, were known to the early pathfinders of Latin indexing and concordances. Masoretic Bibles were certainly in circulation in France, whence the earliest concordances originated, and by 1271 at least one was available in Lincoln, where Robert Grosseteste was bishop. Furthermore, Hebrew dictionaries had been translated in France, to help with accuracy in biblical scholarship. Perhaps most importantly, Hugh of St. Cher (c. 1200–1263), of the Dominican priory of St. Jacques in Paris, the home of concordance-making, was known to have studied Hebrew Bibles.[18] Yet while these associations are possible, we can say only that Masoretic scholarship *may* have influenced the creators of these first concordances as they struggled to find a satisfactory way of indexing the Bible.

It was Hugh of St. Cher who in 1239 oversaw the creation of the first known Latin concordance.* There is one solitary reference, dating from

---

*At least, this is how the story has come down to us, although the earliest surviving mention of his involvement dates from 1315. Whether he was involved, and to what degree, cannot be stated with certainty. Essentially, the design and creation of concordances was a project of overwhelming teamwork, not of the independent, solitary scribe.

the 1240s, to a subject-ordered index to the Scriptures compiled by "the preaching friars" at St. Jacques, but nothing of that version has survived, and we hear no more about it.[19] For the next attempt, each word of the Bible was written down together with its chapter number—those numbers now being in common use—and with a subsection letter derived from the now also standard division of each chapter into sections lettered from A to G. A few of the compilers' working notes have survived, and so we know that each person was charged with gathering words beginning with a single letter, which were then alphabetized to the first or second letter. Once gathered and ordered, however, the words were given no context, no surrounding words to help locate the reader. Instead, a given word was listed—say, "lamb"—followed by a long string of chapter numbers.[20]

This concordance was not therefore terribly useful, but the working habits of these compilers were known more widely, at least to clerics in the 1320s—we hear of one Franciscan preacher urging his flock to take responsibility for their own actions and shortcomings, using the compilers as an analogy: "Wherefore I would that each one did as did once the brothers who compiled concordances. Each took charge of the letter that was committed to him. He who had A had nothing to do with B, and he who had charge of B did not intermeddle with C."[21]

A third attempt at a concordance, also at St. Jacques, was begun under the supervision of the Englishman Richard of Stavensby, and possibly of his compatriot John of Darlington, confessor of Henry III, the work therefore becoming known as the *Concordanciae anglicanae*, The English Concordances. In this version, each word was given context by repeating the phrase it appeared in. But this time the phrases were too long, completely overwhelming the search terms. Finally, in the 1280s, a fourth attempt found a happy medium, each keyword being accompanied by a brief tag of fewer than half a dozen words from the original citation. This was a success. The manuscripts were copied many times by the university stationers in Paris and spread across

Europe: the Sorbonne alone owned at least fifteen manuscript copies, and another eighty or more that were made in the following half century have survived.[22] By 1302, concordances were considered so crucial that the Dominicans' Roman provincial chapter ordered that a copy must be held in each of their monastic houses, paid for, if necessary, by the sale of other manuscripts.[23]

The 1240s saw the arrival of a new type of concordance, the "real" concordance, which indexed not the words of the Bible, but *realia*, or theological concepts. It worked differently from the verbal concordance, where users began by searching for a word, moving from there to its context; with a real concordance users began with an idea and searched for examples of how it had been deployed.[24]

Amaury de Montfort (1242/3–1301, the son of Eleanor of England and Simon de Montfort, briefly England's ruler if not its king), was for six years held prisoner in Dorset.* He had studied at the University of Padua and received an appointment as a papal chaplain. In his imprisonment he whiled away his time by writing a treatise "on the principles and divisions of theology," to which he appended a series of "schematic divisions," summarizing the teachings of the Gospels. His third manuscript, a concordance of biblical citations concerning the behavior of good Christians, set out in ninety-one sections by subject, far exceeded both of these in length and was clearly his major preoccupation.[25] It may have been the tedium of captivity that made this task worthwhile to de Montfort, or perhaps that captivity had left him unaware of the abundance of florilegia that were now being reorganized, making the subject-based reference work he was producing increasingly unnecessary. For real concordances never gained the readership of their verbal counterparts. Instead, as alphabetical order appeared more routinely in the new genres of concordances, *distinctiones*, and subject indexes, older forms

---

* He was undoubtedly a prisoner, but he was also a nobleman: his retinue included eight grooms and four valets, supervised by a single guard.

of literature like florilegia, which had previously had little or no time for alphabetical order, began to follow the fashion.

By the fourteenth century, *distinctiones* and florilegia were being joined by compendia, which drew material from both these sources, as well as from encyclopedias of the churchmen, canon law, and sometimes even works of contemporary thinkers such as Grosseteste. All of these continued to be primarily of use to preachers. But now, instead of relying on a single volume, the would-be sermon writer might begin by identifying his *dictio*, the element on which he was basing that part of his sermon, "as it might be, *Humilitas*, [or] *Patientia*." This he would look up in a *distinctio* or in Lombard's *Sentences*, or in any of the multitude of florilegia and compendia, forming his argument "on the basis of the multitude of authorities written therein."[26] For ease of use, most of these now had headings arranged in alphabetical order, although the prejudice against this nonhierarchical structuring continued to surface from time to time. One author pretended that his alphabetical ordering was incidental, even accidental, or possibly invisible: "Nobody attains to the palm in the spiritual conflict who does not first . . . cleanse away the filthy sins of the body . . . therefore it would seem most fitting to [begin] . . . with the chapter on 'Abstinence,'" he wrote, even as, of course, the reality was that he began with "Abstinence" because "ab" headed his alphabetical list.[27]

Readers had come to expect these works to be in alphabetical order, and this expectation gradually spread to other genres. Those that did not as easily lend themselves to alphabetization instead frequently had indexes, produced either by their owners or by the manuscripts' copyists. One manuscript of the *Legenda aurea*, The Golden Legend, a mid-thirteenth-century collection of saints' lives, had a note appended to it by its scribe: he had added an index, he wrote, so that preachers "may more quickly and easily find an example" when they needed one.[28]

The center for the creation of alphabetical tools was now without question Paris. The university's masters and pupils came from all over

Europe, drawing on a deep well of knowledge fed by many different influences: Cistercian indexes, Dominican concordances, and Oxford's line-numbering systems with their radical new reliance on Arabic numerals. Out of this, by the mid-thirteenth century, came full subject indexes to the works of Augustine and Aquinas—and of Aristotle, the first time in Europe that a reference tool had been created for an entirely secular subject.[29]

This appearance of secular, in addition to ecclesiastical, material was important: by the thirteenth century reading was no longer necessarily, or primarily, a form of devotion or meditation, nor did the works being read have to be treated as sacrosanct authorities, handed down by God or the Church Fathers.[30] The act of reading could now simply be *utilitatis*, useful. Hugh of Pisa, who wrote on grammar and etymology, carefully distinguished between the contemplative and the purposeful reader, although he continued to feel reading ought to have an end result, a measurable outcome that was public, not simply private improvement or enjoyment: "We do not call *literator* or *literatus* [a scholar, or someone who is erudite] he who possesses a lot of books, and looks into them . . . Instead, we call *literator* or *literatus* he who thanks to his ability can . . . shape letters into words, and words into orations."[31]

This new desire to investigate texts, to highlight specific elements found therein or to focus on single subjects, led to new ways of physically laying out the words on the page. Today we take for granted many of the features that first began to emerge in books in the fourteenth century, whether in new manuscripts or appended to older ones: tables of contents and indexes; chapter, section, and paragraph breaks; and annotations to assist the reader, whether marginalia (which later turned into footnotes) or separate studies, précis, and summaries.[32] Books were simply no longer acceptable without.

The appearance of these new elements was facilitated by a system of manuscript copying originating in Italy, one that by the second half of the thirteenth century had been adopted and was flourishing at the

Université de Paris. Using this *pecia*, or piece, system, manuscripts were divided into four-page sections, *peciae*, and each section was hired out to a different student for him to copy. While each student, obviously, wrote no faster than a scribe, another student was at the same time copying the next, or previous, four pages, and another the next four, and the next, together ensuring that each manuscript copy was produced far more quickly than could be achieved by a single scribe copying an entire work. And, while the primary aim of the *pecia* system was to speed up the copying process, a by-product was that the layout innovations now appearing were incorporated far more rapidly than would have occurred if all copying had been done in the scriptoria spread across Europe, frequently located in rural or isolated monasteries.

The spread of manuscripts utilizing these modern search tools reinvigorated florilegia, as they now received indexes and tables of contents, or were reordered alphabetically. They also began regularly to include secular as well as religious works, which brought with it further organizational issues. Lombard's *Sentences* and its successors had, it is true, entertained arguments and examined contradictions but, apart from Abelard's *Sic et non*, they had nevertheless always ended by handing down conclusions. Now readers were beginning to use the array of reference tools available to them to discover new arguments, and to draw their own conclusions. The order of citations, therefore, had to be considered anew. No longer was the older hierarchical ordering—from the Bible, to the Church Fathers, to more recent commentary—a given, since in some works religious texts might no longer predominate, while a set hierarchy for secular authors was barely established. The German theologian Hugh of St. Victor (c. 1096–1141) examined the question of organization in florilegia, or commonplace books, as they were coming to be: "As you study all knowledge, store up for yourselves good treasures. . . . In the treasure house of wisdom are various sorts of wealth, and many filing places in the storehouse of your heart. . . . Their orderly arrangement is clarity of knowledge. . . . Confusion is the mother of all ignorance . . . but orderly arrangement illuminates the intelligence."[33]

"Arrangement illuminates the intelligence"—not a thought Peter Lombard would have had. Nor, indeed, a thought we would have today. To modern readers, commonplace books can be delightful, but we rarely think of them as contributing to, much less illuminating, knowledge. But in the thirteenth century they were viewed, at least in part, as containing material concerned with original thought, and their arrangement was an important component of that expression. The florilegium of Arnold of Liège was even entitled *Alphabetum narrationum*, Alphabetic Extracts (1297–1308), as though the organizing system was the key element.

St. Bonaventura (1221–1274), an Italian theologian and leader of the Franciscan order, was steeped in the Université de Paris's teaching of Lombard: he may have been a student of Alexander of Hales, whose summary of the *Sentences* was the university's standard text, and Bonaventura himself later wrote a commentary on it. His careful categorization of the types of writer that existed, and their importance, can therefore be considered to be the—or at least an—established view:

> There is a fourfold method of making a book. One can write without adding or changing anything; this is merely a scribe. Another writes by adding, but not his own work; this is a compiler. Another writes his own text and others', but the others' [text] constitutes the principal element . . . and this is [also] called a compiler, not an author. Another writes his own and others' texts, but as though his own text were the principal element and the others' were only appended to confirm his views: this must be called an author.[34]

So while Bonaventura gave original thought preeminence, it also appeared that in terms of quantities of books produced, he expected that for every author producing original work, there would be another two compilers creating composite texts.

One of the most influential florilegia of the period was Thomas of Ireland's *Manipulus florum*, A Handful of Flowers (1306), whose success ensured it continued to be reprinted throughout the Renaissance— at least twenty-five editions appeared in the sixteenth century, and a dozen more in the seventeenth.[35] It is likely that Thomas came from Ireland, although we do not know for sure; he was, however, definitely educated at the Sorbonne, and afterward was probably a priest in Paris until his death sometime between 1329 and 1338. Thomas's *Manipulus* was designed to serve as a source book for sermons, but in retrospect it can also be seen to have unconsciously taken on something of the secular approach of the times, in that it did not describe, nor prescribe, doctrine, but simply provided examples and learned citations to be used however the reader might decide. For content it drew on two earlier florilegia, the *Florilegium gallicum*, The French Posy, and the *Florilegium angelicum*, The Angel's Posy. These twelfth-century works, both probably French, had themselves been influential, Vincent of Beauvais having included large sections of the *Florilegium gallicum* in his *Speculum historiale*, right down to the order in which the extracts appeared.[36]

Now Thomas rearranged the extracts from both, grouping his thousands of citations into 266 topics, based on theology, doctrine, morals, and ethics, but marking a departure from earlier styles, which would have seen the extracts ordered according to some form of value system: from the heavens to mankind; or good versus evil; or in pairs of virtues and vices; or according to the relative authority vested in the citations' authors. Instead, Thomas arranged his topics in absolute alphabetical order "in the manner of the concordances," as he wrote in his prologue, assuming his audience of sermon writers would know what a concordance was, so quickly had these volumes been assimilated as standard works for the ministry—although in case they didn't, he also gave a quick explanation of alphabetical order.

For this was still a new way of ordering, and one Thomas did not always find appropriate. Occasionally, therefore, he switched from alphabetical to what he clearly viewed as simply logical order: *gloria bona* and *gloria mala* are in opposition, so he placed them together, but followed them with *gloria eterna*, which, as the summation, he put last, despite e coming before m.* (Although, oddly, he also placed *vita humana*, human life, before *vita eterna*, eternal life, which runs counter to alphabetical order as well as to the hierarchy of religious priorities.)[37] Within his subject categories, too, Thomas moved between the older pattern of presenting his citations hierarchically and newer organizational systems. For the first time ever that we know of, he set sources that did not fit into one of the older categories in the order that the works appeared in the lists of books owned by the Sorbonne.[38] Then, instead of repeating an extract under different headings when it dealt with several subjects, he included each extract just once, with a letter of the alphabet in the margin beside it, producing a network of what would later become known as cross-references.[39]

While Thomas did not invent cross-referencing, he was among the first to use it extensively and systematically, to make it a feature of a work. And, as with alphabetical order, cross-referencing suggests a new way of looking at writing, and manuscripts. With alphabetical order, letters are no longer just a representation of a word, and words are no longer indivisible with their meaning. They become individual units that can be manipulated by both writer and reader to indicate and guide, as well as having meaning.[40] Cross-references do the same with larger units, enabling blocks of information to be considered under various headings through the abstract use of letters of the alphabet. Content and position were thus no longer inextricably bound. Perhaps these notions came more easily to those, such as the (probably) Irish Thomas, whose mother tongues were not based on languages of Latin origin. Latin, to

---

Gloria eterna is "eternal glory," a religious concept; *Gloria bona* or *mala*, however, could refer not merely to the virtues and vices, but also to the secular values of temporal renown and honor, which could turn into pride and arrogance.

them, was an acquired language, and much of their early experiences of it would have been written, not spoken. Seeing rather than hearing the words might perhaps have made the leap from meaning (the sense of the words) to the abstract (their appearance and construction, via letters of the alphabet, textual references, and page layout) more natural than it was for those whose mother tongues were cognate with Latin, and who had therefore heard the words long before they learned to read.[41]

AS THE CENTURY PROGRESSED, governments reorganized their archives to enable documents to be located as well as stored. So too did scholars and theologians produce increasing quantities of manuscripts that could be searched, whether by original design or through later intervention. One school of study, medical writing, had long been focused on compilation and categorization—on anatomization, in fact—and it now began to expand a genre of its own, which was in many ways itself a formula for searching.

Galen, as we have seen, may well have used alphabetical order in some of his writing on herbal or plant cures, known as "simples," and other medieval works on the same subjects had followed this style. But here too alphabetical order was by no means the only organizational possibility. Other works were organized into the types of remedy needed, whether salve, pills, powders, or tinctures, and only then, within these, was alphabetical order sometimes on display. General medical treatises continued to use different systems, including ordering diseases and cures by the affected part of the body, working downward *a capite ad calcem*, from head to heel. Others mixed their methods: six volumes of the *Chirurgia magna*, The Great Book of Surgery, by the French physician Guy de Chauliac (1300–1368), were in head-to-heel order, while the seventh, listing antidotes, was alphabetical.[42]

Medical dictionaries were often florilegia in all but name, collections of extracts covering various diseases and cures; by the thirteenth century they were sometimes referred to as medical concordances. The

Concordanciae Johannis de Sancto Amando was arranged in second-letter alphabetical order, with extracts on everything from *abstinentia* to *ydromel* (abstinence to hydromel, another word for mead). A revised version from the fourteenth century, renamed *Concordanciae Petro de Sancto Floro*, was reorganized into third-letter order, and the preface promised that its author, Peter of St. Fleur, had "gathered the flowers [note the florilegium metaphor] which are most esteemed by zealous physicians from all the authors of medical books . . . and following the arrangement made by John of St. Amand . . . he has added other quotations . . . and arranged them all in alphabetical order."[43]

But it was herbals, books that describe plants and their medicinal properties, that were most commonly arranged in alphabetical order. The basis for many of these works was *De materia medica*, On Medical Material, by the first-century Greek physician and botanist Dioscorides (c. 40–90 CE). In its original form, this compilation of remedial preparations had not been set in alphabetical order, but sometime before the fourth century those producing new manuscript copies of the text substantially rearranged them. One of the first herbals to be produced from inception in this manner, in the first century, was by Pamphilus of Alexandria.[44] (Perhaps, given what we know about alphabetical order in the classical world, it is no surprise to find that this early contribution came from Greek Egypt.) Probably because of the existence of these copies of Dioscorides, which by the eleventh century were known as *Dioscorides alphabeticus*, Dioscorides Alphabetized, by the following century writers in this genre seemed almost automatically to adopt an alphabetical arrangement, long before authors of other types of books did: the *Laud Herbal Glossary* and the *Durham Plant Glossary*, both of which offered Latin–English translations, were in mostly second-letter alphabetical order.[45]

Possibly readers found it easier to accept alphabetical order in these technical books because they were created as part of the professional world that was now emerging and becoming dominant. Measuring, ruling, ordering—all became abiding concerns of everyday life, not merely in the rarefied world of books. Clocks, for example, had been in use in China from at least the tenth century, but it was the thirteenth century before news of these time-measuring machines began to be rumored in Western Europe. By the early fourteenth century, they were more than a rumor. In the *Divine Comedy* (c. 1308–1320), Dante compared a soul in Paradise to synchronized clockwork: he knew how clocks worked, and furthermore he assumed his readers also knew of this extraordinary invention and its workings.

These early clocks had neither hands nor faces: time was marked by bells. In the fourteenth century, both Richard of Wallingford in St. Albans and Giovanni Dondi in Padua constructed astrological clocks, among the earliest in Europe, that told not just the hours, but also the minutes. And swiftly, at least in urban areas, hours consisting of sixty minutes began to replace the more fluid hours that had expanded and contracted with the seasons. As currency had made money abstract, as the letters of the alphabet were severed from the content they spelled out and used for abstract purposes in indexes and dictionaries, so too time was now being severed from the sun and the seasons. It could be noted down, and referred back to. If a clock ran fast or slow, it could even be manipulated. Time had become an abstract symbol and sign. Just as "Aaron" was now at the beginning of most biographical dictionaries because his name began with "Aa," not because he was older than his brother Moses, so too noon was becoming a fixed point, rather than "more or less when the sun is at the highest point depending on the time of year."[46]

CHAPTER 5

 IS FOR EXPANSION

The Reference Work in the Thirteenth and Fourteenth Centuries

---

By the thirteenth century, knowing how to search *through* a book for a particular piece of information, rather than reading it from start to finish, had become commonplace for clergy and scholars. How to search *for* a book, however, was something that had yet to be addressed. Until this date, it had been a question that had barely needed a solution.

Monasteries, the location of most books in Europe, had historically possessed relatively few books, even in the larger, more important religious centers: in the twelfth century, Christchurch, the cathedral priory in Canterbury, seat of the archbishop, owned 223 volumes; Durham Cathedral library had 352. In the few monasteries with larger collections, individual works remained easy to locate: many were duplicate copies of the Bible, or service books. Back in the ninth century, the Benedictine Fulda Abbey in Hesse had owned forty-six complete or partial manuscripts of the Bible, thirty-eight copies of St. Jerome, and twenty-six of Augustine.[1]

From the early tenth century, the Benedictines at Cluny Abbey in southeast France appointed an *armarius* to be in charge of the books—the *armarius* being responsible for the *armarium*, or cupboard, where the books were kept. It was his job to oversee the annual book distribution at Lent, when the monastery's collection was spread out on a carpet and each book checked against a list to ensure that nothing had gone missing over the previous twelve months. Once the *armarius* was assured of the safety of the abbey's treasures, a book was allocated to every member of the community, his to study for the next twelve months. By the eleventh century the same ceremony was replicated in Benedictine priories in England, right down to the carpet. Many houses began to maintain two collections: one comprising books to be lent to the monks each year, or, if there was anything to spare, to lay people outside the community; and a second collection made up of more valuable manuscripts that could be read only under supervision in the monastery.

At this date the Benedictine *armarius* still checked his collection every Lent against an inventory, and not yet a library catalog. Whereas the main purpose of an inventory is to serve as a complete list of possessions, to verify that nothing is missing or has been stolen, a catalog is a finding tool, helping the user to locate a specific copy of a specific book. As inventories, therefore, many of the monastery book lists itemized the author and title of each manuscript, and also its *incipit*—the first few words of the text of an individual manuscript—or, if a number of manuscripts had been bound together, as was common, the individual incipit of each. Since every manuscript of the same work was slightly different—a scribe might include more or fewer words per line, and more or fewer lines per page—checking an incipit was a way to ensure that a different, potentially inferior, copy had not been substituted for a valuable one.

Most of these book lists divided manuscripts first by genre or sub-ject, then in the now familiar hierarchical order. One of the earliest lists to have survived, setting out the contents of Rochester Cathedral Priory, which at the beginning of the twelfth century owned fewer than a hun-dred books, is missing a page at the start, where the priory's Bibles are likely to have been listed; it now begins with manuscripts by Augustine, then the other Church Fathers: Jerome, Ambrose, and Gregory, in the type of order established earlier in florilegia.[2] Some monasteries, on the other hand, listed their books in chronological order of acquisition, oth-ers grouped by the names of the donors of these valuable manuscripts. Apart from purposes of inventory, the order selected was also intended to act as a memory prompt: the books were few enough that those in charge were expected to remember their locations. The librarian of the Benedic-tine Admont Abbey, in what is now Austria, advised his fellow librarians what to do if, unusually, they found themselves looking after "a rather large quantity of books, so that it is not possible to grasp their number or their titles, or retain them in memory." If that were the case, then "a small book should be made in which each and every book is recorded."[*3]

The collections of private individuals, even those of great church-men or scholars, had previously numbered at most in the dozens. By the thirteenth century, however, their libraries were increasing in both importance and quantity. In 1272, Gerard of Abbeville, a theologian at the Université de Paris, bequeathed some three hundred volumes to the Sorbonne. It was an enormous gift, but the novelty was that he had that many to donate. Public collections, too, were becoming larger, partly through gifts like these, partly owing to the *pecia* system and the conse-quent number of utilitarian, rather than luxury, copies of manuscripts.

---

*As late as the early sixteenth century, librarians continued to rely on their memories. In a catalog of c. 1500–1510 from a monastery in Basel, a librarian advised his successors to spend their spare time regularly reading over the catalog, in order to impress the library's holdings onto their memories.[4]

By the early fourteenth century, the Sorbonne had become one of the largest libraries in Europe, with 1,722 volumes; Christchurch, Canterbury, which in the twelfth century had owned barely more than 200 books, now listed 1,800. (The Papal Library was at this stage very much an also-ran, with fewer than 650.)

Among the monastic orders, the Dominicans and the Cistercians had previously led the way both in their emphasis on reading and in book ownership. The original Franciscan rule had taken monastic vows of poverty to extremes. Until 1230, Franciscans were barred not just from owning luxury items such as manuscripts, but from owning any possessions at all, right down to the food they ate, instead relying entirely on donations from the faithful to whom they preached. After that date, while individuals still could not own anything personally, a less stringent interpretation of the rule permitted the ownership of goods by the community as a whole, and manuscripts for libraries were among their very first purchases.[5]

Just how wholeheartedly they embraced this change can be seen in the Franciscan *Registrum librorum angliae*, A Register of Books in England, compiled in the early fourteenth century.[6] This was a very early forerunner of what later came to be called a union catalog—a single catalog listing the holdings of a number of different libraries.* A century after the Franciscans first received permission to own any books at all, the *Registrum* shows that 183 of their monasteries in England had libraries. The *Registrum* appears to have been created in order to inform the community's preachers where to find specific books, organized as it was by district, library, and author, although within those categories, it is today not possible to discern any further organizational principle. In another innovation, however, the list made use of Arabic numerals to

---

*Online union catalogs today take the notion to extremes never before imagined: World-Cat combines the catalogs of 72,000 libraries in 170 countries; the smaller UK-based Library Hub Discover claims that its 137 specialist and research library catalogs contain more than forty million book records.

record which manuscripts each monastery owned. The *Registrum* thus radically extended the function of the book list, not only now serving as an inventory but well on the way to becoming a finding tool.

This Franciscan innovation was followed by another, their *Tabula septem custodiarum super bibliam*, an index of biblical passages and patristic commentaries on them.[7] (The Franciscan order divides itself into geographical provinces and "custodies," of which seven were then extant in England. The title, *An Index to the Bible in the Seven Custodies*, therefore indicates that the contents concern the English Franciscan religious houses only.) Used in tandem, the *Registrum* and *Tabula* enabled Franciscan preachers to identify biblical passages and their commentaries, and then locate the libraries that held the relevant works.

It was not, however, the purpose of the *Registrum*, nor of the majority of other lists of that date, to guide the reader from the title of a work on the page to a physical copy on the shelf, as we now expect. Similarly, we know from surviving book lists that in the twelfth century the books owned by the Cistercian Meaux Abbey in Yorkshire were stored in a variety of places, probably wherever was convenient: service books were kept in cupboards in the church, psalters in another cupboard in the cloister. The remainder of the collection was placed on shelves marked with letters of the alphabet. Although no further information has survived, it is thought that the letters on these shelves had no connection with the author's name or with the book's title—Augustine was not placed on the shelf lettered A, nor Gregory the Great on the shelf lettered G. A hundred years later, little had changed: a 1396 inventory shows the abbey's books categorized first by their location, then by subgroups called *thecae*, cases or caskets, which were each allocated a letter of the alphabet, but still without any correspondence between the letters and the ordering of the books themselves.[8]

Even so, two streams were converging and bringing change with them. These were the increasing number of books owned by monasteries and universities, in some places more than any librarian could remember, and the increasing use of reference tools designed to help readers locate what they needed in each individual book. With the latter becoming common, it may have begun to feel natural for libraries to attempt to order their books in such a way as to enable them to be searched for as a unit, as individual books could be. The question was, how was that ordering to be achieved?

The most obvious method was to continue to group manuscripts by category as before, creating subcategories where a single group—patristic writings, say—had become so large that the search for a single volume was now unwieldy. Humbert of Romans, Prior General of the Dominicans in the mid-thirteenth century, thought it rational, even natural, that books should be "kept according to the branches of study; that is to say, different books and [separate manuscript glosses, called] postils and treatises and the like which belong to the same subject should be kept separately and not intermingled." To aid a reader searching for a particular manuscript within those subject categories, he recommended "signs made in writing" (the very clumsiness of the phrase makes evident the novelty of this idea) which could "be affixed to each section, so that one will know where to find what one seeks."[9]

University libraries frequently divided their collections into two, as the Dominicans had done, with a primary collection holding books for students and teachers to consult in the libraries themselves, and a secondary, smaller collection with duplicates or less valuable works that could be borrowed. By 1300, the Sorbonne, and at Oxford both Merton College and possibly University College, kept many of their books that fell into that first category chained to lecterns, to make consultation easier. By the 1320s, the Sorbonne library held three hundred chained books, many, possibly most, of them reference books, including *distinctiones*, concordances, and indexes: the chained books had become their own library of search tools.[10]

Christchurch, Canterbury, also divided its collection. One part was distributed to members of the community at Lent in the long-established manner. But while the distribution was long established, something entirely novel was happening to the book list that around 1326 itemized this collection. It began conventionally enough with the cathedral's Bibles, followed by Augustine, and so on. Then, instead of moving on to Jerome, the list continued, for the first time that we know of, in first-letter alphabetical order, without regard for hierarchy: Angelomus, Aldhelm, Ambrose, Answelf, Amalarius, Achard, Alcuin, Aelred, Arator, it read, before moving on to Boethius, and continuing in first-letter alphabetical order right up to V. At that point it returned to subject categories, putting the collection's history books in subject order until, with another about-face, the remainder of the books were sorted under the names of their donors." The way the list moved back and forth between ordering systems suggests that those compiling it knew they had a problem. Their solution, interim and partial as it was, must have been both confusing and difficult to use, but the recognition that there were choices to be made was telling.

The Christchurch list was first, but it was not unique for long: the use of alphabetical order to sort and locate books was beginning to appear in many different regions of Europe, each time apparently independently, and using a variety of methods. Alphabetization was an idea that was in the air, rather than being the product of a single direct line of influence and imitation. The bibliographical work of Henry Kirkestede, prior of Bury St. Edmunds (c. 1314–after 1378), shows how the evolution of library tools more generally was a process: not a single decision but the result of many small changes. Kirkestede began by reorganizing his monastery's library, allocating each volume what today is known as a shelfmark, or accession number, a code unique to one single volume and no other. First came a letter that corresponded to the name of the author (or, presumably, where several manuscripts were bound together, to the first, or primary, author). A was for Augustine, Y for Isidore of Seville, and so on. A second letter indicated the subject or type of book: M for *medica*, C for *consuetudines*, or customs. Finally, each volume was given an

Arabic numeral, making that individual copy distinct from any other copy of the same work. To further distinguish each volume, particularly those with multiple authors, Kirkestede drew up a title page for every book in the library.[12] The resulting product could now, almost for the first time, be called a catalog, rather than an inventory or a book list. (The catalog has not survived, but some of Kirkestede's notes have.)

Kirkestede's second, and equally important, work was a bibliography, *Catalogus scriptorum ecclesiae*, A Catalog of Writings of the Church [Fathers]. A bibliography is a further stage in the development of reference tools. An inventory lists the goods—in this case books—that a person or institution possesses; a catalog gives the location of each of the books in the person's or institution's possession; while a bibliography outlines all known works on a single subject, or by an individual author, wherever they might be. A bibliography might include the location of the material it refers to, but it is more concerned with recording and describing the extant copies of a work, at this date also often appending a brief biography of the author. (From the fifteenth century and the arrival of printing, variations in editions, printers, places of publication, etc., also became the concern of bibliographers.) Not content simply to describe the works that made up the library at Bury St. Edmunds, Kirkestede drew on a range of sources for his *Catalogus*: he included manuscripts he had seen in other libraries in the region, noting their incipits to identify specific works; he incorporated the information held in the *Registrum librorum angliae* as well as information on manuscripts described in the works of authorities such as Isidore of Seville and Vincent of Beauvais.[13]

By the fifteenth century, both alphabetical order and the use of library lists to indicate the location of a book had become common. A concordance of c. 1425, written in England, probably in the Midlands, is prefaced by a paean to the alphabet and the order it brings: "Man's mind, that is often robbed of the treasure of cunning by the enemy of science—that is, by forgetting—is greatly assisted by tables and indexes created in the order of the a, b, c."*[14] Library lists from the monastery of St. Sebald in Nuremberg show how remarkably quickly change could happen: in 1486/7 a list of the monastery's books was drawn up "in the order of the pulpits," that is, following the physical layout of the church, noting where the books were stored on shelves and in cupboards. In 1489/90, however, this list, so recently completed, was superseded by a new one that put the books "into alphabetical order, so that everybody who looks for a book can find it more easily," thereby moving from inventory to catalog in just four years.[15]

This same progression was occurring spontaneously across Western Europe, as the use of indexes, florilegia, and other reference works became ever more widespread. A catalog from a priory in Hertfordshire, dating from 1400, shows its collection housed in four "columns," or bookcases, of eight shelves, each assigned a letter of the alphabet; the books on each shelf were then marked with a corresponding letter and recorded thus in the catalog, to make it possible—as the St. Sebald cataloger had observed of his own list—for "everybody who looks for a book [to] find it more easily." As at St. Sebald, too, there was no connection in the Hertfordshire catalog between the letters on the shelves and the names of the authors—shelf A did not house copies of Augustine and

---

*A modern transcription of this preface does not do justice to the charm of the original: "Mannes mynde, þat is ofte robbid of þe tresour of kunnyng bi þe enemye of science, þat is, forgetyng, is greetly releeued bi tablis maad bi lettre aftir þe ordre of þe a, b, c. Ensaumple: If a man haue mynde oonly of oon word or two of sum long text of þe Newe Lawe & haþ forgetyn al þe remenaunt, or ellis if he can seie bi herte such an hool text but he haþ forgeten in what stede it is writen, þis concordaunce wole lede him bi þe fewe wordis þat ben cofrid in his mynde vnto þe ful text & shewe him in what book & in what chapitre he shal fynde þo[se] textis whiche him list to haue." [*Man's mind, that is often robbed of the treasure of cunning by the enemy of science—that is, by forgetting—is greatly assisted by alphabetical indexes. For example: If a man remembers just one or two words of some long text from the New Testament, having forgotten the rest, or if he can recite by heart an entire passage, but cannot remember where it comes from, this concordance will lead him, from the few words that have stuck in his mind, to the full text, giving him the book and chapter references he needs to find the texts.*]

Anselm. Instead, books continued to be organized hierarchically, with the Bibles shelved first, although here they were unexpectedly followed by biblical glossaries, and only then by commentaries: works of reference were given priority over the Church Fathers.

But of course the speed of the changes, and of the acceptance of sorting tools and alphabetical order, were not uniform: one catalog of 1481 suggests the Vatican library was continuing to use hierarchical arrangements, while as much as a decade earlier a Carthusian monastery at Mainz had drawn up its catalog in alphabetical subject order.[16]

THE SPREAD OF REFERENCE TOOLS generated new interest in that primary reference tool, the dictionary. In 1150, the rationale behind Papias's alphabetical dictionary had been much misunderstood, some copies transcribed without his guiding marginals, others reordered entirely. Now a new wave of dictionary makers was better equipped to return to his pioneering notion. Even so, initially each dictionary compiler seems to have thought he was alone in inventing alphabetical order, explaining the system in a preface to his, presumably, uncomprehending readers.*

---

*That alphabetical order was neither natural nor instinctive can be gathered by these repeated directions, which continued for more than a century. In 1547, William Salesbury's Welsh-English dictionary carried an introduction to explain that a "Wordbook or Dictionary" was a collection of words "in which if you carefully notice, order and arrangement are kept: for the words are not mixed helter skelter in it, as they might happen to tumble to my mind at first thought. But with constant reflection, for the sake of the unlearned, every word . . . was chased to its own proper position. Thus all the words having *a* for the first letter were at the outset collected into the same place. Then all words beginning with *b* were placed apart. So with *c*, and *ch*, and *d*. Thus also of all the rest, every word is ranged under the standard of its captain [*sic*] letter."

As late as 1604, what has been called the first English nontranslating dictionary, Robert Cawdrey's *A Table Alphabeticall*, was published, listing "hard usuall English words . . . for the benefit and help of all unskilfull persons." Nearly half a millennium after Papias, and in the same year *Othello* was first performed and *Don Quixote* published, the author felt that "unskilfull persons" still needed to have it explained that "thou must learn the Alphabet, *to wit*, the order of the Letters as they stand, perfectly without booke, and where every Letter standeth," so that they would know "if the word,

In the twelfth century, Hugh of Pisa's *Magnae derivationes*, The Great Book of Derivations, had examined the etymology of words, which he arranged in first- or second-letter alphabetical order, depending on the manuscript copy. But for Hugh alphabetical order was not a fixed organizing principle; it could easily be interrupted or overturned in favor of other, more important, elements. Longer entries were given precedence over shorter ones, as were etymological concerns over alphabetic—*brevio*, or "abridge," for example, was not under "b," but under "a," for *abbrevio*, which also meant "shorten," as well as "abstract" or "précis."[18] These etymological groupings made the dictionary difficult to use as a reference tool, although that appeared to have had little impact on its success: nearly two hundred manuscript copies have survived, indicating its large circulation. The majority of these copies, however, include indexes that were compiled later, either by the scribes who copied the work or by their subsequent owners, to make the dictionary functional. Durham Cathedral library owned three copies, and Dover Priory six: of these nine, six had indexes.[19]

Hugh of Pisa's great work was followed sometime before 1272 by William Brito's *Summa*, or *Expositiones difficilorum verborum de Biblia*, Explanations of Difficult Biblical Words, where the 2,500-odd entries are, almost for the first time in a work of this nature, in absolute alphabetical order. William the Breton, another dictionary maker in this fertile period, originated a method that ignored suffixes and other grammatical variants, alphabetizing just the root of a word. (Thus "discovered" and "discovering" would both appear under "discover," as we would expect today.) Yet a hundred years later, alphabetical order still remained only one possibility among many: dictionary makers continued to use an array of organizing systems, often etymological or grammatical, sometimes

which thou art desirous to finde, begin with (*a*) then looke in the beginning of this Table, but if with (*v*) looke towards the end. Again, if thy word begin with (*ca*) looke in the beginning of the Letter (*c*) but if with (*cu*) then looke towards the end of that Letter."[17]

by, say, making separate sections for nouns, verbs, and other *indeclinabilia*—adjectives, adverbs, and prepositions.[20] Others turned to much older styles. In the mid-thirteenth century, one Anglo-Norman knight wrote an old-fashioned interlinear gloss to teach the children of the English-speaking gentry to differentiate similar-sounding French words:

> *Lippe*   *the hare*
> Vous avez la levere et le levere,
>
> *the pount*   *book*
> La livere et le liv[e]re.[21]

Then in 1286 came the *Summa grammaticalis quae vocatur catholicon* of the Dominican Giovanni Balbi, or John of Genoa (d. c. 1298), his Compendium of Grammar that is Called Universal (usually referred to as the *Catholicon*, the Universal). Balbi drew on the work of both Papias and Hugh of Pisa to produce this hugely popular Latin dictionary in absolute alphabetical order: nearly two hundred copies have survived, and two centuries later, in 1460, it was to become one of the very earliest books to be printed.

The single focus of Balbi's work made it notable. Other dictionary makers retained a fondness for organizational complexity, such as, "from the land of Engleterre," Moses ben Isaac Hanessiah's *Sefer ha-Shoham*, The Onyx Book,* a dictionary structured into a series of "gates," in which nouns, for example, were subdivided into a web of 162 interlocking categories.[22] Multilingual dictionaries were well known elsewhere on the Continent from possibly the thirteenth century, but they used alphabetical order only in part, relying on other categorizing systems as

---

* *Shoham*, meaning onyx in Hebrew, is an anagram of "Moshe" in the Hebrew alphabet, where vowels are a secondary notation: Sh-h-m becoming M-sh-h. It was very probably this wordplay that guided his choice of title, rather than any connection with the stone.

well. The *Codex Cumanicus*, for example, probably produced near Caffa (today Feodosiya in Ukraine, then a Genoese colony), was a guide for travelers and missionaries, translating Latin, Persian, and Cuman (or Kipchak), the now-dead language of the Cumans, a nomadic people of Central Europe. In it, words were divided first into categories, as in a modern phrasebook, to help travelers or merchants by grouping together vocabulary for food, or other words they might need on the road. Only then were they alphabetized.[23]

Balbi's *Catholicon* rejected these and other possibilities. In his preface Balbi was explicit as to how to use his book, going into such detail it is as though he were attempting to set out instructions for future dictionary makers rather than guiding his own readers. He began simply, with first-letter sorting, using as his examples the words *amo* and *bibo*, "I love" and "I drink": "I will discuss *amo* before *bibo* because *a* is the first letter of *amo* and *b* is the first letter of *bibo* and *a* comes before *b* in the alphabet." This type of first-letter alphabetization was not uncommon by this date, and so Balbi moved swiftly on to second-letter sorting: when two words began with the same letter, such as *abeo*, "I depart," and *adeo*, "I approach," "I will discuss *abeo* before I do *adeo* because *b* is the second letter in *abeo* and *d* is the second letter in *adeo*, and *b* is before *d*." He continued: "You may proceed everywhere according to the alphabet," reminding his readers that they must take note of every letter of each word, as he labored through the same idea for the third letter of a word, then for the fourth, the fifth, and the sixth. Only then did he feel he had made his point: "And so in like manner you will understand the letters of which all the words included in this part are composed, for the arrangement always follows the order of the alphabet." Even after all that, he still thought it necessary to explain that when a word included a repeated letter—"ss" or "tt"—then each letter had to be considered individually. He ended, sounding quite exhausted, with both a boast and a plea: "I have devised this order at the cost of great effort and strenuous application . . . I beg of you, therefore, good reader, do not scorn this great labour of mine and this order as something worthless."*[24]

By the fourteenth century, certainly, few in Europe in the world of books scorned this great labor, or this order, as something worthless. The next major development in organizing, and alphabetical ordering, however, was first seen outside Europe, in places where no alphabet existed. This was printing, and it brought with it a revolution. As a modern scholar of the history of writing said: "Writing makes civilization possible. Printing makes science possible. Indexing makes them [both] accessible."[26]

---

*Balbi's long explanation brings into focus the work that goes into dictionaries, which, when we use them, seem straightforward, as though the dictionary maker has simply had to perform a mechanical task: Ab before Ac, and so on. For while alphabetical order is the most useful tool to find a word in a dictionary that has so far been devised, it is by no means the easiest tool to *create* a dictionary. Grouping words by type (slang, or technical words, or fields of knowledge), or by entry size (words like "go" and "run," which require lengthy definitions and have a large number of meanings), or grammatically (verbs, nouns, adjectives) is far easier for the dictionary writer to implement. In addition, endless decisions are required to alphabetize usefully. Where do abbreviations get placed?—does DIY go under "di," or under "do" for "do it yourself"? What about compound or hyphenated words? Post / Postilion / Post office, or Post / Post office / Postilion? What about words that have no letters, like 9/11? What happens to words with accents? Are those letters treated as though there is no accent, or are they ordered as though the accented letter is a separate entity? Alphabetization is easier to use than to produce, as Balbi's explanation made clear.[25]

 IS FOR FIRSTS

From the Birth of Printing to Library Catalogs in the Fifteenth to Sixteenth Centuries

---

BY THE FIFTEENTH CENTURY, PRINTING WITH MOVABLE TYPE HAD BEEN in use for more than two hundred years, although it had been unknown in Europe. China had long been familiar with various ways of mass-producing texts: in the second century, to promote Confucianism as the state ideology, the Han emperors had had the Analects of Confucius and the Five Classics carved onto stone steles, from which were produced rubbings of individual sections or texts.[1] By the ninth century, copies were being printed from engraved woodblocks, a method well suited to capturing the detail of calligraphic brushstrokes. The earliest known block-printed work, from 868 CE in the Western calendar, was the Buddhist Diamond Sutra from Dunhuang in western China, which was "reverently made for universal free distribution by Wang Jie, on behalf of his parents," according to its printed inscription.[2]

It was the eleventh century, however, that saw the emergence of printing with movable type. This century was one of extraordinary invention in China, which among other wonders delivered the world's first magnetic compass, and while paper had been used for writing from the third century—the Diamond Sutra was printed on paper—it now became the material for something startlingly novel: currency. Those who were creating mass-produced written works—who from here onward can be denominated "printers"—began to experiment with different materials to manufacture text images, or ideograms, that could be replicated in bulk, whether made of ceramic, clay, paste, wood, tin, or bronze, although woodblocks were soon deemed best suited to the thousands of characters needed for each work.[3]

The idea of movable type continued to spread and was modified and improved on as it traveled. By the 1230s it was employed in Korea, where *hanja*, a writing system based on Chinese characters and adapted to suit the requirements of the Korean language, was in use. In 1377, at Heungdeok Temple, the *Jikji*, an anthology of Buddhist teachings, was printed in movable type, some of which has survived. And in 1403 King Taejong (1367–1422), who was consolidating power as an absolute monarch, initiated the printing of the country's laws using copper plates as a symbol of their permanence.[4]

It was among the alphabetic writing systems of Western Europe, however, that print was to predominate. The Western printing press was born of several elements, none of which was individually an innovation, nor even out of the ordinary. Gold- and silversmiths had long utilized the punch, a tool used to impress specific shapes into metal. For printing, the punch was used to cut a desired shape—in this case, an individual letter of the alphabet—into a soft metal to create a matrix; the matrix was then set in a mold into which molten metal was poured, which, when cooled, resulted in a single letter, a process that could be repeated ad infinitum, permitting endless replications of each letter of the alphabet.

These metal letters were then arranged as words in rows, after which the rows were locked into an iron brace the size and shape of a page, called a "form." The text was covered with ink, and a page placed over it to receive its impression. The process was mechanized with the printing press, also modified from an older invention, the wine press used to crush grapes. These adapted presses replaced the need for each sheet to be individually smoothed over the inked form by hand, making printing faster and delivering more uniform pages. Afterward the forms could be saved for subsequent printings of the same book, or they could be broken up—taken apart—and the letters returned to the typesetter's case to be used in another book (for more on type cases, see pages 173–174).

It was the genius of Johannes Gutenberg (c. 1400–1468) to take these disparate and well-known elements—the goldsmith's punch (Gutenberg appears to have had some background as a goldsmith), the mold, and the method of creating letters—and combine them with the use of the agricultural press. In repurposing these ordinary tools, Gutenberg changed the world. Between 1450 and 1455 in the town of Mainz on the river Rhine, Gutenberg printed a Bible with the new movable type, a book he carefully designed to resemble as closely as possible the manuscripts his invention was so soon to render obsolete. In 1460, three hundred copies of Balbi's *Catholicon* were printed. This may well have been printed by Gutenberg himself, "without the help of reed, stylus or pen but by the wondrous agreement, proportion and harmony of punches and types," as the inscription on the dictionary's first edition read, but it is not certain. For even before his Bible was completed, he had lost control of his printing house, having borrowed money for the project from one Johann Fust—money he was unable to repay. Gutenberg's business was therefore taken over by Fust and his son-in-law, Peter Schöffer, who had been a scribe in Paris and had then worked for Gutenberg. Schöffer (c. 1425–c. 1503) became an innovator in his own right, designing some of the earliest typefaces, being the first to include the date each book was published, establishing the idea of a printer's colophon—a symbol or inscription that identified the printer (or, later, the publisher), and often the place of publication—as well as devising new methods of punch-cutting letters. Meanwhile, Gutenberg set up a new printing house, and it was there that he may have printed the *Catholicon*.

Europe embraced print. A decade after Gutenberg's Bible, Italy's first printing press was established. Within another ten years France, Spain, the Netherlands, and England had presses too. This brought a change beyond anything that had gone before. In the thousand years before printing, it is estimated that perhaps five million manuscripts had been produced in Europe. In the half century following the arrival of printing, up to twenty million copies of books entered circulation, four times more in fifty years than throughout the previous millennium. And between 1500 and 1600, as many as two hundred million more were printed.[5]

Books therefore became both more widely available and much less expensive. They were still items for the well-to-do, but we know that in Paris by the first half of the sixteenth century, more than sixty tradesmen had book collections large enough to be considered libraries. Access to books was no longer a privilege confined to the nobility, or to distinguished scholars, or religious orders.[6] The middle classes, especially the new professional middle classes, could now assemble their own collections. This expanding readership in turn brought about a change in the type of books that were being produced: the proportion of religious texts declined, while Latin, Greek, and humanist works became increasingly prevalent.

Conveniently enough, Frankfurt, a mere twenty-five miles from Gutenberg and Schöffer in Mainz, was already one of the Continent's most significant trade centers, the site of a fair held biannually from the early Middle Ages—a fair so crucial to trade that by 1240 it had been put under imperial protection. Within three decades of Gutenberg's Bible, the Frankfurt fair had become the heart of Western Europe's printing and associated trades: papermakers, woodblock artists, bookbinders, and, eventually, type founders all flocked to the city, as did scholars.* By the early sixteenth century, the printer Henri Estienne (1528/31–1598) hailed the fair as the "Frankfurt Athens." Erasmus (1466–1536), arguably the greatest Renaissance humanist of all, was concerned enough to ask his printer if his *Adagia* (for more on that book, see page 127) would be ready for the fair of 1521.[7]

Now, with the increased output this new technology enabled, printers had to work out how to sell multiple copies of one work, instead of single copies of many. Reference books, they discovered, were nice steady sellers, finding buyers not only among the religious orders and universities but also among students and schools, as well as private individuals. No longer was it necessary for university students to copy out entire manuscripts to have what they needed for their courses. It was now the producers—the printers—who needed to entice buyers to favor their wares. To do so, they began to produce broadsides—printed single pages listing the works they had for sale and the places where they could be purchased—which were posted in public places.

Scholars of print history have estimated that many hundreds, possibly thousands, of broadsides were printed in the fifteenth century; of those hundreds or thousands, a mere forty-seven are known to have survived. In the next century, even more were produced, numbering in the thousands, if not the tens of thousands. Yet in all of Europe, just thirteen of these sixteenth-century broadsides have survived, eleven of them from north Italy, preserved by chance when they were bound together to serve as a bookseller's reference work.[8] Thus what we know about how booksellers sold their stock can be, at best, a guess based on scanty evidence. The extant broadsides indicate that as yet booksellers

---

*The Frankfurt Trade Fair continues to be a major economic force today, with over €600 million in sales annually, the five days dedicated to books drawing more than seven thousand exhibitors each year.

did not feel the need to categorize their wares any more than libraries had in centuries past: they listed their books in seemingly random order, neither alphabetically nor by subject. One Nuremberg bookseller listed thirty-one works, beginning with a gloss, followed by two parts of Vincent of Beauvais's *Speculum maius*, Balbi's *Catholicon*, and then the Old and New Testaments.[9]

It is easy to assume that standardization, organization, regularization—and alphabetization—followed hard on the heels of the arrival of printing, but the reality was less tidy, as reality usually is. It took some time even to arrive at what we think of as a standard page of text: black ink on white paper, a centered text in roman type, intermittently interspersed with italic or bold, broken up into paragraphs by indented spaces, surmounted by running heads and page numbers. Nor were other elements of the book—chapter headings to mark text divisions, tables of contents, title pages to announce the book title, the author, publisher, and date and place of publication—any more formalized at this date. Instead, in the fifteenth and well into the sixteenth centuries, texts were designed to resemble manuscripts, often with no title page, and with red initial letters, headings, and glosses underlined. Paragraphs or other breaks in the text were rarely used, and most frequently unknown, although paragraph marks—¶—were sometimes used as marginalia, to give an indication of the text's structure. Indented paragraphs would not become commonplace for another half century.

The Venetian printer Aldus Manutius (1449/52–1515) was an innovator: in his *Hypnerotomachia Poliphili*, The Dream of Poliphilus, printed in 1499, he used the paragraph indents we would recognize; and two years later, he introduced italic typefaces (see page 119).[10] Other symbols that we take for granted appeared more gradually. In manuscripts, a diple (which resembles our mathematical symbol meaning "less than": <) had often hitherto been used as a marginal notation to guide readers' attention to something important in the text. In the sixteenth century, the symbol moved into the text itself, indicating those lines of text that included *sententiae*, or citations from the authorities. And then, around the 1570s, the diple migrated again, to the beginning of a citation, to indicate direct speech or quoted material: it had become an inverted comma, or quotation mark.[11]

Pagination—numbering each page with consecutive Arabic numerals—came relatively swiftly, although it was not originally a matter of marking first page 1, then its reverse page 2, and so on to the end of the work.* At first, printers used these numerals to guide themselves, not their readers. From the early days of printing (and still today), the technology of the printing press was such that eight, sixteen, or thirty-two pages were printed together on a single sheet, which was then folded to produce pages 1 to 8, 1 to 16, or 1 to 32 of a book. That folded section was, and is, called a signature (the equivalent for a manuscript was a quire, which was usually made up of between four and six folded sheets), and multiple signatures were gathered in order and bound together to produce a book. These gathers can best be seen today along the top or bottom edges of most hardback books, where the pages meet the spine. To ensure the signatures were kept in the correct order during the binding process, printers gave each signature a number, or, today, consecutive letters of the alphabet, printing them inconspicuously at the bottom of each signature's first page. The signatures could then be dispatched to a bindery in any order, and by following the progression of the numbers or letters, the book, even without numbered pages, would still easily be bound in the correct order.

---

*Page numbers may have come swiftly, but as always there were those who disapproved long after the novelty had become the norm. As late as the seventeenth century, the diarist and writer John Evelyn distinguished the "Roman Figure," or roman numerals, from what he dismissed as "the Barbarous," or Arabic numerals.[12]

Printed books were originally bound in plain paper covers, with the expectation that their owners would have them rebound in different styles or qualities of leather according to their resources and tastes. To ensure that the order of the signatures was maintained during this second binding, printers included a "register," or list, of the first words of each signature, placing it at the beginning of the text in the position that a table of contents later came to occupy. And not long after the establishment of printing houses, some began to do more than give each signature a numeral for internal use. In printers' technical vocabulary, a folio is the sheet of paper consisting of two sides, or pages, the front and reverse. Once the sheets have been bound into a book, the right-hand, uneven-numbered page is called the recto; the left-hand, even-numbered page the verso. (This page, for example, is a verso.) At first, it was the folios themselves that were numbered, followed by an "r" for recto, or "v" for verso.* Whichever style was chosen, the numbers were no longer internal printers' indicators, but were there for the convenience of the readers.

In 1450, fewer than a tenth of manuscripts used any system to indicate pagination. In 1499, a reference work to the epigrams of the Roman poet Martial, *Cornu Copiae*, The Horn of Plenty, by the Italian humanist Niccolò Perotti, may have been the first book to include numbering on every page, a novelty highlighted by the accompanying explanation at the head of the index: "[E]ach word that is sought can be found easily, since each half page [that is, each recto and verso] throughout the entire book is numbered with arithmetical numbers [meaning Arabic, not roman, numerals]." A century later, most printed books included page numbers as a matter of course.[13] Yet even then, printers assumed that many readers would be unfamiliar with the concept. In England in

---

*The explanation is more complicated than the reality. This book is numbered by the page—pages 1, 2, 3, etc. If it were numbered by folio, then the current page 1 would be folio 1r (1 recto), the current page 2 would be 1v (1 verso), pages 3 and 4, folios 2r and 2v, and so on.

1576, the poet Barnabe Googe (1540–1594) translated a contemporary satirical Latin epic, *Zodiacus vitae*, as *The Zodyake of Life*.* "[F]or the Readers aduantage," the volume announced, it included "A large table alphabeticall" in which, it was carefully explained, each entry contained a "Figure [that] referreth the Reader to the number of the page": the link between a page number and an index entry was not yet automatic.**[15]

Even so, right from the start, printers clearly had a sense of the benefits that pagination was shortly to bring. In the early 1460s, Fust and Schöffer's Mainz printing house produced Augustine's *De arte praedicandi*, On the Art of Preaching, with what was possibly the first printed index.[16] Without the inclusion of page numbers, the text was divided into paragraphs with a marginal letter beside each: the first twenty-five (I and J were still the same letter) were lettered A to Z; the next two bore the symbols for *et*, "and," and *con*, "against"; after which the letters were doubled, AA, BB, to produce a second alphabetical series.[17] This index was alphabetized to the first two or three letters. So was the index to the *Speculum vitae*, The Mirror of Life, by Bishop Rodrigo de Zamora (1404–1470). This book was printed in Rome in 1468, and is the first index in a printed book that carries a date. In its preface, the reader is promised a "repertory or alphabetical table for easily finding subjects in

---

*This work by a minor Italian poet, Pier Angelo Manzolli, became disproportionately important to English literature. Googe's translation was popular in schools, and is credited with influencing many Elizabethan writers, including Shakespeare, who drew on it in *As You Like It* for his "Seven Ages of Man" speech ("All the world's a stage . . ."). And there is a second connection here with Shakespeare. Unusually, we know the name of the indexer of Googe's work: Abraham Fleming (c. 1552–1607), a clergyman, translator, and editor. As well as producing this index for Googe, he is thought to have been the editor who oversaw and contributed to the production of the second edition of Holinshed's *Chronicles*, a work much pillaged by Shakespeare for material used in, among others, *Macbeth*, *King Lear*, and *Cymbeline*.[14]

**Fleming's index was primitive, in first-letter order only, and he indexed the first word of each phrase, no matter how minor. Thus the opening entries run: Aganippe / Avarice causeth care / A beast & no man, that regardes none but himself / Avarice frayeth the riche man . . .

the present book," although when it was reprinted in Germany it carried a postscript about that same repertory, or index: "This is the happy and welcome end of the brief alphabetical table," which sounds rather like a sigh of relief in saying farewell to a new and complex idea.[18] For indexing grew only slowly over the first half century of printing: possibly fewer than 10 percent of the books printed before 1501 included an index. Yet each decade saw an increase, and twice as many books with indexes may have been printed between 1490 and 1499 as between 1470 and 1479.[19]

Many early indexes included small preambles of instruction, as with Fust's and Schöffer's Augustine volume; some explained that they were structured "according to the order of the ABC"; others assumed that this was understood. Even so, how, exactly, an index was to be alphabetized was not yet settled. One of the most successful of early printed books, *The Nuremberg Chronicle*, a history of the world from the creation, included an index sorted, as Fleming's had been, by the first letter not of a word, but of a phrase, no matter how minor that first word might be: *Ars imprimendi libros*, the "art of book printing," was indexed under "a" for art, not "i" for printing, nor "l" for book.[20]

The content of a book, of course, influenced whether or not it was indexed. The sciences were at the forefront of all systems of ordering. In the late 1300s, Greek manuscript copies of the works of the mathematician, geographer, and astronomer Ptolemy (c. 100–170 CE) had circulated in Italy, and in 1477 a version of the *Geographia*, his work on longitude and latitude, maps and mapping, was printed in Bologna. In the following decade Johann Reger, a printer in Ulm in southern Germany, produced an edition with text and maps, as well as an alphabetical index. This edition proved very successful, bringing Ptolemy's mathematical projections, his entirely novel way of envisioning space, to a new audience.[21] A century later, modern cartography was born with the printing of the *Theatrum orbis terrarum*, The Theatre of the World, by the Flemish mapmaker Abraham Ortelius (1527–1598). As well as being considered the first modern atlas, the *Theatrum* was a model reference work, with an alphabetical list of mapmakers and which maps each had produced and where and when, followed by a first- and sometimes second-letter alphabetical list of the maps by country. At the back of the book, place names were cross-indexed under both their classical and their modern names, followed by brief identifications ("region in England," "river in Spain," and so on).[22]

Other fields, too, welcomed and subsequently developed the index. The one in the first Italian edition of Vitruvius's *De architectura*, On Architecture (1521), included not just subheads that read "A," or "B," but "*A. ante B.*" (A before B, *abacus, Abaton*), "*A. ante C.*" (*Accio, Acie*), making clear for its readers the utility of working past first-letter alphabetical order into ever finer distinctions, even though the words themselves were not yet alphabetized past that second-letter order.[23] Books on medicine had long been inclined to use the alphabet for sorting. In the Arabic-speaking world, medical treatises by authorities such as Rasis (854–925) and Avicenna (c. 980–1037) were traditionally accompanied by both indexes and glossaries, and in the sixteenth century these were translated into Latin together with their reference tools. By the 1580s, editions of Guy de Chauliac's fourteenth-century *Chirurgia magna*, the text still organized in head-to-heel order, included five indexes to help medical professionals locate the information they needed in this multivolume work.[24] And in another scientific genre, natural history, an alphabetically ordered collection of citations of 1482, drawing on both Greek and Arabic sources as well as the more usual Latin, was one of the earliest to break with a subject-based order, possibly under the influence of the very Arabic texts it cited.[25]

Or it may have been that the influence of herbals, a favorite genre from the earliest days of printing, encouraged both alphabetical ordering and the use of indexes. By the late thirteenth century, a manuscript herbal, *De virtutibus herbarum*, On the Virtues [or Benefits] of Plants, had already included a first-letter index. The earliest printed herbals appeared in the 1470s and 1480s, frequently editions of much earlier works. The *Herbarium of Apuleius*, printed near Rome in 1480/81, was culled from texts by the first-century Greek physician and botanist Dioscorides: the plants were listed in the most basic alphabetical order by their Latin names, with accompanying translations back into the original Greek (transliterated: printers had not yet started printing non-Latin characters), as well as into Italian, French, "Dacian" (Slavonic), and "Ægyptian," which one modern commentator has dryly described as being "mostly" Arabic.[26]

But far more influential than these early contributions were three entirely new herbals. In 1484, Peter Schöffer's Mainz printing house published a *Herbarius*, with 150 plants in more or less alphabetical order by their Latin names, together with their German translations. Within a year pirated editions were printed in Leuven, with translations into Dutch, and in Paris, into French. In 1485 Schöffer produced a revised and enlarged version in German, without the Latin, entitled *Gart der Gesundtheit*, Garden of Health. This time, however, the text was in the older head-to-heel order, as was its accompanying subject index, which was prefaced: "[A]nd this is an index to find out quickly about all the diseases of people," followed by a rudimentary first-letter alphabetically ordered index of plant names. Six years later, again in Mainz, the printer Jakob Meydenbach produced the *Ortus* [sometimes *Hortus*] *sanitatis*, The Source [or Garden] of Health, which listed 533 plants, 228 animals (divided into land and water animals), and 144 minerals, with four tables of contents and two indexes, one for the plants, one a subject index, and both in relatively consistent second-letter order. These were flagged in the preface, which promised that they were supplied "lest it happen, O reader, that you should have to wander around [the book] tediously."

Herbals were popular, both in Latin and in vernacular languages. The first herbal in French appeared in 1487; in Italian and English, in the 1520s. Many advertised their indexes on their title page—they had become selling points, a tool whereby "one can see the whole contents of this book, as in a mirror," as a German herbal of 1527 boasted. Even so, they often remained unwieldy. *The Vertuose Boke of Distyllacyon*, an English translation of a Latin text compiled around 1527, laboriously, and confusingly, explained: "[T]his present table is dyuyded in xxxi [parts]" that could be searched "by the nōbre of youre chaptyres, and by the regystre of youre [marginal] letters as ABCDE, &c. and seke to this in the xii chapitre in the lettre D after that seke for this in the xxvii chapitre in the lettre J. and in the lxxxix chapytre in the letter A."[27]

By the mid-sixteenth century, almost all books on natural philosophy, or science, included an index, as did many miscellanies and compilations. These indexes were more complex, tending toward absolute alphabetical order, with careful entries and subentries replacing the earlier long lists of proper names. What had once been considered an optional extra produced by an individual—sometimes the book's owner, sometimes its creator—was now regularly expected by readers, in great part owing to the increase in output generated by print.

With the arrival of printing came a marked increase in the production of volumes containing works by a single author, superseding those composite manuscripts where works by several authors were routinely bound together. In the first half of the fourteenth century, for example, nearly half of all manuscripts containing works by Petrarch also included texts by other writers. By the second half of the century, that number had dropped to a third, and in the following century nearly three-quarters of texts featuring Petrarch contained his work only.[28] This growing predominance of single-author volumes, whether in manuscript form or in print, contributed greatly to the spread of ordering—especially alphabetical ordering—systems: it is easier to catalog or shelve multi-author books chronologically by date of production, or by subject, or language, or printer, than it is to organize them alphabetically.

The ever-greater supply of printed volumes meant that the broadsides announcing booksellers' products for sale became increasingly inefficient for both producers and consumers. From 1542 Robert Estienne, the Parisian (later Genevan) printer, issued pamphlets listing his wares, divided by language: books in Hebrew, Greek, and Latin, each in their own section. His contemporary Christoph Froschauer (c. 1490–1564), one of the first printers in Zurich, followed the same model.

The most influential bookseller's catalog in Europe was not that of an individual, however, but was a compilation of all the publications issued by the booksellers who attended the Frankfurt book fair. Printed in the 1560s, that first catalog, like Estienne's, sorted new publications by language, either Latin or German, and then by subject. In 1592, the fair printed a retrospective edition covering the previous three decades of fair catalogs; six years later the town council took over, banning individual booksellers' catalogs at the fair and insisting on its own biannual catalog, again with books grouped by language.[29] The Basel-based printer Johannes Oporinus (1507–1568) refused to conform, though, producing a seventy-six-page catalog in alphabetical order by first name.[30] He was not the only exception: English booksellers also went their own way, organizing their catalogs first by format, that is, by size, and then by subject, well into the eighteenth century.*[31] Across Europe, books were generally sold at auction rather than in shops. The first printed book-auction catalog appeared in the Netherlands in the 1590s. Almost all auction catalogs used format as their primary sorting criterion, with subject categories as a secondary one.[32]

Whether issued by booksellers or the Frankfurt book fair or auction houses, these catalogs announcing new works and old were not intended as ephemeral advertising, as broadsides had been, but were long-lasting and influential. They were kept and referred to by booksellers and collectors not only for current sales, but also as reference

---

*Book formats were, and still are, based on the signature—that folded sheet that is the basis for printed books. The largest format is called a folio, indicating that historically it was a full sheet, or folio, folded just once. The next size down, quarto, indicates the sheet was folded to make a four-folio, eight page, signature, while an octave was printed to create a signature of eight folios, or sixteen pages, and was thus half the size of a quarto, and a quarter the size of a folio.

tools, precursors to what today we call bibliographies: organized lists of books by subject, date, category, or some other defining characteristic, with details of publishing history and sometimes authors' biographical information, as in Henry Kirkestede's fourteenth-century prototype, his *Catalogus scriptorum ecclesiae*. The catalogs' range and variety, and their ubiquity, ensured that booksellers and their customers 'across Europe became familiar with all manner of organizing systems. In 1494/5, Johann Tritheim (1462–1516), the Abbot of Sponheim Abbey in the Rhineland, had compiled a *Liber de scriptoribus ecclesiasticis*, A Book of Ecclesiastical Writers, and a *Catalogus illustrium virorum Germaniae*, A Catalog of the (Lives of) Illustrious Germans, both listing more than three thousand authors and their works in chronological order, with first-name alphabetical indexes appended.[33]

Tritheim's influence was profound: the remit of a bibliography was far greater than a bookseller's catalog, the latter including only new volumes, or those currently available for purchase; bibliographies also enabled readers to survey an entire subject in overview. Many similar works followed in the sixteenth century, for both Latin and vernacular books: in 1548, an English bibliography aimed to list all British writers in chronological order; a couple of years later, a Venetian work listed books written in Italian, with the authors in alphabetical order by first name.[34]

In England, an important milestone was reached with the bookseller Andrew Maunsell's 1595 *Catalogue of English Printed Books*. This he organized in the tried and trusted method, by subject, but he was more innovative with other features, using italic type to distinguish each author's name.* And, instead of alphabetizing by first name, the standard practice for centuries, he announced:

---

* In 1500–1501, Aldus Manutius became the first printer to produce an italic typeface, a cursive that mimicked handwriting, making it more compact than standard roman typefaces and therefore useful for small volumes designed to be carried about rather than read sitting at a desk in a library. The idea of using italics to distinguish elements of a text, as Maunsell did, developed only gradually over the next century, as did its later use for emphasis, that typographic nudge in the ribs.

[I] have to my great pains drawn the writers of any special argument together, not following the order of the learned men that have written Latine catalogs, Gesner, Simler and our countriman, John Bale. They make their alphabet by the Christian name, I by the sirname . . . For example Lambert Danaeus, his treatise of Antichrist, translated by John Swan, printed for John Potter and Thomas Gubbin. . . . The author's sirname, which is Danaeus; the matter of the booke, which is Antichrist; the translator's name, which is Swan; are, or, should be, in Italica letters, and none others, because they are alphabetical names observed in this book: turne to which of these three names you will, and they will direct you to the books.[35]

With this paragraph, Maunsell hurtled into the future. Previously, alphabetical order by first name had made a great deal of sense. Many people had no last names, or the last names by which they were known were not names as such, but the names of places, often their place of origin. The father of English bibliography, Henry Kirkestede, was a man named Henry who came from a place called Kirstead (written Kirkestede or Kerkestede at the time) in Norfolk; Peter Lombard, the author of the famous *Sentences*, was born near Lombardy in northwest Italy. While today we consider looking up Thomas Aquinas under "T" not just odd but confusing, in reality, distinguishing him from Thomas of Bayeux, Thomas of Ireland, Thomas à Becket, or Thomas à Kempis is no more difficult than distinguishing between the William Smith who was a Bishop of Lincoln, the Miles Smith who was Bishop of Gloucester, or the Thomas Smith who was Bishop of Carlisle. Maunsell's focus on the "sirname" was a recognition that while some names still derived from place names, or were patronymics, or other variants of their names—Lambert Danaeus in his example was the Latinate name sometimes used for the French Calvinist theologian Lambert Daneau—more and more people, like his examples of John Swan, John Potter, and Thomas Gubbin, were beginning consistently to use modern forms of both first and surnames.

Maunsell was also looking to the future when he cited Gesner as a "learned" bibliographer. For it was Conrad Gesner (often Gessner, 1516–1565) who took bibliography, and alphabetical order, into the modern world. The Zurich-born Gesner was a doctor and naturalist, professions that indirectly led him to become the foremost guide to the creation of modern bibliography. In 1541/2, Gesner published two botanical volumes: a compendium of plants mentioned in classical writings, with name and subject indexes; and a catalog of plants, with their names in Latin, Greek, German, and French, using strict and absolute alphabetical order in both. Then came his 1545 *Bibliotheca universalis*, The Universal Library, not merely a catalog of every book Gesner could find, or examine, or had heard of, but an attempt to include every work that had ever existed, and with as much detail as he could gather. In the end, the published volumes listed approximately twelve thousand works, in alphabetical order by the authors' first names.*

This was the first of a planned three-part work; the second, referred to as the *Pandectae*, The Compendium, followed three years later.** The *Pandectae* in turn served as a massive subject index to the *Bibliotheca universalis*, but was also much more. It was a list of subjects and keywords, but instead of simply listing everything alphabetically Gesner shaped it carefully into a classified structure. On the title page he described it as "embracing the commonplaces and categories . . . all philosophy and every discipline and area of inquiry," intending the work to function as both an index and a program of reading. So, for instance, the theology volume listed commentators on the Bible, metaphysics, ethics,

---

* In 1555 an index of surnames, for those who could not remember the authors' first names, was appended—a sign, surely, that Maunsell's system a few decades hence was the one that would eventually prevail.

** More formally, it was entitled *Pandectarum sive pàrtitionum universalium . . . libri XXI*, The Compendium or Universal Divisions, in 21 Parts, although only nineteen were initially published. The twentieth, on theology, appeared a year later, and the last, on medicine, was incomplete at the time of Gesner's early death from the plague.

the Church, heresy, Church history, and *varia*. Each was then subdivided: *varia* included *summae*, commonplace compilations, indexes, and glosses; *sententiae* and *distinctiones*; collections of letters; and literature, including satires. These too were further subdivided. Gesner had taken the older ideas of the encyclopedia, but instead of reflecting and reconstructing the image of a hierarchical world, he reconfigured it to meet the needs of natural science and an exploration of the natural world, producing the early shoots that would later grow into the classification systems of scientists such as Linnaeus (see page 198), who sought to establish a classification method that would encompass the entire natural world. This, however, was still in the future, and so, at the very end of the *Pandectae*, Gesner included an alphabetical index of headings for his entire work: his subject index needed an index of its own.[36]

In his section *De grammatica*, On Grammar, the function of an index was explained yet again: "It is now generally accepted," Gesner wrote, "that copious and strictly alphabetically arranged indexes" were of "the greatest convenience to scholars, second only to the truly divine intervention of printing books by movable type," and books with indexes were "deservedly preferred" to those without. This was already a stronger and clearer statement than many other index preambles that laid out their purpose, but Gesner then went further. Nearly three hundred years earlier, Giovanni Balbi had explained painstakingly in the preface to his *Catholicon* how he had ordered each word, letter by letter, teaching his readers how to look things up alphabetically. Gesner now described not how to use an index, but how to make one—the first technical explanation of index-making that we know of. In the past, many book owners had been taught privately, or had taught themselves as they indexed their own manuscript copies. Now, in the age of the mass dissemination of printed books, expectations were changing. A few years after his *Pandectae*, Gesner attempted in a five-volume *Historia animalium*, A History of Animals (1551–1558), to provide a description of every known animal, together with a bibliography of natural-history books, both firsts in their field. Unlike the *Bibliotheca universalis* or the *Pandectae*, which were structured around subject categories, here he relied entirely on alphabetical order, "the utility" of which, he explained, "comes not from reading [the book] from beginning to end, which would be more tedious than useful, but from consulting it." Gesner was no longer thinking of his work as an encyclopedia in the older sense, a mirror of the world, but in the new: it had become a modern reference tool.[37]

Gesner was developing the means to comb through books to find authoritative sources even as print—and search tools themselves—were, in other respects, and counterintuitively, making books seem *less* authoritative than they had been before. Previously, any piece of information was most likely read in isolation. Now, with so many more books available, as well as the new tools to help search them, a single nugget of information could be compared to information on the same subject in another book, and another, and another, all of which might agree—or might not. And print itself, while it made a text appear definitive and unchanging, also encouraged a new questioning of authority. Previously, if a scribe had copied a manuscript incorrectly, it required another reader with access to the original manuscript, or another copy, for that to become apparent. Certainly, later scribes often added marginalia, comparing one manuscript to another, or commenting on sources, or simply indicating that they thought something might be wrong, or missing, in the copy in front of them. Or they might follow the pattern of a concordance of c. 1425, where a scribe ended his explanation of how to use alphabetical order with a warning: if "ony word in this werk" was found to be out of order, the reader was to understand that it was unintentional, the result of "vnkunnyng or neglygence of the writere," who could only hope that it might at some point be "amendid."[38] Because once a manuscript left a scribe's hands, there was nothing more he could do.

Print was different. In 1611, the *Vocabolario degli accademici della Crusca* was published, an Italian dictionary that included literary citations to support what it presented as correct usage. The Accademia della

Crusca, which had sponsored this work, had been founded in Florence in 1583 to advocate for the primacy of Tuscan among all the dialects of the Italian peninsula.* The principal citations in the dictionary were therefore selected from the works of Tuscan writers: Dante, Boccaccio, Petrarch, and Giovanni Villani, the author of a history of Florence. The dictionary also included many of the scholars' new tools: a table of the authors judged to be preeminent, with their cited works; a list of modern authors who were called upon when no citations from the more authoritative writers were available; an alphabetical list of abbreviations; indexes offering Latin and (briefer) Greek translations; and an index of Latin and Greek proverbs. And then, after all this erudition, a list of emendations and errata was printed at the end of the text. Thus, in this new work, scholarship was at one and the same time pronouncing with authority—*this* was the way educated people spoke, and *these* were the authors who were valued—and undermining that very authority—*here* was a list of things that were incorrect. This type of questioning would grow even stronger with the coming Enlightenment.

URBANIZATION, COMBINED WITH THE GROWTH in power and influence of the middle classes, as well as the arrival of print, increased demand for more widely accessible education. From the fourteenth century, early literacy had been taught with the aid of primers, which did little more than outline a set of daily prayers for the student to learn to recognize. In the fifteenth century, horn books were added as a teaching tool. These were wooden boards, generally shaped like small paddles, inscribed with the letters of the alphabet, the Lord's Prayer, and numbers from one to ten. Very often the paddles had a Maltese cross at the top, which in England led to an introductory invocation, "Christ's cross me speed," recited before each reading of the letters of the alphabet.

---

*It was the Accademia and its output that inspired Cardinal Richelieu to found the Académie française in 1635, with a view to producing a similar dictionary to formulate "exact rules" for the French language.

(This became a synonym for the alphabet itself—"How long agoo lerned ye Crist Cross me spede? Haue ye no more lernyd of youre a, b, c?" asked a poem of c. 1430.)*[39]

It must be stressed, however, that learning to read and learning to write were not inextricably tied together until relatively recently. For most of history, reading and writing were distinct acts. As late as the 1870s, Danish army recruits were carefully graded into six categories: those who could write a text of some substance, and read well; those who could write their names, and read both print and handwriting; those who could write their names, but read only print; those who could not write their names, but could read both print and handwriting; those who could not write their names, and could read only print; and those who could write their names, but could not read at all.[41] There appear to have been no recruits who could neither write their names nor read at all; all knew at the very least the letters of the alphabet, probably learned from one of these primers or hornbooks.

Once a child was able to read and write, the copying out of commonplaces, of extracts that conveyed wisdom, became a centerpiece of their learning, an educational practice that was expected to be the start of the habit of a lifetime. Earlier, we saw how florilegia had been a vital resource in the compilation of encyclopedias, their extracts and citations used to support entries that described the world, or a history of the universe; and how essential they had been to preachers, who treated them as sourcebooks for symbols, citations, and analogies. Now their readership expanded in a more secular direction, as theology merged with humanism in new florilegia, for example in the popular *Margarita poetica*, Pearl of Poetry, by the humanist Albrecht von Eyb (1420–1475). This was a compendium of teachings on rhetoric and extracts as in a

---

*Over the centuries the phrase was reduced first to "Christ's cross," then, in nineteenth-century dialect, to "criss-cross," to mean the alphabet, which was possibly reinforced by the convention whereby those who could not write signed documents with an "x," or crisscross.[40]

florilegium, together with *exempla*—in effect, templates for speeches and letters to suit a range of circumstances. Each section had a heading establishing its subject or theme—the topics, or *topoi*, recommended by Aristotle. Schoolchildren were taught to lay great importance on the selection of the appropriate *topoi*, which would enable them to marshal their arguments, structure their essays, or even just lend a speech or letter some apposite rhetorical flourishes. An influential series of essays on education by the humanist Rodolphus Agricola (1444–1485), *De formando studio*, On Forming (Habits of) Study, utilized the headings from *distinctiones*, but replaced their alphabetical ordering with thematic headings that could be set in opposition to each other. Careful selection from these pairs then helped budding scholars to build formal arguments structured with a thesis and an antithesis.[42] Other ordering systems could be more symbolically laden, including ordering the *topoi* by the virtues and vices as laid down by Aquinas in his *Summa theologica*, or by Aristotle's *Nichomachean Ethics*, or even using ten headings, one for each of the Ten Commandments.[43]

However it was done, the expectation was that all schoolchildren would as a matter of course create a commonplace book of their own. Jan Ludovicus Vives (1493–1540), a Spanish scholar who lived most of his life in the Netherlands (not surprisingly: his Jewish father and grandparents were murdered under the Inquisition), gave precise instructions on the creation of the ideal commonplace book:

> Make a book of blank leaves of a proper size. Divide it into certain topics. . . . In one, jot down the names of subjects of daily converse: the mind, body, our occupations, games, clothes, divisions of time, dwellings, foods; in another, idioms or *formulae dicendi* [forms of speech, or ways of speaking]; in another, *sententiae* [commonplaces]; in another, proverbs; in another, difficult passages from authors; in another, matters which seem worthy of note to thy teacher or thyself.[44]

The possibilities were endless, and so how these *topoi* were to be organized, and how the extracts so carefully copied out were later to be located, was a matter of equally endless discussion. In 1512, Erasmus recommended an organizing principle based on "the main types and subdivisions of the vices and virtues," which could be further divided into pairs of what he called "similars and opposites," although later he dismissed this approach: headings could be "arranged . . . in whatever order you prefer," he advised. In his own *Adagia*, Adages (1500), he deliberately chose a random arrangement, eschewing both thematic and alphabetical order, and appending a list of *topoi* in order of appearance as the book's sole search tool.

However, the *Adagia*'s phenomenal success—it went through more than 150 editions in the next two centuries—ensured a series of subsequent modifications that attempted to impose some form of order on his carefully disordered original text. As early as 1508, Erasmus himself had already included a list of his adages in alphabetical order by the first word of each adage, whether it was a keyword or "the" or "but"; by 1515, one printer had rendered that more user-friendly by creating an alphabetical index of *topoi*. A subject index was added by 1550, long after Erasmus's death. This was followed swiftly by an additional index of material that had been overlooked, and soon after by an index of the authors he had cited. Erasmus's random gathering of blossoms was now a regimented bouquet.

The increasing power of print ensured that individuals' commonplace collections, intended to be gathered over a lifetime's reading, conformed more and more to what was coming to be seen as a norm. Many readers did indeed build up their commonplace collections in notebooks they ordered and organized according to their own systems and interests. Many more, however, followed the systems prescribed in printed examples. And for those who wanted or needed even more assistance, printers soon began to produce books in which the pages were blank apart from a series of *topoi* printed at the top—the owner of such a book simply selected the page with a *topos* appropriate to the extract he wished to copy. For many, the convenience of preselected and preordered *topoi* won out over their need to give some subjects more, or less, space.

Commonplace books, whether handmade or purchased, were intended to be a storehouse from which the boy, and later the man, could draw throughout his life. Thus there was also a market for books ready-filled with extracts and commonplaces to fit a variety of situations. Erasmus was one of many to produce a subject-organized manual, *De conscribendis epistolis*, On Letter-Writing (1521), which provided templates of letters to fit a variety of circumstances. The ideal letter of condolence, he instructed, began with an expression of sympathy, before moving on to remind its recipient of the philosophical arguments for moderating grief, complete with *sententiae* selected from the classics, anecdotes from history, and the thoughts of the philosophers.[45] He covered a variety of subjects and eventualities in a similar manner, supplying ready-digested and categorized citations of the kind students were expected to gather over the years.

Other pre-printed commonplace books were narrower in focus, gathering citations from the writings of a single author. The works of the Roman playwright Terence (c. 195/85–c. 159 BCE), for example, had long been heavily mined for *sententiae* by schoolboys when, in the sixteenth century, Dutch and English booksellers produced volumes of his plays to which they appended collections of the playwright's best-known phrases and tags, for schoolchildren to copy into their commonplace books before regurgitating them in their own writing—an early form of intensive literary recycling.[46]

COMMONPLACE BOOKS COULD BE FILLED with far more than moral exhortations, or lofty instructional *exempla* from the classics and the Church Fathers. The *Officina*, Workshop, of Johannes Ravisius Textor (Jean Tixier, c. 1470–1524), rector of the Université de Paris, was an extraordinary compilation of extracts, superficially organized by affinity or opposition, but in reality almost random, beginning cheerfully enough with *exempla* of famous deaths, ordered by method: suicides, parricides, death by drowning (with a detour to consider bodies of water that had been named after those who had drowned); those killed by horses (with a subsection on those killed specifically by falling horses), or by snakes, by boars, by lions, by dogs, or other animals; those struck by lightning, killed by hanging, by crucifixion, by starvation, or by thirst; by falling off a cliff, or down stairs; or in earthquakes, or by poison or even by "sudden" death.*[47]

Although the *Officina* was not originally in alphabetical order, within a dozen years of its first publication a new edition appeared with an index, to assist the beleaguered reader who urgently needed to locate a death by snakebite rather than by falling down stairs, in order to insert the appropriate citation in a letter or speech.

By now, many books announced on their title pages that they were "digested into commonplaces," that is, they contained indexes with entries that matched those of many commonplace *topoi*. Printers further assisted their readers by using an italic typeface for those phrases that lent themselves to being extracted as *sententiae*, or added a pointing-finger symbol, known as a manicule (☞), in the margin to indicate a sentiment ripe for copying.** As we have seen, the commonplace habit was expected to be lifelong, and for many it was, but that same lifetime habit of extracting brought with it a raft of new problems, just as the plenitude of print had done. The philosopher Francis

---

*The scholar who translated this list does not fail to note the inadvertent humor in "sudden" death being given a separate category after all that has come before.

**This marginal system of notation survived, at least humorously, into the twentieth century. In Stella Gibbons's comic classic, *Cold Comfort Farm* (1932), the author helpfully assists readers in distinguishing "a sentence [that is] Literature" from one that "is sheer flapdoodle" by inserting stars in the margins next to her self-described "finer passages." She adds pragmatically: "It ought to help the reviewers, too."[48]

Bacon (1561–1626) commended the practice of extracting as "a matter of great use and essence in studying," even as he warned against those pre-printed headwords in commercial commonplace books that "follow an Alphabet, & fill the Index with many idle Heads," because they encouraged the commonplacer to "fill his paper-Book as full of idle marks." [49] A commonplace book, he said, was only as good as the *topoi* selected. And the *topoi*, and the extracts below them, were in turn useful only if the book's owner was able to locate the citation he wanted from among the great mass of others he had collected. Organizing, and locating, were becoming increasingly urgent problems.

 IS FOR GOVERNMENT

Bureaucracy and the Office, from the Sixteenth Century to the French Revolution

IN ORDER FOR SYSTEMS OF ORGANIZATION, WHETHER ALPHABETICAL OR otherwise, to become pervasive, they had to be needed; for them to be needed, the material that required organizing had to reach critical mass. A single page of entries on no matter what subject rarely demands an organizing principle. Even dozens of pages do not necessarily require organizing, or they may be organized more opportunistically—for example, chronologically. In the Middle Ages, administrative systems for many courts and states functioned without too much difficulty via tax registers, tenant rolls, charters, and other documents, few of which were maintained in any type of ordering system that enabled them to be easily searched.

The Papal Chancery, which possesses by far the most complete, and complex, archival collection in Europe, was organized almost entirely chronologically. From the fourteenth century, alphabetical indexes of some of the holdings in the papal camera, the Vatican's financial hub, were occasionally compiled, but it was not until the fifteenth century that this occurred with any regularity, and it was always instated retrospectively.[1] Alphabetical order, when it was used, was the independent inspiration of individuals rather than the bureaucratic norm. For example, John the Saracen, the chamberlain to Louis IX of France (1214–1270), drew up a single list of debtors in first-letter alphabetical order, but he was neither influenced by the ordering methods of Louis's administration, nor did he influence them.[2]

For the practice to gain a foothold, before all else alphabetical order required the ready availability of a relatively inexpensive writing material: ordering a mass of material via the alphabet can take several drafts to achieve. By the end of the fourteenth century, a quire (twenty-five sheets) of paper cost the same as a single parchment skin, and had eight times the writing surface. And by 1500, the price of paper was a quarter of what it had been a century earlier, and its use in the manufacture of what were referred to as "paper books"—what we call notebooks—made alphabetization accessible to individuals of relatively modest means as well as to wealthy institutions.[3] Some of the earliest paper books to have survived in the Low Countries contain abbreviations and symbols that indicate their owners were clerks in merchants' offices.[4]

While the ready availability of paper and its relatively low price were elements in the development of alphabetization, this is not to overlook another writing medium that lent itself to multiple drafts, one that has today largely been forgotten: the erasable surface. In the classical period, wax tablets, two wax-covered pieces of wood or ivory, joined with a hinge, were in regular use. The tablets' owner incised notes into the wax with a stylus, or metal stick, before folding them closed to preserve the wax surface, which could later be smoothed over and new notes inscribed. This temporary writing system was well known for centuries: one eleventh-century Benedictine abbot even wrote poems addressed to his wax tablet and stylus.[5]

By the sixteenth century, the writing table, an updated version of the wax tablets, had been devised. These tables were in fact bound books made using paper coated with size, a gelatinous material that, once dry, produced a matte surface that could be written on with a metalpoint stylus, ink, or even the newly developed pencil, before being wiped or rubbed clean and reused.* These writing tables were in use in the Low Countries by the 1520s, and their practicality, ease of manufacture, and consequent low price ensured that they quickly spread throughout Europe. Even so, a hundred years later they still appeared to be a novelty to the naval administrator and diarist Samuel Pepys (1633–1703), who described seeing "some sheets of paper varnished on one side, which lies very white and smooth . . . and I am apt to believe will be an invention that will take in the world." So impressed was he that he had some of the paper "made up [into] a little book," as a gift for his superior, the Commissioner of the Navy Sir William Coventry.[7]

---

*It is difficult for us today to remember that, for much of history, impromptu writing was an impossibility. To write in ink required a great deal of equipment, far more than today's pen and paper: paper and a pen, to be sure, but also a knife to sharpen the pen's nib; ink in an inkwell; sand or pounce (pumice) in a shaker to dry the ink; a cloth to wipe excess ink from the pen; wax or wafers to seal documents; a seal; and a candle or other type of fire to heat the wax. In 1663, Samuel Pepys heard news of "a Silver pen . . . to carry inke in," which was likely an early prototype of the fountain pen, but either he never got his hands on one or it was unsatisfactory, for two years later he reported that on a hackney-coach journey, suddenly "thinking of some business, I did [a]light . . . and by the help of a candle at a [market] Stall . . . I wrote a letter . . . and never knew so great an instance of the usefulness of carrying pen and ink and wax about one." It was not until the nineteenth century, with the arrival of mass-produced steel nibs and pens containing ink reservoirs that drew on vacuums or air pressure, that permanent writing could be an easy, impulsive act. Even temporary writing instruments—pencils—come late in history, when, in the sixteenth century, it was discovered that graphite made a fine writing medium (there is, despite its name, no lead in a lead pencil). Enveloped in a string casing, the pencil appeared first in England. Half a century later, in Italy, the string was replaced with a more practical wooden casing, and Gesner the bibliographer may have been the first person to leave a written description of what we know as a pencil.[6]

Both the old-style wax tablets and the new writing tables continued to be used for centuries: one scholar has suggested that in the early seventeenth century, Don Quixote's *librillo de memoria*, his "little memorandum book," in which he plans to write a letter that will later be transcribed "on paper," was a set of wax or ivory tablets, while as late as the 1840s, the poet Matthew Arnold (1822–1888) assumed that writing tablets would generally be understood to be a metaphor for something impermanent, such as the action of the passage of time: "Ere the parting hour go by, / Quick, thy tablets, Memory!"[8] Even into the twentieth century, little plaques made of ivory were used by women to record the names of their partners at a ball, or their shopping expenses as they went about town.

Sixteenth-century writing tables could also be plain blank books, used for anything temporary: extracts from one's reading, to be transferred at a more convenient date to a commonplace book; notes on lectures, or sermons; lists of vocabulary. More often, a number of the specially treated pages were interleaved into commercial works such as almanacs, or lists of weights and measures, distances between towns, dates of fairs, how to calculate servants' wages, or multiplication tables (multiplication was no easy feat using roman numerals).[9] When bound in leather, with extravagant decoration, writing tables were luxury items; in plain paper covers they were the tools of clerks, used for keeping accounts, for running tallies, for contemporaneous transactions and jottings—and they may well have been used to prearrange material into alphabetical order.

Merchants' and traders' account books had originally been kept in chronological order: business transactions that transpired the previous day appeared on the page before those of the current day, and the following day's transactions would be written on the next page. As trade increased, however, and as businesses became more complex, crossing borders and engaging with a multitude of partners and currencies, so the need arose for a system where assets were no longer recorded indiscriminately alongside liabilities, where suppliers were distinguished from customers and, importantly, where a single client, shipment, or purchase could be located with ease. The solution was double-entry bookkeeping, a method whereby each transaction is entered at least twice, as a credit or as a debit, in separate columns which must, at the end of the day, reconcile.

By the early fourteenth century some northern Italian merchants, many of them trading in the southern reaches of France, were independently feeling their way to this possibility. Ledgers dating from 1299/1300 and belonging to the Florentine merchant Amatino Manucci, based in Provence, display a clear knowledge of a double-entry system, while surviving account books of the agent to a Florentine banker living in Champagne, and those of a number of Tuscan merchants in Nîmes, show that they too had begun to maintain separate ledgers for their incomings and outgoings. By 1366, money changers in Bruges were known to order their accounts with assets and liabilities in separate columns on a single page, or on facing pages, a system called *alla venezia*, indicating that they considered this method to have originated in Italy.[10] By 1383, the merchant Francesco di Marco Datini (1335–1410), who had spent years in business in Avignon, returned to his native Prato in Tuscany, where he dealt in luxury goods, and began to keep his books in rudimentary double-entry style; by the end of the decade, his employees were all versed in this new system.[11]

As with so much to do with organization, it was printing that taught clerks and merchants across Europe how to keep accounts in this manner. In 1494, Luca Pacioli, tutor to the children of a Venetian merchant (and later mathematical teacher to, and collaborator with, Leonardo da Vinci), published a textbook on mathematics and geometry that included a chapter entitled *De computis et scripturis*, On Computation and Writing, describing double-entry bookkeeping as it was practiced at that period. Within a few years the chapter was published separately as an instructional pamphlet, translated into English, German, French, and Dutch. As late as the nineteenth century, Russian and American editions were still commercially viable.

Pacioli's system was laborious but straightforward: the merchant was to begin by inventorying his business, listing all of its assets, whether merchandise, cash currently on hand, or already expended; then he was to list all his debts. After that, each day's business was to be written out in triplicate: in a memorandum book (sometimes called a waste book), in a journal, and in a ledger. The memorandum book was to be used by the merchant and his clerks to jot down each transaction as it occurred, one after the other. The journal was also kept chronologically, although arranged more carefully, with the transactions separated into incoming and outgoing, debit and credit, as they were transferred from the memorandum book. The ledger also drew on the information in the memorandum book but was organized by client, supplier, manufacturer, or however best suited the specific business. Its main function was to take every transaction recorded so hastily in the memorandum book and more carefully in the journal, and establish it as either an asset or a liability. Pacioli called the ledger the *quaderno grande*, the large, or important, notebook, and instructed bookkeepers to "enter all the debtors and creditors according to the letter with which they begin, along with the sheet [page] number for each," suggesting that the clerks were expected to create an alphabetical index rather than ordering the entries themselves alphabetically.[12]

Double-entry bookkeeping is a system that takes an undifferentiated mass of small units—in this case business transactions—and systematizes and arranges them so that anyone, not merely the person who oversaw the transactions, but even a person who knows nothing of the business or its processes, can re-create what has occurred. In other words, it is a system of data management, just as alphabetization is. It is a system that divides, subdivides, and recombines, just as the handbooks of *distinctiones* divided, subdivided, and recombined theological writings in order to help preachers assemble their sermons.[13]

Pacioli was describing a system of bookkeeping that had been used by some of his countrymen for two centuries and was now becoming more widely known, even as alphabetization had, and for the same reason—substantial increases in data, in population, and in the number of people who needed to use the material but who possessed no comparable increase in specialist knowledge. In the thirteenth century an account book belonging to one Jehan d'Ays, who may have been a soldier, was kept in approximate and intermittent first-letter alphabetical order—one small exception out of the many thousands that have come down to us that have hewed more usually to geographical or chronological systems. By the 1440s, the papers of the family of two successive doges of Venice, Marco and Agostino Barbarigo, had been rendered accessible by first-letter alphabetical indexes, and in the same century the ledgers of the Medici in Florence were completely alphabetized: Giuliano de' Medici appeared under "G," *Avanzi e Disavanzi* (surpluses and deficits) under "a." (Although again, the system we use today, where words we deem irrelevant or minor are treated as though they are invisible, was not yet in place: *Una Mandata di panni*, a delivery of clothes, was entered under "u," for "Una.")[14] In the same year that Pacioli's work was published, the household of the Infante Juan, in Spain, was governed by four household books: the Diary, the Book of Everything, the Great Book, and the Book of Inventory. The Great Book used bookkeeping methods to reconcile the Diary and the Book of Everything, while the Book of Inventory was a master list in alphabetical order of all correspondence, incoming and outgoing.[15]

INTO THE SIXTEENTH CENTURY, throughout Europe, there was no guarantee as to organizational method in any area, no consistency from country to country, church to church, individual to individual—a single person might use a patchwork of systems, whether alphabetical, chronological, or hierarchical, or no order at all. For example, during the English Civil War, a government committee was charged with tallying the financial burdens the army had laid upon civilian communities, drawing on accounts submitted by those communities. One district in Warwickshire produced, over 134 pages, an alphabetical list of every soldier with the costs attributed to each.[16] Yet a similar pamphlet listing the costs in Hereford organized them geographically; and a decade later other assessments followed the time-honored system of ordering their entries hierarchically, with the most socially eminent or the richest inhabitants heading the list.[17]

This mélange was not unique to England. As late as the eighteenth century, lists of parishes in Moldavia itemizing the number of parishioners, church assets, and other key information for the centralized Catholic Church were neither alphabetical nor geographical, nor even hierarchical, appearing instead to be organized by a series of interlocking and on-the-ground decisions: frequently the largest parish was at the head of the list; sometimes the most politically important; some lists were organized by the routes the census takers had followed to gather the information; others along major transport arteries.[18] Yet at exactly the same period in Lower Austria, houses had for the first time been given numbers, to assist in the compilation of military conscription records. For some time afterward, however, the construction of new buildings failed to lead to a renumbering of the houses on any particular street. Instead, the new houses were given supplementary alphabetical tags: those, for example, between the old 9 and 10 being denominated 9a, 9b, 9c, as if alphabetical order were natural, and naturally understood.[19]

A similar range of systems can be seen in two royal archives. In Portugal under Manuel I (r. 1494–1521), the Crown authorized a compendium of archival documents and royal decrees: beginning in 1504, forty-seven volumes were organized under the geographical areas they dealt with, with the remaining nineteen focused on the person and prerogatives of the ruler. Just half a dozen years later, at Würzburg in what is now Franconia in Bavaria, the secretary to the prince–bishop was creating a series of finding tools for his ruler's archive, with alphabetical

registers and indexes carefully linked to boxes given identifying numbers, and all tied to a three-volume alphabetical guide outlining all the
business that was in the ruler's purview, with keys to where the relevant documents to carry out any particular business might be found.
Two royal archives, two entirely different organizational principles. (It
is worth noting, however, that both sets of registers were inaccessible
to virtually everyone: they were still, to a degree, princely treasure to be
guarded rather than working tools to be shared.)[20]

Thus the administrative world sat on the cusp, straddling the old
and the new. The advantages of the new were tipping the balance as the
avalanche of paper gathered pace. It is estimated that between 1565 and
1613, ambassadors to the Venetian republic may have dispatched some
quarter of a million pages of reports, and received a similar quantity in
return. In the mid-sixteenth century, two cabinets were sufficient to
store all of the previous century's dispatches; a hundred years later that
number had increased to fifteen. And with this increase, so came the
need for sorting.

Across the Italian city–states, different methods were explored:
organizing by incoming and outgoing correspondence, by the geographical regions covered, by whether the documents dealt with matters of
internal or external policy. Envelopes were not in use before the nineteenth century. Instead, a letter was written on one side of the page,
which was then folded and sealed with the blank side, known as the
cover, facing out, on which the address was written. Many government
archives took advantage of this mostly blank space by bundling together
letters and dispatches chronologically, or by subject, jotting a brief summary—sender, date of receipt, points outlined—on each cover. As the
quantity of documents grew, these summaries were sometimes transferred to ledgers, organized chronologically or by subject, by sender or
by type of business, and then indexed.[21]

The diaries of Samuel Pepys demonstrate how these many systems
coexisted in the seventeenth century. England at this date had no state

archive, and therefore no state archiving systems. Those, like Pepys, who worked on government business had no obligation to collect and store the documents that they produced or received; much less were they required, or even expected, to make those documents available to others. In his work as a senior naval clerk, Pepys relied on his own modified version of the commonplace method—and, in a way, of double-entry bookkeeping—jotting entries in a notebook as events transpired before, at the end of each day, transferring them to separate ledgers depending on their content: account books, naval contracts, or his own personal diary. (At the end of each month, his clerks copied any material not reordered elsewhere into a clean notebook, for the process to begin again: a luxury not enjoyed by many.) His "navy book," a collection of reports of Navy Board deliberations, lists of ships, and other ongoing details of his work, was evidently kept in some sort of nonalphabetical order, as several times over the years he wrote of creating an "alphabet"—either an index or an alphabetized table of contents—which was later bound into the completed ledger. He also kept an "abstract book" of précis of contracts and other documents, presumably finding it easier to refer to this than to his other nonalphabetized files.[22]

Altogether, Pepys was an industrious and enthusiastic organizer, an able civil servant, and an early adopter of filing, a system of organization that came in modern times to be almost inseparable from alphabetization. The word "file" comes from the Latin *filum*, meaning string. Documents dealing with a single subject were quite literally strung together, tied with a needle and twine, as can be seen in Jan Gossart's *Portrait of a Tax-collector* (c. 1530; see insert), which may be the first ever depiction of filing. Behind the sitter's right shoulder is a file, or string of documents, entitled *Alrehande Missiven*, miscellaneous letters, presumably ones he has received; behind his left, *Alrehande Minuten*, miscellaneous drafts, presumably copies of the letters he had sent. Both files appear to be otherwise blank, for they have been hung facing backward as well as upside down, for the sake of both confidentiality and convenience:

sitting in front of them, the tax collector can reach behind and flip them over to find the information he seeks. Above his head, behind the dagger (which indicates his status as a gentleman), hang three balls of string to create further files as necessary, as well as a loop of tape with which to bind packets of documents. A ledger rests on the table in front of him, from which he appears to be copying information onto one of two sets of folded sheets, which would be bound into another notebook when complete. The book lying at the very front of his table, on the extreme right of the painting, has been identified as a set of writing tables, those books containing washable pages interspersed with printed tables of weights and measures, almanacs, and other material; set on top are the metalpoint styluses used for writing on the treated pages.[23]

Pepys would have had almost identical office supplies: parchment and paper, ink and quill pens, seals, wafers, wax and candles, tape, needles and string. There were now always piles of paper to be filed: printing had produced not only books, but had ushered in the age of documents and forms. As early as the 1580s, Philip II of Spain—whose first biographer claimed he changed "the world by means of paper"— had ordered a series of forms to be disseminated to his regional governments, to be filled in and returned: today a tiresome request, in the sixteenth century an astonishing novelty. Nearly a century later, a portrait of one of Amsterdam's great merchant princes, Daniël Bernard (1626–1714), depicted him at work in his study, although he is wearing suspiciously sumptuous robes for this supposedly informal portrait (see insert). On his writing table, scattered next to a bundle of bound ledgers, are a series of filled-in printed forms, with the string threaded through the holes so that they can be filed: by now a routine part of the life of a merchant.

Across the globe two decades later, William Bradford, the son of the first governor of the Plymouth Colony in what was to become Massachusetts, recorded his gratitude for the bounty that the "great Art and Mystery of Printing" had brought with it to the new world: blank forms, including those, he specified, for land deeds, bonds, patents, and bills.[24] Yet without organizational systems all this "Art and Mystery" would have remained mostly mystery. And so, twenty years before Bradford, Pepys was already "setting [his] papers to rights" by commissioning "two things to file papers on" from a turner, an artisan who made objects out of wood or metal (turning them on a lathe).[25] What precisely these "things" were is not known. (Neither is it known whether Pepys expected to file his papers *on* or *in* them: the vowels in his private shorthand are not always distinguishable.) They might, of course, have simply been tables or other flat surfaces on which to sort his papers into piles, but as he specified that they were for filing, it is more likely that they were in some way specialized. A legal dictionary published a decade after Pepys wrote about this commission defined a file as "A Thred or Wier [wire], whereon Writs or other Exhibits in Courts and Offices are fastened, properly called *Filed*, for the more safe keeping them."[26] And so, Pepys's "things to file papers on" might have included some arrangement to facilitate threading them or for hanging them afterward.

We do know that he had been experimenting with different approaches to ordering. A few years previously he had spent time and "much pains in sorting and folding" his papers, writing a summary of the contents on the outer fold of each.[27] This method, in effect a forerunner of the modern cardboard file folder, had been widely used in Europe during the previous century. The office of Sir Francis Walsingham (1532–1590), secretary to Elizabeth I, had done something similar, summarizing on the blank covers the salient points in all incoming correspondence, together with the name of the sender and the date, as we saw in some Italian states. When a specific document was needed, the searcher simply flicked through each bundle, referring to the summaries for assistance.[28] And, as Pepys was to do later, Walsingham's office kept a "Table Book" (one survives, dating from around 1588), which consisted of three indexes: lists of books, with their locations; summaries of some of them; and indexes of papers, divided by type of document—"treatie," "diarie," register, memorial—and then subheads, either by territory or by government department; and ending with a shrug: "Books of Diverse Matters." These indexes indicated the locations of documents and sometimes included page references, which suggests that at least some of the bundles of letters and loose papers were later bound into volumes.[29]

Roughly contemporaneously, an English merchant in Antwerp wrote a pamphlet outlining what he considered to be the best method of keeping records and accounts, recommending that when a memorandum book was full, the clerk should "glewe on a peace of parchement and to writ apon the same what it doth containe."[30] It is doubtful that Pepys would ever have come across this pamphlet, nor that he knew of the 1592 manuscript by Walsingham's private secretary, Nicholas Faunt, whose "Discourse touching the Office of Principal Secretary of State" was never published but outlined what he thought were the best methods of organization for a diplomat's office. Within Pepys's lifetime too, in France, Jean-Baptiste Colbert de Torcy (1665–1746) was to take this further, establishing under Louis XIV the basis for a government run by paper, right down to introducing pieces of vellum, mounted on boards, to carry the abbreviated titles of every ledger in his department—what might be described as a map of the government archive.[31]

As with alphabetization, it is likely that each of these systems was invented and reinvented independently, rather than there being any one accepted method—or at most, not more than a handful—concerning how documents were to be kept or, even more importantly, how they were to be arranged so as to be easily located by those who came later, who had had no hand in the original sorting.

European scholars, in particular, had already developed their own systems of organizing. Many continued to favor the commonplace-book method, elaborating on it to enable them to keep track of their experiments or studies as well as their reading. But others broke away from the bound book. Gesner cut up his notes and filed the resulting individual slips under appropriate headings. He was quick to recognize that it was

the sorting itself that made his material valuable: while it was "important to have material at hand on all things and from all over," he wrote,
" . . . of what use is this material, if it is not ordered, and organized?"[32]
Like Gesner, the mathematician Georg Joachim Rheticus (1514–1574),
a pupil of Copernicus, also kept his notes for his books and lectures
on slips. When he was ready to write he shuffled them around until he
was satisfied they were in the correct order, then pinned each one in
place, producing his final text before "restor[ing] the slips of paper to
their place for reuse."[33] We know too that Abraham Ortelius, the author
of that heavily indexed first modern atlas, kept notebooks he organized
into alphabetical order under geographical headings, which he made
flexible by writing his notes on slips and gluing them into the notebooks
in a single column, while leaving a second column blank for additional
material to be added later.

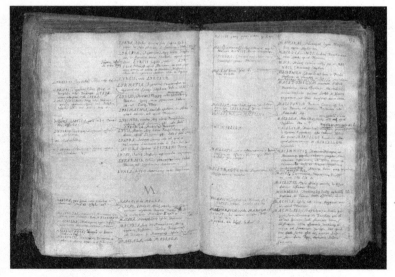

Abraham Ortelius, Thesaurus geographicus, *Geographical Treasure-house.*

Ulisse Aldrovandi (1522–1605), who oversaw one of the earliest botanical gardens in Europe and was the first professor of natural history at the University of Bologna, compiled natural history encyclopedias in multiple volumes, to that end creating a filing system in ledgers that he entitled *Pandechion epistemonicon*, Scientific Innovations. In his youth Aldrovandi had worked as a bookkeeper, and some of his practices were very obviously based on bookkeeping principles. One volume, entitled *Observationes*, was, like a merchant's waste book, kept for notes that he jotted down in the order he came across them in his reading or observations. When he was sure that an observation held or that the material was significant, he carefully copied it onto a paper slip and placed it in one of a number of linen bags. Such bags had long been used to store documents. The Venetian Chancery did so until the eighteenth century. The court treasury of the Holy Roman Emperor Ferdinand I (1503–1564) used leather sacks painted with red letters: "B" for Bohemia; "R" for matters pertaining to the empire, presumably for *Reich*; "K" for military, presumably for *Krieg*, war.[34] On a less grand scale, so too did many businesses as far north as the Low Countries, as can be seen in Gerrit Berckheyde's 1672 painting, *A Notary in His Office* (see insert). Bags hang on the wall above the notary's head, and he also used the method of threading documents together on a string, which can be seen behind the head of his assistant on the right. A trinity of organizing systems is completed by the pigeonholes above the files.

While Aldrovandi's bags were no innovation, the naturalist used them in a novel way by assigning a letter of the alphabet to each bag—not, as in Ferdinand's treasury, to represent a subject category, but as a purely alphabetical sorting tool. The sacks thus both stored his slips and at the same time sorted them into first-letter alphabetical order. From there, he could sort them once more before pasting them into his *Pandechion*, which ultimately reached over eighty volumes, organized in alphabetical order by keyword. As in the bookkeepers' ledgers, and as did Ortelius, Aldrovandi divided his pages into two columns, to leave space for later information. He also used only a light fixative when pasting in his slips; that way they could be moved, to maintain alphabetical order when new entries were added.[35]

It is likely that Aldrovandi came to these solutions himself, for they were not in more general use. Some half century later in England, Pepys's near-contemporary, the scientist Robert Boyle (1627–1691), left a chaos of papers behind him on his death. Boyle was one of the founders of modern chemistry and the formulator of Boyle's law, which relates the pressure and volume of a gas; he also worked on questions involving gravity, refractions, crystallography, sound waves, electricity, color, and more. Unlike many at this date, he did not keep his notes in bound ledgers or commonplace books, but on loose sheets—not for their organizational schema, like Gesner, but because he feared losing them: one lost ledger would represent possibly years of work, whereas one lost page was relatively easily replicated.

To keep track of his many and varied projects, therefore, he spent decades experimenting with different sorting systems. He used different-colored strings to tie up documents associated with different fields of research; when he ran out of colors he used letters and numerals; he even wrote little mnemonic verses to remember the order in which he had put various papers. He kept lists to remind him what was where. Some documents were "In a white pastboard cover with parti-coloured ribands," others "In a Marble-paper Cover," or a "Gray Past-board, black & green strings." Still others were stored in boxes, some of which were referred to by their colors, while others were lettered. His lettering system, however, was a simple matter of labeling: there was no connection between the letters and the contents of each box. For alphabetical order seems to have been one of the few systems Boyle left untried, while the elements of filing that to the modern mind are completely natural—are the files grouped by general categories? or for the type of work being undertaken? were they notes on Boyle's own publications, or on the work of others?—were likewise not matters he appears to have considered.[36]

Boyle's colleague at the Royal Society, Robert Hooke (1635–1700), who came up with the word "cell" to describe the cavities, or chambers, he saw in his pioneering microscope studies of biological forms, had a tighter grip on his research material, creating an interwoven series of books, slips, papers, and more to keep his work in order. He wrote out what he called "Schedules," summaries of scientific observations or experiments, which like Aldrovandi he then glued into a large bound ledger with "Moth Glew"—glue more commonly used to trap moth and butterfly specimens, which remained sticky and thus did not permanently affix items onto the page, permitting new material to be added later: what "was plac'd first may be plac'd middle-most, or last, or transpos'd to another Head." Where possible, Hooke also included diagrams and what he called "small schedules," conjectures or deductions rather than certitudes, for which he used "an Ink of some other Colour, as Red or Green . . . for this will much assist the Memory and Ratiocination." He also wrote ongoing "Queries" on small pieces of paper or in a separate notebook, checking them regularly against the ledger containing his schedules as new information was discovered.[37]

This complex method of cross-referencing and highlighting served the needs of a single mind with multiple projects and reading sources well. But governments, civic bodies, or institutions needed to establish systems that served the needs of many minds dealing with information and documents from multiple sources. These systems had to be comprehensible not just to those who created them, but also to those who used them without knowing either the creators or their intentions. The key concern was being able to lay hands on any particular document, as governments and the law were becoming increasingly reliant on paper records rather than on oral or sworn oaths.

One historian suggests that it was during the reign of the Holy Roman Emperor Maximilian I (1459–1519) that governing became an act of documentation, not of imperial presence or of spoken decrees. Over the following century, more and more governmental and legal rulings were set down in writing, and this became the expectation rather than the exception. Soon, only written rulings were considered to have legitimacy: the state had become a bureaucracy, its memory made out of paper.[38] The registers maintained by the court of Maximilian I were sometimes called *slossil* or *slötel*, derived from the German for "key," *Schlüssel*, and they were indeed keys—keys that by means of their indexes enabled government officials to unlock bureaucracy and lawmaking by identifying the location of any document as it was needed to carry out the business of state.

In an early stage, these indexes and registers were generally maintained in chronological order, but their users, armed only with a date, found it difficult—or impossible—to navigate the increasingly complex documents of state.[39] Subject headings therefore gradually replaced chronology as the main ordering system, especially after the number of government documents doubled once it became routine to keep copies of outgoing, as well as incoming, letters, as the canny tax collector in Jan Gossart's portrait had done. With the rising practice of documenting ongoing business—keeping records of done and gone transactions, as well as current paperwork containing information that might influence the actions of tomorrow—both how, and where, documents were stored had to change. No longer could they be stuffed away in chests, where every subsequent layer of papers had to be removed to reach those stored first, at the bottom.

The government archives of Lucerne, part of the Swiss Confederation, show how this transformation played out over two centuries. In the early fifteenth century, access to all the city's documents was controlled by a single clerk, who maintained a simple list of copies of important documents; these were kept accessible while the originals were carefully stored. By midcentury, more complex registers itemizing these documents were arranged chronologically, and then subdivided according to a variety of principles: by local, regional, or foreign government; by trade or profession, or whether the matter was rural or urban; or by a hierarchy based on the status of the sender. It would be another hundred years or so before such documents were indexed, and even then each index was specific to a single box of documents, so the searcher had first to know which box to go to, while the boxes were sometimes organized by subject, sometimes by correspondent. In the late sixteenth century, these boxes were assigned letters of the alphabet, and subcategorized by numbers, the beginning of a more comprehensive outline of the archives' contents. It was not until the end of the seventeenth century, however, that an overarching system was in place: the boxes were now reordered into categories—commerce, urban administration, religious matters, foreign affairs—and itemized in a single index, complete with cross-references. And then, finally, the material was alphabetized.

Thus over time the archive's organization had moved from an inventory, a list; to a catalog that pinpointed a document's physical location, a map, or other spatial plan; to a method of indexing and alphabetization that made the information abstract.[40]

It is perhaps not coincidental that furniture was simultaneously evolving to meet the new needs of paperwork, and of archives too. Desks and drawers emerged only in the late fifteenth and early sixteenth centuries, initially as luxury items for the highest echelons of society. Essentially, these early desks were boxes that held the multifarious accoutrements needed for writing, as well as providing a sloped surface on which to write. Isabella I of Castile (1451–1504) imported desks and writing cabinets from Germany, and both Henry VIII of England and Isabella's grandson the Holy Roman Emperor Charles V (1500–1558) also owned some fine examples.[41]

Chests were the primary repository for documents for the less exalted, or the merely prosperous, having been standard items of European

A writing desk belonging to either Henry VIII or Catherine of Aragon, c. 1525.

furniture for households across the social spectrum for a thousand years. And, as searchable archives came into being, they began to evolve. In the Low Countries in the late fourteenth and early fifteenth centuries, some chests were raised slightly off the ground on stubby legs, to make it easier to reach down to the bottom of the storage space. In the sixteenth century, the legs were lengthened, to bring the storage area up to eye level. As a consequence, side-hinged front panels replaced the earlier rear-hinged lids, effectively becoming doors. Shelves, until now affixed only to the walls of a room, were repurposed and incorporated into the newly raised chests' interiors, which allowed for the layered contents to be separated: no longer did everything have to be removed to reach an item at the bottom. The constraints of medieval joinery meant that these shelves were, of necessity, supported by thick posts and rails, limiting their use to larger chests, until technical innovations in the sixteenth century enabled joiners to create dozens of tiny compartments, drawers, and shelves in even the most delicate pieces.

The chest was thus utterly transformed, becoming an entirely new item of furniture: the cupboard.[42] Chests had been single-unit objects; the new cupboards permitted—even encouraged—classification, division, and separation. Papers could be sorted and folded, with a contents résumé written on the outside, as had been the case in both England and Italian city-states. Placed on a shelf in a cupboard, a number of these folded and summarized documents could be flipped through in minutes, even as many administrators now routinely sat at desks and put things away in drawers.

The world was growing more organized, more bureaucratized, more reliant on paper, not merely physically, but mentally too. And with that new systematization came new ways to map the paper world, new ways to locate individual elements as and when needed. Customs, and even laws, incorporated these changes, and then came to rely on them. Finally, they came to be the very basis of the law themselves.

As a consequence of the law courts' now almost routine expectation of documentary evidence, and of the legal profession's long reliance on precedent, on past rulings, and on court decisions, it had become increasingly useful, even necessary, for lawyers and judges to be able to cite previous cases and judgments as well as statutes. This, in turn, required better search tools. In England, some parliamentary statutes and law books had included second-letter alphabetical indexes as early as the thirteenth century.[43] Before the arrival of printing, these indexes were mostly produced for individual manuscripts and were not transferable. One copyist, or perhaps a subsequent owner, of a late thirteenth-century manuscript of Henry of Bracton's treatise *De legibus et consuetudinibus angliae*, On the Laws and Customs of England (written before c. 1235), made a painstaking attempt to overcome this limitation by drawing up a detailed table of contents that précised the entire work, and which was therefore applicable to any manuscript copy of that work, although the user would still have to read through the entire list.[44]

By the sixteenth century, the pragmatic nature of alphabetical ordering had led to its increasing use in the study of law. The standard teaching method of the time saw law students attending lectures and carrying
out their own program of reading in what today is called case law, the
body of past judgments. They were then expected to copy extracts from
both their reading and their lectures into commonplace books, alphabetically ordered by type of law, statute, judgment, or however each
student chose to manage his notes. In Germany, a preacher instructing
students on commonplacing methods recommended the use of folded
sheets of papers set between cardboard covers, but not permanently
glued or stitched in, so that more pages could always be added; and all
prefaced by an index of the books the extracts were drawn from inserted
at the front of the volume, also unbound, so that alphabetical order
could be maintained.[45] Most English law students, though, used bound
commonplace books, and therefore had to find other ways to control
their material.

In 1668 Matthew Hale, a barrister and later a judge, set out what
he designated the best way to study: "[L]et [the student] get him a large
Common-place Book [and] divide it into Alphabetical-Titles," which
he could copy from the indexes of other law texts. Under each of these
heads, "let him enter the Abstract or Substance [of what he reads] thereof."[46] This instruction figured in the preface to what was to become one
of the standard legal textbooks of the period, Henry Rolle's *Abridgment
des plusieurs cases et resolutions del Common Ley*, An Abridgement of
Many Cases and Judgments in Common Law.* This was laid out like a

---

*This title is in what is known as "law French," a relic of the French that had been
spoken in England after the Norman invasion of 1066. From the fourteenth century,
English had gradually replaced Norman French in the general population, leaving it
to become increasingly a language of the law only. Three hundred years later even the
courts had switched to English, and law French was restricted to case reports and legal
textbooks. Today many legal words in English owe their origins to law French: a jury is a

commonplace book, with headings of legal terms instead of *topoi*, and a series of references to statutes and case law instead of commonplace extracts. The copy of this work that is today in the British Library was very obviously used, by two successive students, in just such a manner. It was bound with blank folios interleaved between the printed pages, as well as five blank folios before the title page, on which the book's owners produced their own dense, double-column combined table of contents and index; in the text itself they made marginal comments, added cross-references and, on the blank pages, remarked on various points regarding their studies. (Some things, of course, never change: both students began well, but their notes diminish in frequency, stopping no more than halfway through the book.) For the even less industrious student, booksellers produced legal commonplace books, blank books with the various legal terms pre-printed in alphabetical order, or pamphlets listing alphabetically all possible legal headings, for the student to transfer to his own commonplace book.[47]

Reference works for those already practicing law were becoming recognized as a profitable genre for the book trade. In 1557 the printer William Rastell published a *Collection of All the Statutes*, set out in alphabetical order; in 1594 it was expanded with the addition of two new tables, one again ordering the statutes alphabetically, the other listing them chronologically, divided by reign. The first law dictionary in England was published in 1572: the *Expositiones terminorum legum Anglorum*, The Exposition of English Legal Terms—known colloquially in law French as the *Termes de la ley*—in second-letter alphabetical order. Fifty years later the Latin title had been dropped in favor of the law-French title only, and alphabetical order had been extended to the

---

group of people who have sworn, *juré*, an oath; a person on parole is someone who has given his word, or *parole*. Other phrases, such as attorney general, are in reversed order for standard English, but match that of old (and modern) French.

fourth letter. Furthermore, while the index of 1572 had merely repeated the title entries, in the seventeenth-century edition, it was now relocated to serve as a table of contents; absolute alphabetical order followed only a few years later.

The explosion of legal publishing was just one consequence of the bureaucratizing of government, both cause and effect of the increasing power of the middle classes in civic life. Much of the material published was devoted to trial judgments, from which precedents could be drawn in new cases. Once again, the successful publications were those that contained finding tools to navigate the mass of information. In 1588 the judgments of Sir James Dyer (1510–1582) were tabulated and published as a standalone index to the decisions of this judge, who was known for his use of precedents he had located in old manuscript sources, as well as for his prodigious memory. The table had been drawn up by another legal mind, that of Thomas Ashe (c. 1556–1618), who went on to edit the volumes known colloquially as *Coke's Reports*. Edward Coke (1552–1634), later Sir Edward, was progressively Solicitor General, Speaker of the House of Commons, Attorney General (as such, the prosecutor of both Walter Raleigh and Guy Fawkes), and ultimately Chief Justice of the Common Pleas. From his student days in the 1570s, Coke had compiled a register of trial judgments for his own use—the sort of legal commonplacing that was encouraged. Presented in chronological order, parts of it were published in 1600 and 1602. Four years later, Ashe produced a set of tables that indexed and cross-referenced these registers, thereby enabling them to be fully searched for the first time, making half a century of precedents readily accessible to legal practitioners and students alike. In 1614, Ashe's own *Table Generall del Common Ley Dengleter &c.*, General Table of the Common Law of England, alphabetized the cases by title, under which appeared references to the relevant statutes and cases, cross-referenced to other relevant legal texts, to produce what was perhaps the first general index to English law itself, as well as to its practical application.[48]

Naturally, there were many who disapproved of these innovations, complaining that learning from textbooks that chopped the law into alphabetized paragraphs was a sort of cheating. The barrister Abraham Fraunce (c. 1559–c. 1592/3), whose greater fame was as a poet under the patronage of Philip Sidney, trumpeted his discontent in an I-had-to-learn-the-hard-way-so-you-youngsters-should-too outburst:

> I could heartily wish the whole body of our law to be rather logically
> ordered, than by alphabetical breviaries torn and dismembered. If any
> man say it cannot be . . . then I do not so much envy his great wisdom,
> as pity his rustical education, who had rather eat acorns with hogs,
> than breed [bread] with men, and prefer the loathsome tossing of an
> A.B.C. abridgement, before the lightsome perusing of a methodical
> coherence of the whole common law.*[49]

This was not merely a generational quarrel, the old versus the young; it was, rather, the resistance of tradition to a new world order. Printing had brought with it unforeseen changes. As books spread, so did ideas—and ideas, whether secular or religious, are always problematic. As early as 1469, Pope Innocent VIII had decreed that all books must receive Church approval before they could be published, and from the 1520s European secular rulers also began to compile registers of forbidden books. Universities that held civic or religious authorization to print books were careful to produce their own lists of banned books: the first

---

*It is worth noting that this is not merely a reactionary opinion of the time, nor is it unsound even in modern legal practice. Justice Nicholas Kasirer, of Canada's Supreme Court, wrote in 2003 that to divide the law of obligations (which includes contracts and torts) into chunks so as to fit it into an alphabetical dictionary "results in a dulling of the law—substantively, technically, [and] epistemologically. . . . Outside the dictionary, they are tied together by the question of the relative degree of their binding character. Inside the dictionary, this shared *lien de droit* is not strong enough to bind them to the same page as they are considered separately, as linguistic phenomena."[50]

was issued by the Sorbonne in 1544, alphabetized by author, followed shortly by lists from universities, from Leuven in the Low Countries to Venice and Portugal. One of the earliest editions of the Vatican's *Index librorum prohibitorum*, Index of Prohibited Books, appeared in 1559 under the authority of Paul IV. It was divided into three sections: authors who were entirely forbidden; individual works that were forbidden, although other works by the same authors might be acceptable; and anonymous banned works. The lists were compiled in alphabetical order, by author for the first and second parts and by title for the third.*

Rulers knew that books could be revolutionary. And equally, that revolutions could affect books. It might seem a long way from the cabinets of curiosities prized by great men—those helter-skelter collections of objects encompassing art and history, architecture and archaeology, geology and botany—to the French Revolution, and certainly the path that takes us there is long and winding, but the two were connected by one tangible object: the catalog.

A cabinet of curiosities, also known as a *Wunderkammer*, wonder room, or *Kunstkammer*, art room, became a status symbol for the powerful in the sixteenth century. They, or their displays, were a crossroads, an intersection in the history of categorization and organization. One view is that these rooms stuffed full of objects—all visible, set out on shelves or hung from ceilings—were seen by their creators and owners as

---

*The *Index* was still being published in the twentieth century, heeded more or less, depending on the reach and power of the Church in each location. As early as the seventeenth century Oxford's Bodleian librarian claimed to find it "invaluable" for bringing to his attention books that were "particularly worthy of collecting." Yet the list, and who was included, and who ignored, was always patchy. While the works of Copernicus and Galileo were (mostly) removed from the list in the eighteenth century, writers such as Hobbes, Montaigne, and Voltaire continued to be banned until the *Index* was discontinued in 1966. Erasmus Darwin's 1794–1796 precursor to his grandson Charles Darwin's theory of evolution remained permanently prohibited, yet his grandson's work never made the list at all, even as Simone de Beauvoir's shocking assertion in *The Second Sex* (1949) that women are human too, and not merely failed men, ensured her inclusion to the *Index*'s final days.[51]

The Wunderkammer of Ole Worms (1588–1654), in Aarhus.

microcosms of the universe, a way of showing the plenitude of the natural world, as with the great encyclopedias of the Middle Ages. But unlike those encyclopedias, cabinets of curiosities were not organized so as to show God's purpose, moving in strict sequence from God, to angels, to saints, to men, to animals, and finally to plants and minerals. Instead, their layout tended to be aesthetically determined, or organized by the fragility or size of the objects, with the largest or most breakable hung overhead, and the smaller items on the open shelves.

Unsurprisingly, the catalogs that itemized the contents of these collections were almost never organized in the manner of medieval encyclopedias, nor in display order. They were instead products of modernity, with the objects organized by genre and type, manmade or natural: paintings, drawings, or sculpture; medals or coins; minerals or seashells or fossils. Within those groups, the objects were divided once more, by creator, author, method, material, chronology, or—remarkably frequently to our eyes—by price, the most valuable items

A piece of specialist furniture for categorizing and displaying a collection,
illustrated in Levinus Vincent, The Wonders of Nature *(1706).*

appearing first, just as rent rolls had listed the richest residents first. It was only gradually that the displays themselves followed this sorting method, as new furniture containing shelves and subdivided compartments became more popular. Soon specialist pieces were built for collectors, to hold very specific items in very specific niches, separated, itemized, and categorized, as the catalogs had been.[52]

This evolution in display mirrored developments in libraries of the period, which were undergoing similar changes as they gradually moved toward lists that both inventoried the contents of their shelves and also helped librarians and readers find their way around them. In 1560 Florian Trefler, a Benedictine monk from an abbey in southern Bavaria, wrote that every library needed five catalogs to function well: an author list, in alphabetical order; a subject list in the order the books were shelved; a subject index, order unstated; an alphabetical index to the subject index; and finally a list of books that had been withdrawn from circulation.[53] Only a few decades before, in Spain, Hernando Colón, the son of Christopher Columbus and the creator of one of the largest libraries in the world at that time, had cataloged his fifteen thousand volumes into a Book of Epitomes, or summaries and extracts, a Book of Materials, or subject index, and a Table of Authors and Sciences, which was made up of ten thousand slips containing Colón's own symbols, like Grosseteste's half a millennium before, but this time looking forward, to convey author, title, subject, and publication details—a proto–card catalog that would not see fruition for another two hundred years.[54]

Meanwhile in England, a chance to start almost from scratch precipitated one of the first and most influential printed library catalogs. Following the devastation caused by Henry VIII's Dissolution of the Monasteries, Oxford University's library lay more or less in ruins. Sir Thomas Bodley (1545–1613), who in his younger years had been a fellow of Merton College and Oxford's first lecturer in ancient Greek, became a Member of Parliament and a diplomat under Elizabeth I. In his retirement he turned again to his alma mater, envisioning a rejuvenated library, toward which he immediately and enthusiastically began to buy books. To assist him, he employed Thomas James (c. 1573–1629), later to become the newly named Bodleian's first librarian. Before they began to work on a catalog of Bodley's copious purchases, James traveled to other libraries to examine different sorting methods. By this date, a history of Cambridge University written by John Caius (1510–1573) had been published posthumously the year after his death. It had included a list of the university's book collection, which is often referred to as the first institutional library catalog, but it was perfunctory, incomplete, and closer to an inventory than a catalog. Bodley and James had higher aims.

Bodley was acquainted with Sir Robert Cotton (1571–1631), whom he approached in the hope that Cotton's extraordinary manuscript collection might find its way to Oxford.[55] While Bodley wanted the manuscripts, he probably would have disdained Cotton's by now old-fashioned cataloging system, based as it was on the layout of his bookcases, each of which was surmounted by the bust of a Roman emperor. Ultimately Cotton did give a few manuscripts to Bodley, but the bulk of his collection later formed the nucleus of the British Museum's library (now the British Library).*[56] There, those items that originated in Cotton's library continue to bear his system of cataloging as their modern shelfmark. The sole known manuscript of *Sir Gawain and the Green Knight*, for instance, carries the British Library shelfmark "Cotton Nero A.x," indicating it was originally owned by Cotton, who stored it in a bookcase surmounted by a bust of Nero, the tenth ("x") book on the shelf marked "A." Ralph de Diceto's manuscript (illustrated on page 55) at some point found its way into Cotton's collection, and today its British Library shelfmark is "Cotton Claudius E.iii": the third book on shelf "E" in the bookcase surmounted by a bust of the emperor Claudius. Cotton's method, still in use in the twenty-first century, searchable at the click of a mouse, is one that very likely has its origins as far back as Isidore of Seville's shelving method in the seventh century (see page 33).

In Germany, other private collectors were more up to date, at least in some respects. A 1572 catalog of the library of one Jeremias Martius, a doctor in Augsburg, is the first known printed European catalog. It was a simple one, the books divided into three subject categories, and then listed in no discernible order and with no index.[57] Apart from the sheer

---

*Cotton bequeathed his collection to his grandson; it was he who, to protect the manuscripts from his own "two illiterate grandsons," sold it to the nation, whence it found its way to the British Museum as one of its foundational collections on its formation in 1753.

fact of its publication, it is an old-fashioned production, even if a few centuries in advance of Cotton—it too was one that Bodley would not have admired. The first printed catalog of an institutional library was created for the University of Leiden, which in 1595, just before Bodley set to work, cataloged its books first by their size, then by subject; and with two indexes, one in alphabetical order by first name, the second chronological with subsections for individual donors.*[58] Five years later, the Augsburg City Library produced a printed catalog arranged in a standard hierarchical manner: Bibles first, followed by theology, and so on, although it intermittently broke into alphabetical order, as though hesitantly interested in dipping a toe into modern organizing systems. The catalog also contained an index that aimed at absolute alphabetical order by first name.[60]

Bodley concerned himself with all the details of Oxford University library's catalog as it progressed, and the issue of alphabetization was one that continued to vex him. He wrote to Thomas James in 1599, asking him to let him know whether Cambridge's library shelved its books "by the Alphabet, or according to the [university] Faculties" (theology, medicine, law and the arts, which was indeed Cambridge's choice). Two years later, he informed James that his organizing solutions were inadequate: the catalog, he wrote, should order the books first by format and only then put them into alphabetical order. Months later, he was still pressing the matter: now it was James's version of alphabetical order that was "defectiue," failing as it did to list every author in each of the many multi-author volumes. In any case, he continued, "I did always wishe, that in the setting down of an Autours title, yow would place

---

*Monastery libraries, as we have seen, had used donors as one possible cataloging category. If Bodley was aware of the Leiden catalog, the books listed by donor might have inspired him. In 1600 he placed a lavish "Register of Donations," with names carefully inscribed, on display in the Bodleian, a way of trumpeting gifts publicly and thus encouraging further donations.[59]

his surname first."[61] (His wish was not fulfilled: none of the first three seventeenth-century editions used this system.)

When the catalog finally went to press in 1605, it was ordered first by faculty, then alphabetically. The 1620 edition, by contrast, did away with the faculties and followed Bodley's plan for surnames, creating the first general library catalog to be organized entirely by author surnames in one single A–Z run, with no subdivisions. While Bodley's desire to see surnames precede forenames—"Bodley, Thomas," not "Thomas Bodley"—continued to be ignored, the catalog broke new ground by printing the surnames in a different type style, to make it easier to pick them out.* After 1674, copies of the Bodleian's catalog were dispatched to many European libraries, ensuring that the unfettered A–Z system with highlighted surnames became widely known.

At the time, however, this was at odds with the practices of most European catalogs, many of which had been influenced by the precepts of the French librarian Gabriel Naudé (1600–1653), one of the most important writers on library systems of his time. As librarian to Cardinal Mazarin, Naudé had acquired and cataloged profusely, and his *Advis pour dresser une bibliothèque*, Advice on Setting Up a Library (1627), was greatly respected. (It was translated into English by the diarist and writer John Evelyn [1620–1706], whose own plan for a "Method for a

---

*The convention of putting the surname first was not entirely unknown at the time. A copy of a play by James Shirley dated 1637 has his name handwritten on the title page as "Shirley, James." In 1697, a collector in Denmark, Frederik Rostgaard (1671–1745), devised his own library scheme, his catalog ending with an alphabetical index of subjects and authors in which he listed the surnames first: possibly the first time this had been systematically done. (It is notable that as a young man Rostgaard had studied in both Leiden and Oxford.) But Rostgaard was a private collector, and his work was not widely known. In 1788, an unnamed Carmelite monk in Bavaria also suggested that his monastery library's catalog might place first names under surnames. As with alphabetization itself, the reversed-surname-and-first-name style had to be reinvented several times before it became standard.[62]

Librarie According to the Intellectual Powers," that is, by faculty, followed Naudé in spirit.)[63]

Naudé stated, as Bodley had before him, that an alphabetical catalog was essential, although in Naudé's view its main function was to serve as a tool for the librarian, to prevent the purchase of duplicate copies. (Bodley had also nagged at James about this, grumbling that unsystematic alphabetization had caused him unintentionally to buy additional copies of books the library already owned.)[64] That was the sole reason for alphabetical order, Naudé thought; otherwise he recommended that library catalogs be organized according to university faculties: it was both the "most natural" and the most often used, and was therefore familiar to the most readers. Within the divisions by faculties he advocated an older, hierarchical system of ordering: in theology, Bibles were to come first, then "Ecclesiastical constitutions" (decrees, synods, councils), standing as they did in "the second place of authority" after the Bible; these were followed by the writings of the Church Fathers, and so on, in the usual order. Precedence was always, according to Naudé, to be given to authority, and to age: "[T]he most universal & antient, do alwayes march in front."[65]

Naudé's outline strongly influenced another important librarian. While Gottfried Wilhelm Leibniz (1646–1716) is better known to posterity as a philosopher and, simultaneously with Newton, the inventor of calculus, for much of his life he held posts as a librarian. He was first employed by a diplomat, for whose library he created an alphabetically ordered subject catalog, in which he dealt with the problem of works that fell into more than one category by heavy cross-referencing, although he backtracked and also used duplicate entries: some works were repeated as much as a dozen times. He then produced a bibliography that outlined the approximately 2,500 volumes he deemed essential for any good library, arranged in chronological order of publication. It was after 1691, when he took up a post at Wolfenbüttel, the home of the Dukes of Brunswick-Lüneburg, that Leibniz's library classification skills flourished.

The Wolfenbüttel library had long been organized according to the system recommended in Gesner's *Pandectae* (see pages 121–122), to which the duke's librarian was formally obliged to adhere.* There was, however, no bar to the new appointee creating additional finding tools, and so Leibniz hired two assistants to copy out the entire catalog so that it could be cut into slips, which would then be alphabetized and copied into bound ledgers. Leibniz always thought of this alphabetical stage as a preliminary one in his plan for a single overarching subject-ordered catalog, which was to be accompanied by a chronological index "to reveal the development of scholarship." But neither the subject catalog nor the chronological index ever materialized. Instead, this preliminary alphabetical, author-based catalog, in one single A–Z sequence without subject divisions, was his library legacy: the first fully alphabetical catalog in the German-speaking lands.[66]

From the earliest Middle Ages, librarians had been expected to be the institutional memory of their libraries, with catalogs as their aides-mémoires: an assumption that lasted well past the arrival of detailed catalogs. Humfrey Wanley, an assistant at the Bodleian and later keeper of the Harleian Library,** wrote in 1710 that a major task of "The Library-Keeper's business" was "fixing [the contents of the library] in his Memory . . . [A]s the Catalog is what is contained in a Library, So the Library-Keeper should be the Index to the Catalog."[67] But in Germany Leibniz and his catalogs had plainly demonstrated the difference

---

* Or rather, it was organized according to Gesner's system up to a point: the catalog used standard subject categories—theology, jurisprudence, philosophy, and so on—but suddenly, in midmanuscript, reverted to a style that had been extinct for centuries, turning itself into an inventory as it itemized the contents of one of the library's rooms—"Red Curtains made of chargette," globes, tables, chairs, and a bed—before returning to cataloging the library's books.

**As with Cotton's collection, the manuscript collection of Robert Harley (1661–1724) and his son Edward (1689–1741) was purchased by the British government to become a nucleus of the manuscript collection of the newly founded British Museum.

between the shelf list, a written replication of actual objects, and the catalog, whether alphabetical or subject-based, which placed concept over object. No longer tied to either collector or donor, or to the shelf by the size of the book, the catalog became, as the index had been for the printed book, a transferable object. In the following century, at the University of Göttingen between 1763 and 1812, the librarian Christian Gottlob Heyne in turn tied catalog and shelf list together by formalizing what has become the modern shelfmark, or call or accession number, which links the abstract concept in a catalog to the physical copy of a book.[68] This was reinforced by another librarian to the German nobility, Albrecht Christoph Kayser (1756–1811), employed by the Princes of Thurn und Taxis, whose *Über die Manipulation bey der Einrichtung einer Bibliothek und der Verfertigung der Bücherverzeichnisse*, On the Arrangement of a Library and the Production of Catalogs, broke from current practice in its conviction that what mattered was having a shelf list *and* a catalog; once in existence, the layout of the shelves themselves, previously considered to be paramount, became purely a matter of convenience.[69]

In earlier centuries, descriptions of idealized libraries had imagined the physical layout of a library to be a spatial re-creation of a commonplace book: one could, using the headings of either the commonplace book or a shelf list, locate the appropriate text for every imaginable instance.[70] Once the catalog became paramount, however, with efficient search tools, the books themselves no longer had to be tied either to location or to subject, or even to author. They could now be free-floating units, without hierarchical constraints. Just as the reading world had taken a conceptual leap forward when *deus* no longer meant only "God" but also the letters *d-e-u-s*, which could be rearranged and reordered at will, and just as double-entry bookkeeping had taken concrete transactions and rendered them into abstract units in the debit and credit columns, so too books had become units to be manipulated, building blocks of something greater than the sum of its parts.

Kayser's plan for a perfect library arrangement was published in 1790, and the date was not insignificant, for in the previous year the biggest revolution by far had begun. The French Revolution was a revolution in politics, of course, but it also precipitated a revolution in organization. The Middle Ages had found comfort in the concept of a hierarchical world, both religious—tracing a line of descent from, or a connection to, God, through the angels, to the saints, to mankind, and to the animal kingdom; and civil—from the king, God's anointed, to the nobility, then down via the clergy to the workers. More recently these hierarchies had been under stress from, among other things, the impact of humanism through the rediscovery of Aristotle and advances in scientific discovery, as well as the rising power of the middle classes and the consequent decline in the prestige of the nobility. Economically, religiously, and politically, traditional worldviews were being discarded. With the French Revolution, they were overturned.

Within five months of the Revolution's outbreak, the National Assembly had brought all clerical property, including monastery and convent libraries, under the ownership of the state; the libraries of many of the nobility were confiscated as their owners fled or fell to the guillotine. And, as is the way of revolutions, those in charge did something that was at one and the same time backward and innovative: they centralized. They put the state, the ruler, at the center of everything (an old idea), and then bureaucratized all of it (a new one). To do so, they broke with thousands of years of custom, moving from the bound manuscript and the printed ledger to the most basic unit, the precursor to so much of alphabetization in the future: the index card.

A fifteen-century depiction of Grammar, Rhetoric, and Logic (the *trivium*) pulling a cart bearing Theology (holding the head of Christ), surrounded by Mathematics, Geometry, Music, and Astronomy (the *quadrivium*). The figure at the rear, flogging them onward, may be a portrait of Peter Lombard (see p. 59)

The presentation of an index to the Gospel Commentary of William of Nottingham to Thomas Arundel, Archbishop of Canterbury. The indexer, the small kneeling figure on the left, holds up his work, while his master the Archbishop, the large seated figure, gestures towards the commentary that has been indexed.

Jan Gossart, *Portrait of a Tax-collector* (c. 1530)

A fifteenth-century manuscript from Bruges
showing a study complete with bookshelves

The eighteenth-century library at Admont Abbey

Bartholomeus van der Helst, *Portait of Daniël Bernard* (1669). Note the printed forms (front left), which have been "filed" on a string.

Detail from Gerrit Berckheyde, *A Notary in His Office* (1672), showing three filing systems: documents threaded with strings and hung on the wall; placed in pigeonholes; and sorted into sacks.

Detail from Chardin, *The House of Cards* (1736/7), showing the blank reverse of eighteenth-century playing cards.

A collector's cabinet with miniature apothecary pigeonholes, 1730.

A Wooton desk, produced after 1875; closed (left), and open (below).

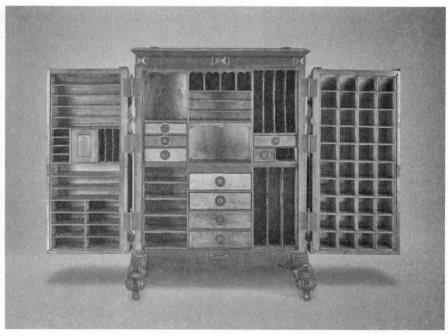

Gospels of Maél Brigte, or the Armagh Gospels, c. 1138,
the central text surrounded by commentaries, and with interlinear glosses.

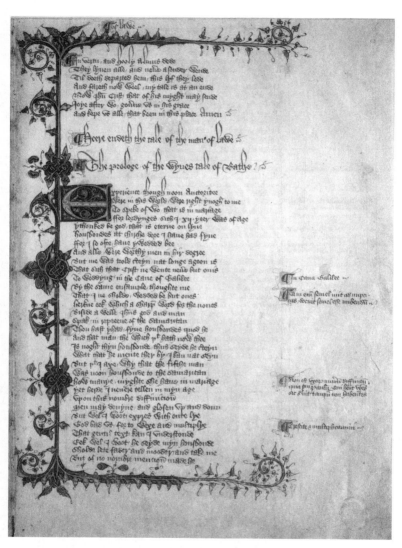

An early fifteenth-century manuscript of Chaucer's
Canterbury Tales, known as the Ellesmere Chaucer,
showing the opening of the Wife of Bath's tale.

CHAPTER 8

H IS FOR HISTORY

Libraries, Research, and Extracting in the Seventeenth and Eighteenth Centuries

---

In the mid-twentieth century, the medievalist C. S. Lewis summed up his view of the period he had studied for so long:

> [M]ediaeval man was not a dreamer. . . . He was an organizer, a codi-
> fier, a builder of systems. He wanted a "place for everything and every-
> thing in its place." Distinction, definition, and tabulation were his
> delight. . . . There was nothing mediaeval people liked better, or did
> better, than sorting out and tidying up. Of all our modern inventions, I
> suspect they would most have admired the card index.[1]

Lewis was, if anything, understating the matter. It may well be
that medieval minds would not merely have admired the card index,
but instead it is possible that they invented it. When Giovanni Balbi

compiled his *Catholicon* in the thirteenth century, his description of the process of alphabetization was so detailed that it may have been written not to help the reader new to alphabetical order, but to instruct those who wanted to create their own dictionaries in the same way.[2] Balbi's guidance suggests that he was using something like slips of paper, one headword per slip, which he could then shuffle around into alphabetical order.

If Balbi did use slips for his notes, he would have been more than two centuries ahead of his time. Yet it might nevertheless have been the case. By the thirteenth century, Genoa, Balbi's home, was a well-known center of paper production. It was also a city of merchants, and a city, therefore, of bookkeepers and bookkeeping. Furthermore, 250 miles along the coast of the Mediterranean, some notaries in Marseille had already adopted the use of inexpensive notebooks made of paper offcuts for their hasty scribbles, those rough drafts to be polished before being transferred to their registers. A system of alphabetization via slips of paper might therefore have already been in use, unnoted and unrecorded.[3]

We do, in fact, have two pieces of evidence that suggest slips might have been used this early, one from France, one from across the Channel. Thirty years after Balbi's *Catholicon*, in 1316–1317 a chronicler reported that "when some noteworthy thought occurred" to Bishop Robert Grosseteste (see page 75), he jotted it down in the margin of the manuscript he was reading, *"just as he also wrote many slips of parchment."*[4] Whether he actually did, or whether this chronicler was simply assuming that the bishop had in an earlier century used the slips that were now becoming current, cannot be known for certain. But virtually contemporaneous with this account was the work of Jean de Fayt (c. 1320–1395), a French Benedictine abbot who compiled an alphabetized commonplace book of Aristotle's writings on morals, which, from his descriptions of copying and ordering extracts, may also have been written on slips.[5]

After this, there is silence for the next quarter of a millennium. The first concrete information we have of *how* items were put into alphabetical order does not appear until 1548, when Conrad Gesner, in the second installment of his *Pandectae*, laid out "A method by which anyone may compile an index":

> Whatever one wishes to refer to in an index is written down, after first having been excerpted, in no particular order on a sheet of paper of good quality, on one side only . . . At last, all that has been written down is cut up with scissors, and then you divide the cut slips in the desired order, first into larger parts, then subdivide again and again, however many times this is needed. . . . [These] are separately laid out on different places on a table, or are arranged in small boxes on a table. . . . When all has been arranged in the desired order, it may either be copied immediately or, if the original entries have been written sufficiently well . . . they may be mounted with glue made from flour . . . [which allows] the mounted slips [to be removed] when wetted with water if an error has been made, or if you wish to consider another use in a new order.[6]

The idea that entries were units that could be moved and manipulated was one that librarians, too, were now welcoming, not just for books, which had always been open to being recategorized and reshelved, but for the great ledgers that commonly comprised the catalogs. This was transformative, opening up a world of new possibilities. In the 1720s, a Swede in Paris visited the library of the Pères de l'Oratoire, a theological teaching institution. There, to his amazement, he found a library that contained "no catalogs, but only *bundles of paper slips*" about the size of playing cards, as he recorded, fifty or sixty tied together in a packet, each "representing one letter of the alphabet." He considered the system to be impractical: "[A] light draught, when the string is broken, might easily scramble the neat order, so that one could say with some reason that this beautiful library *hangs by a thin thread*."[7]

Hanging by a thread or not, this modest library's ordering system was a harbinger of an entirely new way of looking at cataloging: the card catalog. And the card catalog was to bring with it an increased interest in alphabetical order. More than a century before, Hugo Blotius (1534–1608), a Dutch librarian, had begun working in a routine manner on a catalog for the Royal Court Library in Vienna, producing an array of slips that were filed in boxes in alphabetical order by subject, as a preparatory stage before they were to be transcribed into bound ledgers. Before that final stage was undertaken, however, political and economic events intervened, and without financial resources or political will, the library slumbered for nearly 150 years. It was not until the 1760s that fresh impetus saw Blotius's slips reemerge, to be rearranged from subject order to alphabetical by author.

In the following decades, a change of ruler brought increased funds to the library, and its holdings were greatly expanded with the acquisition of several major collections. In 1780 work began on a new catalog of this enlarged collection, now known as the Josephinian after the Habsburg ruler Joseph II (1741–1790). A slip was created for each book, and by 1781 over three hundred thousand slips were ready and waiting, boxed up in alphabetical order until such time as they could be copied into bound ledgers. By 1787 there were more than two hundred boxes, which, it was estimated, would fill sixty volumes when transcribed. Yet neither the money, nor the time, nor the staff, was ever quite available, and so the slips remained in their boxes in what had been planned as an interim stage. Instead, they served as a functioning card catalog in all but name and intent.[8]

In a similar fashion, further revolutionary change came about through the equally unrevolutionary world of royal societies, when the Abbé François Rozier (1734–1793), a botanist and friend of Jean-Jacques

Rousseau, was commissioned by the Académie des Sciences in Paris to produce an index of its publications. Rozier did not think he was doing anything revolutionary; in fact, had he been asked, it is likely he would have described his method as traditional, even old-fashioned, following as it did Gesner's description of how to create a bibliography. He organized his work, which he referred to in turn as an index, a dictionary, and a concordance—"the name doesn't matter," he wrote—in a patchwork of unwieldy systems that demanded substantial preliminary knowledge of anyone using it. He rejected pure alphabetical order in favor of keywords, although even then he indexed the members of the Académie chronologically by the date of their election to the society, with further subcategories based on their membership rank.* To find, say, Leibniz in this work, the searcher needed to know the year the philosopher had joined the Académie; that, as a foreigner, he had been given only associate membership; and that he was indexed under the French variant of his name, Godefroy-Guillaume Leibnitz.[9] Despite this, the material on which Rozier wrote out his old-fashioned catalog was one that looked forward—was, indeed, path-breaking: "Playing cards are best for creating these tables," he decreed.

Rozier's choice of medium for his unwieldy jottings was a stroke of organizational genius. Eighteenth-century playing cards were printed with the suits and values on one side, as ours are today, but the reverse was left blank (see insert). Nor did eighteenth-century cards have the shiny high finish of modern ones. Playing cards were also easily available, and inexpensive; they were designed for constant handling, and

---

*It is worth reminding ourselves that the word "catalog," which to modern ears implies sorting as part of its essence, did not necessarily mean the same in the eighteenth century. A decade after Rozier's work was published, the "Catalogue Aria" in Mozart and his librettist Da Ponte's opera *Don Giovanni* was a recapitulation of the Don's conquests: 640 Italian women, 231 German, 100 French, 91 Turkish, and 1,003 Spanish, a précis that follows neither alphabetical, nor geographical, nor numerical order.

were therefore more durable than paper; they did not stick together, as pieces of paper often do, so they were easier to flick through; and they were a standard size, making storage simpler.

As with the librarians of the Josephinian, Rozier's expectation was that these cards would serve as an interim measure to help him order his material before the finished indexes were bound and published, and in his case this is exactly what happened. But when, two decades later, the Bastille was stormed and the French Revolution overturned the ancien régime, information concerning a defunct royal society was of little moment to a new republic. Nonetheless, Rozier's choice of writing medium was adopted wholesale.* A year after the nationalization of the clerical libraries, the government planned a nationwide survey of its new possessions, hoping to amalgamate all holdings into a single central catalog of all books in all libraries throughout France.

Initially, questionnaires were sent to each of the eighty-three *départements*, or administrative regions, that had just been established. It did not go well: fifteen regions responded with fairly accurate information; several more claimed, implausibly, that their districts contained not a single book collection; most did not trouble to reply one way or the other. The central government persisted, however, and in 1791 each local government district received instructions on how to catalog its library holdings. Every library was to number its entire collection consecutively, from the first book on the top shelf in the first case on the left, to the last book on the bottom shelf in the final case on the right. Each book's number, followed by the author's name, underlined (or, if a work was anonymous, a title or keyword was to be underlined), its title, place, and date of publication, size, volume number, and the name of

---

*Rozier himself welcomed the Revolution, and ended up as its victim. A botanist and the compiler of a twelve-volume encyclopedia of agricultural methods, he petitioned the new National Assembly to found a national institute for agriculture in Lyon, but before this could be accomplished he was killed in an attack on the city by Republican forces.

the library, were all to be inscribed on a playing card, one per book. The cards were then to be ordered alphabetically by the underlined words, tied in batches, and sent to Paris. And once more, the expectation was that these cards would serve as the preliminary material for bound ledgers. Again, as with Rozier and with the Josephinian, reality caught up with this pretty fantasy. The country's libraries contained between ten and twelve million books, but just 1.2 million cards arrived in Paris; and of those, many were illegible, or incorrect, or incomplete. Or all three.*[10]

And so, in the way of governments through the ages, nothing much happened. The cards sat unused, unfiled, and unvalued. The plan was too grand and the resources finite. Governmental attention turned elsewhere, but the connection between cards and books had been established.

The card or slip turned information into physically manipulable chunks of knowledge. From the days of Gutenberg the metal letters, or type, used for printing had been stored in type cases, each letter kept separate from the next. These cases were organized not alphabetically, but by utility. Large sections held the letters most frequently used, the smallest ones the least—thereby turning the letters of the alphabet, for millennia understood as symbols of sounds, into physical, tangible objects. Now, in the sixteenth century, units of information similarly began to be understood as objects that could equally be housed in specialized furniture to aid their sorting.

Early in the sixteenth century, a Flemish writer on grammar and rhetoric, Joachim Sterck van Ringelberg (c. 1499–c. 1536), published a volume he entitled *Chaos*, because it contained miscellaneous thoughts, fragments for which he had no other place, and essays that touched

---

* And on the whole very little changes. In 2010, a study undertaken to assess the status of cataloging in research libraries in the UK estimated that across the seventy-seven libraries surveyed, thirteen million volumes were entirely uncataloged, or an average of more than 150,000 ghost books per library.[11]

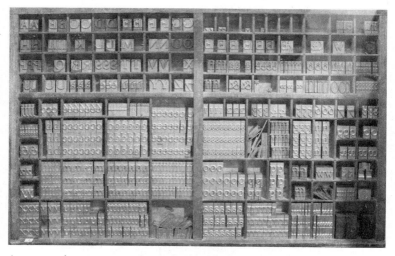

A type case housing a printer's metal type, the largest sections holding the most frequently used letters (e in French, English, German, and Spanish), the smallest the least common (z in English, k in French and Spanish, q in German). The accented letters (top and third rows, right), and the two lone k's in their tiny pigeonhole (third row from the bottom, right), suggest that this might be a French typesetter's case.

upon more than one topic. In one of those essays he described his system for mapping out a new work:

> First and foremost, I make a complete plan of the work, after which I write out the headings of the chapters on a very large board*. . . . I add or remove some as needed, modify others, or move them around. . . . I roughly expand each title, scribbling on scraps of paper, and pin these rough notes below the corresponding headings; then I write out the headings in large letters. In this way, I have the entire outline for the work in front of me, and can take it in at a glance. [13]

*Writing slates—small, handheld tablets of slate stone—were in use from at least the fourteenth century in Europe, possibly several centuries after they had appeared in Egypt. Sixteenth-century European classrooms contained larger boards, but if they were used elsewhere by individuals to organize material, I have not seen any earlier reports. [12]

One can today imagine authors using computer software to give them the same freedom to draw arrows and make connections—to sort out and represent their thoughts in physical form.

The most basic kinds of "sorting furniture," if we can call it that, arrived in the following century, at first as an addendum to the notebooks that had been the basis of information collecting for so long. An Italian doctor, Marcello Malpighi (1628–1694), known for his foundational work on microscopical anatomy, kept two notebooks, one for his own anatomical research, the other for extracts from his medical reading. By gluing tiny paper labels onto the side of the notebooks' right-hand pages, inscribed with the letters of the alphabet from A to T, he had invented the tabbed notebook.[14] And, as so often in this story of organization, his invention was re-invented elsewhere almost simultaneously. In England, Sir William Trumbull (1639–1716), a politician and diplomat as well as a lifelong commonplacer, in the 1700s began to record his extracts in volumes with hand-cut tabs to separate the pages alphabetically.[15]

This simultaneous development is unsurprising. The combination of the abundance and ready availability of reading materials, and the new spirit of scientific inquiry that would only gain impetus as the Enlightenment spread across Europe, meant readers and researchers were finding that the basic "paper book," such a thrilling innovation when it had first arrived, was no longer sufficient for their purposes.

As early as the mid-sixteenth century, Gesner had felt the need for more. He described the notebook that he would like to have: one that held glued slips or, even better, one made of thick paper and cardboard, with strings running down each page, behind which slips could be inserted, allowing the commonplacer to move them from page to page as desired.[16]

This was barely a notebook at all anymore; rather, it was a machine for sorting. Perhaps it was Gesner's ideas that made other constructions for sorting, constructions not of paper, but of wood, seem plausible, although what was next contemplated appears in retrospect to be

implausible in the extreme. That it became known of at all was owing
to the efforts of the gregarious Samuel Hartlib (c. 1600–1662), an intelli-
gencer, or person who produced what today would be called a newslet-
ter, copying out and translating learned correspondence and pamphlets
on a variety of subjects—the sciences, engineering, trade, travel—and
circulating the result to friends and admirers as well as to the general public.[7] In this way Hartlib spread the news of his discovery of a
"booke-Invention" by one Thomas Harrison. A copy of Harrison's plan,
with diagrams, was later reproduced in a work by Vincentius Placcius
(1642–1699), a professor of "morals and eloquence" in Hamburg, who
captioned it "The Ark of Studies: or, a repository, by means of which it is
proposed that all the things one has read, heard, or thought can be more
speedily arranged, and more readily used."

Harrison's Ark was, in effect, a wooden commonplace book, a piece
of furniture designed to improve on the paper commonplace notebook:
a sturdy unit for filing, storage, and retrieval. It aimed to hold all those
extracts normally copied into commonplace books, from all the important works, of all periods, but without any of the problems that were built
into the nature of those books: namely, that as material was added the
commonplace books had to be indexed and re-indexed to be searchable;
that the extracts were fixed on a single page, and could not be manipulated and merged with other extracts, on other pages or in other books;
and that if one wished a friend to read an extract, it had to be copied out,
or the entire precious, one-of-a-kind notebook had to be lent.

To achieve his vision, Harrison envisioned a cabinet fitted with
wooden rods, one for each letter of the alphabet. Each rod was to hold a
number of hooks, each in turn labeled with a brass plate inscribed with
a keyword or *topos*, as used in commonplace books. His plan called
for the cabinets to be manufactured with three thousand of these
pre-printed plates, and three hundred more plates left blank, to be
inscribed to suit their owners' particular interests. Once in possession
of an ark, the owner would carry a supply of narrow paper strips instead

of a notebook, on which he would copy any passages worthy of preservation, together with a keyword. Back home, he would simply open his cabinet and attach each strip to its relevant hook; to find an extract later, he looked for the label printed with the appropriate keyword; and if he was working on a larger project, all the strips on a specific subject could be gathered and ordered and reordered as necessary. In addition, Harrison's Ark enabled groups of scholars, such as those in Hartlib's circle, or university students, or members of a learned society, to work collectively on a single project, thereby producing a physical, as well as virtual, storehouse of knowledge.[18]

It is said that two prototypes of this cupboard were built, one of which, a "modified" version, was owned by Placcius, and the other ultimately acquired by Leibniz. Whether they were in fact built and, if they were, whether Leibniz ever owned one, is not entirely clear.* While he was known to have made notes on slips as he read—he referred to them as *Zetteln*, small slips of paper—some think he put them into alphabetical order and then copied them into ledgers, organized by subject.[20] However, Leibniz himself wrote that he routinely lost track of his notes, and rather than searching for them he found it more efficient to do the work again, which suggests that he used neither a ledger nor an ark.[21] Half a century later, we do know that the philosopher G. F. W. Hegel (1770–1831) kept his notes alphabetically by commonplace headings in a *Zettelkasten*, or slip box.[22] For Leibniz, all that has survived are some preliminary records that he owned but probably did not himself create: over three hundred pages of slips glued into bound volumes in preparation for a historical etymological dictionary of standard and dialect German. These appear to be closer in appearance and method to Gesner's card-and-string notebook than to Harrison's Ark.[23]

---

*Harrison recorded that he had used an ark for five years before writing about it, although his dates appear suspect: he was imprisoned for contempt of court from 1638 until his death in 1649, and he most likely began to write *The Ark of Studies* in 1640 or 1641.[19]

Harrison's Ark, as illustrated in Vincentius Placcius, The Art of Excerpting (1689). Left: a single rod with several hooks and their paper slips attached. Below: the cabinet itself, with its multiplicity of rods.

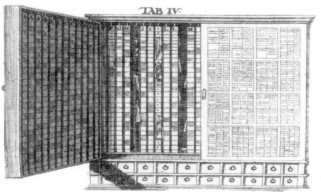

While the ark would have been a huge object, it was not unusual for a wealthy scholar or collector to commission a smaller piece of sorting furniture for his work, often to his own design. Martin Fogel (1631–1675), a German doctor and linguist, used "little holes" to store his papers in, while the poet Georg Philipp Harsdörffer (1607–1658) filed his notes alphabetically in "one box with twenty-four drawers, each of which bears a letter. When one wants to index, one . . . puts [the notes] in their letter drawer, later, one takes them out, sorts one letter after another, and either glues the little papyri together, or copies them again."[24] In other words, both men used some form of furniture containing pigeonholes. The jurist Johann Jakob Moser (1701–1785) described his own sorting furniture: "I have many small open boxes, a little over a foot long, [and] four fingers high," each divided by "cardboard strips a finger and a half wide and a little higher than the half sheets" on which he recorded his thoughts and extracts from his reading. Just as Malpighi and Trumbull had created their own tabbed notebooks, so too a century and more later Moser had invented his own handmade card-index tabs, items that were not to be seen again until 1896 (see pages 215–216).[25]

Whether or not Harrison's Ark was ever built, whether or not Leibniz owned a version of it, it remained at best a one-off, an oddity barely known even to specialists. If anything, it resembled the astounding "typographical desk" dreamed up by the French educator Louis Dumas (1676–1744), who promoted this novelty as a tool to teach children to read: a long, pigeonholed desk (see next page) into which the student sorted what today are called flash cards, printed with the letters of the alphabet, or words separated into grammatical elements—verbs, nouns, pronouns—in both French and Latin. The confection was very much designed for the children of the aristocracy.[26] Or perhaps, like Harrison's Ark, it was a work of the imagination, a sorting fantasia.

Far more influential in teaching children their letters was what has been called the first children's picture book, *Orbis sensualium pictus*, The Visible World in Pictures, by the Moravian educator Jan Comenius (1592–1670). It was originally published in 1658 in Latin and German, but its extraordinary success ultimately ensured that nearly 250 editions were printed across Europe over the next three centuries. Primers had been in use from the fourteenth century, but they were neither specifically for children, nor illustrated. While Comenius's book was not in fact

An illustration of the typographical desk from Louis Dumas, La biblioteque des enfans, ou les premiers elemens des lettres, The Children's Library, or, First Elements of Writing *(1733).*

the first illustrated book for children, its ubiquity established it and its method as *the* way to teach children, a melding together of alphabetical order and commonplace-book systems. Comenius divided the text by subject categories that might have been drawn directly from commonplacing—Temperance, Providence, and so on; even more influentially, he linked each phoneme—the sound that each letter of the alphabet represents—to the real world, using, for example, the noises that animals make. An early English translation begins, "The Crow cryeth á á, The Lamb blaiteth bé bé, the grasshopper chirpeth ci ci, the Whooppoo saith du du."[27] It was then only a small step to the teaching system that is now so familiar across the world: "A is for Apple" in English children's books, for *Apfel* in German ones, for *avventura* in Italian, and for *anaar*, or "pomegranate," in Hindi reading primers.

Later in the book Comenius included an illustration of a student at work, a book propped open before him, and captioned it: "The *Study* . . . is a place where a *Student* . . . sitteth alone, addicted to his

Studies, whilst he readeth *Books*, which . . . he layeth open upon a *Desk* and picketh all the best things out of them into his own *Manual*."[28] Each of the italicized words had a small number beside it, to match a number in the illustration, and was translated into Latin. As well as teaching vocabulary, this caption simply assumed, and in turn taught its readers to assume, that a student was by definition one who read books and copied extracts—"all the best things"—from them into a commonplace book, or "manual."

This may appear no different from the practice recommended for centuries—as we have seen, commonplace books had been in regular use by students from classical times. There was now, however, an important change. In the Middle Ages, memory had been considered as an art on a par with learning, and the *topoi* of a commonplace book had served, at least in part, as a memory prompt, a way of bringing a relevant passage to mind by its *topos*—literally, its place—in the reader's memory. Richard Holdsworth (1590–1649), Master of Emmanuel College, Cambridge, followed in this tradition in his manual for new students, recommending that they copy out extracts from their reading, or the salient points from their lectures, into a "paper book" so that by "frequent[ly] reading [these passages] over on evenings . . . they will offer themselves to your memory."[29] Yet even as he promoted this old-fashioned method of learning, he was aware that there had been a shift from memory to print, from rote learning to search tools. In addition to expecting the students to transcribe their notes into commonplace books under appropriate *topoi*, he recommended that a second book be kept to serve as an index to the first.[30] This approach prefigured the method of John Locke (1632–1704), the philosopher of the Enlightenment, and of education, who was to conceive and popularize what would become the principal method of sorting commonplace books, a method whose influence would be felt as a new wave of organizers made their appearance.

In 1523, the humanist scholar Jan Ludovicus Vives, who had published his own instructions for keeping a commonplace book, had referred to *topoi* as *loci ac velut nidi*, places, and, as it were, nests. "Places" was traditional, but the "nests" now became pigeonholes, which was new.[31] Vives's work may well have been known to Locke, who by the 1680s was turning his mind to how readers should best organize their notes, and he initially expressed his admiration for physical sorting cabinets, seeing they could serve a multitude of purposes. For example, he thought that they might be a way of teaching a child to read: using a cabinet with twenty-four holes, he suggested, pasting "over the first . . . an A, over the second, a B," and so on.[32] But he soon moved away from concrete sorting objects—of necessity, as such specially designed furniture would be confined to the prosperous, who could afford it and had the luxury of space. Instead, Locke took the physical pigeonholes of Harrison and others and transformed them into metaphorical ones. In so doing, he foreshadowed the new lease on life that encyclopedias were to enjoy as they gradually became information-sorters par excellence.

Locke was himself a voluminous commonplacer, having started to keep commonplace books as a student in 1652 and continuing the practice until his death half a century later.[33] At any one time, he maintained a number of notebooks: six were topical, covering subjects such as natural philosophy, medicine, and "moral knowledge"; others were mixed, reflecting the broad range of his interests.[34] But a mere eight years after he began commonplacing, he already had concerns that the quantity of material he was gathering was so vast that he would not be able to locate specific extracts. He therefore began to create indexes, managing to control the notebooks' contents and the decades of reading they represented by means of a system of his own devising. Locke's method was put before the public in a French pamphlet in 1687, and translated into English in 1706 as "A New Method of Making Common-Place Books." The essence of the system was a simple table that he drew in the front of each of his notebooks, listing the letters of the alphabet vertically, then subdividing each letter by the five vowels.

When Locke read a passage he wanted to copy, he selected a subject heading—"On beauty," say. If he had no previous extracts in his notebooks with that heading, he began a fresh page, writing "On beauty" at the head, and under that, copying the extract. Then he turned to the index table he had created at the front of each notebook, and in the space for "B," subdivision "e"—the first letter and first vowel of "beauty"—he noted down the page number the extract appeared on. That page subsequently became the "B/e" page, where he copied any future entries for *topoi* beginning with "B" where the first vowel was "e," whether "beauty," or extracts concerning the cities of Berne or Bremen.[35] When he came across a new extract that he wanted to place under the heading "Beauty" or any other "B/e" word, he referred to his table, which confirmed that he had a "B/e" page, and its page reference. Once that page was full, he continued all further "B/e" entries on the next blank page, adding that page number to his table.[36] It was a reversion to an older time, when readers made their own indexes, for Locke's system was nothing less than a basic second-letter alphabetical index.

A page illustrating Locke's indexing system for commonplace books. Each consonant is followed by a vowel (curiously, themselves not alphabetically ordered): A/i, A/o, A/u, A/a, A/e, and so on. When Locke made an entry in a notebook under, say, the topic "Abstinence," he would note the relevant page number beside "A/i" in the book's index, "A" being the first letter of the word, "i" the first vowel.

Yet it became hugely influential, an indication of the number of commonplace books that continued to be compiled: not only did other writers use it, but printers used it as a promotional tool. Three-quarters of a century after the pamphlet's publication in England, a luxury edition of *A Common Place Book Form'd generally upon the Principles Recommended and Practised by Mr. Locke* found a ready market; elsewhere, a shorthand manual had, prefaced to it, "A specimen of Mr. Locke's index to a common-place book"; and well into the nineteenth century publications still advertised themselves as being based on Locke's system.[37]

Locke's alphabetical method spread widely, but perhaps for that very reason it proved a cause for concern. Many of the learned who otherwise admired Locke balked at the notion of one entry following another without any structure or order other than the happenstance of the sequence of the alphabet, all tenuously linked by nothing more than a hand-drawn table. The poet and hymn writer Isaac Watts (1674–1748) provides a good example of this ambivalence. He presented a method he described as Locke's, but in reality he had returned to an older style, giving each headword its own page: he was using the popularity of Locke's idea even as he removed its rationale, attempting to make it, as he saw it, less random, more premeditated.[38]

But if a commonplace book is premeditated, if the entries are shaped and organized systematically, the content preselected to fit a pattern, then what results is no longer a commonplace book. It is, in truth, an encyclopedia.

NEAR THE BEGINNING OF THE CENTURY that ended with Locke's commonplacing method, Christopher Marlowe's play *Dr. Faustus* (1592) told the story of a man who sold his soul to the devil in exchange for universal knowledge, contained in a single magic book that included everything that it was possible to know about Aristotle, analytics, disputation, logic, economy, Galen (medicine), Justinian (the law), the works of Jerome (theology), metaphysics, necromancy, and the "heavenly" books of prognostication.[39] (It might even be possible to say that Marlowe, and Faustus, listed many of these in first-letter alphabetical order, although there are a number that do not fit the pattern.) Faustus's magic book, his compendium of all knowledge, was to all intents and purposes an encyclopedia.

The idea of being able to capture all the learning of the world in a book was timely. In 1620, the philosopher Francis Bacon planned out his *Instauratio magna*, The Great Instauration (meaning restoration, or renewal), in high medieval style, to be spread over six parts to echo the six days of creation. The second part, *De augmentis scientiarum*, On the Arrangement (or Survey) of Knowledge, attempted to organize and classify knowledge as previous encyclopedists had classified minerals or plants. It too was to have six parts, three to cover divine learning, encompassing sacred history, parables, and doctrines, and three for human learning: memory and history; imagination and poesy; and reason, philosophy, and science, or as we might call them, history, arts and poetry (or literature more broadly), and philosophy and science.[40] Bacon never finished this work, but its influence on later encyclopedists was profound, the scaffolding for many later ambitious edifices.*

A few years later in Central Europe, Johann Heinrich Alsted's *Encyclopaedia septem tomis distincta*, An Encyclopedia in Seven Volumes (1630), was the first to use the word "encyclopaedia" in its title in the sense we use it, to mean a reference book that attempts to encompass, and organize, the totality of the world's knowledge. Alsted's book looked backward, in that it was structured hierarchically, to mirror the structure

---

*This scaffolding, barely recognized, continues to support edifices we use today, some four hundred years later. "Lord Bacon's table of science" underpinned Thomas Jefferson's own private library catalog. After the United States' embryonic Library of Congress was destroyed in the War of 1812, the government purchased Jefferson's library to serve as its replacement, and with it his catalog and organizing system. Melvil Dewey later adapted the Library of Congress's system when planning his own Dewey decimal system of library cataloging. Thus Bacon's outline survives in both of those systems, still used in so many libraries.[41]

of the world; but it also looked forward, with some subjects divided into distinct essays, located via an index.[42]

But until the alphabet became the encyclopedia's principal organizing system, these works could not be seen as truly modern. Not because one system of organizing is better than any other, but because the use of alphabetical order, once more, marks a transition in worldview. Just as the spread of alphabetically organized dictionaries and indexes had indicated a shift from seeing words purely as meaning to seeing them as a series of letters, so too the arrival of alphabetically ordered encyclopedias indicated a shift from seeing the world as a hierarchical, ordered place, explicable and comprehensible if only a person knew enough, to seeing it as a random series of events and people and places.[43]

An early step on this path was Louis Moréri's *Grand dictionaire historique*, an encyclopedia covering history, biography, and the sciences that began to appear in 1674. One of the earliest to be organized alphabetically, the *Grand dictionaire* ultimately spread over ten volumes and went through more than twenty editions, being translated into English, German, Dutch, and Spanish. In his preface, Moréri humbly set out his stall: some of his writings on history had been well received, he wrote, and therefore his friends "imagined that it would not be too troublesome for me to put these into alphabetical order, and so produce the book which you see here." His subtitle, *Le mélange curieux de l'histoire sacrée et profane*, The Intriguing Medley of Sacred and Secular History, stresses the novelty of such a work being organized in neither hierarchical nor chronological order: it is instead a *mélange*—a medley, or mixture. And yet his "friends" appear to have automatically assumed the work would be alphabetical. There were few contemporary comments on the arrangement of the work, perhaps because of Moréri's claim that it was merely a reorganization of earlier material. But later it was suggested that its origins were to be found in the commonplace books he had compiled throughout his life.[44] And as commonplace books were by then routinely alphabetized, so it might have seemed natural to alphabetize an encyclopedia deriving from that genre.

However it came about, the assumption that encyclopedias were alphabetized was reinforced with the work of Pierre Bayle (1647–1706), who from 1689 kept a list of errors he had found in Moréri's work, and which from 1695 he published as an alphabetical *Dictionaire critique*. Bayle's biographer later recounted how he had relied on his own commonplace books for these corrections and emendations, containing as they did "everything historically curious or remarkable that Mr. Bayle has read . . . organized alphabetically. For example, under 'A' he deals with Antiquity. . . . Under 'B' he describes memorable Battles."[45]

Bayle's book, modest in its original plan of correcting Moréri, expanded wildly, establishing itself as an encyclopedia in its own right, with articles on more than two thousand subjects. As it did so, the *Dictionaire critique* became a force in establishing many of the norms modern readers have come to expect in reference works, in great part owing to the fact that Bayle began his publication as a corrective to a previous work. Thus his text had to find a way visually to distinguish Bayle's own thoughts, additions, and amendments from his citations of Moréri. This ultimately produced an elaborate typographic structure: citations and references were given discrete space on the page; notes were set in a different typeface from the main text; Moréri's original text was reproduced in a single column, while Bayle's *remarques*, his comments on Moréri, were in two; the notes were also numbered, a relative novelty.*

---

*Using different type sizes to distinguish different elements of the text was not in itself a novelty, having been common in manuscripts before printing. The *Omne bonum*, All That Is Good, was a second-letter alphabetically ordered encyclopedia compiled by an exchequer scribe in England c. 1360–1375. He used, among other devices, larger script for citations from the Gospels and smaller script for commentary. It was also standard for marginalia and glosses in manuscripts to be written in a smaller script, or with the lines of writing set more closely together.[46]

A sample page from Bayle's Dictionaire critique, showing how typographical layout was used to distinguish the different levels of text.

Bayle was also forced to wrestle with new problems, which compilers of the earlier hierarchical encyclopedias had never had to consider. Ensuring that entries in the first part of the text did not occupy more than their fair share of space was always going to be a challenge in alphabetically ordered endeavors. In Bayle's first edition, entries for the letter A sprawled across more than 20 percent of the finished work, and would have taken up even more had he not altered the headwords of several A articles. For example, Alexander the Great was transferred from A for Alexander to M for Macedonia, while all entries beginning Æ were relocated to E. In his second edition, Bayle continued to smooth out the proportions, renaming and redistributing entries, although even then A still took up a good 10 percent of the finished work.[47]

Following the success of these two encyclopedias, similar works appeared in other European countries. In Italy, the theologian and globe maker Vincenzo Maria Coronelli (1650–1718) began to publish his

Bibliotheca universale sacro-profano, antico-moderna, Universal Library: Sacred and Secular, Ancient and Modern, in 1701. Coronelli took an additional step toward the modern encyclopedia by putting himself in the role of editor, rather than author: although he planned the book's structure, he did not expect to write all the entries himself, pioneering the concept of the expert contributor.

While the contributor model virtually precludes a hierarchical structure, or at least intensifies its difficulties, Coronelli nonetheless presented alphabetical order as a positive choice, the best way of displaying the manifold discoveries of the modern world. Alphabetical order was in his view a reflection of this modernity. Despite his position as Father General of the Franciscan order, in this work the religious no longer automatically took precedence over the secular, kings over subjects, or man over animals: the alphabet was to Coronelli a democratizer (although the word was not one he used).[48] And, like Bayle, he was forced to wrestle with the new problems that arrived with alphabetization—in his case, the use of foreign languages, both ancient and modern: it is difficult to imagine that even the scholars of his day would have thought to search for an entry on "earrings" under the headword *Aantha*, his transliteration of the Greek.[49]

Alphabetical encyclopedias were gaining ground in England too, particularly after the very successful publication in 1704 of John Harris's *Lexicon Technicum, or, An Universal Dictionary of the Arts and Sciences*. Harris (c. 1666–1719) was a clergyman and lecturer on science and mathematics, and this volume was the first in the genre to concentrate on science and technology rather than religion, philosophy, or history. In turn, it heavily influenced a young mapmaker's apprentice named Ephraim Chambers (c. 1680–1740).

Chambers was ambitious, and he saw that by using Harris's methods but concentrating on subjects more appealing to general readers he could produce a book that aimed at a commercial as well as a critical success. Ultimately, Chambers's *Cyclopaedia, or, An Universal*

Dictionary of the Arts and Sciences was indeed the success he was looking for, earning him both sales and praise for an encyclopedia that was a resource to educate the neophyte as well as for the learned to refresh their memories "without the labour and the loss of time, which it would require to recur to a great number of distinct treatises, whence their knowledge was originally derived."[50]

Chambers's early plans for his "cyclopaedia" already demonstrated his double ambition and how to achieve it, including drawing on commonplace books for alphabetical ordering, and extensive cross-referencing both to direct readers to other entries, and for ideas or subjects that did not merit their own entries but were mentioned within longer ones. While Chambers seemed to have had few doubts that alphabetical order was the correct way to structure his book, at the same time he clearly retained a yearning for the certainties of a hierarchical system that described a balanced and ordered universe, as he included a diagram reminiscent of a Baconian tree of knowledge, as well as drawing on the commonplace tradition by turning *topoi* into his headwords.* "The Character of this Work," he wrote, aiming to have his cake and eat it too, "is to be a DICTIONARY, and a SYSTEM at the same time. It consists of an infinite Number of Articles, which may either be consider'd separately, as so many distinct *Parts* of Knowledge; or collectively, as constituting a *Body* [of knowledge] thereof."

Yet alongside this implicit desire for Baconian order, Chambers accepted that there was no longer a place for the inflexibility of the hierarchical model of Bacon and his predecessors, whose elaboration of a "Natural Order" he dubbed "unwieldy." This he replaced with separate alphabetized entries that could be "taken asunder, and . . . re-compos'd in a different Order." He was acknowledging the modern worldview— that the universe was not a perfect organic structure, and that man

---

*Chambers also included an entry for commonplace books themselves, as well as a full description of Locke's commonplacing method, praising him as "the great Master of Order."

cannot grasp all knowledge; in many cases, and on certain subjects, discrete chunks of knowledge might be all we may ever possess.

Even so, when his first edition was published, he felt it necessary to pay homage to hierarchy: while he was sure alphabetical order was the correct decision, some things were lost by its use, most importantly the sense of the interconnectedness of things, "From Generals to Particulars; from Premises to Conclusions; from Cause to Effect . . . i.e. in one word, from more to less complex, and from less to more."[51] This he resolved for the most part by extensive cross-referencing. In following the cross-references, those who wished could build complete pictures of any subject, while the already learned could use alphabetical order to carve out paths of their own.

Not everyone was persuaded. Following Chambers's great success, two even more famous encyclopedists also acknowledged the fear of the atomization of knowledge that alphabetization might herald: the French Enlightenment philosopher Denis Diderot (1713–1784) and the mathematician and physicist Jean le Rond d'Alembert (1717–1783). Their work was formally entitled *L'Encyclopédie, ou dictionnaire raisonné des sciences, des arts et des métiers*, The Encyclopedia, or, A Systematic Dictionary of the Sciences, Arts and Trades (published 1751–1772), but its great renown has ever after led to it being known simply as "the" *Encyclopédie*.

In truth, the fame of Diderot's and d'Alembert's great project has cast a shadow over its origins, which lay heavily in Chambers's work. Chambers was middle-class and a businessman, not a scholar or an intellectual. And while the two Frenchmen acknowledged Chambers handsomely, they preferred to highlight their debt to the better-born and more scholarly Francis Bacon: "If we emerge successfully from this vast undertaking," they announced in their prospectus to the *Encyclopédie*, "we will owe it principally to Chancellor Bacon, who sketched out a plan for a universal dictionary of sciences and art at a time when, so to speak, there were neither sciences nor arts."[52]

Yet even so, Diderot was obliged to acknowledge that he and d'Alembert would not be using Bacon's schema at all, but would instead conform to what had become the standard: they would be organizing their encyclopedia alphabetically for "good reasons." It was, he said simply, *"plus commode et plus facile"*—more convenient and easier—for readers. This was increasingly regarded as obvious, simply a statement of fact, as was the notion that it was the editor's task to ensure that the organization and layout of each essay, as well as the volumes' multiple cross-references, were sufficiently robust to compensate for any lack of overarching structure.[53]

Diderot and d'Alembert estimated that their magnum opus would fill seventeen volumes of text and an additional eleven volumes of plates and engravings. The length of the text, combined with its eminent contributors—drawn from the leading thinkers of the Enlightenment such as Voltaire, Rousseau, and Montesquieu—were intended to produce a work far more ambitious in scope than Chambers's technocratic descriptions of mechanical innovations and discoveries. Diderot's own essays for the volumes included entries for "Nature," "Political Authority," and "Free Will," as well as others—"Enjoyment" and "Chastity," for example—that sounded remarkably like commonplace *topoi*. In retrospect, the arrival and great success of both Chambers's and Diderot's and d'Alembert's encyclopedias can be taken as an affirmation of the rise to preeminence of the bourgeoisie. Whereas Chambers may well have addressed himself to the aspirant and ambitious, those hoping to climb the ladder, his French counterparts wrote for those more firmly established on the higher rungs. Yet both were directly addressing their readers, sharing their views and concentrating their attention on the subjects that concerned them: commerce, scientific discovery, technology, free trade, and free thinking.*

---

*The reach of these pioneers, together with that of the *Encyclopaedia Britannica* (see below), was long-lasting and widespread: Jorge Luis Borges, whose imaginary Chinese encyclopedia I cited in the preface, recalled the impression that "the steel engravings in Chambers's *Encyclopaedia* and in the *Britannica*" made on him as a child in Argentina

The critical success of the *Encyclopédie* ensured that the choices it had so carefully made were often afterward no longer regarded as one possibility among many, but taken for granted as almost immutable laws of encyclopedia-making and -reading. That encyclopedias were ordered alphabetically, like dictionaries, was one of those laws, and the reality, that there were other possibilities, receded, abandoned and all but forgotten. A few made valiant attempts to subvert this new normal: the Parisian bookseller and publisher Charles-Joseph Panckoucke (1736–1798) asked Diderot to create an addendum to his *Encyclopédie*. When Diderot refused, Panckoucke went ahead on his own, announcing his *Encyclopédie méthodique, ou par ordre des matières*, Encyclopaedia Arranged Systematically, or, by Subject, taking Diderot's and d'Alembert's material, but rejecting their chosen method of organization. Even so, alphabetical order remained, in part: while Panckoucke rearranged the work into subject categories, unlike Bacon or his medieval predecessors he set his subjects—"Agriculture," say, or "Classics"—and all their subdivisions into alphabetical order, not hierarchical.[55]

Those who continued to reject alphabetical order out of hand mainly did so by returning to the longstanding—and to many the long-superseded—objection that because alphabetical order was random, it was therefore meaningless. The *Encyclopaedia Britannica*, which in the twentieth century was to become what the English-speaking world thought of when the word "encyclopedia" was mentioned, was a commercial venture that followed on the success of Diderot and d'Alembert. The first edition, the work of two Edinburgh printers and an engraver, was an alphabetically ordered encyclopedia covering seventy-five main

---

at the turn of the twentieth century. His contemporary in Europe, the playwright Bertolt Brecht (1898–1956), also used the *Britannica* as an example of something found in every home: in his *Threepenny Novel* (1934) a character "for his amusement read an old tattered volume of the *Encyclopaedia Britannica* which he had found in the lavatory. Only about half the volume was there, and it was not the first volume. Nevertheless, one could learn quite a lot."[54]

topics and many more shorter ones; it was issued between 1768 and 1771 in a hundred parts, and later collected in three volumes. The second edition, between 1777 and 1784, contained more than two hundred main essays, some so long they were given their own indexes.[56] Yet a full decade after it began to appear, the poet and essayist Samuel Taylor Coleridge (1772–1834) remained a vehement opponent of the work—and of alphabetization—storming against what he saw as nothing more than a "huge unconnected miscellany . . . in an arrangement determined by the accident of initial letters."[57]

So convinced was Coleridge of the superiority of the older model that he planned to undertake his own rival work, to be entitled the *Encyclopaedia Metropolitana*. In a prospectus for it he promoted its "philosophical arrangement," which would be "most conducive to the purposes of intellectual research and information" and would "most naturally interest men of science and literature," designed as it was to "present the circle of knowledge in its harmony."* There was no comparison, he thought, with those inferior alphabetically ordered works, "where the desired information is divided into innumerable fragments scattered over many volumes, like a mirror broken on the ground, presenting, instead of one, a thousand images, but none entire."[58]

Coleridge was exposing the fault line that had opened in intellectual circles, one that the use, or not, of alphabetical order merely highlighted. The older model of the encyclopedia was one designed by, and for, the learned. An encyclopedia organized on traditional hierarchical or symbolic models could be read through to discern the shape of divine providence in its creation of a perfect universe; it could not,

---

*Coleridge here was harking back to the origins of the word "encyclopedia," an erroneous transcription of the Greek in the works of Pliny, among others, for ἐγκύκλιος παιδεία, encyclical education, the notion that the arts and sciences formed a circle encompassing the ideal education.

however, be used to locate immediately an explanation of the names and numbers of, say, the archangels, or their order of eminence. Similarly, a chronologically ordered encyclopedia could show how the divine right of kings unfolded according to God's plan; it could not necessarily quickly be used to determine the causes of, and participants in, the Siege of Constantinople. (Speed was also the bugbear of the Académie française, which at this same date was bewailing the reality that the public preferred alphabetical dictionaries to the Académie's own etymologically organized one—a system, it insisted, that was far more pleasant for educated readers, even if the lesser public "gets annoyed, when opening a Dictionary, if it cannot immediately find the word it is seeking." Indeed.)[59]

But by the end of the eighteenth century, the expectation that every well-educated man had a capacious memory—or at least a well-indexed commonplace book—in which to store everything he had ever read was long gone. So much so that the coining of the phrase "a walking encyclopedia" signified a new disdain for reliance on memory. Instead, the idiom implied that no one any longer needed to remember everything, and anyone who claimed that they were a master of recall, a storehouse of knowledge, was now an object of mockery.[60] Coleridge himself was satirized precisely for that in the novel *Headlong Hall* (1816) by Thomas Love Peacock, who depicted him as Mr. Panscope, "the chemical, botanical, geological, astronomical, mathematical, metaphysical, meteorological, anatomical, physiological, galvanistical, musical, pictorial, bibliographical, critical philosopher, who had run through the whole circle of the sciences, and understood them all equally well; that is, not at all."[61] Memory had been replaced by alphabetical order, by indexes, by catalogs, and by encyclopedias. Just half a century after Coleridge's last-ditch attempt to save the medieval unity of mind and memory, a German scientist remarked proudly on the splendors of the "mechanical" utility of "catalogs, lexicons, registers, indexes, digests . . . and the like," which had freed mankind from its reliance on memory, something he saw as an unquestioned good.*[62]

As late as the 1778–1788 edition of Chambers's *Cyclopaedia*, the stated expectation was that educated readers would use the work "as they would refer to a common-place book, in order to assist their memories." But in reality, the book was simply not structured for that kind of reading, and never had been. For in the new world of science and technology, of the Enlightenment and of secular values, it had become obvious to many that there was not one single, divinely ordained route to knowledge, nor one single path of learning. Rather, readers, students, and the learned could all, via the neutrality of alphabetical order, carve out a place of their own.

---

*This is not to say that no analphabetical encyclopedias were ever published again. Between 1933 and 1962, the great French historian Lucien Febvre oversaw the production of the *Encyclopédie française*, which was divided into sections entitled "The Social Universe," "Psychological Life," "Heaven and Earth," and so on. The *Encyclopaedia Britannica* also returned to the Middle Ages in 1974, when it divided its content into a "Macropaedia," a "Micropaedia," and a "Propaedia." The Macropaedia comprised a series of long essays exploring subjects in depth; the Micropaedia was for brief overview entries; while the Propaedia mimicked a Baconian taxonomy of all knowledge. This analphabetical reordering, however, also required a two-volume alphabetical index.

 IS FOR INDEX CARDS

From Copy Clerks to Office Supplies in the Nineteenth Century

---

BETWEEN 1750 AND 1850 THE POPULATION OF EUROPE INCREASED BY 70 percent, from around 167 million to 284 million. In North America over the same period, the population soared from 2 million to 26 million.[1] Driving this demographic boom, and in turn being driven by it, was increased trade. Sugar, cotton, textiles, grain, timber, and wool became world products, even as luxury goods were transported in ever greater quantities to new markets across the globe. The shipowners and sailors who moved these goods, the merchants who traded them, the bankers who extended lines of credit to both, the shopkeepers who sold them, the customers who bought them—all relied on maps, charts, price lists, shipping manifests, goods inventories, bank ledgers, and notes of credit.

Meanwhile, the new modern states that were being run by bureaucracies created and staffed by the middle classes required laws and statutes, with a legal apparatus of lawyers and judges to support them. They too relied on paper, on deeds, charters, wills, inventories, law books, and records; and on an army of tax gatherers, with their lists of residents and incomes, their ledgers and payment processes; they depended on actual armies and navies, which necessitated charts, maps, inventories of food and other supplies shipped across the world; and on scientific navigation instruments and weather forecasts too. The middle classes themselves floated on a tide of documents: registers, price lists, invoices, bills of lading, almanacs, shipping forecasts, and insurance registers, to list only a few.[2] The modern world was awash with paper.

In the sciences, individuals were building on the new ordering systems that had been developing over the previous century. It is perhaps appropriate that Carl Linnaeus (1707–1778), the Swedish botanist known as the father of modern systems of classifying and naming plants, in his own work moved from methods rooted in the classical commonplace book to newer systems of organization. Early in his career, Linnaeus recorded his findings in bound notebooks in the time-honored fashion. Then, in the 1740s, he made a radical shift, noting his observations on sheets of paper that he bundled together by subject or type, together with dried botanical specimens, fixing those too onto loose sheets rather than in the bound ledgers that were common at this date. These he kept in a cabinet that—shades of Thomas Harrison—he referred to as an "*arca*," or ark. It had adjustable shelves and vertical dividers, which he numbered in a system that might have been based on commonplace-book ordering.[3] In the following decade, however, Linnaeus took a step backward, having his own copies of his published books re-bound with interleaved blank pages for handwritten additions and corrections. But from 1767 he returned to slips of paper, this time cut to a standard size, which he could arrange and rearrange to suit the demands of the material. (The slips are today kept in alphabetical order, but it is not known how Linnaeus himself arranged them.)[4]

Linnaeus's pupil, Daniel Solander (1733–1782), moved from his native Sweden to England, and in the 1770s he and the naturalist Joseph

A modern solander box.

Banks traveled with Captain Cook on his first great voyage, to South America, Tahiti, New Zealand, and Australia. Solander ordered his notes on slips, the practice he had learned from Linnaeus, except that instead of Linnaeus's portrait-shaped slips, Solander turned his sideways; and he used thicker paper, practically card. He had boxes made for the slips, too, so they could be kept in order. Solander had taken a giant step toward the index card.*

Other less famous scientists were also organizing their records in new ways. Édouard de Villiers, an engineer on Napoleon's Egyptian expedition of 1798, later spent his time botanizing more serenely in Switzerland and Italy. He used a bound travel diary in the field, and on his return home transferred his observations into a register, as

---

*Solander made another significant contribution to archiving, although not to classification and ordering, with what became known as the "solander box," which is today a staple of libraries and archives across the world: a cardboard, book-shaped case with a three-sided lip to protect rare manuscripts, maps, archival material, or botanical specimens.

commonplacers had been doing for millennia. But in a modern twist to this old-fashioned practice, he cut away the edges of the register's pages, gluing on a series of homemade alphabetized cardboard thumb tabs, to give him an easier way to sort his notes and tie them to an index he created at the back.[5]

This drive to order one's papers, the feeling that life was filled with too many documents to leave them in disarray, was widespread, but the solutions remained multifarious, and alphabetical order was by no means the first resort. Goethe (1749–1832) was a Renaissance man, acclaimed in turn as poet, novelist, statesman, and scientist. He kept notes covering all these subjects on loose pages, and over the years his diary reveals his many and various attempts to sort them—into incoming and outgoing letters, under subject headings, by drawing up outlines, by separating drafts from fair copies. He then stored this variety of attempts at efficiency into what he referred to as "capsules," or "sacks," or "paper pouches"—an unconscious return to those canvas bags used by merchants and bankers in the Middle Ages and the Renaissance. Goethe's pouches, however, were paper, not linen, a precursor to our large manila envelopes, and he combined their use with what he called *Tecturen*, possibly file folders. With these, too, his repeated references to "arrang[ing] them differently," to "number[ing] the drawers," and to registers that were "bound and paged" all suggest that alphabetical order was not one of his organizational choices.[6]

Goethe's near contemporary, George Washington (1732–1799), as a landowner, slaveholder, revolutionary general, and first president of the United States, also found himself awash in paper, and he was a careful and committed organizer. (He was known to spend the Christmas season alternating between hunting and doing his end-of-year accounts.)[7] His private household accounts tended to be organized by subject, geography, or some other sorting order that made sense to him: in his "List of Taxed Lands, Slaves, and other Possessions," for example, the enslaved people are initially grouped by their work location (house, home plantation, etc.), and only then by first names, in an order that we cannot now discern: "Ben, Will, Will, Jack, Jack, Charles . . . " Washington's military ledgers were organized on bookkeeping principles, with memorandum books for hastily jotted-down expenses, and ledgers where incomings and outgoings were balanced more carefully. Some of these ledgers contain handmade tabbed alphabetical pages at the start, where names were entered with the relevant page numbers, probably by his secretary.[8]

For governments themselves were moving only slowly toward alphabetical schema, even as the need to organize their overflowing archives became ever more urgent. In 1751 Cardinal Giuseppe Garampi (1725–1795) had been appointed Prefect of the Vatican Secret Archive. ("Secret" here means "privy," as in Britain's "privy chamber" and "privy council," indicating not something clandestine or underhanded but merely something accessible to only a specific group of people.) The archive, founded in the early seventeenth century, had intermittently been inventoried, but its contents had never been indexed or cataloged—those in charge knew what was there, but not necessarily where, or in what order or arrangement the material was to be found. To remedy this, the cardinal's instructions were that a single slip, or *scheda*, was to be created for every document, on which were transcribed its date, subject, physical location, and a newly denominated archival reference. As at the Josephinian in Vienna, these *schede* were expected to serve as a preliminary stage in the creation of printed ledgers, in this case containing a calendar of all papal decrees, a statistical survey of the Curia, and, ultimately, a history of the Christian world.

After more than eight hundred thousand slips had been generated, however, Garampi was moved to another position in the Vatican and the *schede* were literally shelved, stuck away and ignored for more than a century, exactly as the Josephinian library slips and those cards collected by the French government after the Revolution had been. It was only in 1880, a period of intensive library cataloging, when the Secret Archive was opened to scholars, that the usefulness of the *schede* were recognized, and they were brought back into the light of day, dubbed the Schedario Garampi.* But instead of continuing to keep them as loose slips, as other libraries were doing by this date, the Vatican had them pasted into 125 ledgers organized by subject. Within those subject categories, however, many of the slips were sorted alphabetically, rather than into the more old-fashioned chronological order the Vatican had previously favored.[9]

For while the Vatican had been at the forefront of indexing in the High Middle Ages, now it was looking backward, even as other governments had long since moved on. The sheer quantity of documents produced by a modern state required a flexibility and interleaving possibility that could be achieved by nothing except loose paper. This did not necessarily mean that the default setting for government departments everywhere was, or indeed should have been, alphabetical order. From 1839, France's central government issued every local département with detailed instructions regarding the arrangement of their archives. They were to be organized into *fonds*, a system that prioritized keeping together documents that had originated or been collected from or by a single source, whether that source was "a [government] body, an organization, a family, or an individual."**[10] Within each *fonds*, the papers were to be separated by subject and ordered according to their connection with

---

*Today in Italian a *scheda* is a record card or form, and a *schedario* is a file, or register, or index card. A modern *schedario* is both a file index and a filing cabinet, although in the eighteenth century such furniture was unknown, except to specialists like Harrison and Leibniz. The verb *schedare* now means "to file," and also to keep an eye on someone in the sense of surveillance, although that was not the eighteenth-century understanding of the word.

**This formulation, and the principle behind it, continue to form the internationally recognized basis of archival organization, known today as *respect des fonds*, principles of provenance, which says that documents are best left organized in the organic order in which they were created, or at least in which they were received. Today many archives use *fonds* as their primary organizational category, with subcategories and divisions that distinguish between types of records and by whom they were produced or created.

other groups in that category. Nonetheless, despite these precise orders from above, many archives, even central government ones, paid little attention, dividing their holdings first by category (financial, judicial, public works, etc.), then by location (département, for instance) or by governmental body (municipal, etc.). Even the Archives nationales, the official archive of the French state, in part disregarded its own rules: it kept to the firmly set and prescribed *fonds*, but gave each one "an alphabetical symbol" to simplify ordering and locating them."

Much of Europe followed suit throughout the century: the Prussian state archives adopted the system of *fonds* in 1881; the Dutch did the same shortly afterward, as did the Swedish and Danish state archives. The British national archives followed in laggardly fashion in the 1920s, and were perhaps less committed to what their instructions referred to as "original arrangements," that is, keeping files in the order in which they were created or received. If that were not possible, the instructions ran, the files could be rearranged into a number of systems: "alphabetical, chronological, formal, *or what not*" (my emphasis).[12]

While British record-keepers might have felt comfortable producing regulations that included this oh-well-you-decide shrug of a category, organizational systems were far more rigid in other countries— sometimes so rigid that they became ripe for satire. The Austrian novelist Heimito von Doderer (1896–1966), in his *Die erleuchteten Fenster*, The Lit Windows (1950), mocked civil-service fixity with his creation of a bureaucrat who in retirement became a Peeping Tom, clandestinely watching women through their windows to classify them as he had once classified his office documents: "126. II 98 15 1030 f" was his reference for the 126th woman he spied on, whom he saw at the second window of her apartment, located at 98 degrees longitude, 15 latitude, at 10:30 A.M. under lighting conditions categorized as "f."[13]

Leaving farce aside, archives and offices were wholeheartedly incorporating new cataloging systems and methods. Just as the pigeonhole had followed the appearance of the practice of making notes on paper slips, so new forms of office furniture began to appear alongside new sorting tools. For much of the nineteenth century and well into the twentieth, the spindle, or spike, was crucial to office organization. This was a stiff wire or thin rod, sharpened to a point at one end, and set upright into a stable base, usually a piece of wood or plaster. These sat on clerks' desks, for one category of document, or documents of the same date, to be punched down onto them.* When the spike was full or the series of documents complete, they were pulled off and either filed in the old style by tying a string through the holes the spindle had made, to keep that batch together, or they were folded and the salient details—sender or recipient, date, type of document, or other identifying detail—were written on the outside fold, to help identify the bundle without having to open it, the method in use from the seventeenth century.

In the nineteenth-century office, the initial attempt to create new ways to store and retrieve documents was in reality a return to a much older method: the ledger. As had been the case from the sixteenth century in much of Europe, outgoing correspondence for most offices was copied into a bound volume before it was dispatched, while incoming letters were pasted into guard books—bound volumes that, instead of paper pages, had narrow paper strips or guards onto which the correspondence was glued. Both of these systems were therefore almost always chronologically based, and were used in conjunction with an index in which the recipients' or senders' names were inscribed, together with page references. To follow the course of a single correspondence, the reader had to use both ledgers, both indexes, and then turn to the different pages by date. If the piece of business involved more than two correspondents, to reconstruct the process each reference had to be

---

*These spikes are the origin of the journalistic term "spiked," to refer to an article that had been commissioned but was not ultimately printed. In the second half of the twentieth century, when computer punch cards came into regular use, the phrase "Do not fold, spindle or mutilate" was printed on many documents: the holes made by a spike or spindle rendered them machine-unreadable.

This view of the New York Times newsroom in the 1920s includes two spindles, one almost empty (front right), and one that has been more than half-filled (center).

marked in the index, with cross-references to the incoming and outgoing correspondence between the various senders.

And yet the first innovation in office filing increased, rather than decreased, reliance on these books, an indication of how conceptually difficult it was to move away from the idea of ledgers. Copybooks, also known as letterpress books, were technological innovations, but they were not organizational advances. These books were bound with tissue-paper pages, replacing regular paper; outgoing correspondence was written in a special copying ink on regular paper, the letter was placed under a tissue-paper page in the letterpress book, the tissue paper was dampened with a sponge and the book closed and placed in a copy press; the resulting pressure transferred the ink from the letter to the back of the tissue paper, from which it could be read through on the reverse. Copy-press, as this was called, was cheaper than employing a correspondence clerk to copy every letter before it was dispatched, and it ensured that no errors were incorporated in the copy when a transcription was being made.

An advertisement for a copy press showing the press in use (above); and (below) an 1890s office that includes a copy-press machine (left) next to a tightly stacked spindle sitting on bound ledgers or guard books.

This system, however, was built on the assumption that most business was carried out by two correspondents, one in the office, one elsewhere. In reality, of course, much business involved several people, or groups or businesses, all contributing. As companies grew, there was also an increase in interoffice correspondence, with memos and schedules, budgets and statements circulating between departments. Office administration produced quantities of other kinds of documents as well, not just letters in and out—such as invoices, inventories, purchase orders, sales receipts, employment documents, contracts, time sheets—and these too had to be stored so that they could easily be located. For many in the nineteenth century, this meant a return to the old pigeonhole system.

As early as 1708, a German trade economist had recommended that merchants commission a chest or cabinet to use as a "reference work," or, for those who traded in tangible goods, a sample case. He gave as an example of the former a chest partitioned into one drawer for each letter of the alphabet, with each drawer divided into a further sixty-four sections, giving altogether 1,536 cubbyholes in which to order notes.[14] We do not know if such a chest was ever built, and it sounds like a fantasy until one considers the output of the thriving business that was the Wooton furniture company, founded in Indiana in 1870. Until the late nineteenth century, two types of office desk had predominated: long tables known as counting-house, or bookkeepers', desks, which sometimes had slanted tops, at which a copyist stood or sat on a high stool; and small, slanted, portable writing desks or slopes that were placed on tables or flat-top desks, where more eminent persons sat. (The bottom photograph on page 206 shows both a counting-house desk on the right, with its accompanying stool, and two flat-topped desks at the rear. In addition, the woman may be using a portable writing slope.) Some slopes had a small storage space underneath as well as a drawer or two, and the desks they sat on frequently also had drawers. But now offices began to replace these with a new style of desk better suited to storage: the cylinder, and then the rolltop, desk.*

---

* These two styles have been merged today into the generic term "rolltop desk." To those who built and used them, however, they were distinct: a cylinder desk had a single, solid cover that pulled down over the working area, while a rolltop cover was made of wooden slats and was therefore pliable.

A pigeonhole-style desk in use, with the wings folded open.

The writing surface of these desks was much as before, a flat surface on which, if wanted, a writing slope could be placed. But this area was backed by a built-up section of pigeonholes for the sorting and storage of documents. Furthermore, at the end of the day the desk's user pulled the cover down from the top of the pigeonholes over the entire writing area, and with one lock and key secured all his paperwork without having to move any of it. These desks became popular choices, not merely for the security they offered, but for the way the pigeonholes freed their users from the binary in/out divisions of the bound ledger.

Patented in 1874, the Wooton desk (see insert) was an advance on the rolltop, not in kind, but in capacity, as the Wooton Company marketed an almost infinitely expandable abundance of places to store paperwork. There were drawers, small square pigeonholes, tall narrow pigeonholes, large flat racks for plans and charts, upright racks for bound ledgers, even reinforced safes—and all theoretically within easy reach of the desk's occupant, who sat and folded out the requisite sections to meet his needs.

In the 1880s, the Wooton Company was advertising its most recent model: "One hundred and ten compartments, all under lock and key. A place for everything and everything in its place. Order Reigns Supreme. Confusion Avoided. Time Saved. Vexation Spared."[15]

But while a Wooton or rolltop desk solved the problem of sorting, storage, and retrieval, and permitted increasingly precise categories into which to separate papers—adding to Locke's pigeonholes lettered A to Z with, perhaps, different pigeonholes for Aa, Ab, Ac—it did not solve the problem that was increasingly arising in the modern office: that more than one person needed access to a single set of documents. For that, a simpler solution appeared almost simultaneously with the excruciatingly expensive Wooton desk, one that in the long term made a far more conspicuous contribution to organizational methods: a modified version of the solander box, or what we know today as a box file. Early versions were in use by the mid-nineteenth century, all moving toward a standard model: a box with a hinged top that opened upward, in which letters or contracts or other paperwork could be piled. This system had the advantage over letterpress and copybooks in that incoming letters could be interleaved with copies of the outgoing correspondence, as well as with any other relevant paperwork, which could all be gathered and organized in one place. Yet papers stored in these boxes for the most part continued to be filed chronologically, each new item laid on top, until a box was full, at which point it was dated and stored.

Thus box files, while a great improvement on bound ledgers, still did not solve the problem of categorizing, or sorting, nor did they necessarily make it easier to locate a single document from among a mass of others. To reach an older document, all the more recent ones had to be lifted out, and by lifting them one risked them slipping out of order. Each box, too, was a unit in itself, and the chronological or other ordering system had to begin again with each new box. While an early version of the filing cabinet had been produced in 1868—the first one possibly being sold by the Amberg File and Index Co. in the United States—this prototype simply replicated the box file in a piece of furniture, being little more than a series of drawers in which papers were laid flat, and were, therefore, as with the box file, commonly arranged in chronological order.[16] A leap of imagination was required, and that came, as with the box file, from a modest innovation.

In 1871 a solution to the conundrum had arisen simultaneously in Germany and the United States. It quickly spread, indicating how universal the problem, and how necessary a solution. In Germany the innovator was one Louis Leitz (1846–1918), in the United States it was a business, the Shannon Company, but both took the spindle as their starting point, both incorporating a double metal shaft to replace the single spike, and capping them off to seal them, making it possible to store documents more permanently. Leitz's version was the more radical reworking. He removed the spindle's base, adding a mechanical lever to the shafts so that they opened and closed, then enclosed these in a cardboard case that protected the documents and also made the file transportable. The Shannon Company kept the spindle's base but bent one of the metal shafts into an arch, with one end permanently fixed, the other hinged, to enable it to open and close. Shannon soon modified their prototype by attaching the arches to a board. From these two innovators, the lever-arch file, or ring binder, was born, and its immediate acceptance can be measured by the fact that, just fifteen years later, a patent was filed for a new item of office stationery, the two-hole punch.

Leitz's version was sold with an alphabetical inlay divider, advancing the file folder from something that merely held documents in a set order to a tool that *created* that order, enabling users to locate documents more efficiently.[17] This ready-made alphabetized insert, furthermore,

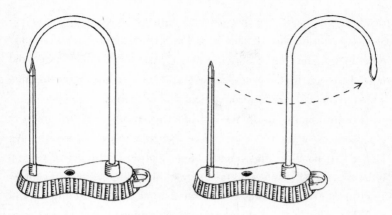

The Shannon lever-arch file in its first incarnation, in the closed and open positions.

silently informed all offices, large and small, that *the* way to organize papers was through the sorting power of the alphabet.

It was no coincidence that typewriters developed in tandem with lever-arch files and ring binders. The first viable typewriter was manufactured in the United States in 1868, and machines were factory-produced from 1874, in the same decade as Leitz's and the Shannon Company's filing innovations. It takes far less time to type a document than to write it out by hand. Once the speed of the typewriter was harnessed to the duplicating powers of carbon paper, producing an original document and multiple copies became not merely quick but inexpensive, neither of which could be claimed for the copy-press ledger.* Unsurprisingly,

---

*Carbon paper, now heading into obsolescence, was an office mainstay for more than a century. Consisting of flimsy paper coated with pigment on one side, carbons were inserted between as many sheets of paper as desired; as the original document was typed on the first sheet, the intervening carbons imprinted copies on the multiple pages behind it. Although carbon paper became ubiquitous with the spread of the typewriter, it was actually invented more than half a century earlier: an Italian, Pellegrino Turri, and an Englishman, Ralph Wedgwood, vie for this honor, although it was Wedgwood who filed the first patent, in 1806.

this influx of typed loose sheets sounded the death-knell for bound led-gers. Typewritten pages had either to be glued into guard books, or some other filing system would have to emerge.[18] And another filing system did indeed emerge. Yet the next changes that were to transform organization systems were to come not from offices, but once more from libraries.

Private libraries or, in Britain, subscription libraries—commercial organizations of greater or lesser size that for a weekly or monthly fee loaned out books to the general public—often continued to rely on older organizing systems. One survey of surviving eighteenth-century English catalogs estimates that fewer than a quarter had any form of alphabetical ordering at all; the main organizational principle continued to be subject, then size.[19] Things were changing, however, in university libraries. Of nearly two dozen printed library catalogs that have survived from institutions in colonial America, most show that their books were arranged in a combination of alphabetical order, format, and subject classifications. A single library might well switch back and forth over time, but overall no single system was favored. Harvard College's catalog of 1723 divided its collection first by size, then alphabetically; in 1773, it moved to full alphabetical order before seventeen years later chang-ing again, to a subject classification system. Yale College in 1743 went with subject classification, with many subcategories—so many that the catalog required its own index to navigate.[20] In general, libraries that used alphabetical order tended to apologize for it.[21] It was considered a poor relation, used when neither time nor money was available for what were generally accepted to be more advanced sorting methods. Catalogs that relied on alphabetical order were regarded as halfway houses, failed subject-classification catalogs.

In 1812, Harvard College hired William Croswell, a morose, unful-filled ex–mathematics teacher with no library experience, to compile its library catalog. Croswell spent the next five years intermittently draw-ing up desultory lists, seemingly spending as much time recording in his diary how little he had achieved. Finally in 1817, when pressed, he "beg[an] to cut [his] Manuscripts," chopping up the lists he had managed to produce with a view to ordering the entries alphabetically, as a preliminary to the bound ledgers that were to be both alphabetically ordered "and also [in] the order of time" (presumably, by date of publication). Before he could reach that stage, however, he was summarily sacked, and replaced by Joseph Cogswell.

Cogswell was far better versed in library organization, having visited many German libraries, including that of the University of Göttingen. Yet lack of both time and funding prevented the adoption of more elaborate schemes and forced him back to Croswell's "Seventeen boxes of folio half-sheets, each containing the name of a single author and abbreviated titles of his work," in alphabetical order. This was a compromise situation, one he hoped was an interim measure. Twenty years later, however, across the Atlantic and on a national scale, Antonio Panizzi (1797–1879), the famed librarian of the British Museum, in London, was expressing adamant opposition to these systems:

> [T]he question of the strictly classified [that is, subject] catalog versus the strictly alphabetical, may indeed be considered as decided. The former . . . may have answered in the library of Alexandria; but the multiplicity of the departments of knowledge, their intricacy, and the nicety with which they blend and shade into each other, render cataloging solely by subjects a delusion.[22]

For Panizzi, and the British Museum, alphabetical order was seen as a pragmatic, modern solution—in fact it was *the* pragmatic, modern solution.

These questions arose in American university libraries just as the institutions themselves were moving toward a grading system that used the alphabet. Yet universities had not naturally been a home to ordering by alphabet more generally. Even in the New World, supposedly freed from old caste systems by its revolution, society continued to be viewed hierarchically: the earliest surviving lists of students at Harvard and Yale Colleges show them ranked not according to their own merits, by examination results or by their conduct, but by their families' social status. It was not until 1886 that Yale began to list graduating students in alphabetical order.[23]

At the same time, many colleges had used descriptive phrases to indicate pass or fail marks. In the late eighteenth century, Yale had used "*Optimi*," best; "second *Optimi*," second best; "*Inferiores (Boni)*," lower (good); and "*Pejores*," worse. In the nineteenth century this was replaced by a scale of 1 to 4. Harvard, on the other hand, switched from numbers to letter grades in descending order from A to C just as it was adopting an alphabetically ordered card catalog. The University of Michigan initially simplified its system to pass or fail, later replaced with P for passed, C for "conditioned" (presumably some form of conditional passing grade), and A for absent. Mount Holyoke, in Massachusetts, founded in 1837 as the Mount Holyoke Female Seminary, used A for excellent, B for good, C, fair, D, passed ("barely"), E for failed, before changing to pass grades A to E, with F becoming the new "failed."*[24] With none of these changes does there appear to have been any discussion as to why A was almost always the best—it just seemed obvious that it was.

In some ways, that supremacy of the start of the alphabet was ancient: the Mishnah, the collection of rabbinic laws—written down in the third century CE but recording an oral tradition that might date back to the sixth century BCE—graded wine and oil into different qualities, the best being "aleph," or A.[25] And it was still taken for granted two millennia later, in the eighteenth century, when Lloyd's of London used

---

*It is again not coincidental that this period also saw the arrival of the "alphabet song," a song that has no name, but that every Anglo-American child can sing, which dates back to sometime before 1835 when a Boston music publisher issued "The A.B.C., a German Air with Variations" by one Louis Le Maire. The tune is that of the folksong on which Mozart had in 1761 based his variations, "Ah, vous dirai-je, Maman," and by 1806 it had been borrowed once more, to accompany the English nursery rhyme "Twinkle, Twinkle, Little Star."

the classification A1 to designate ships that were in the best condition and constructed from the best materials.

Harvard's librarian agreed that alphabetical order was useful—but only useful for certain categories of users. In 1840, the work on the college's catalog that had been in progress for nearly three decades was brought to an end. The details of every title were written out on a single slip, each slip was glued onto a standard-sized card, and all were filed in alphabetical order in wooden drawers. But these cards were considered to be a working tool for the use of the library staff, not for the library's readers, who had to muddle through with the older catalogs, ordered by format and subject as well as alphabetically. It was not until 1861 that the library made its working card catalog available to Harvard's academic staff and students as well as to the library's employees. To withstand the increased—and less skilled—handling, the drawers that held the cards were redesigned: wooden dividers were inserted to indicate the start of each letter of the alphabet; and a rod inserted through a hole punched near the bottom of each card kept them in order.[26] Now for the first time, a library had a catalog of standardized cards, each containing a single unit of information, all ordered in a single sequence—and, furthermore, a sequence that was physically infinitely expandable with more cards and drawers.

The idea of maintaining library records on cards has often been attributed to Charles Coffin Jewett, the librarian of the Smithsonian Institution in the 1850s, although, in reality, it had a long European history as well as being preceded in the United States by Harvard's staff library system.[27] Similarly, the tabbed card, or divider, was another of the many contributions to organization that was invented and reinvented several times. One historian has even suggested its origins might go as far back as the seventeenth century, to a man named Daniel Schwenter (1585–1636), a mathematician and linguist from Nuremberg, who refers in his writings to a marker he called a "nose" or a "rider" because it sat proudly above the mass of his notes.[28] It may be relevant, too, that a posthumous work of his, a compilation of puzzles and "fun" mathematical equations, was updated and continued after his death by Georg Philipp Harsdörffer, whose pigeonhole system was discussed in Chapter 8. If Schwenter did invent the tabbed divider, though, he was a radical outlier; apart from the few homemade tabbed alphabetical indexes that were created independently over the centuries, nothing more was seen of it until Leitz's tabbed alphabetic separators in his lever-arch files, which might be considered an influence on their emergence in the card index.

In its modern form, a divider for cards was born in 1896. There are, once more, two parallel points of origin for the honor of its creation. One of these, the secretary of the Akron, Ohio, YMCA, kept the association's membership details on cards that he divided with a progressive system of tabs, similar to the one still current, in which the projecting elements of the tabs on which the identifying information is written are staggered along the cards' top edges, enabling the user to see all of them at once. The tabs could be marked with the letters of the alphabet, or with finer gradations of each letter—Aa, Ab, Ac, and so on. In 1897, this patent was sold to the Library Bureau, which may have acquired it because it was preparing to market something that closely resembled these tabs: that same year, a patent had been issued to James Newton Gunn, a Library Bureau employee who, a decade later, was to become one of the first lecturers at the newly established Harvard Graduate School of Business.[29]

The Library Bureau had been founded in 1876 by Melvil (born Melville) Dewey (1851–1931), whose work radically altered American libraries and their systems. Dewey had studied at Amherst College in New England, and on graduation in 1876 he was hired by the college to catalog its library. Possibly unaware of the advances in cataloging that were occurring in Europe, he returned to Bacon's notion of the hierarchy of knowledge, based on the classical *trivium* and *quadrivium*. He divided the world, and therefore the library, into ten classes, giving philosophy precedence, followed by theology, social sciences, philology, natural sciences, "useful arts" (technology, or applied sciences), fine arts, literature and history (which included geography), plus a catch-all "generalities," or miscellaneous class for everything else. Each of these categories was given a number from 0 to 9, followed by two digits that refined the category further, then a decimal point and yet more numbers, each number and decimal point dividing the subject into smaller and smaller categories.* To find books on butterflies, the progression a reader follows is:

> 500s Natural sciences
> 590 Zoology
> 595 Other invertebrates
> 595.7 Insects
> 595.78 Lepidoptera
> 595.789 Butterflies

But while Dewey's system will lead any readers desirous to learn more about butterflies directly to the shelves where such books are housed, it is unable to guide them to one specific book on butterflies

---

*While all systems are inevitably biased, making more space for some elements and overlooking others, Dewey's was particularly so, and has proved troublesome in the modern world. Being based on Baconian hierarchies, it is predisposed to an Anglo-centric worldview. More, it is almost laughably Christian-centric: religion, allocated the 200s in Dewey's system, sees 200–289 devoted to Christianity, while all of Islam is contained in just 297. Women, meanwhile, are patronizingly categorized alongside etiquette. (Dewey himself had chronic woman trouble, or, rather, women had chronic trouble with Dewey: he was forced to resign from the American Library Association after no fewer than four women complained that he had assaulted them in a single ten-day period in 1905. He was, in addition, a notable anti-Semite and racist, even for those notably anti-Semitic and racist times, also being requested to stand down from his position as librarian for New York State owing to his endorsement of clubs that operated on Christian-whites-only policies.)

by one specific author. For that, it has to be backed up by an alphabetical catalog.

In the same year that Dewey created his system, he had helped found the American Library Association, which set up a division to sell supplies directly to libraries. That offshoot itself swiftly broke away and established itself as an independent commercial entity, marketing index cards, the drawers and cabinets to house them, and other library necessities. By 1888, it was known simply as the Library Bureau and had greatly extended its brief, doing business not merely with libraries but with every kind of commercial business, pioneering the idea that library systems *were* business systems. It promoted the card catalog in particular as ideal for businesses, the key to all types of office systems. By 1896, the Library Bureau had entered into partnership with the Tabulating Machine Company, which produced cards for government census records and office equipment for the railways (and was later to change its name to International Business Machines, or IBM for short).[30] "The two great systems which have revolutionized accounting and record keeping; viz., the card system and the loose leaf system," said one of Dewey's partners, "had their origin in library work."[31] This wasn't entirely accurate, as we have seen with the development of the lever-arch file, but by the time he made this comment, in 1907, it no longer mattered: businesses had embraced card systems, and therefore the alphabet.

As early as 1886, the head of the US military records and pensions office had transferred the information he held for veterans onto a card system, but primary alphabetical order was still not automatic: the men were listed first by regiment, and only then alphabetically by name.[32] Sometimes not even that happened. The War Department's 1889 directory listed everyone by rank, from the Secretary of War at the head, right down to the watchmen and messengers. When multiple individuals held the same "rank"—the office charwomen, for example—they were carefully listed not in alphabetical order, but chronologically by their date of employment.[33] The first step toward disseminating card indexes—and alphabetical order—in the business world was taken in 1889, when the Library Bureau targeted insurance companies in New England, demonstrating how customer accounts could be accessed more easily via a card catalog. But the main impetus came when the Bureau devised a subscription scheme to induce companies to adopt a card-based system. Under this scheme, the details of all "refused risks"—the potential buyers of insurance who had already been turned down by insurance assessors—were printed onto standardized cards, alphabetized, and mailed out monthly to subscribers. Subscribing insurance companies thus had what today we would call a database, enabling them to cut down the time spent on the most cost-intensive element of their business—risk assessment.

The Library Bureau soon began to create similar systems for banks, and by 1892 it was advertising a card-based method of indexing all types of business correspondence.[34] These alphabetical systems meshed neatly with new types of office supplies such as ledgers and account books, which were no longer bound but were now available as loose-leaf binders. Pages could be inserted or removed when new customers or suppliers began to do business with the company, or old ones left, making maintaining alphabetical order effortless.

In 1893, at the Chicago World Fair, the Library Bureau displayed the next important organizational innovation: the vertical, or hanging, file.[35] Unlike the lever-arch file and the box file, vertical filing freed offices from chronology. No longer was it necessary to lift all the more recent documents out to get to the older material; it could easily be taken out and reordered; pages could be added to, or removed and filed elsewhere. Vertical filing allowed documents to be organized in any way the user desired: by subject, by sender or by recipient, by region, by cost, by supplier, or by project. Or a mixture of any of those, depending on what suited each individual department or company.

What vertical filing did unintentionally, more than anything else, was promote alphabetization. Between 1910 and 1913 a US-government-appointed body conducted an extensive survey of business practices, aimed at improving efficiency. Its report was categorical: in offices across the country, numerically ordered files were routinely being replaced by alphabetically based ones. "There were several instances of changes from the numerical to the alphabetical," but "[i]n no case did we find that an alphabetical . . . file had been supplanted by a numerical [one]."[36]

The alphabet reigned supreme.

CHAPTER 10

 IS FOR Y2K

From the Phone Book to Hypertext in the Twentieth and Twenty-first Centuries

---

IN THE TWENTIETH CENTURY, ALPHABETICAL ORDER APPEARED TO BE immortal. No longer could anyone at home in an alphabetic writing system remember a time when the automatic response to ordering had *not* been alphabetical. In fact, it often seemed that the chaos and fecundity of the world could be tamed by the power of alphabetization alone.

Paul Otlet (1868–1944) was a Belgian visionary who wanted to—and believed he could—categorize all the information in the world. Anything ever written in a book, everything ever known, could be compressed, he believed, into a card system: one nugget of knowledge per index card, all filed in alphabetical order, whence any information about anything, anyone, anywhere, at any time, could be retrieved. Otlet began modestly in the 1890s, creating a bibliography of sociological literature. He then spread his wings to found the International Institute of Bibliography in Brussels, which drew on as many library catalogs and bibliographies as could be consulted to compile a summary, and summation, he hoped, of all libraries and all books: "an inventory of all that has been written at all times, in all languages, and on all subjects." Just as the Library Bureau had done, Otlet then established a subscription service that supplied his customers monthly with standardized cards filled with newly précised information. By 1900 he had 300 full members, and by the outbreak of the First World War another 1,500 people annually were approaching the Institute for information.[1]

The Second World War saw utopian dreams wane, to be replaced by pragmatism. In Germany in 1940, the government ordered the seizure of any books from across occupied Europe that might contribute to the stock of the projected library of the Nazi Hohe Schule, or University of the Third Reich. But Otlet's Universal Bibliography, comprising nearly fifteen million cards after almost half a century of indexing and summarizing, was spurned: "It is an impossible mess," it was reported back to headquarters, "and [it is] high time for this all to be cleared away." Nevertheless, there were elements that the Nazis thought worth preserving: "The card catalog might prove rather useful."[2] This sounds harsh, and must have been unbearable for the elderly Otlet, but in retrospect it is worth noting that it was the card catalog, the engine of his system, that was deemed worthy of preservation.

For in the preceding half century, alphabetical systems had spread everywhere. Even when the great medieval encyclopedists were aware of alphabetical order, they had frequently disdained it. By contrast, at the start of the twentieth century *Nelson's Encyclopedia* (1909), soon to be retitled *Nelson's Perpetual Loose-leaf Encyclopedia*, had leapt on alphabetization as its savior in an attempt to find a solution to the bane of encyclopedists of all eras, that of becoming out of date. *Nelson's* volumes consisted of pages of alphabetically ordered entries, like any other modern encyclopedia. The difference was that those pages were not permanently bound into their covers as with regular books, but manufactured as a loose-leaf system and held in place with pins in the binding that opened with a special key. *Nelson's* was "a modern book," trumpeted the publisher's preface, with "a new and special emphasis . . . on subjects which are of wide and active interest to-day": namely, the sciences and technology, as well as biographical essays on living people, all of which needed regular updating. Each volume included "Our Guarantee": "no less than 500 removable pages" would be sent "without further cost to each subscriber" for at least three years after purchase.[3] As has now become unsurprising, however, and despite their very product hinging on alphabetization, and it being its main selling point, the system itself was apparently invisible even to *Nelson's*: the encyclopedia contained an entry for "Alphabet," covering the history of writing, but none for "alphabetization."

It might well be that alphabetical order, even in a perpetually updated reference work, had by 1909 become invisible because it was so routine and so ordinary, just as it had in that other beacon of alphabetical order, the telephone directory, or phone book. Street guides, and later post office directories, precursors to phone books, had appeared in the eighteenth and nineteenth centuries in many cities. These publications listed the names, occupations, and addresses of residents and businesses, arranged in alphabetical order or, occasionally, in street order that was itself organized alphabetically within districts. Even so, most of these early directories had included prominent analphabetical components: for instance, they were prefaced by registers of government officials, magistrates, aldermen, or other civic leaders or institutions, almost all of whom were listed hierarchically or chronologically.

The first telephones were sold in pairs, the owner of one of a pair able to communicate only with the owner of the other. Customers therefore had no need for directories. It was 1877 before the telephone "exchange" was conceived, a method of routing calls from one subscriber to a central exchange, from which they were transmitted onward to any of the other subscribers to the same exchange. These exchanges typically consisted of people in linked occupations. One early exchange, for example, included a pharmacist, six doctors, and a livery stable: a business arrangement for all of them.

In 1878 George Coy, who had earlier worked for a telegraph company in Connecticut, designed and built a "switch board," where calls could be "switched" from one exchange to another, vastly increasing the reach of any one subscriber, who was now no longer tied solely to a single exchange. These switchboards housed a series of jacks, one per subscriber. When a subscriber rang through to the exchange, the operator answered, the caller asked for a fellow subscriber, and the operator plugged the caller's jack into that linked to the requested subscriber.[*4]

Coy signed up twenty-one subscribers to his switchboard service in his first year. Subscribers were no longer tight-knit groups who worked together, as with the pharmacist and doctors; in fact, they might not know their fellow subscribers at all. Thus all were provided with a list of those served by Coy's switchboard, which included doctors, dentists, the post office, a police station, a club, and some shops and markets. These subscribers' names filled a single page in no particular order that can be determined in retrospect. (It might have been an order that made sense to Coy, perhaps that in which his subscribers had joined his service, or following the layout of his switchboard connections.) There was, of course, no need for numbers to be associated with each name: a subscriber would call the exchange and ask to speak to another subscriber by name or occupation: "Put me through to the post office," or "Mr. Smith, please." Within a few years, Coy was employing four operators to

---

*A charming, frequently repeated, and possibly even true anecdote tells how the occupation of switchboard operator came to be dominated by women. Initially, the story runs, these jobs went to the boys who had previously been employed to deliver telegrams. However, when confined indoors at an exchange they tended to become raucous and play practical jokes on callers. Women, one report is supposed to have found, "are steadier, and do not drink beer." What is certainly true is the 1886 Boston phone book's warning: "Ladies are employed as operators; we ask for them courteous treatment."[5]

connect two hundred subscribers across several switchboards, and his much-expanded list now appeared in alphabetical order.[6]

By 1880, the first known printed list of telephone subscribers in Britain—in effect, the first phone book—had appeared. It had 407 sub- scribers, still with no numbers linked to the names. (Unfortunately, the historian who commented on it in the 1920s was oblivious to matters of sorting, and made no mention of how it was arranged.)[7] In one respect these early switchboard operators were very like the medieval monastery librarians: where they had oversight of a few dozen, or a hundred, units, be they manuscripts or phone subscribers, the individual in charge could remember their location; but once there were more, some form of finding tool became necessary. In general, the early phone books used a variety of systems. Some were arranged in the order subscribers had joined the exchange or by the date they had purchased their telephone. Others grouped entries by trade or profession. At this point it was still rare for individual subscribers to have numbers: the 1883 phone book for the city of Montreal simply reminded those placing a call to pronounce the name of the subscriber they were requesting slowly and clearly.[8]

Numbers began to replace names once switchboards signed up so many subscribers that their operators could no longer remember all their customers' names. These names, presumably, could have been written below each subscriber's jack in alphabetical rather than numer- ical order. Perhaps names took up too much space. Or perhaps it was thought operators could run their eyes along a line of numbers more quickly than they could names. More likely, the deterrent to retain- ing names was the alphabetical reordering that would have been nec- essary each time a new subscriber signed up. For whatever reason, at the point where an exchange reached critical mass, subscribers were given "telephone numbers" to use and to disseminate to those who might want to reach them. Yet even then, telephone directories used a variety of sorting methods. The Boston phone book of 1886, published by the New England Telephone and Telegraph Company, began with a list of "pay stations"—public phones—by location, that is, grouped geographically rather than alphabetically by location. And, the directory warned, subscribers' phone numbers, which were allocated geographically by exchange, might be altered by the company at will, presumably as exchanges expanded and divided into subexchanges. (The first three digits of phone numbers, in use in some places until the 1960s, matched the letters printed beside them on the phone's dial, and referred to the exchange they were connected to: "Hunter" was 486, "Regency" 734, "Mayfair" 629.) Boston subscribers were therefore advised not to put these ephemeral numbers on their office stationery, or in their advertisements, but simply print "Connected by Telephone." Anyone looking for them could ring the appropriate exchange, and ask for them by name.[9] This expectation, that name rather than number was the key finding unit, continued well into the 1950s for many smaller rural exchanges, where subscribers were supposedly well known by name. ("Ethel is outside getting her laundry in before that storm hits, but I'll tell her you want her mother's boysenberry jam recipe when she next dials in," runs a typical fantasy of small community switchboards, perhaps only somewhat exaggerated.)*

In the United States by the 1960s and 1970s, the Bell Telephone Company claimed that more than ninety-three million people looked up at least three phone numbers annually in the Yellow Pages, the classified directory that listed people by trade or profession; slightly fewer turned to the White Pages, or residential directory. Yet as many as 10 percent of all listings were known to be incorrect, adding up to something in the region of fifty million wrong numbers annually. In the UK, the telephone system came under the aegis of the Post Office, and by the 1960s

---

*Some versions of this fantasy were a reality even into the second half of the twentieth century. A personal anecdote: In 1963, my father gave a phone number to a Jerusalem hotel telephone operator without mentioning any associated name. "You want Teddy?" was the response. "He goes to Tel Aviv on Wednesdays, but I'll let you know when he gets back."

directory corrections were the responsibility of one post office employee for every fifty-six phone book districts. These clerks used the current printed phone books as their starting point, making corrections in the margins, writing in new listings and removing numbers no longer in use, then amending the alphabetical order of entries as necessary. However reluctantly, though, the post office was rethinking its system, considering the possibility of transferring corrections onto card indexes—"prepared on typewriters," the head of the department charged with compiling the directories noted with a flourish of modernity, just as those scribes who moved from interlinear glosses to separate dictionaries must have felt.[10]

This post office employee was also, unusually, profoundly aware of how invisible the work his staff undertook was, how the country as a whole relied on the accuracy of those alphabetical listings without ever giving them their due. When he was appointed to his job, he later recounted, he felt that he was insufficiently versed in matters alphabetical, much less in what the experts considered to be best alphabetical practices. He therefore left a message for the librarian of the British Museum, asking for a list of authorities to consult. By return, the library supplied him with a single phone number, that of the man they said was the foremost expert in the field—only for him to discover it was his own.[11]

BY THE MID-TWENTIETH CENTURY, alphabetical order was no longer considered a historical quirk, a creation that over seven hundred years had spread its tentacles into a fair number of different fields. Instead, it was seen, unthinkingly, as something intrinsic, and, more importantly, something that developed nations all shared. According to the original International Olympic Committee rules of 1921, the opening ceremony to each Olympic Games saw the national teams entering "in alphabetical order by country." In 1949 that was clarified, the regulations now specifying that the teams were to enter "in the alphabetical order of the language of the host nation." Yet when the 1964 Olympics were held in Japan, for the first time in a country with a nonalphabetic script, the IOC simply shrugged its institutional shoulders and team entry was ordered by English-language place names, as written in the roman alphabet. By then, at least to western European minds, anywhere without an alphabet was not just different; instead, it was that dreadful thing—*not modern*. It was not until 1988, when South Korea hosted the games, that a nation stood up and made the alphabetic world aware that alphabetical order was not Holy Writ, and many countries and civilizations had managed perfectly well for millennia without it and, every bit as importantly, were continuing to do so, while still thriving in the capitalist market economy. In Seoul, Ghana entered first, followed by Gabon, *ga* being the first syllable of the Korean *han'gul* syllabary. At the Beijing Olympics in 2008, the Chinese hosts followed traditional fourth-century classifying systems, which sorted each ideogram first by a single radical, used as its primary identifier, and then by the number of brushstrokes it contained.[12] And the world did not come to an end, nor did China stop being the world's second-largest economy simply because it had historically sorted and organized by systems the West no longer used. In fact, the sole result was a minor panic among Western television networks as they attempted to work out where to slot their advertising breaks in order not to miss their own country's appearance. Not really an alphabetical existential crisis.

For, while modern communications might have spread the knowledge of languages that are not written in alphabetic scripts to those places that do use alphabets, in modern times the sorting products that in Western Europe have been based on that alphabet—indexes, catalogs, dictionaries, encyclopedias, phone books—have tended to treat alphabetical order as though no other possibilities exist, indeed, as though all other, nonalphabetical sorting methods are somehow deficient, and need to be forced into the sole system that is somehow "right," modern—alphabetical.* The West has discarded many, even most,

---

*That this is firmly ingrained into alphabetic cultures can be seen in a comment made by one of the few people to write an extended work on alphabetical order. The classicist

reference books that were not in alphabetical order, regarding them as unusable. A few have managed to retain their now unrecognizable order, but only after acquiring an alphabetical scaffolding via an index. *Roget's Thesaurus* is perhaps the most frequently consulted analphabetical reference book in English. Based on an eighteenth-century view of the natural-history classification system, its layout is organized by phyla, classes, orders, and families—a system that is impenetrable to the great majority, if not to all, of its modern-day users. The alphabetical index, which all twentieth- and twenty-first-century editions of *Roget* contain, is considered so necessary today that it typically occupies more than half the book. [14] Other things that we regard as language-neutral, and, especially, alphabet-neutral—a great deal of recent technology, including the telegraph code, Morse code, braille, typewriters, punch-card processing, text coding, word processors, ASCII, and OCR—in reality rely on the roman alphabet as their starting point.[15] Yet we alphabetic cultures remain blind to our bias, and none is considered to be alphabet-based by readers of alphabetic languages: we consider them to be neutral or, worse, "universal."

Such is the Anglo-American dominance of modern technology that many countries that use non-alphabetic writing forms have been forced to create work-arounds. The typewriter, and subsequently the computer keyboard, are glaring examples of this bias: they have a strictly limited number of keys; limited abilities to superimpose diacritics or letters that alter their form depending on their position in a word without going into separate keyboards or using special codes; and the direction of the writing is left to right. Typewriters and keyboards for alphabetic languages that do not adhere to these basics have long been available, but they

---

W. Lloyd Daly quoted a fellow classicist who claimed that, to be able to read, a student "*has*" [my emphasis] to learn the alphabet in order—that "alone guarantees the mastery of our letters"—somehow overlooking entire civilizations, such as those of China or Japan or ancient Egypt—civilizations with mighty reading heritages, yet whose readers have no possibility, or need, to learn an alphabet in any order.[13]

are "modified"—the twenty-six-letter alphabet, with at most minimal accents, written left to right, is considered to be the norm; all else is a variant. Analphabetic scripts that cannot be made compatible with an alphabetic keyboard are simply dismissed as absurd or unmodern, which in today's world can be considered to mean the same thing.[16] It is only recently that the World Wide Web Consortium (known as W3C), administered jointly in the United States, France, Japan, and China, has produced changes to the system of creating URLs that permit the use of non-Latin-alphabetic scripts.[17]

Modern Japanese script is a mixture of *kanji*, a logographic script (each character represents a word or an idea), and *hiragana* and *katakana*, which are both syllabaries (where the characters represent a syllable). Dictionary compilers in nineteenth-century Japan based their sorting method on the "Iroha," a poem written sometime between the ninth and eleventh centuries. This poem uses every *kana*, or character, of the Japanese syllabary just once. Learning the poem by heart therefore meant learning the *kana* in a set order, which dictionaries then borrowed. (The "Iroha" was used as the basis, too, for the Japanese telegraph system when it was established in the 1870s.)[18] Today, however, modern Japanese dictionaries have for the most part abandoned this elegant literary solution, instead following an order based on the Brahmic scripts that in Japan were used for Buddhist sutras.[19]

Yet alphabetic script continues its march. Japanese writing scripts also include *rōmaji*, or roman script, which is used in airports and train stations, for street signs, and sometimes for advertising and logos. Many government documents and forms also use *rōmaji*, as do passports—in other words, all those places and pieces of paper that come into contact with those who regularly use an alphabetic script.

Chinese lacks the range of different character sets that Japanese has, instead maintaining a single logographic system. For sorting it long relied, as we saw, on a system of ordering by radicals and brushstrokes, a system used in directories, dictionaries, and encyclopedias. In the twentieth century, after the founding of the People's Republic of China, script reform was instituted to ease the learning process. The result was pinyin (literally, "sounds spelled-out"), which both simplified the forms of many of the written characters and created a romanized system of phonetic renderings, for use in telegrams, road signs, corporate logos, and much of the impedimenta of modern life, including computers.*[20].

Indeed, computers, phones, and other digital media are once again separating reading from writing, in a way that has not been seen since the Middle Ages, when some could read but far fewer could write. Today, many Chinese do much of their writing by typing phonetic versions of words on pinyin keyboards, then selecting the correct characters from the range of possibilities brought up on their screen. They can, therefore, recognize—read—a character with no difficulty, but can have trouble reproducing—writing—the more complex graphemes on their own.[21]

With ideograms, of course, what you see is not what you get. In English, if I type "E-n-g-l-i-s-h" on a keyboard, my screen displays the word "English." In China, typing in pinyin produces a number of possible characters on the screen, which is more akin to turning on a ceiling light via a switch on the wall: do one thing—flick a switch—and an entirely different thing ensues—a light goes on overhead.[22] This separation between cause and effect that technology has recently enabled means that in China dictionaries, encyclopedias, other reference works, and indexes no longer rely on radicals for their ordering principle. The 1979 edition of Jinrong Wu's *The Pinyin Chinese–English Dictionary*, published in Hong Kong, gives the Chinese in characters and pinyin, but both are arranged in an order entirely based on pinyin romanization.[23]

In other ways too, in both alphabetic and analphabetic cultures, computers and technology are returning us to possibilities last engaged with

---

*The simplification of characters has caused its own difficulties: it was a product of mainland China, and so those outside can have trouble reading the simplified forms, while those on the mainland in turn cannot always read the older characters in material printed elsewhere.

in the Middle Ages. While the word "hypertext," meaning "beyond text," was coined in the 1960s following the development of computers, the idea goes a long way back. Medieval and Renaissance texts too went "beyond" their main texts. Today, nonfiction books like this one you are reading tuck most, if not all, of the notes away at the back, alongside the index. It might be necessary for the reader to use additional works as well: a dictionary for the definition of an unknown word, or an encyclopedia entry to elaborate on one of the people, places, or things mentioned. Electronic texts accommodate these external sources, and the end material, onscreen: click the superscript note number on the page to check the source of a quotation; click a link to take you to a dictionary definition, or to an illustration of the material on a different website. In a similar fashion, the manuscripts of the Middle Ages were themselves hypertexts as well as main texts: arguments, references, counterarguments, and digressions were all laid out in front of the reader on every page. An example of this can be seen in an Irish manuscript of 1138 (see insert), which reproduces the Gospels in the center, surrounded by interlinear glosses and commentaries, a few poems here and there (in Irish, rather than Latin), and assorted marginalia.[24] This page differentiates the types of commentary by enclosing some in red boxes, and by using linking rubrication (red highlighting) between the Gospel and the accompanying notes.

One of the most frequently copied manuscript versions of *The Canterbury Tales* included Chaucer's text, together with glosses and marginalia for its readers written in different colors, and aligned in separate columns (see insert). The main text on the left and the notes on the right are generally the same size—one is not presented as being more important than the other—although Chaucer's verses are more widely spaced. Now, in the twenty-first century, with a click of a mouse, just as in the early fifteenth century, readers of today can open up their Chaucer and trace "The Wife of Bath's Tale" back to the *Roman de la Rose*, and then further, to St. Jerome's *Contra Jovinianum*, and finally to its origins with St. Paul.[25]

This hypertextuality, as we know, did not come to a grinding halt as print replaced manuscripts. On the contrary, what became known as the Age of Reason embraced its possibilities. Pierre Bayle's *Dictionaire critique* of 1697 (see pages 187–188) was a virtual argument on a page, as through typography the author set out his predecessor Moréri's views, his own counterviews, and then sources and references for the latter, differentiated by type size, marginalia, and layout, exactly as the medieval scribes had done.

Yet just as this revival has occurred with the age of the computer, the same age of the computer has moved alphabetical order from the center of our lives—as we looked up an address or a phone number, used a card catalog in a library, searched a cookbook index for a recipe to finish up the leftover chicken—to the periphery. Bookshops today can decide to highlight "Our Staff's Picks" or current fiction in no order at all, or even shelve the entirety of their stock, more fancifully, by the country of origin of the books' authors, because a quick check of their computer database will locate every title, with all its details, in seconds. Phone numbers, too, are now found on a website, or at most, keyed into an online "White Pages" website that is neither white nor a page. And no one any longer needs to know whether D comes before or after E when searching for the history of Diderot's and d'Alembert's *Encyclopédie* on Wikipedia, the online encyclopedia that has a readership the pair could never have dreamed of—in 2014, half a billion unique users a month, according to Wikipedia itself.[26]

It is all credit to Wikipedia, then, that it has paid quiet homage to its illustrious predecessors, those careful, hopeful, orderly organizers and alphabetizers. Wikipedia originally named its multiple servers after various categories and types of classifier, among them the encyclopedists in these pages—Alsted, Isidore of Seville, and Bayle—as well as the inventor of italic type, Aldus Manutius, plus mathematicians, philosophers, and other quantifiers, including Locke and Linnaeus.[27]

If most people give alphabetical order any thought at all, it might be described as an organizational Stonehenge: something that always has been, and always will be. Yet historically, once alphabetical order was devised, it continued to evolve and change. Our views on the subject, too, have evolved and changed as we notice, or fail to notice, this great organizing tool of our world and, just like Stonehenge, we wonder if it really serves any purpose. In Molière's play *Le Bourgeois Gentilhomme* (1670), the bourgeois M. Jourdain is enchanted to discover that for forty years, all unknown to himself, he had been speaking in prose. So too today we tend to assume that those things we have not actively learned are not important. As children we learn to sing the alphabet song, but we are far less frequently taught to alphabetize: yet somehow, as with M. Jourdain's prose-speaking, we find that we have been doing it all along.

ALPHABETICAL ORDER IS A MEANS, not an end in itself. It is a system that permits us to organize large quantities of information, and to make it available to others whom we do not know, and who have no information regarding the people or ideas or intentions of those who originally produced and arranged it. There continue to be many ways of organizing, storing, and retrieving information, sometimes in the same way it originated, sometimes in a way that transforms it. Linnaeus's taxonomy, and the periodic tables, are naming and classifying systems. The Dewey decimal system classifies, but does not name. Most museum exhibits are organizing, classifying, *and* displaying systems. Maps are displaying and also transforming systems, as are graphs and pie and bar charts. The importance is not the method, but *a* method, any method. "The human mind works by internalizing such arbitrary and useful tools, as a kind of grid onto which knowledge can be arranged, and from which it can be retrieved," wrote the novelist A. S. Byatt.[28] We think, therefore we sort.

For there is organization, and then there is the perception of that organization. One historian has recorded a nineteenth-century German country saying, "*Wie man berichtet, so geschehe*," which can be translated as "As things are reported, so they happened"—that is, the report, or perception, of an event creates its reality.[29] For all its ubiquity, alphabetization has rarely been perceived, or reported. Rather, it has been overlooked, to all intents and purposes remaining invisible through its eight centuries of active duty. To most people, therefore, it cannot have been very important, a system that has at one and the same time been valueless, and valued above all others.

In 1947, Winston Churchill famously declared, "Many forms of government have been tried, and will be tried, in this world of sin and woe. No one pretends that democracy is perfect, or all-wise. Indeed, it has been said that democracy is the worst form of government, except for all those other forms that have been tried from time to time."[30] And so too, perhaps, with organizing and sorting. Of all the methods that have been explored—hierarchical, categorical, geographical, chronological, alphabetical—we might say that alphabetical is as close as we can get to a universally accessible, nonelitist form of sorting, and therefore it is the worst form of classification and organization that has ever been devised, except for all those other forms that have been tried.

Our exploration of the meandering road to alphabetization suggests the wisdom in the Book of Revelation, written more than two millennia ago. "I am the Alpha and Omega, the beginning and the end, the first and the last": the first and last letters of the alphabet, and all that comes in between, represent a universe that we can order, knowledge we can pin down and later return to, and pass on to others. Isidore of Seville understood this: writing was created, he said, "in order to remember things. For lest [things] fly into oblivion, they are bound in letters."[31]

For us in the West, our knowledge, our learning, everything we see or do or remember in our lives has been created, stored, retrieved, and recalled in some form by alphabetical order. Lest all these things fly into oblivion hereafter, let us, with Isidore, bind them in letters.

TIMELINE

The dates below, particularly in the early period, can be approximate.

BCE

C. 4800	Fragments found in China bearing incisions that may represent precursors to writing.
C. 3500	Sumerian cuneiform becomes ideographic.
C. 3000	Egyptian hieroglyphics develop.
AFTER 2350	Akkadian–Sumerian word lists compiled.
2050–1550	Inscriptions in Egypt show what is probably the world's first alphabet.
C. 2000	Egyptian hieroglyphics comprise around 700 standard symbols; 2,000 years later, increased to 5,000-plus.
C. 1500	Forerunners to Chinese ideograms appear on oracle bones.
C. 1400	A proto-alphabet, in fixed order, written on a clay tablet.
LATE 9TH–EARLY 8TH. CENT	The Greek alphabet develops.
6TH CENT.	First appearance of money, in Lydia, Asia Minor.
	A precursor to Arabic script in use in the Arabian Peninsula.

4TH CENT.	The Etruscans, and their alphabet, assimilated by the Roman republic.
	Parchment begins to be manufactured, initially in Pergamum.
3RD CENT.	The Great Library of Alexandria flourishes.
C. 220	The first Chinese dictionary, organized by subject.
2ND CENT.	The ancestor of modern Arabic script appears.

CE

C.100	A Chinese dictionary containing around 9,500 characters sorted by 540 radicals.
105	Legendary date of the creation of the first true paper in China.
3RD CENT.	Chinese *leishu*, embryonic dictionaries and encyclopedias.
6TH CENT.	Founding of the first Western monastery library, at Vivarium in southern Italy.
600S	Isidore of Seville compiles his *Etymologies*, the first Western encyclopedia.
8TH CENT.	Glossaries in first- or second-letter alphabetical order appear in monasteries.
C.750	Paper exported from China to the Arab world.
868	The first known block-printed work, the Diamond Sutra, produced in China.
10TH CENT.	Books of medical remedies organized *a capite ad calcem*, from head to heel.
	First Hebrew dictionary, in first- and last-letter alphabetical order.
LATE 10TH CENT.	The *Suda*, a Byzantine encyclopedic compilation.
1053	Papias's *Elementarium doctrinae rudimentum*.
1086	The Domesday Book.

11TH CENT.	Printing with movable type appears in China.
11TH–12TH CENT.	"Arabic" (in reality Hindu–Arabic) numerals in use in Western Europe.
12TH CENT.	Greek and Arabic works begin to be translated into Latin in quantity.
LATE 12TH– 13TH CENT.	*Distinctiones*, reference works for use in composing sermons, proliferate.
C. 1180	The Bible is broken up into chapters.
13TH CENT.	The spread of florilegia.
C. 1200	Paper arrives in Western Europe.
1230S	Printing with movable type used in Korea.
1230–1244	Concordances to the Latin Bible created by the Dominicans in Paris.
C. 1235–1250	Robert Grosseteste's and Adam Marsh's table of symbols.
1240	Frederick II Hohenstaufen establishes the first European chancellery as a physical space.
1244–1255	Vincent of Beauvais's *Speculum maius*.
1250S	Subject indexes to the works of Aristotle and Augustine are created.
1273	Konrad of Mure's *Fabularius*, possibly the first Western encyclopedia to be entirely alphabetical.
1286	Giovanni Balbi's *Catholicon*.
1306	Thomas of Ireland's *Manipulus florum*.
1450–1455	Johannes Gutenberg's printing press produces the first printed book in Western Europe.
EARLY 1460S	The first printed index, to the works of Augustine, appears.
1494	A book on double-entry bookkeeping spreads the practice across Europe.

1499	The first book with indented paragraphs printed by Aldus Manutius, followed by italic type and books with pagination on both sides of each leaf.
16TH CENT.	Graphite pencils come into use.
	Filing by threading documents on a string.
	New carpentry techniques enable the creation of cabinets with pigeonholes.
1500	Erasmus's *Adagia*, a commonplace book, published.
1545–1548	Conrad Gesner's *Bibliotheca universalis*.
1551	Conrad Gesner's *Historia animalium* sets out the rationale for reference books.
1570	The first modern atlas, Abraham Ortelius's *Theatrum orbis terrarum*, with multiple indexes.
1595	London bookseller Andrew Maunsell develops the English bibliography, alphabetizing by surname.
1604	Robert Cawdrey's *A Table Alphabeticall*, the first English nontranslating dictionary.
1620	The Bodleian Library, Oxford, produces the first entirely alphabetical institutional catalog.
1630	Johann Heinrich Alsted's *Encyclopaedia*.
1658	Jan Comenius's children's book, *Orbis sensualium pictus*, prefigures the "A is for Apple" system of teaching.
1687	John Locke's method of organizing commonplace books.
1720S	The Library of the Pères de l'Oratoire uses paper slips, bundled, as a library catalog.
1728	Chambers's *Cyclopaedia* (1768–1771).
1751–1772	Diderot's and d'Alembert's *Encyclopédie*.
1771	George Washington's records kept in an "alphabetted" ledger.
1780	The catalog of the Josephinian library, Vienna, on paper slips.

1791	Nationalized libraries in France requested to catalog their books on playing cards.
19TH CENT.	Appearance of the rolltop desk, with pigeonholes.
1835	The alphabet song copyrighted.
1839	The French government archives to be organized by *fonds*.
1840	Harvard College creates an inadvertent card catalog.
1841	Antonio Panizzi, librarian of the British Museum, rejects subject organization for alphabetical.
1871	Lever-arch files invented in the United States and Germany.
1874	Typewriters mass-produced; with carbon paper (patented 1806), multiple document copies proliferate.
1876	First version of Dewey decimal classification system.
1878	Telephone switchboard invented.
1879	List of subscribers to a telephone exchange: forerunner to the telephone directory.
1893	Vertical hanging files.
1896	Tabbed index card dividers patented.
1921	International Olympic Committee establishes alphabetical order by country for entry ceremony.
1988	Olympic teams organized for the first time by an order other than alphabetical.

BIBLIOGRAPHY

Abate, Frank. "Alphabetic Order and Disorder." *Dictionaries: Journal of the Dictionary Society of North America* 27 (2006): 133–136.

Abbot, Ezra. *Brief Description of the Catalogs of the Library of Harvard College.* Cambridge, MA: Harvard, 1867.

Alexander, J. J. G., and M. T. Gibson, eds. *Medieval Learning and Literature: Essays Presented to Richard William Hunt.* Oxford: Clarendon Press, 1976.

Alfonso-Goldfarb, Ana M., Silvia Waisse, and Márcia H. M. Ferraz. "From Shelves to Cyberspace: Organization of Knowledge and the Complex Identity of History of Science." *Isis* 104, no. 3 (2013): 551–560.

Allan, David. *Commonplace Books and Reading in Georgian England.* Cambridge: Cambridge University Press, 2010.

Arnar, Anna Sigrídur. *Encyclopedism from Pliny to Borges.* Chicago: University of Chicago Library, 1990.

Atiyeh, George N., ed. *The Book in the Islamic World: The Written Word and Communication in the Middle East.* Albany: State University of New York Press, 1995.

Bakar, Osman. *Classification of Knowledge in Islam: A Study in Islamic Philosophies of Science.* Cambridge: Islamic Texts Society, 1998.

Bakewell, K. G. B. *A Manual of Cataloging Practice.* Oxford: Pergamon, 1972.

Baldwin, F. G. C. *The History of the Telephone in the United Kingdom.* London: Chapman & Hall, 1925.

Barney, Stephen A., W. J. Lewis, J. A. Beach, Oliver Berghof, with Muriel Hall. *The Etymologies of Isidore of Seville.* Cambridge: Cambridge University Press, 2006.

Baron, Sabrina Alcorn, et al., eds. *Agent of Change: Print Culture Studies after Elizabeth L. Eisenstein.* Amherst: University of Massachusetts Press, 2007.

Beal, Peter. "Notions in Garrison: The Seventeenth-century Commonplace Book." In *New Ways of Looking at Old Texts: Papers of the Renaissance English Society, 1985–1991*, edited by W. Speed Hill. Binghamton, NY: Medieval & Renaissance Texts and Studies, 1993.

Becker, Peter, and William Clark, eds. *Little Tools of Knowledge: Historical Essays on Academic and Bureaucratic Practices*. Ann Arbor: University of Michigan Press, 2001.

Becq, Annie, ed. *L'Encyclopédisme: Actes du Colloque de Caen, 12–16 janvier 1987*. Paris: Éditions aux Amateurs de Livres, and Klincksieck, 1991.

Béjoint, Henri. *The Lexicography of English: From Origins to Present*. Oxford: Oxford University Press, 2010.

Bell, Hazel. *From Flock Beds to Professionalism: A History of Index-Makers*. New Castle, DE: Oak Knoll, 2008.

Bergenholtz, Henning, Sandro Nielsen, and Sven Tarp, eds. *Lexicography at a Crossroads: Dictionaries and Encyclopedias Today, Lexicographical Tools Tomorrow*. Bern: Peter Lang, 2009.

Berger, Jean. "Indexation, Memory, Power and Representations at the Beginning of the Twelfth Century: The Rediscovery of Pages from the Tables to the *Liber de Honoribus* . . . " Translated by Maureen MacGlashan. *The Indexer* 25, no. 2 (2006): 95–99.

Berry, Mary Elizabeth. *Japan in Print: Information and Nation in the Early Modern Period*. Berkeley: University of California Press, 2006.

Berthold, Arthur Benedict. *On the Systematization of Documents in Ancient Times*. Philadelphia: n.p., 1938.

Bertius, Petrus. *Nomenclator. The first printed catalog of Leiden University Library (1595)*. A facsimile edition with an introduction by R. Breugelmans and an author index compiled by Jan Just Witkam. Leiden: 1995, online.

Bijker, Wiebe E., Thomas P. Hughes, and Trevor J. Pinch, eds. *The Social Construction of Technological Systems: New Directions in the Sociology and History of Technology*. Cambridge, MA: MIT Press, 1987.

Bing, Peter. "The Unruly Tongue: Philitas of Cos as Scholar and Poet." *Classical Philology* 98, no. 4 (2003): 330–348.

Binkley, Peter, ed. *Pre-Modern Encyclopaedic Texts, Proceedings of the Second COMERS Congress, Groningen, 1–4 July 1996*. Leiden: Brill, 1997.

Birks, Peter, ed. *The Classification of Obligations*. Oxford: Clarendon, 1997.

Blair, Ann. "Note-Taking as an Art of Transmission." *Critical Inquiry* 31, no. 1 (2004): 85–107.

———. "Organizations of Knowledge." In *The Cambridge Companion to Renaissance Philosophy*, edited by James Hankins, 287–303. Cambridge: Cambridge University Press, 2007.

———. "Reading Strategies for Coping with Information Overload, ca. 1550–1700." *Journal of the History of Ideas* 64, no. 1 (2003): 11–28.

————. *Too Much to Know: Managing Scholarly Information Before the Modern Age*. New Haven, CT: Yale University Press, 2010.

Blair, Ann, and Jennifer Mulligan, eds. "Toward a Cultural History of Archives." Special issue, *Archival Science* 7, no. 4 (2007).

Blair, Ann, and Peter Stallybrass. "Mediating Information, 1450–1800." In *This Is Enlightenment*, edited by Clifford Siskin and William Warner. Chicago: University of Chicago Press, 2010.

Blair, Ann, and Richard Yeo, eds. "Note-Taking in Early Modern Europe." Special issue, *Intellectual History Review* 20, no. 3 (2010).

Blok, Aad, Jan Lucassen, and Huub Sanders. *A Usable Collection: Essays in Honour of Jaap Kloosterman on Collecting Social History*. Amsterdam: Amsterdam University Press, 2014.

Bloom, Jonathan M. *Paper Before Print: The History and Impact of Paper in the Islamic World*. New Haven, CT: Yale University Press, 2001.

Blum, Rudolf. *Kallimachos: The Alexandrian Library and the Origins of Bibliography*. Translated by Hans H. Wellisch. Madison: University of Wisconsin Press, 1991.

Bodley, Thomas. *Letters of Sir Thomas Bodley to Thomas James, First Keeper of the Bodleian Library*. Edited by G. W. Wheeler. Oxford: Clarendon Press, 1926.

Bolzoni, Lina. *The Gallery of Memory: Literary and Iconographic Models in the Age of the Printing Press*. Translated by Jeremy Parzen. Toronto: University of Toronto Press, 2001.

Borges, Jorge Luis. "The Analytical Language of John Wilkins." In *Other Inquisitions, 1937–1952*. Translated by Ruth L. C. Simms. London: Souvenir Press, 1973.

Bornäs, Göran. *Ordre alphabétique et classement méthodique du lexique: Étude de quelques dictionnaires d'apprentissage français*. Malmö: CWK Gleerup, 1986.

Boulanger, Jean-Claude. *Les inventeurs de dictionnaires. De l'eduba des scribes mésopotamiens au scriptorium des moines médiévaux*. Ottawa: Presses de l'Université d'Ottawa, 2003.

Bowen, James. *A History of Western Education*. Vol. 2, *Civilization of Europe, Sixth to Sixteenth Century*. London: Methuen & Co., 1975.

Bowett, Adam. "The Vigani Specimen Cabinet by John Austin, a Cambridge Joiner." *Regional Furniture* 8 (1994): 58–63.

Braudel, Fernand. *Civilization and Capitalism*. Vol.1, *The Structures of Everyday Life: The Limits of the Possible*. Translated by [Miriam Kochan]. Revised by Siân Reynolds. London: Collins, 1981.

Brendecke, Arndt, ed. *Praktiken der frühen Neuzeit: Akteure, Handlungen, Artefakte*. Cologne: Böhlau, 2015.

Brisman, Shimeon. *A History and Guide to Judaic Dictionaries and Concordances*. Hoboken, NJ: Ktav, 2000.

Britnell, Richard, ed. *Pragmatic Literacy, East and West, 1200–1330*. Woodbridge: Boydell, 1997.

Broadberry, Stephen, Bruce M. S. Campbell, and Bas van Leeuwen. "English Medieval Population: Reconciling Time Series and Cross-Sectional Evidence." July 27, 2010, accessed online.

Broecke, Marcel van den, Peter van der Krogt, and Peter Meurer, eds. *Abraham Ortelius and the First Atlas: Essays Commemorating the Quadricentennial of His Death, 1598–1998*. Utrecht: HES Publishers, 1998.

[Brokesby, Francis]. *Of education With respect to Grammar Schools, and the Universities; Concluding with Directions to young Students in the Universities,* "by F.B. B.D." London: John Hartley, 1701.

Brooks, John. *Telephone: The First Hundred Years*. New York: Harper and Row, 1975.

Brosius, Maria, ed. *Ancient Archives and Archival Traditions: Concepts of Record-Keeping in the Ancient World*. Oxford: Oxford University Press, 2003.

Brownrigg, Linda L., ed. *Medieval Book Production: Assessing the Evidence, Proceedings of the Second Conference of the Seminar in the History of the Book to 1500, Oxford, July 1988*. Los Altos Hills: Anderson-Lovelace/Red Gull Press, 1990.

Burger, Konrad. *Buchhändleranzeigen des 15. Jahrhunderts in getreuer Nachbildung*. Leipzig: Verlag von Karl W. Hiersemann, 1907.

Burns, Charles. "Cardinal Giuseppe Garampi: An Eighteenth-century Pioneer in Indexing." *The Indexer* 22, no. 2 (2000): 61–64.

Burnyeat, M. F. "Postscript on Silent Reading." *Classical Quarterly* 47, no. 1 (1997): 74–76.

Burton, Antoinette, ed. *Archive Stories: Facts, Fictions, and the Writing of History*. Durham, NC: Duke University Press, 2005.

Buzás, Ladislaus. *German Library History, 800–1945*. Translated by William D. Boyd, with the assistance of Irmgard H. Wolfe. Jefferson, NC: McFarland, 1986.

Caius, John. *De Antiquitate Cantebrigiensis Academiae*. London: John Day, 1574.

Calder, George, ed. *Auraicept na nÉces: The Scholar's Primer, being the texts of the Ogham Tract . . .* Dublin: Four Courts, 1995.

Carruthers, Mary J. *The Book of Memory: A Study of Memory in Medieval Culture*. Cambridge: Cambridge University Press, 1990.

———. "How to Make a Composition: Memory-craft in Antiquity and in the Middle Ages." In *Memory: Histories, Theories, Debates*, edited by Susannah Radstone and Bill Schwarz. New York: Fordham University Press, 2010.

Casson, Herbert N. *The History of the Telephone*. Freeport, NY: Books for Libraries, 1971. First published 1910.

Casson, Lionel. *Libraries in the Ancient World*. New Haven, CT: Yale University Press, 2001.

Cavallo, Guglielmo, and Roger Chartier, eds. *A History of Reading in the West*. Translated by Lydia G. Cochrane. Amherst: University of Massachusetts Press, 1999.

Cevolini, Alberto, ed. *Forgetting Machines: Knowledge Management Evolution in Early Modern Europe*. Leiden: Brill, 2016.

———, ed. *Thomas Harrison: The Ark of Studies*. Turnhout: Brepols, 2017.

Charmantier, Isabelle, and Staffan Müller-Wille. "Carl Linnaeus's Botanical Paper Slips (1767–1773)." *Intellectual History Review* 24, no. 2 (2014): 215–238.

———. "Worlds of Paper: An Introduction." *Early Science and Medicine* 19 (2014): 379–397.

Chartier, Roger. *Inscription and Erasure: Literature and Written Culture from the Eleventh to the Eighteenth Centuries.* Translated by Arthur Goldhammer. Philadelphia: University of Pennsylvania Press, 2007.

———. *The Order of Books: Readers, Authors, and Libraries in Europe Between the Fourteenth and the Eighteenth Centuries.* Translated by Lydia G. Cochrane. Cambridge: Polity, 1994.

Châtillon, Jean. "Désarticulation et restructuration des textes à l'époque scolastique (XIᵉ–XIIIᵉ siècle)." In *La notion de paragraphe*, edited by Roger Laufer. Paris: Éditions du Centre National de la Recherche Scientifique, 1985.

Chibnall, Marjorie. *Select Documents of the English Lands of the Abbey of Bec.* London: Offices of the Royal Historical Society, 1951.

Christ, Karl. *The Handbook of Medieval Library History.* Revised by Anton Kern. Translated by Theophil M. Otto. Metuchen, NJ: Scarecrow, 1984.

Christin, Anne-Marie, ed. *A History of Writing: From Hieroglyph to Multimedia.* Translated by Josephine Bacon, Deke Dusinbere, and Ian McMorran. [Paris]: Flammarion, 2002.

Clanchy, M. T. *From Memory to Written Record: England 1066–1307.* London: Edward Arnold, 1979.

———. "Literacy, Law, and the Power of the State." In *Culture et idéologie dans la genèse de l'état modern.* Collection de l'École Française de Rome, no. 82. Rome: École Française de Rome, 1985.

Clark, John Willis. *The Care of Books: An Essay on the Development of Libraries and Their Fittings, from the Earliest Times to the End of the Eighteenth Century.* Cambridge: Cambridge University Press, 1909.

Cole, Richard Glenn. "The Art of History and Eighteenth-century Information Management: Christian Gottlieb Jöcher and Johann Heinrich Zedler." *Library Quarterly* 83, no. 1 (2013): 26–38.

Collison, Robert. *Encyclopaedias: Their History Throughout the Ages.* New York: Hafner Publishing, 1966.

———. *A History of Foreign-Language Dictionaries.* London: André Deutsch, 1982.

Comenius, John Amos. *Orbis Pictus: A Facsimile of the First English Edition of 1659.* Edited by John E. Sadler. London: Oxford University Press, 1968.

Connolly, Philomena, and Geoffrey Martin, eds. *The Dublin Guild Merchant Roll, c. 1190–1265.* Dublin: Dublin Corporation, 1992.

Considine, John. *Academy Dictionaries, 1600–1800.* Cambridge: Cambridge University Press, 2014.

———. *Adventuring in Dictionaries: New Studies in the History of Lexicography.* Newcastle-upon-Tyne: Cambridge Scholars, 2010.

———. *Small Dictionaries and Curiosity: Lexicography and Fieldwork in Post-Medieval Europe*. Oxford: Oxford University Press, 2017.

———, ed. *Words and Dictionaries from the British Isles in Historical Perspective*. Newcastle-upon-Tyne: Cambridge Scholars, 2007.

Cooper, Michael. "Review of *The Nippo Jisho: Vocabulario da Lingoa de Iapam . . . .*" *Monumenta Nipponica* 31, no. 4 (1976): 417–430.

Corens, Liesbeth, Kate Peters, and Alexandra Walsham, eds. *Archives and Information in the Early Modern World*. Proceedings of the British Academy, no. 212. Oxford: Oxford University Press, 2018.

———, eds. "The Social History of the Archive: Record-keeping in Early Modern Europe." *Past and Present*, supplement 11 (2016).

Cormack, Bradin, and Carla Mazzio. *Book Use, Book Theory: 1500–1700*. Chicago: University of Chicago Library, 2005.

Cowell, John. *The Interpreter, 1607*. Menston: Scolar, 1972. Facsimile of *The Interpreter: or, Booke Containing the Signification of Words . . .* Cambridge: John Legate, 1607.

Cowie, A. P., ed. *The Oxford History of English Lexicography*. Oxford: Clarendon Press, 2009.

Cowling, David, and Mette B. Bruun, eds. *Commonplace Culture in Western Europe in the Early Modern Period: Reformation, Counter-Reformation and Revolt*. Leuven: Peeters, 2011.

Crain, Patricia. *The Story of A: The Alphabetization of America from* The New England Primer *to* The Scarlet Letter. Stanford, CA: Stanford University Press, 2000.

Crane, Mary Thomas. *Framing Authority: Sayings, Self, and Society in Sixteenth-century England*. Princeton, NJ: Princeton University Press, 1993.

Crane, William G. *Wit and Rhetoric in the Renaissance: The Formal Basis of Elizabethan Prose Style*. New York: Columbia University Press, 1937.

Crosby, Alfred W. *The Measure of Reality: Quantification and Western Society, 1250–1600*. Cambridge: Cambridge University Press, 1997.

Curtius, Ernst Robert. "Goethe as Administrator." In *Essays on European Literature*. Translated by Michael Kowal. Princeton, NJ: Princeton University Press, 1973.

Daly, Lloyd W. *Contributions to a History of Alphabetization in Antiquity and the Middle Ages*. Brussels: Latomus, 1967.

———. "Early Alphabetic Indices in the Vatican Archives." *Traditio* 19 (1963): 483–486.

Daly, Lloyd W., and B. A. Daly. "Some Techniques in Mediaeval Latin Lexicography." *Speculum* 39, no. 2 (1964): 229–239.

Dana, John Cotton, and Henry W. Kent. *Literature of Libraries in the Seventeenth and Eighteenth Centuries*. Metuchen, NJ: Scarecrow, 1967.

Daniels, Peter, and William Bright, eds. *The World's Writing Systems*. New York: Oxford University Press, 1996.

Darnell, John Coleman, F. W. Dobbs-Allsopp, Marilyn J. Lundberg, P. Kyle Mc-Carter, and Bruce Zuckerman. "Two Early Alphabetic Inscriptions from the Wadi el-Ḥôl: New Evidence for the Origin of the Alphabet from the Western Desert of Egypt." *Annual of the American Schools of Oriental Research* 59 (2005): 63–124.

Daston, Lorraine. "Taking Note(s)." *Isis* 95, no. 3 (2004): 443–448.

Datta, Bimal Kumar. *Libraries and Librarianship of Ancient and Medieval India*. Delhi: Atma Ram and Sons, 1970.

Davis, R. H. C. *The Kalendar of Abbot Samson of Bury St. Edmunds and Related Documents*. Camden Third Series, vol. 84. London: Royal Historical Society, 1954.

Daybell, James. *The Material Letter in Early Modern England: Manuscript Letters and the Culture and Practice of Letter-writing, 1512–1635*. Basingstoke: Palgrave Macmillan, 2012.

Daybell, James, and Peter Hinds, eds. *Material Readings of Early Modern Culture: Texts and Social Practices, 1580–1730*. Basingstoke: Palgrave Macmillan, 2010.

Décultot, Élisabeth, ed. *Lire, Copier, Écrire: Les bibliothèques manuscrites et leurs usages au XVIIe siècle*. Paris: CNRS Éditions, 2003.

[Dekker, Thomas]. *Lanthorne and Candle-light, or, The Bell-Mans second Nightswalke*. London: John Busby, 1609.

Delbourgo, James, and Staffan Müller-Wille. "Introduction to Isis Focus Section, 'Listmania.'" *Isis* 103, no. 4 (2012): 710–715.

Déroche, François, and Francis Richard, eds. *Scribes et manuscrits du Moyen-Orient*. Paris: Bibliothèque Nationale de France, 1997.

Derrida, Jacques. *Archive Fever: A Freudian Impression*. Translated by Eric Prenowitz. Chicago: University of Chicago Press, 1996.

Dick, R. P. "The Compiling of the Telephone Directories." *The Indexer* 3, no. 1 (Spring 1962): 10–16.

Didier, Béatrice. *Alphabet et raison: Le paradoxe des dictionnaires au XVIIIe siècle*. Paris: Presses Universitaires de France, 1996.

Dilworth, Thomas. *A New Guide to the English Tongue: In Five Parts*. 38th ed. London: Henry Kent, 1776.

———. *The Young Book-Keeper's Assistant . . .* York: Thomas Wilson and Sons, 1839.

[Dilworth, Thomas], and S. James. *Dilworth Improved, or, A New Guide to the English Tongue . . .* 70th ed. London: Sherwood, Neely and Jones, 1810.

Diringer, David. "The Origins of the Order of the Letters." *The Indexer* 6, no. 2 (1968): 54–58.

Diringer, David, with Reinhold Regensburger. *The Alphabet: A Key to the History of Mankind*. Rev. ed. London: Hutchinson, 1968.

Dodsley, Robert. *The Correspondence of Robert Dodsley, 1733–64*. Edited by James E. Tierney. Cambridge: Cambridge University Press, 1988.

Dolbeau, François. "La bibliothèque des Dominicains de Bâle au XVᵉ siècle: Fragment inédit d'un catalog alphabétique." In *Medieval Manuscripts, Their Makers and Users: A Special Issue of* Viator *in Honor of Richard and Mary Rouse*. Turnhout: Brepols, 2011.

Doležalová, Lucie, ed. *The Charm of a List: From the Sumerians to Computerised Data Processing*. Newcastle-upon-Tyne: Cambridge Scholars, 2009.

Dover, Paul M., ed. "Philip II, Information Overload and the Early Modern Moment." In *The Limits of Empire: European Imperial Formations in Early Modern World History. Essays in Honor of Geoffrey Parker*, edited by Tonio Andrade and William Reger. Farnham: Ashgate, 2012.

———. *Secretaries and Statecraft in the Early Modern World*. Edinburgh: Edinburgh University Press, 2016.

Dury, John. *The Reformed Librarie-Keeper* (1650), in Dana and Kent, *Literature of Libraries* . . . (above).

Eddy, M. D. "Tools for Reordering: Commonplacing and the Space of Words in Linnaeus's *Philosophia Botanica*." *Intellectual History Review* 20, no. 2 (2010): 227–252.

Edwards, Edward. *Memoirs of Libraries, of Museums, and of Archives*. London: n.p., 1901. First published 1885.

Eisenstein, Elizabeth L. *Divine Art, Infernal Machine: The Reception of Printing in the West from First Impressions to the Sense of an Ending*. Philadelphia: University of Pennsylvania Press, 2011.

———. *The Printing Press as an Agent of Change*. Cambridge: Cambridge University Press, 1979.

Elayyan, Ribhi Mustafa. "The History of the Arabic-Islamic Libraries, 7th to 14th Centuries." *International Library Review* 22, no. 2 (1990): 119–135.

Elsendoorn, Ben, and Herman Bouma, eds. *Working Models of Human Perception*. London: Academic Press, 1989.

Elsner, John, and Roger Cardinal, eds. *The Cultures of Collecting*. London: Reaktion, 1994.

Enenkel, Karl A. E., and Wolfgang Neuber, eds. *Cognition and the Book: Typologies of Formal Organisation of Knowledge in the Printed Book of the Early Modern Period*. Leiden: Brill, 2005.

Erünsal, Ismail E. "A Brief Survey of the Development of Turkish Library Catalogs." *Libri* 41, no. 1 (2001): 1–7.

Esbester, Mike. "Nineteenth-century Timetables and the History of Reading." *Book History* 12 (2009): 156–185.

Evangelatou, Maria. "Word and Image in the 'Sacra Parallela' (Codex Parisinus Graecus 923)." *Dumbarton Oaks Papers* 62 (2008): 113–197.

Evelyn, John. Evelyn Papers, vols. CLXI, CLXIV, British Library, Add MS 78328, Add MS 78331.

Faraday, M. A., ed. *Herefordshire Militia Assessments of 1663*. Camden Fourth Series, vol. 10. London: Royal Historical Society, 1972.

Farge, Arlette. *The Allure of the Archives*. Translated by Thomas Scott-Railton. New Haven, CT: Yale University Press, 2013.

Farnaby, Thomas. *Index Rhetoricus*. Menston: Scolar, 1970. First published 1625.

Febvre, Lucien, and Henri-Jean Martin. *The Coming of the Book: The Impact of Printing, 1450–1800*. Translated by David Gerard. Edited by Geoffrey Nowell-Smith and David Wootton. London: Atlantic Highlands/Humanities Press, 1976.

Feller, Joachim Friedrich. *Otium Hanoveranum, sive, Miscellanea, Ex ore et schedis Illustris Viri, piae memoriae, Godofr. Guillielmi Leibnitii . . .* Leipzig: Johann Christian Martin, 1718.

Flanzraich, Gerri Lynn. "The Library Bureau and Office Technology." *Libraries and Culture* 28, no. 4 (1993): 403–429.

Foucault, Michel. *The Order of Things: An Archaeology of the Human Sciences*. [No translator named.] London: Tavistock Publications, 1970.

Frängsmyr, Tore, J. L. Heilbron, and Robin E. Rider, eds. *The Quantifying Spirit in the Eighteenth Century*. Berkeley: University of California Press, 1990.

Frasca-Spada, Marina, and Nick Jardine, eds. *Books and the Sciences in History*. Cambridge: Cambridge University Press, 2000.

Frost, Carolyn. "The Bodleian Catalogs of 1674 and 1738: An Examination in the Light of Modern Cataloging Theory." *Library Quarterly* 46, no. 3 (1976): 248–270.

Fuchs, James Lawrence. "Vincenzo Coronelli and the Organization of Knowledge: The Twilight of Seventeenth-century Encyclopedism." PhD thesis, University of Chicago, 1983.

Garberson, Eric. "Libraries, Memory and the Space of Knowledge." *Journal of the History of Collections* 18, no. 2 (2006): 105–136.

Gavrilov, A. K. "Techniques of Reading in Classical Antiquity." *Classical Quarterly* 47, no. 1 (1997): 56–73.

Gerritsen, W. P. "Het alfabet als zoekinstrument: Een beschouwing over de geschiedenis van de alfabetische index." *Scaliger-Lezingen* 2. Leiden: Primavera Pers, 2006.

Gesner, Conrad. *Mithridates: De differentiis linguarum, tum veterum, tum quae hodie apud diversas nationes in toto orbe terrarum in usu sunt*. Zurich(?): Froschauer, 1555.

Ghobrial, John-Paul. *The Whispers of Cities: Information Flows in Istanbul, London, and Paris in the Age of William Trumbull*. Oxford: Oxford University Press, 2013.

Gilliver, Peter, *The Making of the* Oxford English Dictionary. Oxford: Oxford University Press, 2016.

Gleick, James. *The Information: A History, a Theory, a Flood.* New York: Pantheon, 2011.

Goeing, Anja-Silvia. *Storing, Archiving, Organizing: The Changing Dynamics of Scholarly Information Management in Post-Reformation Zurich.* Leiden: Brill, 2017.

Googe, Barnabe, trans. *The Zodiake of Life, written by the excellent and Christian Poet, Marcellus Palingenius Stellatus . . .* London: Raufe Newberie, 1576.

Grafton, Anthony. *The Footnote: A Curious History.* Cambridge, MA: Harvard University Press, 1997.

Graziaplena, Rosella, with Mark Livesey, eds. *Paper as a Medium of Cultural Heritage: Archaeology and Conservation.* 25th Congress, Rome–Verona, August 30 to September 6, 2002. Rome: Istituto centrale per la patologia del libro, 2004.

Greenspan, Ezra, and Jonathan Rose, eds. *Book History.* Vol. 12. Philadelphia: Pennsylvania State University Press, 2009.

Hanks, David A. *Innovative Furniture in America from 1800 to the Present.* New York: Horizon, 1981.

Harvey, David J. *The Law Emprynted and Englysshed: The Printing Press as an Agent of Change in Law and Legal Culture, 1475–1642.* Oxford: Hart, 2015.

Harvey, Steven, ed. *The Medieval Hebrew Encyclopedias of Science and Philosophy.* Dordrecht: Kluwer, 2000.

Haskins, Charles Homer. *The Renaissance of the Twelfth Century.* Cleveland: Meridian, 1967. First published 1927.

Hausmann, Franz Josef, Oskar Reichmann, Herbert Ernst Wiegand, and Ladislav Zgusta, eds. *Wörterbücher/Dictionaries/Dictionnaires: . . . An International Encyclopedia of Lexicography . . .* Berlin: Walter de Gruyter, 1989–1991.

Havens, Earle. *Commonplace Books: A History of Manuscripts and Printed Books from Antiquity to the Twentieth Century.* [New Haven, CT]: Beinecke Rare Book and Manuscript Library, 2001.

———. "'Of Common Places, or Memorial Books': An Anonymous Manuscript on Commonplace Books and the Art of Memory in Seventeenth-century England." *Yale University Library Gazette* 76, nos. 3/4 (2002): 136–153.

———, ed. "'Of Common Places, or Memorial Books': A Seventeenth-century Manuscript from the James Marshall and Marie-Louise Osborn Collection." [New Haven, CT]: Beinecke Rare Book and Manuscript Library, 2001.

Head, Randolph, ed. "Archival Knowledge and Cultures in Europe, 1400–1900." Special issue, *Archival Science* 10, no. 3 (2010).

———. "Knowing Like a State: The Transformation of Political Knowledge in Swiss Archives, 1450–1770." *Journal of Modern History* 75 (2003): 745–782.

———. "Mirroring Governance: Archives, Inventories and Political Knowledge in Early Modern Switzerland and Europe." *Archival Science* 7, no. 4 (2007): 317–329.

Headrick, Daniel R. *When Information Came of Age: Technologies of Knowledge in the Age of Reason and Revolution, 1700–1850*. New York: Oxford University Press, 2000.

Heesen, Anke te. "The Notebook: A Paper Technology." In *Making Things Public: Atmospheres of Democracy*, edited by Bruno Latour and Peter Weibel. Cambridge, MA: MIT Press, 2005.

———. *The World in a Box: The Story of an Eighteenth-century Picture Encyclopedia*. Translated by Ann M. Henschel. Chicago: Chicago University Press, 2002.

Henisch, Georg. *Bibliothecae inclytae reipub. Augustanae utriusque tum graecae tum latinae librorum impressorum manu exaratorum catalogus, Augustae Vindelicorum*. Augsburg: Valentinum Schönigk, 1600.

Hess, Volker, and J. Andrew Mendelsohn. "Case and Series: Medical Knowledge and Paper Technology, 1600–1900." *History of Science* 48, no. 161 (2010): 287–314.

———. "'Sauvages' Paperwork: How Disease Classification Arose from Scholarly Note-Taking." *Early Science and Medicine* 19 (2014): 471–503.

Higgs, Edward. *The Information State in England: The Central Collection of Information on Citizens Since 1500*. Basingstoke: Palgrave Macmillan, 2004.

Hoogvliet, Margriet. "The Medieval Texts of the 1486 Ptolemy Edition by Johann Reger of Ulm." *Imago Mundi* 54 (2002): 7–18.

Hoole, Charles. *A New Discovery of the Old Art of Teaching Schoole . . .* London: "Printed by J.T., for Andrew Crook," 1660.

Hopkins, Judith. "The 1791 French Cataloging Code and the Origins of the Card Catalog." *Libraries and Culture* 27, no. 4 (1992): 378–404.

Hüllen, Werner. *English Dictionaries, 800–1700: The Topical Tradition*. Oxford: Clarendon Press, 2006.

Huloet, Richard. *Abecedarium Anglico-Latinum*. Facsimile edition, Menston: Scolar, 1970. First published 1552.

Hunt, Richard William. "The Library of Robert Grosseteste." In *Robert Grosseteste, Scholar and Bishop: Essays in Commemoration . . .* , edited by D. A. Callus. Oxford: Clarendon Press, 1955.

Hunter, Michael, ed. *Archives of the Scientific Revolution: The Formation and Exchange of Ideas in Seventeenth-century Europe*. Woodbridge: Boydell, 1998.

Hyde, J. Edward. *The Phone Book: What the Phone Company Would Rather You Not Know*. Chicago: Henry Regnery, 1976.

Illich, Ivan, and Barry Sanders. *ABC: The Alphabetization of the Popular Mind*. San Francisco: North Point, 1988.

Jacobs, Edward H. "Buying into Classes: The Practice of Book Selection in Eighteenth-century Britain." *Eighteenth-century Print Culture* 33, no. 1 (1999): 43–64.

James, Gregory, ed. *Lexicographers and Their Works*. Exeter: University of Exeter, 1989.

Kafker, Frank A., ed. *Notable Encyclopedias of the Seventeenth and Eighteenth Centuries: Nine Predecessors of the Encyclopédie*. Oxford: Voltaire Foundation, 1981.

Kaplan, Steven Laurence, and Cynthia J. Koepp, eds. *Work in France: Representations, Meaning, Organization, and Practice*. Ithaca, NY: Cornell University Press, 1986.

Kasirer, Nicholas. "Pothier from A to Z." In *Mélanges Jean Pineau*, edited by Benoît Moore. Montreal: Éditions Thémis, 2003.

Katz, Bill. *Cuneiform to Computer: A History of Reference Sources*. History of the Book Series, no. 4. Lanham, MD: Scarecrow, 1998.

Kaufman, Paul. "The Community Library: A Chapter in English Social History." *Transactions of the American Philosophical Society*, n. s., 57, no. 7 (1967): 1–67.

Keaney, John J. "The Alleged Alphabetization of Aristotle's *Politeia*." *Classical Philology* 64, no. 4 (1969): 213–218.

Keller, Vera, Annamarie Roos, and Elizabeth Yale, eds. *Archival Afterlives: Life, Death, and Knowledge-making in Early Modern British Scientific and Medical Archives*. Leiden: Brill, 2018.

Kelley, Donald R. *History and the Disciplines: The Reclassification of Knowledge in Early Modern Europe*. Rochester, NY: University of Rochester Press, 1997.

Kenny, Anthony. Introduction to *John Evelyn in the British Library*. London: British Library, 1995.

Kittler, Friedrich. "Authorship and Love." *Theory, Culture and Society* 32, no. 3 (2015): 15–47.

Knight, G. Norman. "Book Indexing in Great Britain: A Brief History." *The Indexer* 6, no. 1 (1968): 14–18.

König, Jason, and Katerina Oikonomopoulou, eds. *Ancient Libraries*. Cambridge: Cambridge University Press, 2013.

König, Jason, and Tim Whitmarsh, eds. *Ordering Knowledge in the Roman Empire*. Cambridge: Cambridge University Press, 2007.

König, Jason, and Greg Woolf, eds. *Encyclopaedism from Antiquity to the Renaissance*. Cambridge: Cambridge University Press, 2013.

Kraemer, Fabian. "Ulisse Aldrovandi's *Pandechion Epistemonicon* and the Use of Paper Technology in Renaissance Natural History." *Early Science and Medicine* 19 (2014): 398–423.

Krajewski, Markus. "Paper as Passion: Niklas Luhmann and His Card Index." In *Raw Data Is an Oxymoron*, translated by Charles Macrum II, edited by Lisa Gitelman. Cambridge, MA: MIT Press, 2013.

———. *Paper Machines: About Cards and Catalogs, 1548–1929*. Translated by Peter Krapp. Cambridge, MA: MIT Press, 2011.

Kuhn, Sherman M. "The Preface to a Fifteenth-century Concordance." *Speculum* 43, no. 2 (1968): 258–273.

Kunoff, Hugo. *The Foundation of the German Academic Library*. Chicago: American Library Association, 1982.

Kusukawa, Sachiko. *A Wittenberg University Library Catalog of 1536*. Binghamton, NY: Medieval and Renaissance Texts and Studies, 1995.

Kwakkel, Erik. "A New Type of Book for a New Type of Reader: The Emergence of Paper in Vernacular Book Production." *Library* 4, no. 3 (2003): 219–248.

Kwakkel, Erik, Rosamond McKitterick, and Rodney Thomson, eds. *Turning Over a New Leaf: Change and Development in the Medieval Manuscript*. Studies in Renaissance Book Culture. Leiden: Leiden University Press, 2012.

Lakoff, George. *Women, Fire, and Dangerous Things: What Categories Reveal About the Mind*. Chicago: University of Chicago Press, 1990.

Langham, Thomas. *The nett duties and drawbacks of all sorts of merchandize, imported and exported, plac'd in alphabetical order. Designed for the use of merchants*. 5th ed. London: T.H., 1727.

Leedham-Green, Elisabeth. "A Catalog of Caius College Library, 1569." *Transactions of the Cambridge Bibliographical Society* 8, no. 1 (1981): 29–41.

Le Men, Ségolène. *Les Abécédaires français illustrés du XIXᵉ siècle*. Paris: Promodis, 1984.

Lendinara, Patrizia, Loredana Lazzari, and Claudia Di Sciacca, eds. *Rethinking and Recontextualizing Glosses: New Perspectives in the Study of Late Anglo-Saxon Glossography*. Turnhout: Brepols, 2011.

Lerner, Fred. *The Story of Libraries: From the Invention of Writing to the Computer Age*. New York: Continuum, 2009.

Lieshout, H. H. M. van. *The Making of Pierre Bayle's* Dictionnaire historique et critique. Amsterdam and Utrecht: APA-Holland University Press, 2001.

Locke, John. "A New Method of Making Commonplace Books." London: J. Greenwood, 1706.

Logan, Robert K. *The Alphabet Effect: The Impact of the Phonetic Alphabet on the Development of Western Civilization*. New York: St. Martin's Press, 1986.

Loveland, Jeff. *The European Encyclopedia: From 1650 to the Twenty-first Century*. Cambridge: Cambridge University Press, 2019.

Lund, Roger D. "The Eel of Science: Index Learning, Scriblerian Satire, and the Rise of Information Culture." *Eighteenth-century Life* 22, no. 2 (1998): 18–39.

Lyall, R. J. "Materials: The Paper Revolution." In *Book Production and Publishing in Britain, 1375–1475*, edited by Jeremy Griffiths and Derek Pearsall. Cambridge: Cambridge University Press, 1989.

Lynch, Jack. *You Could Look It Up: The Reference Shelf from Ancient Babylon to Wikipedia*. New York: Bloomsbury, 2016.

Lynch, Jack, and Anne McDermott, eds. *Anniversary Essays on Johnson's Dictionary.* Cambridge: Cambridge University Press, 2005.

Mack, Peter. *Elizabethan Rhetoric: Theory and Practice*. Cambridge: Cambridge University Press, 2002.

MacKinney, L. C. "Medieval Medical Dictionaries and Glossaries." In *Medieval and Historiographical Essays in Honor of James Westfall Thompson*, edited by James Lea Cate and Eugene N. Anderson. Chicago: University of Chicago Press, 1938.

Makdisi, George. *The Rise of Colleges: Institutions of Learning in Islam and the West.* Edinburgh: Edinburgh University Press, 1981.

———. *The Rise of Humanism in Classical Islam and the Christian West: With Special Reference to Scholasticism*. Edinburgh: Edinburgh University Press, 1990.

Malcolm, Noel. "Thomas Harrison and his 'Ark of Studies': An Episode in the History of the Organization of Knowledge." *The Seventeenth Century* 19, no. 2 (2004): 196–232.

Mandelbrote, Giles. "The First Printed Library Catalog? A German Doctor's Library of the Sixteenth Century, and Its Place in the History of the Distribution of Books by Catalog." In *La biblioteche private come paradigma bibliografico: atti del convegno internazionale, Roma, Tempio di Adriano, 10–12 ottobre 2007*, edited by Fiammetta Sabba. Rome: Bulzoni, 2008.

———. "Proposals for Printing a Catalog of Sion College Library (1721)." *Library and Information History* 32, nos. 1–2 (2016): 20–33.

Manguel, Alberto. *A History of Reading*. New York: Penguin, 1996.

Marbeck, John, *A Booke of Notes and Common Places . . . brought Alphabetically into order*. London: Thomas East, 1581.

Martin, Henri-Jean. *The History and Power of Writing*. Translated by Lydia G. Cochrane. Chicago: University of Chicago Press, 1988.

Martin, Henri-Jean, Roger Chartier, and Jean-Pierre Vivet, eds. *Histoire de l'édition française*. Vol.1, *Le Livre conquérant; Du moyen âge au xviiie siècle*. Paris: Promodis, 1983.

Martin, Michèle. *Hello, Central?: Gender, Technology, and Culture in the Formation of Telephone Systems*. Montreal and Kingston: McGill/Queen's University Press, 1991.

McArthur, Tom. *Worlds of Reference: Lexicography, Learning and Language, from the Clay Tablet to the Computer*. Cambridge: Cambridge University Press, 1986.

McCrimmon, Barbara. *Power, Politics, and Print: The Publication of the British Museum Catalog, 1881–1900*. Hamden, CT: Linnet, 1981.

McEvoy, James. *Robert Grosseteste*. Oxford: Oxford University Press, 2000.

McKenzie, D. F. *Bibliography and the Sociology of Texts*. Cambridge: Cambridge University Press, 1999.

MacKinnon, H. "William de Montibus: A Medieval Teacher." In *Essays in Medieval History Presented to Bertie Wilkinson*, edited by T. A. Sandquist and M. R. Powicke. Toronto: University of Toronto Press, 1969.

McKitterick, David. "Bibliography, Bibliophily, and the Organization of Knowledge." In David Vaisey and David McKitterick, *The Foundations of Scholarship: Libraries and Collecting, 1650–1750*. Los Angeles: William Andrews Clark Memorial Library, 1992.

———. *The Invention of Rare Books: Private Interest and Public Memory, 1600–1840*. Cambridge: Cambridge University Press, 2018.

McKitterick, Rosamond, ed. *The Uses of Literacy in Early Mediaeval Europe*. Cambridge: Cambridge University Press, 1990.

McLuhan, Marshall, and R. K. Logan. "Alphabet, Mother of Invention." *Et Cetera* 34 (1977): 373–383.

Meynell, G. G. "John Locke's Method of Common-placing as Seen in His Drafts and His Medical Notebooks, Bodleian MSS Locke d.9, f.21 and f.23." *The Seventeenth Century* 8, no. 2 (1993): 245–267.

Moore, Lara Jennifer. *Restoring Order: The École des Chartes and the Organization of Archives and Libraries in France, 1820–1870*. Duluth, MN: Litwin, 2008.

Morgan, Nigel J., and Rodney M. Thomson, eds. *The Cambridge History of the Book in Britain*. Vol. 2, *1100–1400*. Cambridge: Cambridge University Press, 2008.

Moss, Ann. *Printed Commonplace-books and the Structuring of Renaissance Thought*. Oxford: Clarendon Press, 1996.

Mulcaster, Richard. *The first part of the elementarie: vvhich entreateth chefelie of the right writing of our English tung*. London: Thomas Vautroullier, 1582.

Mullaney, Thomas S. *The Chinese Typewriter: A History*. Cambridge, MA: MIT Press, 2017.

Müller-Wille, Staffan, and Isabelle Charmantier. "Lists as Research Technologies." *Isis* 103, no. 4 (2012): 743–752.

———. "Natural History and Information Overload: The Case of Linnaeus." *Studies in History and Philosophy of Biological and Biomedical Sciences* 43, no. 1 (2012): 4–15.

Müller-Wille, Staffan, and Sara Scharf. "Indexing Nature: Carl Linnaeus (1707–1778) and His Fact-Gathering Strategies." In *Working Papers on the Nature of Evidence: How Well Do "Facts" Travel?* No. 36/08. London: London School of Economics, 2009.

Munby, A. N. L., and Lenore Coral, eds. *British Book Sale Catalogs, 1676–1800: A Union List*. London: Mansell, 1977.

Mure, Konrad von. *Fabularius*. Edited by Tom van de Loo. Turnhout: Brepols, 2006.

Murphy, Andrew, ed. *The Renaissance Text: Theory, Editing, Textuality*. Manchester: Manchester University Press, 2000.

Myers, Robin, Michael Harris, and Giles Mandelbrote, eds. *Books for Sale: The Advertising and Promotion of Print Since the Fifteenth Century*. London: British Library, 2009.

Naudé, Gabriel. *Advis pour dresser une bibliothèque*. Leipzig: Veb Edition, 1963, first published 1627; also as *Instructions concerning erecting of a library*, "interpreted by Jo. Evelyn." London: n.p., 1661.

———. "News from France, or, A Description of the Library of Cardinal Mazarin, *and* Surrender of the Library of Cardinal Mazarin." In Dana and Kent, *Literature of Libraries* (above). Translated by Victoria Richmond and John Cotton Dana.

Nelson's Perpetual Loose-leaf Encyclopaedia. Edited by John H. Finley. New York: Nelson's, 1909–.

Neng-fu, Kuang. "Chinese Library Science in the Twelfth Century." *Libraries and Culture* 26, no. 2 (1991): 357–371.

Newman, L. M. "Leibniz (1646–1716) and the German Library Scene." *Library Association Pamphlet* no. 28. London: Library Association, 1966.

Nichols, Stephen G., and Siegfried Wenzel, eds. *The Whole Book: Cultural Perspectives on the Medieval Miscellany*. Ann Arbor: University of Michigan Press, 1996.

Noinville, Jacques Bernard Durey de. *Dissertation sur les bibliotheques, avec une table alphabétique, tant des ouvrages publiés sous le titre de* Bibliothéques . . . Paris: Hug. Chaubert, 1758.

Nolcken, Christina von. "Some Alphabetical *Compendia* and How Preachers Used Them in Fourteenth-century England." *Viator* 12 (1981): 271–288.

Norris, Dorothy May. *A History of Cataloging and Cataloging Methods, 1100–1850*. London: Grafton & Co., 1939.

Noyes, Gertrude. "The First English Dictionary: Cawdrey's Table Alphabeticall." *Modern Language Notes* 58, no. 8 (1943): 600–605.

Olson, David R. *The World on Paper: The Conceptual and Cognitive Implications of Writing and Reading*. Cambridge: Cambridge University Press, 1994.

Ong, Walter. *Interfaces of the Word: Studies in the Evolution of Consciousness and Culture*. Ithaca, NY: Cornell University Press, 1977.

———. *Orality and Literacy: The Technologizing of the Word*. London: Methuen, 1982.

———. *The Presence of the Word: Some Prolegomena for Cultural and Religious History*. New Haven, CT: Yale University Press, 1967.

Ortelius, Abraham. *Theatrum orbis terrarum*. Introduction by R. A. Skelton. Facsimile of first, 1570, ed. Amsterdam: N. Israel/Meridian, 1964.

Osselton, N. E. *The Dumb Linguists: A Study of the Earliest English and Dutch Dictionaries*. Leiden: Sir Thomas Browne Institute, 1973.

Painting-Stubbs, Clare. "Abraham Fleming: Elizabethan Maker of Indexes and 'Tables.'" *The Indexer* 29, no. 3 (2011): 109–113.

———. "Abraham Fleming: Writer, Cleric and Preacher in Elizabethan and Jacobean London." PhD thesis, University of London, 2011.

Parkes, M. B. *Pause and Effect: An Introduction to the History of Punctuation in the West*. Berkeley: University of California Press, 1993.

———. "The Provision of Books." In *The History of the University of Oxford*. Vol. 2, *Late Mediaeval Oxford*, edited by J. I. Catto and T. A. R. Evans. Oxford: Oxford University Press, 1992.

Pepys, Samuel. *The Diary of Samuel Pepys*. Edited by Robert Latham and William Matthews. London: Bell & Hyman, 1970–1983.

Petiver, Jacobo [James]. *Musei Petiveriani Centuria Prima Rariora Naturae Continens: viz. Animalia, Fossilia, Plantas . . .* London: S. Smith & B. Walford, 1695.

Pettee, Julia. "The Development of Authorship Entry and the Formulation of Authorship Rules . . . " *Library Quarterly* 6, no. 3 (1936): 270–290.

Pfander, H. G. "Mediaeval Friars and Some Alphabetical Reference-books for Sermons." *Medium Ævum* 3 (1934): 19–29.

Poleg, Eyal, and Laura Light, eds. *Form and Function in the Late Medieval Bible*. Leiden: Brill, 2013.

Pollard, Graham, and Albert Ehrman. *The Distribution of Books by Catalog, from the Invention of Printing to AD 1800 . . .* Cambridge: for the Roxburghe Club, 1965.

Pool, Ithiel de Sola, ed. *The Social Impact of the Telephone*. Cambridge, MA: MIT Press, 1977.

Rabnett, Mark. "The First Printed Indexes: A Study of Indexing Techniques in Some Incunabula." *Cataloging & Classification Quarterly* 2, nos. 3–4 (1982): 87–102.

Ranz, Jim. *The Printed Book Catalog in American Libraries, 1723–1900*. Chicago: American Library Association, 1964.

Ray, John D. "The Emergence of Writing in Egypt." *World Archaeology* 17, no. 3 (1986): 307–316.

Reale, Nancy M., and Ruth E. Sternglantz, eds. *Satura: Studies in Medieval Literature in Honour of Robert R. Raymo*. Donington, Lincolnshire: Shaun Tyas, 2001.

Rolle, Henry. *Un abridgment des plusieurs cases et resolutions del Common Ley: Alphabeticalment digest desouth severall Titles*. London: A. Crooke et al., 1668.

Rosemann, Philipp W., ed. *Expositio in Epistolam Sancti Pauli ad Galatas*. In *The Works of Robert Grosseteste of Lincoln*. Vol. 130. Turnhout: Brepols, 1995.

Rosenberg, Daniel, ed. "Early Modern Information Overload." Special issue, *Journal of the History of Ideas* 64, no. 1 (2003).

Rouse, Mary A., and Richard H. Rouse. *Authentic Witnesses: Approaches to Medieval Texts and Manuscripts*. Notre Dame, IN: University of Notre Dame Press, 1991.

————. "Biblical Distinctions in the Thirteenth Century." *Archives d'histoire doctrinale et littéraire du moyen âge* 41 (1974): 27–37.

————. *Bound Fast with Letters: Medieval Writers, Readers, and Texts.* Notre Dame, IN: University of Notre Dame Press, 2013.

————. "Concordances et index." In *Mise en page et mise en texte du livre manuscript*, edited by Henri-Jean Martin and Jean Vezin. Paris: Éditions du Cercle de la Librairie, Promodis, 1990.

————. "From Flax to Parchment: A Monastic Sermon from 12th.-c. Durham." In *New Science Out of Old Books*, edited by Richard Beadle and A. J. Piper. Aldershot: Scolar, 1995.

————. "History of Alphabetization." In *Dictionary of the Middle Ages*, vol. 1, edited by Joseph R. Strayer, 204–207. New York: Charles Scribner's Sons, 1982.

————. "*Ordinatio* and *Compilatio* Revisited." In *Ad Litteram: Authoritative Texts and their Medieval Readers*, edited by Mark D. Jordan and Kent Emery Jr. Notre Dame, IN: University of Notre Dame Press, 1992.

————. *Preachers, Florilegia and Sermons: Studies on the* Manipulus florum *of Thomas of Ireland.* Toronto: Pontifical Institute of Mediaeval Studies, 1979.

————, eds. *Registrum Anglie de libris doctorum et auctorum veterum.* In Corpus of British Medieval Library Catalogs series. London: British Library, 1991.

————. "The Texts Called *Lumen Anime.*" *Archivum Fratrum Praedicatorum* 41 (1971): 5–113.

————. "The Verbal Concordance to the Scriptures." *Archivum Fratrum Praedicatorum* 44 (1974): 5–30.

Rouse, Richard H. "Cistercian Aids to Study in the 13th Century." In *Studies in Medieval Cistercian History*, vol. 2, edited by John R. Sommerfeldt. Kalamazoo, MI, Cistercian Publications, 1976.

————. "Florilegia and Latin Classical Authors in Twelfth- and Thirteenth-c. Orléans." *Viator* 10 (1970): 131–160.

Rovelstad, Mathilde V. "The Frankfurt Book Fair." *Journal of Library History, Philosophy, and Comparative Librarianship* 8, nos. 3–4 (1973): 113–123.

————. "Two Seventeenth-century Library Handbooks, Two Different Library Theories." *Libraries and Culture* 35, no. 4 (2000): 540–556.

Rozier, M. l'Abbé [François]. *Nouvelle table des articles contenus dans les volumes de l'Académie royale des sciences de Paris, depuis 1666 jusqu'en 1770 . . .* Paris: Ruault, 1775.

Rule, John C., and Ben S. Trotter. *A World of Paper: Louis XIV, Colbert de Torcy, and the Rise of the Information State.* Montreal and Kingston: McGill/ Queen's University Press, 2014.

Saenger, Paul. *Space Between Words: The Origins of Silent Reading.* Stanford, CA: Stanford University Press, 1997.

Sandler, Lucy Freeman. Omne bonum: *A Fourteenth-century Encyclopedia of Universal Knowledge.* London: Harvey Miller, 1996.

Schäfer, Jürgen. *Early Modern English Lexicography*. Oxford: Clarendon Press, 1989.

Schellenberg, Theodore R. *European Archival Practices in Arranging Records*. Washington, DC: National Archives and Records Service, 1975.

Schmitt, Jean-Claude. "Recueils franciscains d'*exempla* et perfectionnement des techniques intellectuelles du xiiie au xve siècle." *Bibliothèque de l'École des Chartes* 135, no. 1 (1977): 5–21.

Schulte-Albert, Hans G. "Gottfried Wilhelm Leibniz and Library Classification." *Journal of Library History* 6, no. 2 (1971): 133–152.

Senner, Wayne M., ed. *The Origins of Writing*. Lincoln: University of Nebraska Press, 1989.

Shapin, Steven. "The Invisible Technician." *American Scientist* 77 (1989): 554–563.

Shapiro, Fred R. "Origins of Bibliometrics, Citation Indexing, and Citation Analysis: The Neglected Legal Literature." *Journal of the American Society for Information Science* 43, no. 5 (1992): 337–339.

Sherman, Claire Richter, and Peter M. Lukehart, eds. *Writing on Hands: Memory and Knowledge in Early Modern Europe*. Carlisle, PA: Trout Gallery, Dickinson College, 2000.

Showalter, J. Camille, and Janet Driesbach, eds. *Wooton Patent Desks: A Place for Everything and Everything in Its Place*. Indianapolis: Indiana State Museum, 1983.

Small, Jocelyn Penny. *Wax Tablets of the Mind: Cognitive Studies of Memory and Literacy in Classical Antiquity*. London: Routledge, 2015.

Smallwood, Mary Lovett. *An Historical Study of Examinations and Grading Systems in Early American Universities: A Critical Study . . .* Cambridge, MA: Harvard University Press, 1935.

Smith, Pamela H., Amy R. W. Meyers, and Harold J. Cook, eds. *Ways of Making and Knowing: The Material Culture of Empirical Knowledge*. Ann Arbor: University of Michigan Press, 2014.

Sorlien, Robert Parker, ed. *The Diary of John Manningham of the Middle Temple, 1602–1603*. Hanover, NH: University Press of New England, 1976.

Stallybrass, Peter, Roger Chartier, J. Franklin Mowery, and Heather Wolfe. "Hamlet's Tables and the Technologies of Writing in Renaissance Italy." *Shakespeare Quarterly* 55, no. 4 (2004): 379–419.

Starnes, DeWitt. *Renaissance Dictionaries English-Latin and Latin-English*. Austin: University of Texas Press, 1954.

———. *Robert Estienne's Influence on Lexicography*. Austin: University of Texas Press, 1963.

Starnes, DeWitt, and Gertrude E. Noyes. *The English Dictionary from Cawdrey to Johnson, 1604–1755*. Revised by Gabriele Stein. Amsterdam/Philadelphia: John Benjamins, 1991.

Stein, Gabriele. *The English Dictionary before Cawdrey*. Tübingen: Max Niemeyer Verlag, 1985.

————. "Lexicographical Method and Usage in Cawdrey's *A Table Alphabeticall*." *Studia Neophilologica* 82, no. 2 (2010): 163–177.

————. *Sir Thomas Elyot as Lexicographer*. Oxford: Oxford University Press, 2014.

Stockwell, Foster. *A History of Information Storage and Retrieval*. Jefferson, NC: McFarland & Co., 2001.

Stolberg, Michael. "John Locke's 'New Method of Making Common-Place-Books': Tradition, Innovation and Epistemic Effects." *Early Science and Medicine* 19 (2014): 448–470.

Tankard, Paul. "Reading Lists." *Prose Studies* 28, no. 3 (2006): 337–360.

Taylor, Archer. *General Subject-Indexes Since 1548*. Philadelphia: University of Pennsylvania Press, 1966.

Teeuwen, Mariken, and Irene van Renswoude, eds. *The Annotated Book in the Early Middle Ages: Practices of Reading and Writing*. Turnhout: Brepols, 2017.

Tenner, Edward. "From Slip to Chip: How Evolving Techniques of Information-gathering and Retrieval Have Shaped the Way We Do Mental Work." *Harvard Magazine*, November–December 1990, 52–57.

————. "Keeping Tabs: The History of an Information Age Metaphor." *Technology Review*, February 2005, 71.

Thomas, David St. John, introduction. *Three Victorian Telephone Directories*. New York: Augustus M. Kelley, 1970.

Todd, John. *Index Rerum, or, Index of Subjects; Intended as a Manual, to aid the Student and the Professional Man in Preparing Himself for Usefulness*. London: Hamilton, Adams & Co. [?1835].

Vincent, David. *The Rise of Mass Literacy: Reading and Writing in Modern Europe*. Cambridge: Polity, 2000.

Vine, Angus. "Commercial Commonplacing: Francis Bacon, the Waste-Book, and the Ledger." *English Manuscript Studies, 1100–1700*. Edited by Peter Beal and A. S. G. Edwards. Vol. 16, *Manuscript Miscellanies, c. 1450–1700*, edited by Richard Beadle and Colin Burrow, 197–218. London: British Library, 2011.

Vismann, Cornelia. *Files: Law and Media Technology*. Translated by Geoffrey Winthrop-Young. Stanford, CA: Stanford University Press, 2008.

Vivo, Filippo de, Andrea Guidi, and Alessandro Silvestri, eds. "Archival Transformations in Early Modern Europe." Special issue, *European History Quarterly* 46, no. 3 (2016).

Walker, Alan. "Indexing Commonplace Books: John Locke's Method." *The Indexer* 22, no. 3 (2001): 114–118.

Wall-Randell, Sarah. "Doctor Faustus and the Printer's Devil." *Studies in English Literature, 1500–1900* 48, no. 2 (2008): 259–281.

Wallis, Faith. "*Communis et universalis*: The *Catholicon* of Giovanni Balbi of Genoa, O.P." Thesis, LMS, Toronto, Pontifical Institute of Mediaeval Studies, 1981.

———. "Structure and Philosophy in Mediaeval Encyclopaedias." Master's thesis, Montreal, McGill University, 1974.

Walters, Betty Lawson. *The King of Desks: Wooton's Patent Secretary*. Washington, DC: Smithsonian Institution, 1969.

Weinberg, Bella Hass. "The Earliest Hebrew Citation Indexes." In *Historical Studies in Information Science*, edited by Trudi Bellardo Hahn and Michael Buckland. Medford, NJ: American Society for Information Science, 1998.

———. "Indexes and Religion: Reflections on Research in the History of Indexes." *The Indexer* 21, no. 3 (1999): 111–118.

———. "The Index of a Sixteenth-century Architecture Book." *The Indexer* 23, no. 3 (2003): 140–148.

———. "Index Structures in Early Hebrew Biblical Word Lists: Preludes to the First Latin Concordances." *The Indexer* 22, no. 4 (2001): 178–186.

Weinberger, David. *Everything Is Miscellaneous: The Power of the New Digital Disorder*. New York: Times Books/Henry Holt, 2007.

Wellisch, Hans. "Early Multilingual and Multiscript Indexes in Herbals." *The Indexer* 11, no. 2 (1978): 81–102.

———. "How to Make an Index, 16th-century Style: Conrad Gessner on Indexes and Catalogs." *International Classification* 8, no. 1 (1981): 10–15.

———. "Incunabula Indexes." *The Indexer* 19, no. 1 (1994): 3–12.

———. "The Oldest Printed Indexes." *The Indexer* 15, no. 2 (1986): 73–82.

White, Hayden. *The Content of the Form: Narrative Discourse and Historical Representation*. Baltimore: Johns Hopkins University Press, 1987.

Wilkins, Ernest H. "Early Alphabetical Indexes." In *The Manly Anniversary Studies in Language and Literature*. Chicago: University of Chicago Press, 1923.

Wilkins, John. *An Essay Towards a Real Character, and a Philosophical Language*. Menston: Scolar, 1968. First published 1668.

Willis, John. *The Art of Memory as it Dependeth upon Places and Ideas*. 1621. Facsimile edition. Amsterdam: Da Capo, 1973.

Wilson, Edward. *A Descriptive Index of the English Lyrics in John of Grimestone's Preaching Book*. Oxford: Medium Ævum Monographs, 1977.

Wilson-Lee, Edward. *The Catalog of Shipwrecked Books: Young Columbus and the Quest for a Universal Library*. London: William Collins, 2018.

Witty, Francis J. "The Beginnings of Indexing and Abstracting: Some Notes Towards a History of Indexing and Abstracting in Antiquity and the Middle Ages." *The Indexer* 8, no. 4 (1973): 193–198.

Wright, Alex. *Cataloging the World: Paul Otlet and the Birth of the Information Age*. Oxford: Oxford University Press, 2014.

———. *Glut: Mastering Information Through the Ages*. Washington, DC: Joseph Henry, 2007.

Xue, Shiqui. "Chinese Lexicography Past and Present." *Dictionaries* vol. 4 (1982): 151–169.

Yale, Elizabeth. *Sociable Knowledge: Natural History and the Nation in Early Modern Britain*. Philadelphia: University of Pennsylvania Press, 2016.

Yates, Frances. *The Art of Memory*. Harmondsworth: Penguin, 1969.

Yates, JoAnne. *Control Through Communication: The Rise of System in American Management*. Baltimore: Johns Hopkins University Press, 1989.

Yeo, Richard. "Between Memory and Paperbooks: Baconianism and Natural History in Seventeenth-century England." *History of Science* 45, no. 1 (2007): 1–46.

———. *Encyclopaedic Visions: Scientific Dictionaries and Enlightenment Culture*. Cambridge: Cambridge University Press, 2001.

———. "Ephraim Chambers's *Cyclopaedia* (1728) and the Tradition of Commonplaces." *Journal of the History of Ideas* 57, no. 1 (1996): 157–175.

———. "John Locke's 'New Method' of Commonplacing: Managing Memory and Information." *Eighteenth-century Thought* 2 (2004): 1–38.

———. "Lost Encyclopedias: Before and After the Enlightenment." *Book History* 10, no. 1 (2007): 47–68.

———. "Notebooks as Memory Aids: Precepts and Practices in Early Modern England." *Memory Studies* 1, no. 1 (2008): 115–136.

———. *Notebooks, English Virtuosi, and Early Modern Science*. Chicago: University of Chicago Press, 2014.

Yong, Heming, and Jing Peng. *Chinese Lexicography: A History from 1046 BC to AD 1911*. Oxford: Oxford University Press, 2008.

Young, Peter. *Person to Person: The International Impact of the Telephone*. Cambridge: Granta, 1991.

Zeegers, Margaret, and Deirdre Barron. *Gatekeepers of Knowledge: A Consideration of the Library, the Book and the Scholar in the Western World*. Oxford: Chandos Publishing, 2010.

NOTES

PREFACE

1. Cited in Wayne M. Senner, ed., *The Origins of Writing* (Lincoln: University of Nebraska Press, 1989), 12.

2. This point is made by Mary A. Rouse and Richard H. Rouse, "History of Alphabetization," *Dictionary of the Middle Ages*, ed. Joseph R. Strayer (New York: Charles Scribner's Sons, 1982), 1:205.

3. The bibliography was by François Grudé, Sieur de La Croix du Maine, whose dedication in his *Bibliothèque du sieur de La Croix du Maine, qui est un catalog général de toutes sortes d'auteurs qui ont escrit en français* . . . (1584) is cited by Roger Chartier, *The Order of Books: Readers, Authors, and Libraries in Europe Between the Fourteenth and the Eighteenth Centuries*, trans. Lydia G. Cochrane (Cambridge: Polity, 1994), 77.

4. Edward Tenner, "From Slip to Chip: How Evolving Techniques of Information-gathering and Retrieval Have Shaped the Way We Do Mental Work," *Harvard Magazine*, November–December 1990, 54. I am grateful to Mr. Tenner for supplying me with a copy of this difficult-to-locate essay.

5. Peter Birks, ed., "Introduction," *The Classification of Obligations* (Oxford: Clarendon, 1997), v. I am grateful to Justice Nicholas Kasirer, whose thoughts on alphabetical order and the law in "Pothier from A to Z," in *Mélanges Jean Pineau*, ed. Benoît Moore (Montreal: Éditions Thémis, 2003), led me to this work.

6. Jorge Luis Borges, "The Analytical Language of John Wilkins," in *Other Inquisitions, 1937–1952*, trans. Ruth L. C. Simms (London: Souvenir, 1973), 104, 103. John Wilkins's 1668 publication is *An Essay Towards a Real Character, and a Philosophical Language* (Scolar, 1968).

7. While "abracadabra" definitely finds its origins in the ABCD opening of the alphabet, more than that cannot be said with certainty. The *Oxford English Dictionary* dates the earliest use of the word to fourth-century Latin, but carefully notes that the evidence regarding its etymology is unverifiable.

8. David Diringer with Reinhold Regensburger, *The Alphabet: A Key to the History of Mankind*, rev. ed. (London: Hutchinson, 1968), 1:1. It must be added that since this was written, the University of London has overseen a flourishing Museum of Writing Research Collection.

9. These forms of reading are parsed by Patricia Wright, "The Need for Some Theories of NOT Reading: Some Psychological Aspects of the Human-Computer Interface," in *Working Models of Human Perception*, ed. Ben Elsendoorn and Herman Bouma (London: Academic Press, 1989), 320–321. Samuel Johnson divided his reading into "hard study," which involved close reading and note-taking; "perusal," or looking something up; "curious reading," for novels or narrative history; and "mere reading" of newspapers, journals, and other current material. These and other types of reading are cited in Ann Blair, "Reading Strategies for Coping with Information Overload, ca. 1550–1700," *Journal of the History of Ideas* 64, no. 1 (2003): 13.

10. The notion that most reading is goal oriented rather than narrative driven comes from Mike Esbester, "Nineteenth-century Timetables and the History of Reading," *Book History* 12 (2009): 159–160.

11. Stephen A. Barney, W. J. Lewis, J. A. Beach, Oliver Berghof, with Muriel Hall, eds. and trans., *The Etymologies of Isidore of Seville* (Cambridge: Cambridge University Press, 2006), 401.

12. Mary J. Carruthers, *The Book of Memory: A Study of Memory in Medieval Culture* (Cambridge: Cambridge University Press, 1990), 43.

13. Cited in Daniel R. Headrick, *When Information Came of Age: Technologies of Knowledge in the Age of Reason and Revolution, 1700–1850* (New York: Oxford University Press, 2000), 4.

CHAPTER 1. A IS FOR ANTIQUITY

1. Diringer and Regensburger, *The Alphabet*, 1:5–11.

2. This is the insight of Don G. Bouwhuis, "Reading as Goal-Driven Behaviour," in Elsendoorn and Bouma, *Working Models of Human Perception*, 344–345.

3. My description of cuneiform is derived from Diringer and Regensburger, *The Alphabet*, 1:18–20; Piotr Michalowski, "Mesopotamian Cuneiform," 33–36, and Jerrold S. Cooper, "Sumerian and Akkadian," 37–57, both in *The World's Writing Systems*, ed. Peter Daniels and William Bright (New York: Oxford University Press, 1996).

4. Tom McArthur, *Worlds of Reference: Lexicography, Learning and Language, from the Clay Tablet to the Computer* (Cambridge: Cambridge University Press, 1986), 21–22.

5. The two paragraphs on Egyptian writing systems come from Robert K. Ritner, "Egyptian Writing," in Daniels and Bright, *The World's Writing Systems*, 73–84; Anne-Marie Christin, ed., *A History of Writing: From Hieroglyph to Multimedia*,

trans. Josephine Bacon, Deke Dusinbere, and Ian McMorran (Paris: Flammarion, 2002), 45ff.; Henry George Fischer, "The Origin of Egyptian Hieroglyphs," in Senner, *The Origins of Writing*, 59–76.

6. Peter T. Daniels, "Grammatology," in Daniels and Bright, *The World's Writing Systems*, 1–2. The three he lists are Sumerian/Egyptian, Chinese, and Mesoamerican. There is some question around the runes of Rapa Nui (Easter Island). These RongoRongo glyphs have yet to be deciphered, and it is not certain that they are a full writing script. If they are, they are the sole independent Polynesian script, and a fourth to be added to the above list.

7. William G. Bolts, "Early Chinese Writing," in Daniels and Bright, *The World's Writing Systems*, 191–194.

8. Floyd G. Lounsbury, "The Ancient Writing of Middle America," in Senner, *The Origins of Writing*, 203ff.

9. Henri-Jean Martin, *The History and Power of Writing*, trans. Lydia G. Cochrane (Chicago: University of Chicago Press, 1988), 37.

10. This is the idea of Walter Ong, *The Presence of the Word: Some Prolegomena for Cultural and Religious History* (New Haven, CT: Yale University Press, 1967), 42–43.

11. A summary of the Wadi el-Ḥôl finds can be found in John Coleman Darnell, F. W. Dobbs-Allsopp, Marilyn J. Lundberg, P. Kyle McCarter, and Bruce Zuckerman, "Two Early Alphabetic Inscriptions from the Wadi el-Ḥôl: New Evidence for the Origin of the Alphabet from the Western Desert of Egypt," *Annual of the American Schools of Oriental Research* 59 (2005): 63–124; and André Lemaire, "The Origin of the Western Semitic Alphabet and Scripts," in Christin, *A History of Writing*, 203–215.

12. These prophets were Isaiah, Jeremiah, Ezekiel, Hosea, Joel, Amos, Obadiah, Jonah, Micah, Nahum, Habakkuk, Zephaniah, Haggai, Zechariah, and Malachi. The first three probably lived in the eighth century BCE, although the biblical texts were possibly written in the sixth century BCE; the remainder were probably written between the sixth and fourth centuries BCE.

13. The idea of the alphabet flourishing in egalitarian or skeptical climes: Frank Moore Cross, "The Invention and Development of the Alphabet," in Senner, *The Origins of Writing*, 77, 86.

14. James A. Bellamy, "The Arabic Alphabet," in Senner, *The Origins of Writing*, 94–96.

15. Diringer and Regensburger, *The Alphabet*, 1:145.

16. McArthur, *Worlds of Reference*, 25.

17. Klaas R. Veenhof, "Archives of Assyrian Traders," in Maria Brosius, ed., *Ancient Archives and Archival Traditions: Concepts of Record-Keeping in the Ancient World* (Oxford: Oxford University Press, 2003), 102–103.

18. Jerrold S. Cooper, "Sumerian and Akkadian," in Daniels and Bright, *The World's Writing Systems*, 40.

19. All these are cited in M. O'Connor, "Alphabet as Technology," in Daniels and Bright, *The World's Writing Systems*, 291–292, although undated. The dates for the examples can be found in: for Nimrud, A. R. Millard, "Alphabetical Inscriptions on Ivories from Nimrud," *Iraq* 24, no. 1 (1962): 41, 50; for the ship, later wrecked off the coast of Sicily, Aïcha ben Abed ben Khader and David Soren, *Carthage: A Mosaic of Ancient Tunisia* (New York: W. W. Norton, 1987), 33; and for Petra, Philip C. Hammond, David J. Johnson, and Richard N. Jones, "A Religio-Legal Nabataean Inscription from the Atargatis/Al-'Uzza Temple at Petra," *Bulletin of the American Schools of Oriental Research* 263, no. 1 (1986): 77.

20. Martin, *History and Power of Writing*, 47.

21. Lloyd W. Daly, *Contributions to a History of Alphabetization in Antiquity and the Middle Ages* (Brussels: Latomus, 1967), 11–15.

22. This is a point made by Ann Blair, *Too Much to Know: Managing Scholarly Information Before the Modern Age* (New Haven, CT: Yale University Press, 2010), 18.

23. Aristotle's *Constitutions*: Daly, *Contributions*, 16–17; Aristotle's *Politics*: John J. Keaney, "The Alleged Alphabetization of Aristotle's *Politeia*," *Classical Philology* 64, no. 4 (1969): 213–218, although he does not make the link to the wider use of alphabetical order in Ptolemaic Egypt.

24. Myrto Hatzimichali, "Encyclopaedism in the Alexandrian Library," in *Encyclopaedism from Antiquity to the Renaissance*, ed. Jason König and Greg Woolf (Cambridge: Cambridge University Press, 2013), 76.

25. Daly, *Contributions*, 22–25, is the voice of sanity in this discussion, as is Rudolf Blum, *Kallimachos: The Alexandrian Library and the Origins of Bibliography*, trans. Hans H. Wellisch (Madison: University of Wisconsin Press, 1991), 226–227, who also attributes the alphabetization to Zenodotus. Others assert without hesitation that Callimachus was the author of the *Pinakes*, and they were ordered alphabetically. See, for example, Margaret Zeegers and Deirdre Barron, *Gatekeepers of Knowledge: A Consideration of the Library, the Book and the Scholar in the Western World* (Oxford: Chandos, 2010), 12–13; Fred Lerner, *The Story of Libraries: From the Invention of Writing to the Computer Age* (New York: Continuum, 2009), 16–17.

26. Hatzimichali, "Encyclopaedism," in König and Woolf, *Encyclopaedism from Antiquity to the Renaissance*, 76–77.

27. Daly, *Contributions*, 23, 40.

28. Ibid., 45–50, 75.

29. Werner Hüllen, *English Dictionaries, 800–1700: The Topical Tradition* (Oxford: Clarendon Press, 2006), 30–31.

30. Daly, *Contributions*, 20–21; Blum, *Kallimachos*, 185.

31. Daly, *Contributions*, 61.

32. Ibid., 41, 10–51.

33. Ibid., 56, 52.

34. Ibid., 34–35.

35. John Wilkins, "Galen and Athenaeus in the Hellenistic Library," in *Ordering Knowledge in the Roman Empire*, ed. Jason König and Tim Whitmarsh (Cambridge: Cambridge University Press, 2007), 83.

36. Daly, *Contributions*, 58, gives the history of these copies. Other historians of lexicography are more cavalier. Robert Collison, *A History of Foreign-Language Dictionaries* (London: André Deutsch, 1982), 31, for example, says merely that Marcus Verrius Flaccus's work "was arranged in alphabetical order," without adding that we do not know when, or by whom.

37. Daly, *Contributions*, 30.

38. Wayne A. Wiegand and Donald G. Davis Jr., *Encyclopedia of Library History* (New York: Garland, 1994), 133–134. On the categories, see also Foster Stockwell, *A History of Information Storage and Retrieval* (Jefferson, NC: McFarland, 2001), 23.

39. Heming Yong and Jing Peng, *Chinese Lexicography: A History from 1046 BC to AD 1911* (Oxford: Oxford University Press, 2008), 28, 35, 52, 69.

40. Francis J. Witty, "The Beginnings of Indexing and Abstracting: Some Notes Towards a History of Indexing and Abstracting in Antiquity and the Middle Ages," *The Indexer* 8, no. 4 (1973): 194, mentions its alphabetical order, but not in terms of memorization. Witty also fails to consider that the copies of this work that survive are all substantially later, and may not reflect the original arrangement.

41. Daly, *Contributions*, 37–38. In another work Athenaeus listed 101 different kinds of drinking vessels in almost absolute alphabetical order, although this more complex ordering system might be owing to later copyists.

42. König and Whitmarsh, *Ordering Knowledge*, 32–33, which also disregards the question of later copies.

43. Peter Barr Reid Forbes, Robert Browning, and Nigel Wilson, "Iulius Pollux, of Naucratis," *Oxford Classical Dictionary*, accessed online, August 3, 2018.

44. König and Whitmarsh, *Ordering Knowledge*, 34.

45. Yang Juzhong, "The Origin of Ancient Chinese Papermaking," in *Paper as a Medium of Cultural Heritage: Archaeology and Conservation*, ed. Rosella Graziaplena, with Mark Livesey, 25th Congress, Rome–Verona, August 30 to September 6, 2002 (Rome: Istituto centrale per la patologia del libro, 2004), 328–336, is one of many who attribute the invention to Cai Lun in 105 CE. Jonathan M. Bloom, *Paper Before Print: The History and Impact of Paper in the Islamic World* (New Haven, CT: Yale University Press, 2001), 32–33, elaborates on its longer history.

46. Cited in Timothy D. Barnes, *Constantine and Eusebius* (Cambridge, MA: Harvard University Press, 1981), 107.

47. Jerome's *Liber Interpretationis*, in Daly, *Contributions*, 65; however, Daly fails to note the reordering of the text that occurred in the thirteenth century, the history of which can be found in Rouse and Rouse, "History of Alphabetization," 205. The suggestion regarding memorization appears in Carruthers, *Book of Memory*, 115–116.

CHAPTER 2. B IS FOR THE BENEDICTINES

1. Jerusalem, Cirta, and Tabennisis: John Willis Clark, *The Care of Books: An Essay on the Development of Libraries and Their Fittings, from the Earliest Times to the End of the Eighteenth Century* (Cambridge: Cambridge University Press, 1909), 52–54; Vivarium: Ladislaus Buzás, *German Library History, 800–1945*, trans. William D. Boyd, with the assistance of Irmgard H. Wolfe (Jefferson, NC: McFarland, 1986), 3.

2. Clark, *Care of Books*, 54–55.

3. Ibid., 96.

4. It is Buzás, *German Library History*, 15, who ventures a guess at the library's contents.

5. Translation by Andrew F. West, *Alcuin and the Rise of Christian Schools* (New York: Charles Scribners' Sons, 1903), 34–35.

6. I am indebted to Tom Holland for alerting me to Gregory of Nyssa's saintly siblings.

7. Clark, *Care of Books*, 47.

8. Stephen A. Barney et al., *The Etymologies of Isidore of Seville* (Cambridge: Cambridge University Press, 2006), 24.

9. The primary sorting via first-letter alphabetization is visible to any reader, and has been widely noted. The secondary sorting method: Jean Berger, "Indexation, Memory, Power and Representations at the Beginning of the Twelfth Century: The Rediscovery of Pages from the Tables to the *Liber de Honoribus* . . . ," trans. Maureen MacGlashan, *The Indexer* 25, no. 2 (2006): 95–96; tertiary sorting: Andy Merrills, "Isidore's *Etymologies*: On Words and Things," in König and Woolf, *Encyclopaedism from Antiquity to the Renaissance*, 319–320.

10. These examples are from Alfred W. Crosby, *The Measure of Reality: Quantification and Western Society, 1250–1600* (Cambridge: Cambridge University Press, 1997), 32–34, 45–46.

11. Rachida el Moussaoui et al., "Effectiveness of Discontinuing Antibiotic Treatment after 3 days v. 8 days in Mild to Moderate-severe Community Acquired Pneumonia," *British Medical Journal*, 332 (2006): 11355, accessed online October 17, 2018, is just one of several papers on the subject.

12. Augustine and Bartholomew are both cited in Faith Wallis, "Structure and Philosophy in Mediaeval Encyclopaedias" (master's thesis, McGill University, 1974), 85, 178.

13. J.-P. Diény, "Les Encyclopédies chinoises," in *L'Encyclopédisme: Actes du Colloque de Caen, 12–16 janvier 1987*, ed. Annie Becq (Paris: Éditions aux Amateurs de Livres, and Klincksieck, 1991), 195ff.

14. This work is cited in Jack Lynch, *You Could Look It Up: The Reference Shelf from Ancient Babylon to Wikipedia* (New York: Bloomsbury, 2016), 84, although many medical texts of the period followed the same organizing principle.

15. Frank Trombley, "The *Taktika* of Nikephoros Ouranos and Military Encyclopaedism," in *Pre-Modern Encyclopaedic Texts: Proceedings of the Second COMERS Congress, Groningen, 1–4 July 1996*, ed. Peter Binkley (Leiden: Brill, 1997), 263.

16. Gabriele Stein, *The English Dictionary before Cawdrey* (Tübingen: Max Niemeyer Verlag, 1985), 8–10.

17. Rosamond McKitterick, "Glossaries and Other Innovations in Carolingian Book Production," in *Turning Over a New Leaf: Change and Development in the Medieval Manuscript*, Studies in Renaissance Book Culture, ed. Erik Kwakkel, Rosamond McKitterick, and Rodney Thomson (Leiden: Leiden University Press, 2012), 46–47.

18. For example, McKitterick, "Glossaries and Other Innovations," in ibid., 53–54, suggests that the Epinal Glossary may well have been copied into what is known as the Erfurt I fragment, dating to the second quarter of the ninth century; Erfurt II and Erfurt III, but not I, are in second-letter alphabetical order.

19. It is McKitterick, "Glossaries and Other Innovations," in ibid., 44–47, who draws this careful distinction. Others, such as Berger, "Indexation, Memory," 96, and Paul Saenger, *Space Between Words: The Origins of Silent Reading* (Stanford, CA: Stanford University Press, 1997), 91–92, write as though all the copies were identical.

20. Bella Hass Weinberg, "Index Structures in Early Hebrew Biblical Word Lists: Preludes to the First Latin Concordances," *The Indexer* 22, no. 4 (2001): 180–181.

21. Shimeon Brisman, *A History and Guide to Judaic Dictionaries and Concordances* (Hoboken, NJ: Ktav, 2000), 2–3, 7–8.

22. McArthur, *Worlds of Reference*, 75.

23. Stein, *English Dictionary before Cawdrey*, 45.

24. The preface to Papias cited in Daly, *Contributions*, 71–72. A discussion of the layout: Mary A. Rouse and Richard H. Rouse, *Authentic Witnesses: Approaches to Medieval Texts and Manuscripts* (Notre Dame, IN: University of Notre Dame Press, 1991), 193–194.

25. M. T. Clanchy, *From Memory to Written Record: England 1066–1307* (London: Edward Arnold, 1979), 160–161.

26. Rouse and Rouse, *Authentic Witnesses*, 194.

27. All the examples in this paragraph, and the citation from Aristotle in the previous paragraph, come from Bill Katz, *Cuneiform to Computer: A History of Reference Sources*, History of the Book Series, no. 4 (Lanham, MD: Scarecrow, 1998), 54ff.

28. A great deal of scholarship exists on this work, because one of the three surviving manuscripts, Codex Parisinus Graecus 923, is the only surviving illustrated Byzantine florilegium, and is both breathtakingly beautiful and an entire anomaly in format. However, little of this scholarship is devoted to the text and its structure. Maria Evangelatou, "Word and Image in the 'Sacra Parallela' (Codex Parisinus Graecus 923)," *Dumbarton Oaks Paper* 62 (2008): 116, is one of the few to give the text even passing notice.

CHAPTER 3. C IS FOR CATEGORIES

1. Buzás, *German Library History,* 9.

2. Ibid., 11–12.

3. These figures appear, passim, in ibid.

4. Ibid., 23.

5. Daly, *Contributions,* 64.

6. Ian Wood, "Administration, Law and Culture in Merovingian Gaul," in *The Uses of Literacy in Early Mediaeval Europe,* ed. Rosamond McKitterick (Cambridge: Cambridge University Press, 1990), 65, cites two early cases, in the Auvergne and Angers, in the sixth century.

7. Rouse and Rouse, *Authentic Witnesses,* 194–195.

8. Thomas F. X. Noble, "Literacy and the Papal Government in Late Antiquity and the Early Middle Ages," in McKitterick, *Uses of Literacy,* 86–87, 90–91.

9. Daly, *Contributions,* 80, dates the ledger and its likely later index. The link to Cardinal Deusdedit is my own.

10. This development is outlined by Crosby, *Measure of Reality,* 50ff.

11. Ibid., 70, 72.

12. Ibid., 123.

13. Clanchy, *From Memory,* 19–20, 56, 31.

14. The change in kind and quantity: ibid., 41–42; the phrase "invisible technicians" is from Steven Shapin, "The Invisible Technician," *American Scientist* 77 (1989): 554–563.

15. Clanchy, *From Memory,* 44.

16. Charters: Ivan Illich and Barry Sanders, *ABC: The Alphabetization of the Popular Mind* (San Francisco, North Point, 1988), 36; population: Stephen Broadberry, Bruce M. S. Campbell, and Bas van Leeuwen, "English Medieval Population: Reconciling Time Series and Cross Sectional Evidence," July 27, 2010, especially Tables 3 and 4, 17–18, accessed online, February 22, 2018.

17. Cornelia Vismann, *Files: Law and Media Technology,* trans. Geoffrey Winthrop-Young (Stanford, CA: Stanford University Press, 2008), 76–77.

18. Kuang Neng-fu, "Chinese Library Science in the Twelfth Century," *Libraries and Culture* 26, no. 2 (1991): 357–367.

19. Richard Britnell, "Records and Record-keeping in Yuan China," in *Pragmatic Literacy, East and West, 1200–1330,* ed. Richard Britnell (Woodbridge: Boydell, 1997), 222–223.

20. Bloom, *Paper Before Print,* 12.

21. Megan K. Williams, "'This Continuous Writing': The Paper Chancellery of Bernhard Cles," in *Secretaries and Statecraft in the Early Modern World,* ed. Paul M. Dover (Edinburgh: Edinburgh University Press, 2016), 64. For the spread of paper in Europe, see also Graziaplena and Livesey, *Paper as a Medium of Cultural Heritage,* which has a number of essays covering different aspects of the subject.

22. Erik Kwakkel, "A New Type of Book for a New Type of Reader: The Emergence of Paper in Vernacular Book Production," *Library* 4, no. 3 (2003): 220–221.

23. Cited in Lucy Freeman Sandler, Omne bonum: *A Fourteenth-century Encyclopedia of Universal Knowledge* (London: Harvey Miller, 1996), 52. Its owner flourished c. 1330s/1340s.

24. Vismann, *Files*, 79–80.

25. Clanchy, *From Memory*, 239.

26. David Crouch, "Robert de Breteuil, third Earl of Leicester," in the *Oxford Dictionary of National Biography*, accessed online, September 2, 2018.

27. Clanchy, *From Memory*, 240.

28. Berger, "Indexation, Memory," 96–97.

29. Clanchy, *From Memory*, 123–124.

30. Nigel Ramsay, "Archive Books," in *The Cambridge History of the Book in Britain*, vol. 2, *1100–1400*, ed. Nigel J. Morgan and Rodney M. Thomson (Cambridge: Cambridge University Press, 2008), 422.

31. Paul D. A. Harvey, "English Estate Records, 1250–1330," in Britnell, *Pragmatic Literacy*, 129.

32. Olivier Guyotjeannin, "French Manuscript Sources, 1200–1330," in Britnell, *Pragmatic Literacy*, 55.

33. Lucy Freeman Sandler, "*Omne bonum*: *Compilatio* and *Ordinatio* in an English Illustrated Encyclopedia of the Fourteenth Century," in *Medieval Book Production: Assessing the Evidence, Proceedings of the Second Conference of the Seminar in the History of the Book to 1500, Oxford, July 1988*, ed. Linda L. Brownrigg (Los Altos Hills: Anderson-Lovelace/Red Gull, 1990), 198.

34. Ralph de Diceto, *Abbreviationes chronicorum* (before 1174), British Library, Cotton Claudius E.iii. The illustration on 55 is f.3v, and the symbols are explored by Laura Cleaver, www.bl.uk/medieval-english-french-manuscripts/articles/history-in-england-and-france.

35. Clanchy, *From Memory*, 142–143.

36. Hotot's estate book is in the British Library, BL Add MS 54228. The marginalia can be seen in an illustration in Clanchy, *From Memory*, plate xv, n.p. These are, of course, not the same as the historical footnote, the development of which in the modern period has been chronicled by Anthony Grafton, *The Footnote: A Curious History* (Cambridge, MA: Harvard University Press, 1997).

37. Cited in Clanchy, *From Memory*, 61–62.

38. These figures are cited by Lerner, *Story of Libraries*, 68–70.

39. Blanche B. Boyer and Richard McKeon, eds., *Peter Abailard:* Sic et Non, *A Critical Edition* (Chicago: University of Chicago Press, 1976), fasc. I, 6. The two complete manuscripts are in the Bibliothèque Municipale, Avranches, and Corpus Christi College, Cambridge.

40. Clanchy, *From Memory*, 84–85.

41. The number of citations is the estimate of Crosby, *Measure of Reality*, 57.

42. Ribhi Mustafa Elayyan, "The History of the Arabic-Islamic Libraries, 7th to 14th Centuries," *International Library Review* 22, no. 2 (1990): 122.

43. Mounira Chapoutot-Remadi, "L'Encyclopédie arabe au Xe siècle," in Becq, *L'Encyclopédisme*, 37–39.

44. Most scholars are silent on the subject of systems of organization. One of the few references I have seen, Elayyan, "Arabic-Islamic Libraries," 130, is worryingly inclusive, saying, "The arrangement of books in the Islamic libraries was [first] by subject" and then acquisition order, as though all Islamic libraries across all territories organized their books in identical fashion over the seven centuries covered by the article. It is possible, even if unlikely, but no sources are cited.

45. Chapoutot-Remadi, "L'Encyclopédie arabe," in Becq, *L'Encyclopédisme*, 42–45.

46. Sergei Shuiskii, "Encyclopedias and Dictionaries, Arabic and Persian," in *The Medieval Hebrew Encyclopedias of Science and Philosophy*, ed. Steven Harvey (Dordrecht: Kluwer, 2000), 444–445.

47. Osman Bakar, *Classification of Knowledge in Islam: A Study in Islamic Philosophies of Science* (Cambridge: Islamic Texts Society, 1998), 10, 21–25.

48. Wadād al-Qāḍī, "Biographical Dictionaries: Inner Structure and Cultural Significance," in *The Book in the Islamic World: The Written Word and Communication in the Middle East*, ed. George N. Atiyeh (Albany: State University of New York Press, 1995), 97–99.

49. Maaike van Berkel, "Opening Up a World of Knowledge: Mamluk Encyclopedias and their Readers," in König and Woolf, *Encyclopaedism from Antiquity to the Renaissance*, 371.

50. George Makdisi, *The Rise of Humanism in Classical Islam and the Christian West: With Special Reference to Scholasticism* (Edinburgh: Edinburgh University Press, 1990), 214.

51. Van Berkel, "Opening Up a World of Knowledge," in König and Woolf, *Encyclopaedism from Antiquity to the Renaissance*, 367ff.

52. Shuiskii, "Encyclopedias and Dictionaries," in Harvey, *Medieval Hebrew Encyclopedias*, 442–446.

53. Brisman, *Judaic Dictionaries*, 15–17.

54. For translators and their locations, Eva Albrecht, "The Organization of Vincent of Beauvais' *Speculum Maius* and of Some Other Latin Encyclopedias," in Harvey, *Medieval Hebrew Encyclopedias*, 58ff.

55. Blair, *Too Much to Know*, 12–13, notes how the rediscovery of these classics led to conservation efforts and therefore new encyclopedic compilations.

56. Good summaries on futhorc and Ogham can be found in Ruth P. M. Lehmann, "Ogham: The Ancient Script of the Celts," in Senner, *Origins of Writing*, 159–170; Damian McManus, "Ogham," in Daniels and Bright, *The World's Writing Systems*, 340–345; and Pierre-Yves Lambert, "Ogamic Script," in Christin, *A History of Writing*, 276–277.

57. The information in this and the previous paragraph is derived from Paul Saenger, "The Twelfth-century Reception of Oriental Languages and the Graphic *Mise en Page* of Latin Vulgate Bibles Copied in English," in *Form and Function in the Late Medieval Bible*, ed. Eyal Poleg and Laura Light (Leiden: Brill, 2013), 32–37.

58. Tamás Visi, "A Science of Lists? Medieval Jewish Philosophers as List-Makers," in *The Charm of a List: From the Sumerians to Computerised Data Processing*, ed. Lucie Doležalová (Newcastle: Cambridge Scholars Publishing, 2009), 18–20.

59. Martin, *History and Power of Writing*, 150–151.

60. Wallis, "Structure and Philosophy," 177.

61. Michael Twomey, "Encyclopaedias," in Morgan and Thomson, *Cambridge History of the Book in Britain*, 2:246–248. Bartholomew's "properties" begin with the great hierarchy, from God to mankind, to animals, to objects, and finally to the senses—color, smell, and so on, or, as the English translation had it: "For þe propirtees of þinges folewyth þe substaunce, þe ordre and þe distinccioun of propirtees schal be ordeyned to ordir and distinccioun of þe substaunce þerof." M. C. Seymour, ed., *On the Properties of Things: John Trevisa's Translation of Bartholomæus Anglicus, De Proprietatibus Rerum: A Critical Text* (Oxford: Clarendon Press, 1975), 1:41.

62. Konrad von Mure, *Fabularius*, ed. Tom van de Loo (Turnhout: Brepols, 2006), Prologue. I am grateful to Simone Mollea for translating this preface for me.

63. Albrecht, "Organization of Vincent of Beauvais' *Speculum Maius*," in Harvey, *Medieval Hebrew Encyclopedias*, 56–57; and Monique Paulmier-Foucart, "Ordre encyclopédique et organisation de la matière dans le *Speculum maius* de Vincent de Beauvais," in Becq, *L'Encyclopédisme*, 223.

64. The manuscript of James le Palmer, and the later index, is examined forensically by Lucy Freeman Sandler, "Index-Making in the Fourteenth-Century: Archbishop Arundel's Copy of the Gospel Commentary of William of Nottingham," in *Satura: Studies in Medieval Literature in Honour of Robert R. Raymo*, ed. Nancy M. Reale and Ruth E. Sternglantz (Donington, Lincolnshire: Shaun Tyas, 2001), 164–175. I am grateful to Professor Sandler for guiding me to this, as well as to the illustration of the index in Bodleian Laud Misc. 165, and the information in the caption that follows.

65. Erik Kwakkel, "The Margin as Editorial Space: Upgrading *Dioscorides alphabeticus* in Eleventh-century Monte Cassino," in *The Annotated Book in the Early Middle Ages: Practices of Reading and Writing*, ed. Mariken Teeuwen and Irene van Renswoude (Turnhout: Brepols, 2017), 323.

66. It has long been stated that this was the work of the Archbishop of Canterbury, Stephen Langton (1150–1228), in his early days in Paris, but Paul Saenger makes a convincing case for St. Albans, including noting that the earliest Bible in continental Europe to have modern numbering, from Cîteaux, dates from before

1200; Paris Bibles with modern divisions appear around 1200–1210, all from the abbey of St. Victor, which had strong ties to St. Albans. For the full discussion, see Saenger, "Twelfth-century Reception of Oriental Languages," in Poleg and Light, *Form and Function*, 31–64.

67. Rouse and Rouse, *Authentic Witnesses*, 202n28. I am grateful to Professor Gregory Hays of the University of Virginia who during the coronavirus quarantine came to my aid via Twitter to verify this citation.

CHAPTER 4. D IS FOR DISTINCTIONES

1. Rouse and Rouse, *Authentic Witnesses*, 211–212.

2. Ibid., 223, cites these examples, from a manuscript now in Rouen dating from before 1249.

3. Cited by Mary A. Rouse and Richard H. Rouse, "La naissance des index," in *Histoire de l'édition française*, vol. 1, *Le livre conquérant; Du moyen âge au xviiie siècle*, ed. Henri-Jean Martin, Roger Chartier, and Jean-Pierre Vivet (Paris: Promodis, 1983), 78. The English translation of Lombard's Latin, translated into French by the Rouses, is my own.

4. The scholars are Rouse and Rouse, *Authentic Witnesses*, 205–206.

5. The dates and numbers are in ibid., 205–206.

6. Cited in Rouse and Rouse, "History of Alphabetization," 205.

7. Cited in Paulmier-Foucart, "Ordre encyclopédique," in Becq, *L'Encyclopédisme*, 222–223. The translation of Vincent's letter is my own.

8. Freeman Sandler, "Index-Making in the Fourteenth-Century," in Reale and Sternglantz, *Satura*, 174.

9. Rouse and Rouse, *Authentic Witnesses*, 232–233; Richard William Hunt, "The Library of Robert Grosseteste," in *Robert Grosseteste, Scholar and Bishop: Essays in Commemoration . . .* , ed. D. A. Callus (Oxford: Clarendon Press, 1955), 121. Carruthers, *Book of Memory*, 118, suggests that the symbols were memory prompts.

10. This is the view of both Alberto Cevolini, "Making *notae* for Scholarly Retrieval: A Franciscan Case Study," in Teeuwen and Renswoude, *The Annotated Book*, 349–350; and Philipp W. Rosemann, in his notes to *Expositio in Epistolam Sancti Pauli ad Galatas*, in *The Works of Robert Grosseteste of Lincoln* (Turnhout: Brepols, 1995), 130:19–21, which I find persuasive.

11. Blair, *Too Much to Know*, 24.

12. Crosby, *Measure of Reality*, 64, for the invention of subcategorization; the quote appears in M. B. Parkes, "The Influence of the Concepts of *Ordinatio* and *Compilatio* on the Development of the Book," in *Medieval Learning and Literature: Essays Presented to Richard William Hunt*, ed. J. J. G. Alexander and M. T. Gibson (Oxford: Clarendon Press, 1976), 119.

13. Rouse and Rouse, *Authentic Witnesses*, 234. Notes made on a series of lectures on Lombard's *Sentences* given at Oxford in about 1256 have survived, in which we can see the new referencing system being tried out, with the text divided by letters in the margins, and every fifth line numbered. By this means, indexes could pinpoint a reference not merely to a page, but even to the line. M. B. Parkes, "The Provision of Books," in *The History of the University of Oxford*, vol. 2, *Late Medieval Oxford*, ed. J. I. Catto and T. A. R. Evans (Oxford: Oxford University Press, 1992), 443–444.

14. Ibid.

15. James Bowen, *A History of Western Education*, vol. 2, *Civilization of Europe, Sixth to Sixteenth Century* (London: Methuen, 1975), 125.

16. Mary A. Rouse and Richard H. Rouse, *Preachers, Florilegia and Sermons: Studies on the* Manipulus florum *of Thomas of Ireland* (Toronto: Pontifical Institute of Mediaeval Studies, 1979), 13; Rouse and Rouse, *Authentic Witnesses*, 226–227.

17. Rouse and Rouse, *Authentic Witnesses*, 236.

18. Bella Hass Weinberg, "Index Structures in Early Hebrew Biblical Word Lists," 185, apart from the information about the presence at the time of a Masoretic Bible in Lincoln, which is noted by Clanchy, *From Memory*, 156, although he does not connect it with Grosseteste and his indexes.

19. Rouse and Rouse, *Preachers, Florilegia*, 13.

20. Blair, *Too Much to Know*, 38–40, discusses the organizational system of concordances based on the pages that have survived.

21. The preacher was Nicholas Bozon, cited in Rouse and Rouse, *Preachers, Florilegia*, 10.

22. This tracing of the development of the concordance is narrated by Rouse and Rouse, *Authentic Witnesses*, 224–225, and in Mary A. Rouse and Richard H. Rouse, "Concordances et index," in *Mise en page et mise en texte du livre manuscrit*, ed. Henri-Jean Martin and Jean Vezin (Paris: Éditions du Cercle de la Librairie, Promodis, 1990), 219–221. Jean Châtillon, "Désarticulation et restructuration des textes à l'époque scolastique (XIe–XIIIe siècles)," in *La notion de paragraphe*, ed. Roger Laufer (Paris: Éditions du Centre National de la Recherche Scientifique, 1985), 32–33, makes a case for the idea that the subsection division A–G was developed by Thomas Gallus, who taught in Paris before moving to Italy in 1219; Mary A. Rouse and Richard H. Rouse, "The Verbal Concordance to the Scriptures," *Archivum Fratrum Praedicatorum* 44 (1974): 9–10, counter that there is no earlier surviving use of the A–G system than that second (first surviving) concordance. It is Clanchy, *From Memory*, 144–145, who adds John of Darlington to the team of concordance creators; Rouse and Rouse, "Concordances et index," 13–14, are less certain. It is they, too, who give the number of eighty for the surviving manuscripts, ibid., 17, and the Sorbonne's fifteen copies, 24. They also give space to the suggestion of those such as Sherman M. Kuhn, "The Preface to a Fifteenth-century

Concordance," *Speculum* 43, no. 2 (1968): 266, that the third version was produced by Conrad of Halberstadt, concluding ultimately, 18–19, that the weight of evidence is with St. Jacques.

23. Faith Wallis, "*Communis et universalis*: The *Catholicon* of Giovanni Balbi of Genoa, O.P." (thesis, LMS, Toronto, Pontifical Institute of Mediaeval Studies, 1981), 19. I am grateful to Professor Faith Wallis for giving me access to a copy of this work.

24. Rouse and Rouse, *Preachers, Florilegia*, 11–12, describes the *Concordancia morales bibliorum*.

25. Leonard Eugene Boyle, O.P., "'*E cathena e carcere*': The Imprisonment of Amaury de Montfort, 1276," in *Medieval Learning and Literature: Essays Presented to Richard William Hunt*, ed. J. J. G. Alexander and M. T. Gibson (Oxford: Clarendon Press, 1976), 379–386.

26. John of Chalons, cited by Christina von Nolcken, "Some Alphabetical *Compendia* and How Preachers Used Them in Fourteenth-century England," *Viator* 12 (1981): 275.

27. The author was Johannes de Mirfield in his *Florarium*, and it is Rouse and Rouse, "History of Alphabetization," 206, who note it. For the *compendia* more generally, von Nolcken, "Some Alphabetical *Compendia*," 271–274.

28. This appears in the copy now in the Bodleian Library, Auct.V.Q.IV 13. H. G. Pfander, "Mediaeval Friars and Some Alphabetical Reference-books for Sermons," *Medium Ævum* 3 (1934): 19.

29. Rouse and Rouse, *Authentic Witnesses*, 229.

30. This opposition is derived from Jacqueline Hamesse, "The Scholastic Model of Reading," in *A History of Reading in the West*, ed. Guglielmo Cavallo and Roger Chartier, trans. Lydia G. Cochrane (Amherst: University of Massachusetts Press, 1999), 110.

31. Hugh of Pisa, *Magnae derivationes*, cited in Wallis, "*Communis et universalis*," 15. There are no certain dates for the Hugh, or Huguccio, who wrote on grammar. In the past, he was assumed to have been the Huguccio (d. 1210) who was a canon lawyer and taught at the University of Bologna, producing a magisterial summary of Gratian, the *Summa decretum*, but today it is generally accepted that this is not the case. The confusion of the two Hughs dates from the eighteenth century, and many works continue to treat them as one. Wolfgang Müller, *Huguccio: The Life, Works, and Thought of a Twelfth-Century Jurist* (Washington, DC: Catholic University of America Press, 1994), in his first chapter, untangles them as much as possible.

32. Parkes, "*Ordinatio* and *Compilatio*," in Alexander and Gibson, *Medieval Learning and Literature*, 135.

33. Hugh of St. Victor, *Chronica*, cited in Earle Havens, *Commonplace Books: A History of Manuscripts and Printed Books from Antiquity to the Twentieth Century* (New Haven, CT: Beinecke Rare Book and Manuscript Library, 2001), 19.

34. Cited in Parkes, "*Ordinatio* and *Compilatio*," in Alexander and Gibson, *Medieval Learning and Literature*, 127.

35. Ann Moss, *Printed Commonplace-books and the Structuring of Renaissance Thought* (Oxford: Clarendon Press, 1996), 39–40.

36. Ibid., 27–28.

37. This breaking up of alphabetical order is noted by Rouse and Rouse, *Preachers, Florilegia*, 118.

38. Thomas's links with the university can be seen from the surviving copies of the *Manipulus florum*: of the 180 copies known today, more than 160 were produced by university copyists. Rouse and Rouse, *Authentic Witnesses*, 252.

39. Rouse and Rouse, *Preachers, Florilegia*, 94–95, 117–124.

40. Two scholars write adeptly on this change: Jean-Claude Boulanger, *Les inventeurs de dictionnaires. De l'*eduba *des scribes mésopotamiens au scriptorium des moines médiévaux* (Ottawa: Presses de l'Université d'Ottawa, 2003), 413–414; and Jean-Claude Schmitt, "Recueils franciscains d'*exempla* et perfectionnement des techniques intellectuelles du xiiie au xve siècle," *Bibliothèque de l'École des Chartes* 135, no. 1 (1977): 14ff.

41. This idea comes from M. B. Parkes, *Pause and Effect: An Introduction to the History of Punctuation in the West* (Berkeley: University of California Press, 1993), 23.

42. L. C. MacKinney, "Medieval Medical Dictionaries and Glossaries," in *Medieval and Historiographical Essays in Honor of James Westfall Thompson*, ed. James Lea Cate and Eugene N. Anderson (Chicago: University of Chicago Press, 1938), 244.

43. These works, and the citation, are from ibid., although I have slightly rephrased the translation found there.

44. Ibid., 255.

45. Stein, *English Dictionary before Cawdrey*, 47–48.

46. The information in this and the previous paragraph is derived from Crosby, *Measure of Reality*, 78–82.

CHAPTER 5. E IS FOR EXPANSION

1. Unless otherwise noted, the numbers of volumes and ordering methods of the catalogs are drawn from three sources: English libraries predominantly come from Dorothy May Norris, *A History of Cataloging and Cataloging Methods, 1100–1850* (London: Grafton, 1939); German from Buzás, *German Library History*; French and Italian from Rouse and Rouse, *Authentic Witnesses*. The list from Fulda is incomplete, with at least the first page missing, but it is indicative of the multiple copies owned by these institutions.

2. The Rochester list is described in Richard Sharpe, "Library Catalogs and Indexes," in Morgan and Thomson, *Cambridge History of the Book in Britain*, 2:199.

3. Cited in Buzás, *German Library History*, 131. I am grateful to Professor Faith Wallis for the translation.

4. The sixteenth-century librarian was Georg Carpentarius of Basel, cited in ibid., 131–132.

5. M. B. Parkes, "The Provision of Books," in Catto and Evans, *History of . . . Oxford*, 431.

6. Suggestions as to the date of the compilation of the *Registrum* have fluctuated over the years. In the 1930s, Norris, *Cataloging and Cataloging Methods*, settled on 1250–1296. Rouse and Rouse, *Authentic Witnesses*, 237, have more recently pushed that forward quite substantially, to sometime before 1331.

7. As with the *Registrum*, different dates have been suggested for the *Tabula*, with earlier scholars dating it to the mid-thirteenth century, while Norris, *Cataloging and Cataloging Methods*, thinks it postdates the *Registrum*. Mary A. Rouse and Richard H. Rouse, eds., *Registrum Anglie de libris doctorum et auctorum veterum*, in Corpus of British Medieval Library Catalogs series (London: British Library, 1991), give a date of the "early years of the fourteenth century," cxxix; for a description of the catalog, ibid., xiii–xv; and Parkes, "Provision of Books," in Catto and Evans, *History of . . . Oxford*, 445.

8. The twelfth-century inventory: Clark, *Care of Books*, 77; the 1396 inventory: Sharpe, "Library Catalogs and Indexes," in Morgan and Thomson, *Cambridge History of the Book*, vol. 2, 223.

9. Cited in Lerner, *Story of Libraries*, 74.

10. Rouse and Rouse, *Preachers, Florilegia*, 26.

11. Sharpe, "Library Catalogs and Indexes," in Morgan and Thomson, *Cambridge History of the Book*, vol. 2, 205–206.

12. Ibid., 207.

13. The bibliography too has vanished, but it was copied, and then extracts were made from that copy in the sixteenth century, those extracts in turn being the source of a later transcript. R. H. Rouse, "Henry Kirkstede," in *The Oxford Dictionary of National Biography*, accessed online, March 5, 2018. For many centuries Henry Kirkestede's identity was lost, and his *Catalogus* mistakenly attributed to a person given the name Bostonus Buriensis, or Boston of Bury, see e.g., Lynch, *You Could Look It Up*, 317. Lynch says that Kirkestede's catalog was divided by the books of the Bible, with each section containing authors who had written on that particular book. Rouse and others make no mention of this, and given that our only knowledge of the original catalog is a copy of some extracts made from another copy, it is probably not safe to judge whether that was Kirkestede's own organizing principle or whether it was reorganized later on.

14. Preface to a concordance in the British Library, BM MS Royal 17. B. 1, cited in Kuhn, "Preface to a Fifteenth-century Concordance," 27–71. The modernization of the text is my own.

15. Cited in Daly, *Contributions*, 78. I am grateful to Tobias Hoheisel for the translation.

16. Hertfordshire and Vatican: Clark, *Care of Books*, 77–79, 192, 217–218; Mainz: Buzás, *German Library History*, 132–133.

17. Stein, *The English Dictionary before Cawdrey*, 2; [Robert Cawdrey], *A Table Alphabeticall, or the English expositor* . . . ([1604], 4th edition, London: Edmund Weaver, 1617), n.p.

18. This example is found in Daly, *Contributions*, 72.

19. Wallis, "*Communis et universalis*," 29.

20. Boulanger, *Les inventeurs*, 415–416.

21. Cited in Clanchy, *From Memory*, 150.

22. Brisman, *Judaic Dictionaries*, 27; and Moses ben Isaac Hanessiah, *The Sepher haShoham (The Onyx Book)*, ed. Benjamin Klar, introduction by Cecil Roth (London: Edward Goldston for the Jewish Historical Society of England, 1947), 5–7.

23. John Considine, *Small Dictionaries and Curiosity: Lexicography and Field-work in Post-Medieval Europe* (Oxford: Oxford University Press, 2017), 11–12.

24. Balbi's full explanation is cited in Daly, *Contributions*, 73, although I have amended the translation slightly here.

25. Some of these decisions and examples are discussed by Henri Béjoint, *The Lexicography of English: From Origins to Present* (Oxford: Oxford University Press, 2010), 16–17.

26. Peter T. Daniels, "Analog and Digital Writing," in Daniels and Bright, *The World's Writing Systems*, 892.

CHAPTER 6. F IS FOR FIRSTS

1. Lerner, *Story of Libraries*, 40ff.

2. Erica Eisen, "The Oldest Printed Book in the World," *London Review of Books*, October 12, 2018, accessed online. The scroll itself, effectively stolen from China in 1907, is now in the British Library and can be viewed online under their "Turning the Pages" project.

3. M. R. Guignard, "The Chinese Precedent," in Lucien Febvre and Henri-Jean Martin, *The Coming of the Book: The Impact of Printing, 1450–1800*, ed. Geoffrey Nowell-Smith and David Wootton, trans. David Gerard (London: Atlantic Highlands/Humanities Press, 1976), 75.

4. Ibid., 76, although I have substituted Taejong for Sejong, as Sejong did not come to the throne until 1418.

5. These figures can be found in Benedict Anderson, *Imagined Communities: Reflections on the Origin and Spread of Nationalism* (London: Verso, 1983), 33–34. Anderson is cautious about the number of books printed between 1450 and 1500, giving an estimate that runs from 8 million to 20 million. More recently others, such as Neil Rhodes and Jonathan Sawday, eds., *The Renaissance Computer: Knowledge Technology in the First Age of Print* (London: Routledge, 2000), 1, state 20 million without hesitation.

6. Febvre and Martin, *The Coming of the Book*, 263–265.

7. Mathilde V. Rovelstad, "The Frankfurt Book Fair," *Journal of Library History, Philosophy, and Comparative Librarianship* 8, nos. 3–4 (1973): 117–118.

8. Graham Pollard and Albert Ehrman, *The Distribution of Books by Catalog, from the Invention of Printing to AD 1800 . . .* (Cambridge: for the Roxburghe Club, 1965), 48–49. Of the forty-seven from the fifteenth century, too, several are duplicates.

9. This can be read on a 1477 broadside, printed by F. Cruessner, that appears as the frontispiece to Pollard and Ehrman, *Distribution of Books*.

10. Frans A. Janssen, "The Rise of the Typographical Paragraph," in *Cognition and the Book: Typologies of Formal Organisation of Knowledge in the Printed Book of the Early Modern Period*, ed. Karl A. E. Enenkel and Wolfgang Neuber (Leiden: Brill, 2005), 9–10, 14ff, 27.

11. Parkes, *Pause and Effect*, 54–55.

12. John Evelyn, Evelyn Papers, vol. CLXIV, British Library, Add MS 78331. Evelyn prefaced his homemade index volume with a note: "The Roman Figure signifies the Tome; the Barbarous the page." He was not consistent—sometimes the volume number was in parentheses or in lowercase roman numerals—but the page numbers were never anything but Arabic numerals throughout the three volumes that his index covers.

13. The figures for 1450 and 1600: Ann Blair and Peter Stallybrass, "Mediating Information, 1450–1800," in *This Is Enlightenment*, ed. Clifford Siskin and William Warner (Chicago: University of Chicago Press, 2010), 139; Perotti: Febvre and Martin, *Coming of the Book*, 88. This book was published by Aldus Manutius the Elder at the Aldine Press, Venice.

14. The attribution of Googe's index to Fleming: Clare Painting-Stubbs, "Abraham Fleming: Elizabethan Maker of Indexes and 'Tables,'" *The Indexer*, vol. 29, no. 3 (2011): 109–113.

15. Barnabe Googe, *The Zodiake of Life, written by the excellent and Christian Poet, Marcellus Palingenius Stellatus . . .* (London: Raufe Newberie, 1576), 243ff.

16. While the volume itself was printed without any date, a copy inscribed "February 1465" has survived, showing it had to have been printed before that. Hans Wellisch, "Incunabula Indexes," *The Indexer* 19, no. 1 (1994): 4.

17. Hans Wellisch, "The Oldest Printed Indexes," *The Indexer* 15, no. 2 (1986): 73–77.

18. Ibid., 80–81.

19. These are the conclusions of Wellisch, "Incunabula Indexes," 3–4, based on his examination of 970 incunabula, which he calculates make up approximately 3 percent of all incunabula. Of these, eighty-three, or 8.6 percent, had indexes (although four were compiled by hand by the books' owners). Between 1470 and 1479 he counted twenty indexes; between 1490 and 1499, thirty-eight.

20. The *Nuremberg Chronicle* by Hartmann Schedel was printed in 1492/3, initially by Anton Koberger (1440/45–1513). Its index: Witty, "The Beginnings of Indexing and Abstracting," 197–198.

21. Margriet Hoogvliet, "The Medieval Texts of the 1486 Ptolemy Edition by Johann Reger of Ulm," *Imago Mundi* 54 (2002): 7–13; Jerry Brotton, "Printing the Word," in *Books and the Sciences in History*, ed. Marina Frasca-Spada and Nick Jardine (Cambridge: Cambridge University Press, 2000), 39–40, 42.

22. Abraham Ortelius, *Theatrum orbis terrarum*, introduction by R. A. Skelton (facsimile of first, 1570, ed., Amsterdam: N. Israel/Meridian, 1964), n.p.

23. Bella Hass Weinberg, "The Index of a Sixteenth-century Architecture Book," *The Indexer* 23, no. 3 (2003): 140.

24. MacKinney, "Medieval Medical Dictionaries," 248.

25. Mary A. Rouse and Richard H. Rouse, "The Texts Called *Lumen Anime*," *Archivum Fratrum Praedicatorum* 41 (1971): 13–21.

26. Hans Wellisch, "Early Multilingual and Multiscript Indexes in Herbals," *The Indexer* 11, no. 2 (1978): 82–83.

27. All details in the previous two paragraphs are from ibid., 83–86.

28. This was traced by Chartier, *The Order of Books*, 57, although his emphasis is on the idea of the birth of "the author."

29. Rovelstad, "Frankfurt Book Fair," 118–119; the Imperial Commission replaced the town council as the catalog's originator in the seventeenth century.

30. Pollard and Ehrman, *Distribution of Books*, 36ff.

31. David McKitterick, "Bibliography, Bibliophily, and the Organization of Knowledge," in David Vaisey and David McKitterick, *The Foundations of Scholarship: Libraries and Collecting, 1650–1750* (Los Angeles: William Andrews Clark Memorial Library, 1992), 37.

32. A. N. L. Munby and Lenore Coral, eds., *British Book Sale Catalogs, 1676–1800: A Union List* (London: Mansell, 1977), ix.

33. Elizabeth L. Eisenstein, *The Printing Press as an Agent of Change* (Cambridge: Cambridge University Press, 1979), 94.

34. Katz, *Cuneiform to Computer*, 308ff.

35. Cited in Norris, *Cataloging and Cataloging Methods*, 136–138.

36. This analysis was made by Archer Taylor, *General Subject-Indexes Since 1548* (Philadelphia: University of Pennsylvania Press, 1966), 50–52.

37. Blair, *Too Much to Know*, 117, notes that while we use the verb "to consult" to mean "to take advice from," as well as "look up," in Gesner's time the first meaning was somewhat broader, and thus he used the slightly awkward phrase "consult from time to time" to indicate looking material up at intervals, rather than reading a work consecutively.

38. Kuhn, "Preface to a Fifteenth-century Concordance," 271.

39. John Lydgate, "Prohemy Marriage," cited in the *Oxford English Dictionary*, "Christ-cross."

40. The term is defined in William Douglas Parish and William Francis Shaw, *A Dictionary of the Kentish Dialect and Provincialisms in Use in the County of Kent* (London: Trubner, 1887). The link to the "x" signature of those who could not write is my own.

41. David Vincent, *The Rise of Mass Literacy: Reading and Writing in Modern Europe* (Cambridge: Polity, 2000), 17. See also Harvey Graff, *The Labyrinths of Literacy* (London: Falmer, 1987), for an extended discussion on the subject.

42. For more on de Eyb and Agricola, and the definitive history of commonplace books: Moss, *Printed Commonplace-books*, especially 67–71, 73–76, 120–123; also, on Agricola: Havens, *Commonplace Books*, 27–28.

43. Ann Moss, "Power and Persuasion: Commonplace Culture in Early Modern Europe," in *Commonplace Culture in Western Europe in the Early Modern Period: Reformation, Counter-Reformation and Revolt*, ed. David Cowling and Mette B. Bruun (Leuven: Peeters, 2011), 3–4.

44. Cited in Peter Beal, "Notions in Garrison: The Seventeenth-century Commonplace Book," in *New Ways of Looking at Old Texts: Papers of the Renaissance English Society, 1985–1991*, ed. W. Speed Hill (Binghamton, NY: Medieval & Renaissance Texts and Studies, 1993), 136.

45. Peter Mack, *Elizabethan Rhetoric: Theory and Practice* (Cambridge: Cambridge University Press, 2002), 25–26.

46. A Dutch edition of Terence, by Cornelius de Schryver (Paris: 1533), and an English one by Richard Bernard (Cambridge, 1598), are cited in Bradin Cormack and Carla Mazzio, *Book Use, Book Theory: 1500–1700* (Chicago: University of Chicago Library, 2005), 53, 55.

47. List compiled by Walter Ong, *Interfaces of the Word: Studies in the Evolution of Consciousness and Culture* (Ithaca: Cornell University Press, 1977), 154.

48. Stella Gibbons, *Cold Comfort Farm* (London: Folio Society, 1977), 6.

49. Cited in Beal, "Notions in Garrison," in Hill, *New Ways of Looking*, 138.

CHAPTER 7. G IS FOR GOVERNMENT

1. Rouse and Rouse, "History of Alphabetization," 1:206.

2. Daly, *Contributions*, 83.

3. Paper prices: R. J. Lyall, "Materials: The Paper Revolution," in *Book Production and Publishing in Britain, 1375–1475*, ed. Jeremy Griffiths and Derek Pearsall (Cambridge: Cambridge University Press, 1989), 11.

4. Kwakkel, "A New Type of Book," 233–234.

5. Roger Chartier, *Inscription and Erasure: Literature and Written Culture from the Eleventh to the Eighteenth Centuries*, trans. Arthur Goldhammer (Philadelphia: University of Pennsylvania Press, 2007), 1–2.

6. Samuel Pepys, *The Diary of Samuel Pepys*, Robert Latham and William Matthews, eds. (London: Bell & Hyman, 1971–83): the silver pen: August 5, 1663, vol. 4, 264; the letter at London Bridge: November 28, 1664, vol. 6, 312. Gesner and the pencil: this can be found, together with an illustration, in Gesner's 1565 treatise on minerals, *De rerum fossilium, lapidum et gemmarum maximè*.

7. Pepys, *Diary*, July 9, 1666, vol. 7, 198. The editors note that Pepys had commissioned a "Varnisher" to produce "some papers fitted with lines, for my use for Tables and the like," May 5, 1665, vol. 6, 97, but despite another mention of the man on May 9, 1666, vol. 7, 120, and his praise for the sheets two months later, Pepys then goes silent on the subject, seeming to be unaware of the availability of writing tables elsewhere.

8. Don Quixote: this is the suggestion of Chartier, *Inscription and Erasure*, 13–21; Matthew Arnold: "A Memory Picture." I am grateful to Philip Mallet for bringing this poem to my attention.

9. Peter Stallybrass, Roger Chartier, J. Franklin Mowery, and Heather Wolfe, "Hamlet's Tables and the Technologies of Writing in Renaissance Italy," *Shakespeare Quarterly* 55, no. 4 (2004): 382ff.

10. Manucci: Geoffrey A. Lee, "The Coming of Age of Double Entry: The Giovanni Farolfi Ledger of 1299–1300," *Accounting Historians' Journal* 2, no. 4 (1977): 79–95. The same Florentine ledger fragment indicates that some of the preliminaries that would lead to double-entry accounting were already apparent in the thirteenth century: Geoffrey A. Lee, "The Florentine Bank Ledger Fragments of 1211: Some New Insights," *Journal of Accounting Research* 11, no. 1 (1973): 47–61. The ledgers of Champagne, Nîmes, and Bruges: Crosby, *Measure of Reality*, 206–207.

11. Michael Chatfield, "Francesco di Marco Datini," in *A History of Accounting: An International Encyclopedia*, ed. Michael Chatfield and Richard Vangermeersch (New York: Garland, 1976), 204–205, accessed online, March 27, 2018.

12. Pacioli's system is explained by Crosby, *Measure of Reality*, 210–211, 217–219. Daly, *Contributions*, 81–82, looks at the phrasing for the organization of the *quaderno grande*.

13. This is the insight of Martin, *History and Power of Writing*, 151.

14. Daly, *Contributions*, 82–83, who notes that the Barbarigo indexes were maintained thus for just four decades.

15. Edward Wilson-Lee, *The Catalog of Shipwrecked Books: Young Columbus and the Quest for a Universal Library* (London: William Collins, 2018), 32.

16. Cited in Ann Hughes, "'The Accounts of My Kingdom': Memory, Community and the English Civil War," in "The Social History of the Archive: Record-keeping in Early Modern Europe," *Past and Present*, ed. Liesbeth Corens, Kate Peters, and Alexandra Walsham, supplement 11 (2016): 315. These records can be found in the UK National Archives, SP 28/182–186, for Warwickshire.

17. Hereford: Miles Hill, *A True and Impartiall Account of the Plunderings, Losses, and Sufferings of the County of Hereford by the Scottish Army . . . 1645* (London: E.G. for L.C., 1650); hierarchical assessments: see, for example, M. A. Faraday, ed., *Herefordshire Militia Assessments of 1663*, Camden Fourth Series, vol. 10 (London: Royal Historical Society, 1972).

18. Rafael Chelaru, "Towards a Missionary Geography: The Lists of Moldavian Catholic Parishes in the 17th and 18th Centuries in the Correspondence of the *Propaganda Fide* Missionaries," in Doležalová, *Charm of a List*, 139, 148–151.

19. Markus Krajewski, *Paper Machines: About Cards and Catalogs, 1548–1929*, trans. Peter Krapp (Cambridge, MA: MIT Press, 2011), 28.

20. The archives of Manuel I of Portugal and the Prince–Bishop of Würzburg are contrasted and described by Randolph C. Head, "Early Modern European Archivality: Organized Records, Information, and State Power, c. 1500," in *Archives and Information in the Early Modern World*, ed. Liesbeth Corens, Kate Peters, and Alexandra Walsham, eds., Proceedings of the British Academy, no. 212 (Oxford: Oxford University Press, 2018), 29–51.

21. A number of Italian states and their methods are examined in Filippo de Vivo, "Archival Intelligence: Diplomatic Correspondence, Information Overload, and Information Management in Italy, 1450–1650," in Corens, Peters, and Walsham, *Archives and Information*, 53–85.

22. Pepys's notebook: Jacob Soll, "From Note-Taking to Data Banks: Personal and Institutional Information Management in Early Modern Europe," in "Note-Taking in Early Modern Europe," ed. Ann Blair and Richard Yeo, special issue, *Intellectual History Review* 20, no. 3 (2010): 355–356; his navy book and alphabetization: Pepys, *Diary*, June 11, 1662, 3:106; February 7, 1662/3, 4:36; March 4, 1662/3, 4:65; July 24, 1667, 8:350; his abstract book: November 27, 1667, 8:551.

23. This painting, with its new attribution of the sitter (previously thought to be an anonymous merchant), and the identification of the writing tables, has been analyzed in great—and fascinating—detail by Heather Wolfe and Peter Stallybrass, "The Material Culture of Record-keeping in Early Modern England," in Corens, Peters, and Walsham, *Archives and Information*, 179–208.

24. Blair and Stallybrass, "Mediating Information," 144, mentions both Philip II and William Bradford; Philip II's biographer cited in Arndt Brendecke, "Knowledge, Oblivion, and Concealment in Early Modern Spain: The Ambiguous Agenda

of the Archive of Simancas," in Corens, Peters, and Walsham, *Archives and Information*, 134.

25. Pepys, *Diary*, September 3, 1661, 2:171.

26. Thomas Blount, *Nomo-lexikon: a law dictionary, interpreting such difficult and obscure words and terms, as are found either in our common or statute, ancient or modern lawes* . . . ([1671], "In the Savoy" [London]: Thomas Newcomb for John Martin and Henry Herringman, 1870), n.p.

27. Pepys, *Diary*, March 12, 1661/2, 3:44; it is the volume's editors, Latham and Matthews, who describe the summarizing on the outer folds of the documents.

28. Arnold Hunt, "The Early Modern Secretary and the Early Modern Archive," in Corens, Peters, and Walsham, *Archives and Information*, 122.

29. Elizabeth Williamson, "Archival Practice and the Production of Political Knowledge in the Office of Sir Francis Walsingham," in *Praktiken der frühen Neuzeit: Akteure, Handlungen, Artefakte*, ed. Arndt Brendecke (Cologne: Böhlau, 2015), 481.

30. John Weddington, *A Breffe Instruction, and Manner, Howe to Kepe, Marchantes Bokes, of Accomptes* (Antwerp, 1567), cited in Angus Vine, "Commercial Commonplacing: Francis Bacon, the Waste-Book, and the Ledger," in *English Manuscript Studies, 1100–1700*, ed. Peter Beal and A. S. G. Edwards, vol. 16, *Manuscript Miscellanies, c. 1450–1700*, ed. Richard Beadle and Colin Burrow (London: British Library, 2011), 204–205.

31. John C. Rule and Ben S. Trotter, *A World of Paper: Louis XIV, Colbert de Torcy, and the Rise of the Information State* (Montreal and Kingston: McGill/Queen's University Press, 2014), 324.

32. Cited in Anke te Heesen, "The Notebook: A Paper Technology," in *Making Things Public: Atmospheres of Democracy*, ed. Bruno Latour and Peter Weibel (Cambridge, MA: MIT Press, 2005), 586.

33. Cited in Krajewski, *Paper Machines*, 13–14.

34. Megan Williams, "Unfolding Diplomatic Paper and Paper Practices in Early Modern Chancellery Archives," in Brendecke, *Praktiken der frühen Neuzeit*, 505.

35. Fabian Kraemer, "Ulisse Aldrovandi's *Pandechion Epistemonicon* and the Use of Paper Technology in Renaissance Natural History," *Early Science and Medicine* 19 (2014): 401–416, 420–421.

36. Richard Yeo, "Loose Notes and Capacious Memory: Robert Boyle's Note-Taking and its Rationale," in Blair and Yeo, *Note-Taking*, 336; Michael Hunter, "Mapping the Mind of Robert Boyle: The Evidence of the Boyle Papers," in *Archives of the Scientific Revolution: The Formation and Exchange of Ideas in Seventeenth-century Europe*, ed. Michael Hunter (Woodbridge: Boydell, 1998), 126–127.

37. Richard Yeo, "Between Memory and Paperbooks: Baconianism and Natural History in Seventeenth-century England," *History of Science* 45, no. 1 (2007): 29–30.

38. Vismann, *Files*, 90–91.

39. Ibid., 91–95.

40. This is a lightly skimmed summary of the work done by Randolph Head, "Mirroring Governance: Archives, Inventories and Political Knowledge in Early Modern Switzerland and Europe," *Archival Science* 7, no. 4 (2007): 321–325, which is meticulously detailed.

41. Wolfe and Stallybrass, "The Material Culture of Record-keeping," in Corens, Peters, and Walsham, *Archives and Information*, 203–205.

42. For the development of the cupboard in a domestic context, see my *The Making of Home* (London: Atlantic, 2014), 132–133. A useful technical explication of the development of divided cabinets can be found in Glenn Adamson, "The Labor of Division: Cabinetmaking and the Production of Knowledge," in *Ways of Making and Knowing: The Material Culture of Empirical Knowledge*, ed. Pamela H. Smith, Amy R. W. Meyers, and Harold J. Cook (Ann Arbor: University of Michigan Press, 2014), 243–279. The conjunction of the development of files and filing, and furniture history, is only just beginning to be explored.

43. Clanchy, *From Memory*, 144.

44. M. B. Parkes, "Layout and Presentation of the Text," in Morgan and Thomson, *The Cambridge History of the Book*, 2:72–73.

45. Helmut Zedelmaier, "Christoph Just Udenius and the German *ars excerpendi* Around 1700: On the Flourishing and Disappearance of a Pedagogical Genre," in *Forgetting Machines: Knowledge Management Evolution in Early Modern Europe*, ed. Alberto Cevolini (Leiden: Brill, 2016), 87–88.

46. Preface by Sir Matthew Hale to Henry Rolle, *Un abridgment des plusieurs cases et resolutions del Common Ley: Alphabeticalment digest desouth severall Titles* (London: A. Crooke et al., 1668), n.p. The British Library copy mentioned later in this paragraph has a note pasted at the front: "Mr. Cay presents his compliments and has sent Mr. Hargrave the interleaved Rolle's Abridgment that he mentioned yesterday. The bulk of the Writing in a small very legible hand-writing is by his Father John Cay Esq. late Bencher of Gray's Inn; there is a small proportion of an older & less legible handwriting: this is by his Grand-father Henry Boult Esq. of Gray's Inn: who probably began the book, & soon tired and left off, & afterwards gave the book to his son-in-law. / Cursitor's Street / 8 July 1793." The catalog attributes this note to Francis Hargrave, a barrister and antiquarian.

47. E.g., Samuel Brewster, *A brief method of the law: being an exact alphabetical disposition of all the heads necessary for a perfect common-place: useful to all students and professors of the law: much wanted, and earnestly desired . . .* (London: [n.p.], 1680).

48. The information on legal publishing is derived from David J. Harvey, *The Law Emprynted and Englysshed: The Printing Press as an Agent of Change in Law and Legal Culture, 1475–1642* (Oxford: Hart, 2015), 202–205; and John Stone, "The Law, the Alphabet, and Samuel Johnson," in *Anniversary Essays on Johnson's Dictionary*, ed. Jack Lynch and Anne McDermott (Cambridge: Cambridge University Press, 2005), 150. It is Harvey who calls Ashton's work a general legal index.

49. Abraham Fraunce, *The lawiers logicke* (London: 1588), f.119, cited in "'Of Common Places, or Memorial Books': An Anonymous Manuscript on Commonplace Books and the Art of Memory in Seventeenth-Century England," ed. Earle Havens, *Yale University Library Gazette* 76, nos. 3/4 (2002): 142.

50. Kasirer, "Pothier from A to Z," 395. I am grateful to Mr. Justice Kasirer for guiding me to this work.

51. Cited in Jonathon Green and Nicholas J. Karolides, *Encyclopedia on Censorship* (New York: Facts on File, 2005), 257.

52. The comparison of these types of display is to be found in Adamson, "The Labor of Division," in Smith, Meyers, Cook, *Ways of Making and Knowing*, 248–252.

53. Norris, *Cataloging and Cataloging Methods*, 135–136.

54. Wilson-Lee, *Shipwrecked Books*, 319, 321.

55. Bodley's letter to Cotton is reproduced in Andrew Kippis, *Biographia Britannica: Or, The Lives of the Most Eminent Persons who have Flourished in Great Britain and Ireland* . . . (London: W. and A. Strahan, 1780), 2:392.

56. Cotton's gift to Bodley: Kevin Sharpe, *Sir Robert Cotton, 1586–1631* (Oxford: Oxford University Press, 1979), 75; Stuart Handley, "Sir Robert Bruce Cotton, 1st baronet," *Oxford Dictionary of National Biography*, accessed online, October 28, 2018.

57. I am grateful to Herr Wolfgang Mayer, of the Staats- und Stadtbibliothek Augsburg, for directing me to this source and for sending me scans of it. The catalog itself is owned by the Staats- und Stadtbibliothek; it is discussed in detail, with biographical information on Dr. Martius, by Giles Mandelbrote, "The First Printed Library Catalog? A German Doctor's Library of the Sixteenth Century, and its Place in the History of the Distribution of Books by Catalog," in Fiammetta Sabba, ed., *La biblioteche private come paradigma bibliografico: atti del convegno internazionale, Roma, Tempio di Adriano, 10–12 ottobre 2007* (Rome, Bulzoni, 2008), 295ff.

58. Petrus Bertius, *Nomenclator. The first printed catalog of Leiden University Library (1595).* A facsimile edition, introduction by R. Breugelmans (Leiden, 1995, available online); again, I am grateful to Herr Wolfgang Mayer of the Staats- und Stadtbibliothek Augsburg for directing me to this material.

59. Louis B. Wright, "Some Early 'Friends' of Libraries," *Huntington Library Quarterly* 2, no. 3 (1939): 357–358. Wright refers to a 1412 instruction to the university chaplains to pray for the souls of Oxford's donors, but is either unaware of, or sees little importance in, the many monastic library catalogs that listed their books categorized by donor.

60. Georg Henisch, *Bibliothecae inclytae reipub. Augustanae utriusque tum graecae tum latinae librorum impressorum manu exaratorum catalogus, Augustae Vindelicorum* (Augsburg: Valentinum Schönigk, 1600). The catalog is owned by the Staats- und Stadtbibliothek Augsburg and is viewable online. Once again, I acknowledge the assistance of, and my gratitude to, Herr Mayer at that institution.

61. Thomas Bodley, *Letters of Sir Thomas Bodley to Thomas James, First Keeper of the Bodleian Library*, ed. G. W. Wheeler (Oxford: Clarendon Press, 1926), letters dated December 24, 1599, July 22, 1601, July 29, 1601, August 26, 1601, pp. 2, 10–11, 13–14, 16–17 respectively.

62. Shirley: Cormack and Mazzio, *Book Use, Book Theory*, 59, mentions this book, although the name was handwritten, so it possibly did not reflect a routine bibliographic practice. Rostgaard: Norris, *Cataloging and Cataloging Methods*, 166–167, notes the style Rostgaard adopted, but seems unaware of its originality. Carmelite monk: Buzás, *German Library History*, 279.

63. Theodore Hofmann, Joan Winterkorn, Frances Harris, and Hilton Kelliher, "John Evelyn's Archive at the British Library," in *John Evelyn in the British Library*, introduction by Anthony Kenny (London: British Library, 1995), 33.

64. Norris, *Cataloging and Cataloging Methods*, 142–143.

65. Gabriel Naudé, *Advis pour dresser une bibliothèque* ([1627], Leipzig: Veb Edition, 1963); taken here from John Evelyn's translation, *Instructions concerning erecting of a library*, "interpreted by Jo. Evelyn" (London: n.p., 1661), 126–128.

66. Writings on Leibniz's library work are scattered, and this section has been gathered from Buzás, *German Library History*, 167–168, 278; L. M. Newman, "Leibniz (1646–1716) and the German Library Scene," *Library Association Pamphlet*, no. 28 (London: Library Association, 1966), 12–13, 17, 21, 24, 29–31; Hans G. Schulte-Albert, "Gottfried Wilhelm Leibniz and Library Classification," *Journal of Library History* 6, no. 2 (1971): 133–152; and Krajewski, *Paper Machines*, 21.

67. Cited in Richard Yeo, *Notebooks, English Virtuosi, and Early Modern Science* (Chicago: University of Chicago Press, 2014), 26.

68. William Clark, "On the Bureaucratic Plots of the Research Library," in Frasca-Spada and Jardine, *Books and the Sciences*, 195–197.

69. Ibid., 202.

70. Ann Moss, "Locating Knowledge," in Enenkel and Neuber, *Cognition and the Book*, 43.

CHAPTER 8. H IS FOR HISTORY

1. C. S. Lewis, *The Discarded Image* (Cambridge: Cambridge University Press, 1964), 10.

2. This is the suggestion of Wallis, "*Communis et universalis*," 32ff. It is her ideas that follow.

3. Ibid. For paper production, see also Henri-Jean Martin, "L'art du papier des Chinois aux Genois," in Martin, Chartier, and Vivet, *Histoire de l'édition française*, 1:28–29.

4. This citation (italics mine) in Hunt, "The Library of Robert Grosseteste," 127.

5. Cevolini, "Making *notae* for Scholarly Retrieval: A Franciscan Case Study," in Teeuwen and Renswoude, *The Annotated Book*, 350.

6. This translation, which I have slightly modified, appears in Hans Wellisch, "How to Make an Index, 16th-century Style: Conrad Gessner on Indexes and Catalogs," *International Classification* 8, no. 1 (1981): 11.

7. Cited in Isabelle Charmantier and Staffan Müller-Wille, "Carl Linnaeus's Botanical Paper Slips (1767–1773)," *Intellectual History Review* 24, no. 2 (2014): 217.

8. The description of the evolution of the Josephinian catalog: Krajewski, *Paper Machines*, 16, 34–42.

9. M. l'Abbé [François] Rozier, *Nouvelle table des articles contenus dans les volumes de l'Académie royale des sciences de Paris, depuis 1666 jusqu'en 1770 . . .* (Paris: Ruault, 1775).

10. The description of this project is compiled from Norris, *Cataloging and Cataloging Methods*, 195–196; Krajewski, *Paper Machines*, 45–46; and Judith Hopkins, "The 1791 French Cataloging Code and the Origins of the Card Catalog," *Libraries and Culture* 27, no. 4 (1992): 390–391.

11. Mike Mertens and Dunia García-Ontiveros, "Hidden Collections: Report of the RLUK Retrospective Cataloging Survey, in association with the London Library," 2013, accessed online, December 10, 2018.

12. I have seen only one reference that might be to boards used to organize material after Ringelberg. Christoph Just Udenius, a preacher from the Harz region, wrote the first book on commonplacing in German, in 1696. This *Excerpendi ratio nova*, A New System of Excerpting [or Commonplacing], recommended that a student carry "a writing board" to jot down noteworthy material, for later transcription into his commonplace book. This may have been a slate, or possibly wax or ivory tablets, or even bound writing tables. Zedelmaier, "Christoph Just Udenius," in Cevolini, *Forgetting Machines*, 79. Zedelmaier cites this passage but makes no suggestion as to what the board in question might be.

13. Biographical information on van Ringelberg, together with this citation, appears in the *Biographie nationale, vie des hommes et des femmes illustrés de la Belgique* (Brussels: Émile Bruylant, 1866–1944), 19:349–350. The translation is my own, with thanks to Frank Wynne for clarifying some idioms unknown to me.

14. Domenico Bertoloni Meli, "The Archive and *Consulti* of Marcello Malpighi: Some Preliminary Reflections," in Hunter, *Archives of the Scientific Revolution*, 110, describes the notebooks; the modern comparison is my own.

15. According to the catalog of Yale's Beinecke Library, which now owns these commonplace books, the first volume and some of the second is in Trumbull's own handwriting, with the remainder written by someone else. I have presumed, therefore, that Trumbull was the guiding intelligence behind the tabs, as there is no sign of any text having been cut off in their creation, suggesting they were made

before the volumes were written in. Beinecke Library, Osborn collection, Osborn fc23 1/2. I am greatly obliged to Sara Powell, research librarian at the Beinecke Rare Book and Manuscript Library, Yale, who looked at these manuscripts for me, and sent me images.

16. This was described in Gesner, *Bibliotheca universalis*, Book 1, "De grammatica"; translated by Wellisch, "How to Make an Index," 11.

17. M. Greengrass, "Samuel Hartlib," *Oxford Dictionary of National Biography*, accessed online, June 18, 2018.

18. The description of the Ark and the information about Harrison and Placcius are derived from Noel Malcolm, "Thomas Harrison and his 'Ark of Studies': An Episode in the History of the Organization of Knowledge," *Seventeenth Century* 19, no. 2 (2004): 196–232; Yeo, "Between Memory and Paper Books," 3, 14; Yeo, *Notebooks, English Virtuosi*, 116–121.

19. The dates appear in Alberto Cevolini, ed., *Thomas Harrison: The Ark of Studies* (Turnhout: Brepols, 2017), 2–3, although Cevolini seems to think Harrison may well have had, and used, an ark. Placcius's modified ark is mentioned in Vincentius Placcius, *De arte excerpendi, vom gelehrten Buchhalten . . .* (Hamburg: Holmiae, 1689), 149ff.

20. Malcolm, "Thomas Harrison," 220, thinks that Leibniz kept his notes in ledgers. Others think Leibniz did have a cabinet and that it was based on Harrison's Ark; among these are Newman, "Leibniz," 13, and Blair, *Too Much to Know*, 93.

21. Yeo, "Loose Notes and Capacious Memory," in Blair and Yeo, *Note-Taking*, 339. Yeo, however, like Blair and Newman, also believes that Leibniz owned an ark, 341.

22. Markus Krajewski, "Paper as Passion: Niklas Luhmann and His Card Index," in *Raw Data Is an Oxymoron*, ed. Lisa Gitelman, trans. Charles Macrum II (Cambridge, MA: MIT Press, 2013), 103.

23. Most of the slips appear to be in neither Leibniz's own hand, nor that of Martin Fogel, whose manuscripts Leibniz had purchased for the library, and whose extract cabinet Leibniz was said, in the eighteenth century, to have adopted. The dictionary and handwriting: John Considine, *Academy Dictionaries, 1600–1800* (Cambridge: Cambridge University Press, 2014), 92–95; the connection of Martin Fogel with the excerpt cabinet: Krajewski, *Paper Machines*, 17, who cites Christoph Gottlieb von Murr, the eighteenth-century scholar, who said it was "likely" Leibniz's cabinet was adopted from Martin Fogel's.

24. Fogel: cited by Malcolm, "Thomas Harrison," 217; Harsdörffer: Krajewski, *Paper Machines*, 21.

25. Helmut Zedelmaier, "Johann Jakob Moser et l'organisation erudite du savoir à l'époque moderne," in *Lire, Copier, Écrire: Les bibliothèques manuscrites et leurs usages au XVIIIᵉ siècle*, ed. Élisabeth Décultot (Paris: CNRS Éditions, 2003), 43–62. The 1896 tabs: Gerri Lynn Flanzraich, "The Library Bureau and Office Technology," *Libraries and Culture* 28, no. 4 (1993): 411.

26. Louis Dumas, *La biblioteque des enfans, ou les premiers elemens des lettres: contenant le sisteme du bureau tipograpfique . . .* (Paris: Pierre Simon, 1733).

27. Jan Amos Comenius, *Orbis sensualium pictus, or, Visible World,* trans. Charles Hoole (London: John Sprint, 1659), in a facsimile edition, *Orbis Pictus,* ed. John E. Sadler (London: Oxford University Press, 1968), 30.

28. Ibid., 200.

29. Cited in Yeo, "Between Memory and Paperbooks," 2.

30. Richard Yeo, "Notebooks as Memory Aids: Precepts and Practices in Early Modern England," *Memory Studies* 1, no. 1 (2008): 127.

31. Cited in Moss, *Printed Commonplace-books,* 116.

32. John Locke, *The Correspondence of John Locke and Edward Clarke* (London: Oxford University Press, 1927), 245. Fiona Skelton, "The Content, Context and Influence of the Work of Juan Luis Vives (1492–1540)" (PhD thesis, University of Glasgow, 1996), makes a case for both a direct and an indirect influence by Vives on Locke, but whether she knows of this particular reference regarding pigeonholes I have been unable to determine.

33. Dates for Locke's commonplace books, and, later in the paragraph, for when he began indexing: G. G. Meynell, "John Locke's Method of Common-placing as Seen in His Drafts and His Medical Notebooks, Bodleian MSS Locke d.9, f.21 and f.23," *The Seventeenth Century* 8, no. 2 (1993): 245.

34. Beal, "Notions in Garrison," in Hill, *New Ways of Looking,* 140.

35. This first-consonant/first-vowel system had been used in a sixteenth-century Latin–Greek dictionary, the *Pseudo-Philoxenus,* in an edition printed by Henri Estienne, which Locke might well have known. Daly, *Contributions,* 69. It should be added that the examples of Berne and Bremen are my own to illustrate the system, and are not drawn from Locke.

36. John Locke, "A New Method of Making Common-place Books" (London: J. Greenwood, 1706), passim.

37. Some of these titles are listed by Beal, "Notions in Garrison," in Hill, *New Ways of Looking,* 242; and Yeo, *Notebooks, English Virtuosi,* 175. The shorthand volume is *Stenography Compendized, or, An Improvement of Mr. Weston's Art of Shorthand* (Glasgow: Montgomerie & McNair, 1780).

38. Yeo, *Notebooks, English Virtuosi,* 218.

39. Christopher Marlowe, *Doctor Faustus,* I.i.1–2, in *The Complete Plays,* ed. Frank Romany and Robert Lindsey (Harmondsworth: Penguin, 2003), 347.

40. This summation is précised from Alex Wright, *Cataloging the World: Paul Otlet and the Birth of the Information Age* (Oxford: Oxford University Press, 2014), 27.

41. Ibid., 29.

42. Blair, *Too Much to Know,* 170.

43. Charles Porset, "L'encylopédie et la question de l'ordre: réflexions sur la lexicalisation des connaissances au XVIIIᵉ siècle," in Becq, *L'Encyclopédisme,* 257.

44. Andrew Kippis in his *Biographia Britannica*, 4:2201, cited in Richard Yeo, "Ephraim Chambers's Cyclopaedia (1728) and the Tradition of Commonplaces," *Journal of the History of Ideas* 57, no. 1 (1996): 162.

45. Pierre des Maizeaux, *La vie de Mr. Bayle* (The Hague: Gosse and J. Neaulme, 1732), 2:326.

46. Sandler, "*Omne bonum*: *Compilatio* and *Ordinatio*," in Brownrigg, *Medieval Book Production*, 183, 188–189. Sandler has written extensively on this unique manuscript: see Sandler, Omne bonum: *A Fourteenth-century Encyclopedia of Universal Knowledge*.

47. H. H. M. van Lieshout, *The Making of Pierre Bayle's* Dictionaire historique et critique (Amsterdam and Utrecht: APA-Holland University Press, 2001), 70–71, 74–77.

48. James Lawrence Fuchs, "Vincenzo Coronelli and the Organization of Knowledge: The Twilight of Seventeenth-century Encyclopedism" (PhD thesis, University of Chicago, 1983), 182–186.

49. Ibid., 215.

50. Cited in Richard Yeo, "Encyclopaedic Knowledge," in Frasca-Spada and Jardine, *Books and the Sciences*, 215ff.

51. *Chambers Cyclopaedia, or, An Universal Dictionary of the Arts and Sciences* (London: James and John Knapton, 1728), 1.

52. Diderot, "Prospectus to the *Encyclopédie*," 2; accessed online, June 25, 2018.

53. "*Si l'on nous objecte que l'ordre alphabétique détruira la liaison de notre systeme de la Connoissance humaine; nous répondrons que, cette liaison consistant moins dans l'arrangement des matières que dans les rapports qu'elles ont entr'elles, rien ne peut l'anéantir, & que nous aurons soin de la rendre sensible par la disposition des matieres dans chaque article, & par l'exactitude & la fréquence des renvois.*" From the Prospectus to the *Encyclopédie*, 8, accessed online, June 25, 2018.

54. Jorge Luis Borges, *The Aleph and Other Stories, 1933–1969, Together with Commentaries and an Autobiographical Essay*, ed. and trans. Norman Thomas di Giovanni (London: Jonathan Cape, 1971), 209, 233; Bertolt Brecht, *Threepenny Novel*. Both cited in Richard Yeo, "Lost Encyclopedias: Before and After the Enlightenment," *Book History* 10, no. 1 (2007): 48.

55. Jean Ehrard, "De Diderot à Panckoucke: deux pratiques de l'alphabet," in Becq, *L'Encyclopédisme*, 244–245.

56. Robert Collison, *Encyclopaedias: Their History Throughout the Ages* (New York: Hafner, 1966), 138ff.

57. Samuel Taylor Coleridge to Robert Southey, July 1803, *The Life and Correspondence of Robert Southey*, ed. Rev. Charles Cuthbert Southey (London: Longman, Brown, Green and Longmans, 1850), 2:220.

58. The prospectus is reprinted in Collison, *Encyclopaedias*, 238ff.

59. Cited in Headrick, *When Information Came of Age*, 166.

60. Yeo, "Lost Encyclopedias," 51, cites examples.

61. Thomas Love Peacock, *Headlong Hall* (London: T. Hookham, 1816), 31–32.

62. This was Hermann von Helmholtz, "Popular Lectures on Scientific Subjects," 1873, cited in Yeo, "Between Memory and Paperbooks," 1.

CHAPTER 9. I IS FOR INDEX CARDS

1. The figures are from Headrick, *When Information Came of Age,* 9–10, but those for North America do not include population numbers for First Nations, as there are few complete or well-sourced (or, often, any) figures for these groups before the 1860s. See, for example, Campbell Gibson and Kay Jung, "Historical Census Statistics on Population Totals by Race . . . ," Population Division, Working Paper No. 76 (Washington, DC: US Census Bureau, 2005), accessed online, June 27, 2018.

2. This idea of demographic requirements is from Headrick, *When Information Came of Age,* 9–10.

3. The description, and the link to commonplace books, is that of M. D. Eddy, "Tools for Reordering: Commonplacing and the Space of Words in Linnaeus's *Philosophia Botanica," Intellectual History Review* 20, no. 2 (2010): 247. The link to Harrison's Ark, however, is my own.

4. Linnaeus, and Solander in the following paragraph: Charmantier and Müller-Wille, "Carl Linnaeus's Botanical Paper Slips," 215–216, 218–220, 227–229; and Isabelle Charmantier and Staffan Müller-Wille, "Worlds of Paper: An Introduction," *Early Science and Medicine* 19 (2014): 381.

5. Marie-Noëlle Bourguet, "A Portable World: The Notebooks of European Travellers (Eighteenth to Nineteenth Centuries)," in Blair and Yeo, "Note-Taking," 395–396.

6. This summary is gathered from Vismann, *Files,* 116; and Ernst Robert Curtius, "Goethe as Administrator," in *Essays on European Literature,* trans. Michael Kowal (Princeton, NJ: Princeton University Press, 1973), 58–60.

7. Penne L. Restad, *Christmas in America: A History* (New York: Oxford University Press, 1995), 13.

8. Household documents: George Washington Papers, Series 5, Financial Papers: Invoices, 1766–1773; Lists of Taxed Lands, Slaves, and other Possessions, 1760 to 1774, 1760, www.loc.gov/item/mgw500005; military ledgers: George Washington Papers, Series 5, Financial Papers: Virginia Military Accounts: Ledger, September–December 1758, 09-/12-1758, 1755, www.loc.gov/item/mgw500007.

9. Charles Burns, "Cardinal Giuseppe Garampi: An Eighteenth-century Pioneer in Indexing," *The Indexer* 22, no. 2 (2000): 62–63.

10. [French] Ministry of the Interior, Circular No. 14, April 24, 1841. I am grateful to Caroline Shenton for sharing her expertise in the matter of *respect des fonds.*

11. Theodore R. Schellenberg, *European Archival Practices in Arranging Records* (Washington, DC: National Archives and Records Service, 1975), 1–4. This is a very bald outline of an extremely complex development, analyzed in detail by Lara Jennifer Moore, *Restoring Order: The École des Chartes and the Organization of Archives and Libraries in France, 1820–1870* (Duluth, MN: Litwin, 2008).

12. Schellenberg, *European Archives*, 5–10 for continental Europe; Britain, with the citation unsourced, 11.

13. Cited in Peter Becker and William Clark, eds., *Little Tools of Knowledge: Historical Essays on Academic and Bureaucratic Practices* (Ann Arbor: University of Michigan Press, 2001), introduction, 2–3.

14. Cited in Anke te Heesen, *The World in a Box: The Story of an Eighteenth-century Picture Encyclopedia*, trans. Ann M. Henschel (Chicago: Chicago University Press, 2002), 146–147.

15. The advertisement is cited in J. Camille Showalter and Janet Driesbach, eds., *Wooton Patent Desks: A Place for Everything and Everything in Its Place* (Indianapolis: Indiana State Museum, 1983), 33. More generally, see 22–23.

16. JoAnne Yates, *Control Through Communication: The Rise of System in American Management* (Baltimore: Johns Hopkins University Press, 1989), 34.

17. Vismann, *Files*, 130–133.

18. Yates, *Control Through Communication*, 37–40.

19. Paul Kaufman, "The Community Library: A Chapter in English Social History," *Transactions of the American Philosophical Society*, n.s., 57, no. 7 (1967): 11–13, 26–28.

20. These, and the remaining surviving catalogs, are examined by Jim Ranz, *The Printed Book Catalog in American Libraries, 1723–1900* (Chicago: American Library Association, 1964), 9ff.

21. Ranz, *Printed Book Catalog*, 25, cites three such preliminary apologetic prefaces: from the New York Society Library, 1793; the library of Allegheny College, 1823; and the Boston Athenaeum library, 1827.

22. Cited in Norris, *Cataloging and Cataloging Methods*, 207–208.

23. Mary Lovett Smallwood, *An Historical Study of Examinations and Grading Systems in Early American Universities: A Critical Study . . .* (Cambridge, MA: Harvard University Press, 1935), 41, 60.

24. Grading is another area of invisibility for the alphabet, and the subject has rarely been explored. The best historical description, although without analysis, is still Smallwood, *An Historical Study of Examinations*, 42–59.

25. Mishnah, Menaḥot 8:1, 3, 6. Cited in Joseph Naveh, "Unpublished Phoenician Inscriptions from Palestine," *Israel Exploration Journal* 37, no. 1 (1987): 28.

26. The Harvard catalog, from 1812 to 1861, Krajewski, *Paper Machines*, 69–82, passim.

27. For an example of the attribution to Jewett, see David Weinberger, *Everything Is Miscellaneous: The Power of the New Digital Disorder* (New York: Times

Books/Henry Holt, 2007), 51, who appears not to know of the Harvard catalog, and makes no reference to any European libraries.

28. Krajewski, *Paper Machines*, 82.

29. The Akron, Ohio patent: Flanzraich, "The Library Bureau and Office Technology," 411–412; James Newton Gunn: Edward Tenner, "Keeping Tabs: The History of an Information Age Metaphor," *Technology Review*, February 2005, 71. Neither author mentions the other patentee.

30. Wright, *Cataloging the World*, 42.

31. Cited in Flanzraich, "Library Bureau and Office Technology," 404.

32. Cited in Tenner, "From Slip to Chip," 54.

33. *Register of War Department*, January 1, 1889 (Washington, DC: Government Printing Office, 1889).

34. Flanzraich, "Library Bureau and Office Technology," 405–407. Flanzraich also says that the Bank of England used a card catalog system as early as 1852, but she gives no source, and despite an approach to the Bank of England archive I have been unable to corroborate this.

35. Flanzraich, "Library Bureau and Office Technology," 416–417.

36. Yates, *Control Through Communication*, 61.

CHAPTER 10. Y IS FOR Y2K

1. Wright, *Cataloging the World*, 69ff.

2. Ibid., 7.

3. *Nelson's Perpetual Loose-leaf Encyclopaedia*, John H. Finley, ed. (New York: Nelson's, 1909–), prelims, passim.

4. This system of boards and jacks survived in offices well into the 1960s, and possibly later.

5. James Gleick, *The Information: A History, a Theory, a Flood* (New York: Pantheon, 2011), 195, is one of several contemporary books that repeat the story of the telegram boys. However, none of the works cites the origins of this report, and I have been unable to locate anything like a source, as with so much concerning telephones (see the following note). Boston phone book: *List of Subscribers, October 1, 1886 . . . New England Telephone and Telegraph Co., Boston Division*, 14.

6. Almost all information about the early days of phones and phone books reads as if it were apocryphal, and very little is sourced. George Coy, and the later switchboard: Gleick, *The Information*, 193–194; the pharmacist and doctors: Peter Young, *Person to Person: The International Impact of the Telephone* (Cambridge: Granta, 1991), 15. Yet neither of these two stories appears in other books on the history of the telephone, such as F. G. C. Baldwin, *The History of the Telephone in the United Kingdom* (London: Chapman & Hall, 1925); John Brooks, *Telephone: The First Hundred Years* (New York: Harper and Row, 1975); or Ithiel de Sola Pool, ed.,

The Social Impact of the Telephone (Cambridge, MA: MIT Press, 1977). The history of the telephone still awaits a serious historian.

7. This historian is Baldwin, *History of the Telephone*, 40–41. Whether the list still survives is unknown, since Baldwin gives no location for it.

8. Michèle Martin, *Hello, Central?: Gender, Technology, and Culture in the Formation of Telephone Systems* (Montreal and Kingston: McGill/Queen's University Press, 1991), 130–132, cites the 1883 directory before moving on to 1899 when, she makes clear, phone numbers had come into use, but possible changes to the arrangement of the directory that may have occurred are not discussed.

9. 1886, 1892, 1895 Boston phone books: *List of Subscribers . . . Boston Edition*.

10. R. P. Dick, "The Compiling of the Telephone Directories," *The Indexer* 3, no. 1 (spring 1962): 11.

11. Ibid.

12. This is recounted in Thomas S. Mullaney, *The Chinese Typewriter: A History* (Cambridge, MA: MIT Press, 2017), 2–4. I am indebted to Mullaney for many of the ideas that follow.

13. Daly, *Contributions*, 11.

14. For the page count, I have used P. M. Roget, *Roget's Thesaurus of English Words and Phrases*, ed. and rev. by Betty Kirkpatrick (Harmondsworth: Penguin, 1987).

15. This very incomplete list, and the idea, from Mullaney, *Chinese Typewriter*, 9.

16. Ibid., 60–65. As can be seen, I have found Mullaney's book invigorating and path-breaking, although my few mentions do little to indicate its breadth and scholarship.

17. See www.w3.org/International/articles/idn-and-iri. I am grateful to Nicholas Blake for pointing me to this information.

18. For a more in-depth explanation of Japanese (and Chinese) telegraph coding, see Mullaney, *Chinese Typewriter*, 201ff.

19. For Japanese scripts and ordering systems I have relied on Janet Shibamoto Smith, "Japanese Writing," in Daniels and Bright, *The World's Writing Systems*, 209–217; and Daniels, "Analog and Digital Writing Systems," in ibid., 892.

20. Victor H. Mair, "Modern Chinese Writing," in Daniels and Bright, *The World's Writing Systems*, 204–205.

21. I am grateful to Jean-Jacques Subrenat for introducing me to this information.

22. I owe this idea, and the literally illuminating analogy, to Mullaney, *Chinese Typewriter*, 239ff.

23. Ladislav Zgusta, "The Influence of Scripts and Morphological Language Types on the Structure of Dictionaries," in Franz Josef Hausmann, Oscar Reichmann, Herbert Ernst Wiegand, and Ladislav Zgusta, *Wörterbücher/Dictionaries/Dictionnaires: An International Encyclopedia of Lexicography* (Berlin: Walter de Gruyter, 1989–1991), 1:298–299.

24. Jean Ritmueller, "The Hiberno-Latin Background of the Matthew Commentary of Maél-Brigte Ua Maéluanaig," *Proceedings of the Harvard Celtic Colloquium* 1 (1981): 1–2.

25. Graham D. Caie, "Hypertext and Multiplicity: The Medieval Example," in *The Renaissance Text: Theory, Editing, Textuality*, ed. Andrew Murphy (Manchester, UK: Manchester University Press, 2000), 35.

26. https://en.wikipedia.org/wiki/Wikipedia#Readership, accessed July 4, 2018.

27. Most of these servers, which were located in Tampa, Florida, were superseded when Wikipedia migrated many of its sites to Virginia. However, the intention remains, and some of the old names can be found at https://wikitech.wikimedia .org/wiki/Obsolete:Pmtpa_cluster, accessed November 1, 2018. These include a server named "Pappas," which I would like to believe is a misspelling of Papias.

28. A. S. Byatt, preface to Hazel Bell, *From Flock Beds to Professionalism: A History of Index-Makers* (New Castle, DE: Oak Knoll, 2008), 11.

29. Cited in David W. Sabean, *Property, Production, and Family in Neckarhausen, 1700–1870* (Cambridge: Cambridge University Press, 1990), 66, 78.

30. Said in the House of Commons, November 11, 1947, *Hansard*, series 5, vol. 444, cols. 206–207; accessed online, June 3, 2019.

31. Cited in Carruthers, *Book of Memory*, 111.

INDEX

Aachen library, 29–30

Abbasid caliphate, 59–60

Abbreviationes chronicorum (Diceto), 55*fig*

Abelard, Peter, 56–57, 65
  Sic et non, 58–59, 84

abjad, 9, 10

Abridgment des plusieurs cases et resolutions del Common Ley (Rolle), 152–153

Académie des Sciences, Paris, 171

Académie française, 124n, 195

Accademia della Crusca, 123–124

accession numbers, 97–98, 165

acrostics, 9, 20

Adagia (Erasmus), 109, 127

Advis pour dresser une bibliothèque (Naudé), 162–163

Aelfric, Abbot, 37

Aeneid (Virgil), 21

Aesop's Fables, 24

Agricola, Rodolphus, *De formando studio*, 126

Akkadian, 11–12

Albertus Magnus, 59, 70

Alcuin of York, 29–30

Aldrovandi, Ulisse, *Pandechion epistemonicon*, 145–146

Alembert, Jean le Rond d', and Denis Diderot, *L'Encyclopédie, ou dictionnaire raisonné des sciences, des arts et des métiers*, 191–193

Alexander II, Pope, 48

Alexander III, Pope, 48–49

Alexander of Hales, 76–77, 85

Alexander Severus, Emperor, 27

Alexandria, 14–15

Al-Khalil Ibn Aḥmad, *Kitāb al-'ain*, 62

alphabetical inlay dividers, 210–211

alphabetical order
  absolute, 17–18, 21, 22
  in dictionaries, 100–101, 103–104
  directions regarding, 100–101, 103–104, 168
  in *distinctiones*, 74
  early use of, 11–21
  early versions of, 31–32, 38–39
  in encyclopedias, 186–195
  establishment of, xxv–xxvi
  first-letter, 17–19, 21, 24, 26, 31–32, 35, 36, 54, 97, 103, 115–116, 137, 145
  hierarchical order mixed with, 86–87, 97
  intermittent use of, 131–132
  justifications for, 82
  for legal documents, 153–154
  for library catalogs, 212–213, 215
  in medical texts, 89
  in modern times, 221, 222–223, 227–229

alphabetical order (*continued*)
  in Muslim world, 61
  neutrality of, xxii–xxiii
  objections to, 70, 184, 193–195
  as overlooked, 234–235
  partial, 17, 18–19
  for purposes of memory, 23–24
  transition to, 99–100
alphabet(s)
  as abstraction, 8
  appearance of term, 11
  of consonants, 9
  ease of learning, 9
  hierarchy of, xx–xxi
  invention of, 7–8
  Latin, 10–11
  non-Latin, 64–65
  set order of, xviii
  syllabaries, 228, 230
alphabet song, 214n
Alphabetum in artem sermoncinandi,
  74
Alphabetum narrationum
  (Arnold of Liège), 85
Alsted, Johann Heinrich,
  *Encyclopaedia septem tomis
  distincta,* 185–186, 233
Amberg File and Index Co., 210
American Library Association, 217n,
  218
Amherst College, 216–218
Analects of Confucius, 105
anthologies, 41. *See also* florilegia
Aquinas, Thomas, St., 59, 65–66, 83,
  120
  Summa theologica, 58, 59, 66 126
Arabic numerals, 65, 65*fig*
Arabic script, 9–10
Arabic translations, 63
Aramaic, 9–10
archives
  etymology of, xxvii

government, 53–54, 202–203
  Papal, 201–202
  royal, 138–139
Archives nationales, France, 203
Aristotle, 39–40, 42, 59, 60, 63, 66, 83
  Constitutions, 14
  Nichomachean Ethics, 126
  Politics, 14
Ark of Studies, The (Harrison), 177n
arks, xxviii, 176–177, 178*fig,* 179, 198
Arnold, Matthew, 134
Arnold of Liège, *Alphabetum
  narrationum,* 85
Art of Excerpting, The (Placcius),
  178*fig*
Arundel, Thomas, Archbishop of
  Canterbury, 69
Ashe, Thomas, *Table Generall del
  Common Ley Dengleter &c.,* 154
As You Like It (Shakespeare), 113n
Athenaeus, 24
atlases, 114–115
Augsburg City Library, 161
Augustine of Hippo, St., 33, 77, 83
  De arte praedicandi, 113
Augustinian order, 72
authority, questioning of, 123–124
Avicenna, 63, 115
al-Aziz Billah, Caliph, 60

Babylonian writing, 5*fig*
Bacon, Francis, 1st Viscount St. Alban,
  129–130, 191–192, 216
  De augmentis scientiarum and
  Instauratio magna, 185
al-Baghdādi, al-Khatib, 61
bags, storage in, 145, 200
Bakhshali manuscript, 65*fig*
Balbi, Giovanni, *Summa grammaticalis
  quae vocatur catholicon,* 102,
  103–104, 107, 122, 167–168
bamboo tablets, 25

Banks, Sir Joseph, 198–199
banned books, 155–156
Barbarigo, Marco and Agostino, 137
Bartholomew the Englishman, *De proprietatibus rerum*, 33, 67
Basil I, Emperor of the East, 44–45
Basilika (Royal Laws), 44–45
Bayle, Pierre, *Dictionaire critique*, 187–188, 188*fig*, 233
Bell Telephone Company, 226
Beauvoir, Simone de, *The Second Sex*, 156n
Benedict, St., and Rule of, 28, 43
Benedictine order, 27–42, 43–44, 53, 70
Berckheyde, Gerrit, *A Notary in His Office*, 145
Bernard, Daniël, 141
Bernard of Clairvaux, St., 58
Bible
    concordances to, 79–81, 86, 88–89
    division of, 70, 80
    Old Testament, 9, 20, 65
    printed editions of, 107
    Psalms, 9, 20
    reference works and, 25–26, 36, 37, 41, 57–58, 59, 73–74
    Revelation, Book of, 235
bibliographies, 17, 98, 119, 120–123, 222
Biblioteque des enfans, ou les premiers elemens des lettres, La (Dumas), 180*fig*
Bibliotheca universale sacro-profano, antico-moderna (Coronelli), 189
Bibliotheca universalis (Gesner), 121
binding process, 111–112
biographical dictionaries, 61
Black Death, 49
block-printed works, 105
Blotius, Hugo, 170

Bodley, Sir Thomas, 159–160, 161–162, 163
    Bodleian Library, 156n, 161n, 162, 164
Bologna, University of, 57
Bonaventura, St., 85
Boniface, Pope, 49
Boniface, St., 43–44
book-auction catalogs, 118
book formats, 118n
bookkeepers' desks, 207
bookkeeping, double-entry
    description of, 135–137
    ledgers and, 51–52, 135–137, 141, 201, 219
    waste books, 136, 145
Book of Commandments (Maimonides), 65
books
    as authorities, 123–4
    chained, 96
    children's picture books, 179–81
    codices, 25
    forbidden/banned, 155–156
    horn books, 124–125
    See also printing; *individual authors*
booksellers/bookshops, xxiv, 109–110, 117–119
Borges, Jorge Luis, xxiv–xxv, 192–193n
Bourgeois Gentilhomme, Le (Molière), 234
box file, 209–210
Boyle, Robert, 146–147
Bradford, William, 141–142
Brecht, Bertolt, *Threepenny Novel*, 193n
Brethren of Purity, 60
British Museum (now Library), 160, 164n, 213, 227
Brito, William, *Summa*, or *Expositiones difficilorum verborum de Biblia*, 101

broadsides, 109–110, 117
Byatt, A. S., 234
Byzantine Empire, 34–35

cabinets of curiosities, 156–158,
    157*fig*
Cai Lun, 25
Caius, John, 159–160
Callimachus
    and authorship of the *Pinakes*, 16
    Local Terms, 18
call numbers, 165
Cambridge University, 57, 159–160
    Cambridge University Library, 161
Canaanites, 9, 10
Cangjie Primer, The, 23
Canterbury Tales, The (Chaucer), 232
capite ad calcem, a, 88, 115, 116
capitulum, 46
Capuchin order, 72
carbon paper, 211
card catalogs, 159, 167–168, 170–173,
    215–216, 219
Carmelite order, 72
Carroll, Lewis, 4*fig*
Carthusian order, 44
catalogs
    alphabetical, 164
    book-auction, 118
    booksellers,' 118–119
    for cabinets of curiosities,
        156–158
    card, 159, 167–168, 170–173, 215,
        219
    instructions for, 172–173
    library, 16–17, 29–30, 97–99,
        159–166
    union, 94–95
"Catalogue Aria," 171n
Catalogue of English Printed Books
    (Maunsell), 119–121
Catalogue of Women, The, 13

*Catalogus illustrium virorum
    Germaniae* (Tritheim), 119
Catalogus scriptorum ecclesiae, 98, 119
categorization by subject, 53–54,
    60–61, 62. See also *topoi*
Cathars, 72
cathedral schools, 56–57
Catherine of Aragon, 150*fig*
Catholicon. See *Summa grammaticalis
    quae vocatur catholicon* (Balbi)
Cato, Dionysius, *Disticha de moribus*,
    40
Cawdrey, Robert, *A Table
    Alphabeticall*, 100–101n
census records, 19
chained books, 96
Chambers, Ephraim, *Cyclopaedia, or,
    An Universal Dictionary of the
    Arts and Sciences*, 189–191, 192,
    196
chancellery of Frederick II
    Hohenstaufen, 50
Chaos (Ringelberg), 173–174
Charlemagne, Emperor of the
    Romans, 29, 44
Charles V, Holy Roman Emperor, 149
Chartres Cathedral school, 56–57
Chaucer, Geoffrey, 40
    The Canterbury Tales, 232
Chauliac, Guy de, *Chirurgia magna*,
    88, 115
Cheng, Emperor of China, 22–23
Cheng Ju, *A Tale of the National
    Library*, 50
chests, for document storage,
    149–151, 207
China, 22–23, 25, 33–34, 50, 105
Chinese writing systems, 6–7,
    230–231
Chirurgia magna (Chauliac), 88, 115
Chronicles (Holinshed), 113n
chronological order, 131

Church Fathers, writings of, 28, 41, 57–58, 59

Churchill, Sir Winston, 235

Cicero, Marcus Tullius, 40

Cistercian order, 44, 58, 72, 77–78

Civil War (English), 137–138

clay tablets, 5, 5*fig*, 12

clocks, 90

Codex Cumanicus, 103

codices, 25

Cogswell, Joseph, 213

Coke, Sir Edward, *Coke's Reports*, 154

Colbert, Jean-Baptiste, Marquis de Torcy, 143

Cold Comfort Farm (Gibbons), 129n

Coleridge, Samuel Taylor, 195
   Encyclopaedia Metropolitana, 194

Colón, Hernando, 159

Collection of All the Statutes, 153

colophon, printer's, 107–108

Comenius, Jan, *Orbis sensualium pictus*, 179–181

commonplaces/commonplace books, 40–41, 84–85, 125–130, 152–153, 181–184, 187.
   See also *topoi*

compendia, 82

computer keyboards, 229–231

concordances, 79–81, 86, 88–89

Concordanciae anglicanae, 80

Concordanciae Johannis de Sancto Amando, 89

Concordanciae Petro de Sancto Floro, 89

Constantine the African, 63

Constitutions (Aristotle), 14

construction and carpentry, 12–13

contributor model, encyclopedias, 189

Cook, James, 199

Copernicus, Nicolaus, 156n

copper plates, 106

copybooks/copy-press, 205–207, 206*fig*, 211

Cornu Copiae (Perotti), 112

Coronelli, Vincenzo Maria,
   Bibliotheca universale sacro-profano, antico-moderna, 188–189

correspondence, 18, 48–49, 137, 139, 142, 204–206, 209, 219

Cotton, Sir Robert, 160

counting-house desks, 207

Coy, George, 224–225

cross-referencing, 61, 87, 154, 163, 190–191

Croswell, William, 212–213

cuneiform, 2–3, 12

cupboards, 151. *See also* chests

currencies/money, 8, 47, 106

cursive scripts, 4–5, 6

Cyclopaedia, or, An Universal Dictionary of the Arts and Sciences (Chambers), 189–191, 192, 196

cylinder desk, 207–209

Dante Alighieri, *Divine Comedy*, 90

Darwin, Charles, 156n

Darwin, Erasmus, 156n

dating, standardization of, 52, 53

Datini, Francesco di Marco, 135

days, divisions of, 32

De architectura (Vitruvius), 115

De arte praedicandi (Augustine), 113

De augmentis scientiarum (Bacon), 185

De computis et scripturis (Pacioli), 135–136

De conscribendis epistolis (Erasmus), 128

Decretum Gratiani, 77, 78*fig*

De formando studio (Agricola), 126

De grammatica (Gesner), 122

De legibus et consuetudinibus angliae,
151
De materia medica (Dioscorides), 89
De naturis rerum (Neckam), 66–67
De proprietatibus rerum (Bartholomew
the Englishman), 33, 67
desks, 149, 150*fig*, 207–209, 208*fig*
determinatives, 6, 7
Deusdedit, Cardinal, 45–46
De verborum significatu, 22
De virtutibus herbarum, 115
Dewey, Melvil, 185n, 216–218
Dewey decimal system, 217–218, 234
dialectical reasoning, 58, 66
Diamond Sutra, 105
Diceto, Ralph de, 52–53, 54–55, 55*fig*,
75, 160
   Abbreviationes chronicorum, 55*fig*
Dictionaire critique (Bayle), 187–188,
188*fig*, 233
dictionaries
   Arabic, 62
   biographical, 61
   Chinese, 23, 33–34
   early, 22
   first Latin, 38–39
   Hebrew, 36–37, 79
   law, 153, 155n
   medical, 88–89
   multilingual, 102
   organization within, 101–103
   precursors to, 11–12
   renewed interest in, 100–101
   rhyming, 37
   See also individual works
dictionary-making, 21
   Balbi, Giovanni, 102–104
   Papias the Lombard, 38–39
   See also index cards, notebooks,
      paper books, slips of paper
Diderot, Denis, and Jean le Rond
   d'Alembert, *L'Encyclopédie, ou*

*dictionnaire raisonné des sciences,
des arts et des métiers,* 191–193
Die erleuchteten Fenster (Doderer), 203
Dioscorides, 116
   De materia medica, 89
   Dioscorides alphabeticus, 89
diple, 110–111
Dissolution of the Monasteries,
   England and Wales, 159
Disticha de moribus (Dionysius Cato),
   40
distinctiones, 73–74, 81–82, 122, 126,
   136
dividers for card catalogs, 215–216
Divine Comedy (Dante), 90
documents
   dating of, 52
   education and, 56
   increased reliance on, 46–50,
      197–198, 207
   indexes for, 142–143, 148–149
   standardization of, 48
   storage for, 149–151
Doderer, Heimito von, *Die erleuchteten
   Fenster,* 203
Domesday Book, xxi–xxii, 47
Dominican order, 72
Dondi, Giovanni, 90
Don Giovanni (Mozart), 171n
donors, organization by, 161n
double-entry bookkeeping, 135–137
Dr. Faustus (Marlowe), 184–185
Dumas, Louis, *La biblioteque des
   enfans, ou les premiers elemens des
   lettres,* 179, 180*fig*
Durham Plant Glossary, 89
Dyer, Sir James, 154

education, 56–57, 124–125
Edward I, King of England, 39, 48,
   53
Egyptian writing, 4–6, 8–9

Elementarium doctrinae rudimentum
  (Papias), 38–39
Encyclopaedia Britannica, 192–193n,
  193–194, 196n
Encyclopaedia Metropolitana
  (Coleridge), 194
Encyclopaedia septem tomis distincta
  (Alsted), 185–186
encyclopedias, 31–34, 39, 60, 66–68,
  145, 182, 184–195, 222–223,
  233. *See also individual works*
*Encyclopédie, ou dictionnaire raisonné
  des sciences, des arts et des métiers,
  L'* (Diderot and d'Alembert),
  191–193
Encyclopédie française, 196n
*Encyclopédie méthodique, ou par ordre
  des matières* (Panckoucke), 193
envelopes, absence of, 139
ephemeral writing media, 12,
  132–134, 141, 174n
Erasmus, Desiderius
  Adagia, 109, 127
  De conscribendis epistolis, 128
Erya, 23
Estienne, Henri, 109
Estienne, Robert, 117–118
Etruscans, 10
Etymologiae (Isidore), 31–32, 35, 39,
  66
Euclid, 63
Euripides, 18
Eusebius of Caesarea, *Onomasticon*,
  25–26, 27
Evelyn, John, 111n
  "Method for a Librarie According to
  the Intellectual Powers",
  162–163
*Expositiones terminorum legum
  Anglorum*, 153
Eyb, Albrecht von, *Margarita poetica*,
  125–126

Fabularius (Konrad of Mure), 68
al-Fārābi, 60–61, 63
Faunt, Nicholas, 143
Fayt, Jean de, 168
Febvre, Lucien, *Encyclopédie française*,
  196n
Ferdinand I, Holy Roman Emperor,
  145
Festus, Sextus Pompeius, 22
filing
  alphabetical inlay dividers for,
    210–211
  bags for, 145, 200
  box files for, 209–210
  copybooks/copy-press and, 205–207,
    206fig, 211
  of correspondence, 204–206, 219
  hanging or vertical files for,
    219–220
  lever-arch files for, 210–211,
    211fig, 216
  paper pouches for, 200
  Pepys and, 140–142
  ring binders for, 210–211
  with string, 140–141, 204
  systems for, 143–147
  two-hole punch and, 210
filing cabinets, 210
Five Classics, 105
Flaccus, Marcus Verrius, 22
Fleming, Abraham, 113n
florilegia, 40–42, 58, 77, 81–82,
  84–85, 86, 125–126
Florilegium angelicum, 86
Florilegium gallicum, 86
Fogel, Martin, 178
folios, 112, 118n
fonds, archival method, 202–203
footnotes, precursors to, 56
form (for typesetting), 107
forms, blank, 141–142
Franciscan order, 72, 94–95

Franciscan library catalogs
Registrum librorum angliae, 94–95,
98
*Tabula septem custodiarum super
bibliam*, 95
Frankfurt book fair, 108–109, 118
Franklin, Benjamin, 40
Fraunce, Abraham, 155
Frederick II Hohenstaufen, Holy
Roman Emperor, 50
French Revolution, 166, 172
Fréteval, Battle of, 49
Froschauer, Christoph, 118
Fulbert, Bishop, 56
furniture, 149–151, 150*fig*, 158*fig*,
173–179, 178*fig*, 204, 207,
208*fig*
Fust, Johann, 107, 113
futhorc (also futhark; runes), 64

Galen of Pergamon, 21, 63, 88
Interpretation of Hippocratic Glosses
and *On the Properties of Food*, 21
Galileo Galilei, 156n
Gaon, Rav Saadiah, 36–37
Garampi, Cardinal Giuseppe, 201
Gart der Gesundtheit, 116
Gates, Bill, xxviii
genealogy, as sorting system, 13
Geographia (Ptolemy), 114
geographical divisions, as sorting
system, 13
Gerard of Abbeville, 93
Gesner, Conrad, 120–121, 133n,
143–144, 175
Bibliotheca universalis, 121
De grammatica, 122
Historia animalium, 122–123
*Pandectarum sive partitionum
universalium...libri XXI*,
121–123, 164, 169

al-Ghazali, 63
Gibbons, Stella, *Cold Comfort Farm*,
129n
Glossarium affatim, 36
glosses/glossaries, 11–12, 15, 18, 22,
34–36, 37
Goethe, Johann Wolfgang von, 200
Googe, Barnabe, *The Zodyake of
Life*,113
Gossart, Jan, *Portrait of a Tax-collector*,
140–141
Göttingen, University of, 165, 213
Grand dictionaire historique (Moréri),
186–187
grading systems, academic, alphabet-
based, 213–214
Great Library of Alexandria, 15–18
Greece/Greek
alphabet of, 10–11
alphabetical order in, 19
rediscovery of classical texts, 59–60,
63–64
writing in, 9, 13
Gregory VII, Pope, 46
Gregory IX, Pope, 57
Grosseteste, Robert, Bishop of
Lincoln, 75–76, 79, 82, 168
Guide for the Perplexed (Maimonides),
65
guidebooks, 103
Gunn, James Newton, 216
Gutenberg, Johannes, 107–108

Hadith, 61
al-Hakam II, Caliph, 60
Hale, Sir Matthew, 152
Hanessiah, Moses ben Isaac, *Sefer ha-
Shoham*, 102
hanging files, 219–220
hanja, 106
Harleian Library, 164

Harley, Edward, 2nd Earl of Oxford
and Earl Mortimer, 164n
Harley, Robert, 1st Earl of Oxford and
Earl Mortimer, 164n
Harris, John, *Lexicon Technicum*,
189
Harrison, Thomas, 176–177, 202n
The Ark of Studies, 177n
Harrison's Ark, 176–177, 178*fig*,
179
Harsdörffer, Georg Philipp, 178–179,
216
Hartlib, Samuel, 176
Harvard College, 212–215
Harvard Graduate School of Business,
216
headings, Aristotle on, 39–40
Headlong Hall (Peacock), 195
head-to-heel, as sorting order, 88, 115,
116
Hebrew codices, 36
Hebrew dictionaries, 79
Hebrew scholars, 62–63
Hebrew script, 9
Hegel, G. F. W., 177
Henry II, King of England, 49
Henry VIII, King of England, 149,
150*fig*, 159
Henry of Bracton, *De legibus et
consuetudinibus angliae*, 151
herbals, 89, 115–117
Herbarium of Apuleius, 116
Herbarius, 116
Hesiod, 13
Heungdeok Temple, Korea, 106
Heyne, Christian Gottlob, 165
hierarchical order
combined with other systems, 87,
93, 100, 149
early use of, 24, 33, 41, 53, 65–66,
67–68

encyclopedias and, 185–186, 188,
190–191, 194
lack of consistent use of, 138
in libraries, 28–30, 161, 163
overturning of, 166
hieratic (sacred) script, Egypt, 4–5, 6
hieroglyphics, 4–6, 8–9
Hippocrates of Kos, 63
Hippolytus of Rome, 11
hiragana (Japanese script), 230
Historia animalium (Gesner),
122–123
Hobbes, Thomas, 156n
Hohe Schule (University of the Third
Reich), 222
Holdsworth, Richard, 181
Holinshed, Raphael, *Chronicles of
England, Scotland and Ireland*,
113n
Homer, *The Iliad*, 13
Hooke, Robert, 147
horn books, 124–125
Hotot, Richard, 56
hours, calculation of, 32
house numbering, 138
Hugh of Pisa, 83, 102
Magnae derivationes, 101
Hugh of St. Cher, 79
Hugh of St. Victor, 84–85
humanism, 166
Humbert of Romans, 96
hypertext, 232–233
Hypnerotomachia Poliphili (Manutius),
110

Ibn Gabirol, 63
Ibn Manẓūr, *Lisān al-Arab*, 62
Ibn Sa'd, *Kitāb al-abaqāt al-kabīr*, 61
Ibn Sīda, *Mukhaṣṣaṣ*, 62
ideograms/ideographic writing, xviii, 1,
5–6, 7, 231

Iliad (Homer), 13
indented paragraphs, 110
index cards, 166, 171–172, 198–199
indexes
    for Aristotle's works, 83
    for commonplace books, 129
    compilation instructions for, 169
    cross-referencing, 61, 87, 154, 163,
        190–191
    development of, 114–116
    for documents, 142–143, 148–149
    early versions of, 36, 69, 74–75,
        113–114
    for Erasmus, 127
    Gesner's, 121–122
    in herbals, 116–117
    importance of, 104
    increased use of, 82–83
    instructions for, 114, 122
    for ledgers, 204–205
    for legal documents, 151, 153, 154
    for library catalogs, 161, 212
    Locke's, 182–184, 183*fig*
    marginal notations for, 75–76
    in medical texts, 115, 116
    precursors to, 45
    for *Roget's Thesaurus*, 229
    section numbers used in, 77–78
Index librorum prohibitorum, 156
Innocent VIII, Pope, 155
Instauratio magna (Bacon), 185
Institutio Oratoria (Quintilian), 40
insurance companies, 219
International Business Machines
    (IBM), 218
International Institute of Bibliography,
    221–222
International Olympic Committee
    (IOC), 227–228
Interpretation of Hippocratic Glosses
    (Galen), 21
inventories, library, 17, 22, 92, 95

"Iroha," 230
Isabella I, Queen of Castile, 149
Isidore of Seville, Archbishop, xxvii,
    30–32, 34, 38, 39–40, 160, 233,
    235
    Etymologiae, 31–32, 35, 39, 66
italic typefaces, 110, 119, 129

James, Thomas, 159–160, 161–162,
    163
James le Palmer, *Omne bonum*, 69
Japanese scripts, 230
Jefferson, Thomas, 185n
Jerome, St., 11, 26
    *Liber interpretationis hebraicorum
        nominum*, 26
Jewett, Charles Coffin, 215
Jiao Chou Luo (Zheng Quia), 50
Jikji, 106
John Balliol, King of the Scots, 39
John of Damascus, *Sacra parallela*, 41
John of Darlington, 80
John of Freiburg, *Summa confessorum*,
    79
John of Genoa. *See* Balbi, Giovanni
John the Saracen, 132
Joseph II, Holy Roman Emperor, 170
Josephinian library, 170, 201
Josephus, Flavius, 41
Juan, Prince of the Asturias, 137
Justinian, Emperor of the East, 44

kalendarium, 69
Kanish tablets, 12
kanji (Japanese script), 230
Kasirer, Justice Nicholas, 155n
katakana (Japanese script), 230
Kayser, Albrecht Christoph, *Über
    die Manipulation bey der
    Einrichtung einer Bibliothek
    und der Verfertigung der
    Bücherverzeichnisse*, 165–166

Kilwardby, Robert, 77
Kirkestede, Henry, 97–98, 119, 120
Kitāb al-abaqāt al-kabīr (Ibn Sa'd), 61
Kitāb al-'ain (Al-Khalīl Ibn Aḥmad), 62
Kitāb iḥsa al-ulûm, 60–61
Kitāb usūl al-shi'r al'Ibrāni, 36–37
Konrad of Mure, Fabularius, 68
Kublai Khan, 50
Kunstkammer, 156–158, 157fig

Læcboc, or Medicinale anglicum, 34
Laon Cathedral school, 56–57
Latin alphabet, 10–11
Laud Herbal Glossary, 89
law dictionaries, 153, 155n
law French, 152–153n
law/legal documents, 44–46, 54,
    151–155, 197–198
ledgers, 51–52, 135–136, 141,
    204–205, 206fig, 212, 219
Legenda aurea, 82
Leibniz, Gottfried Wilhelm von,
    163–165, 171, 177, 202n
Leicester, Robert de Breteuil, 3rd Earl
    of, 52
Leiden Glossary, 35
Leiden, University of, 161
leishu, 33–34
Leitz, Louis, 210, 216
Le Maire, Louis, 214n
Leo VI, Emperor of the East, 45
letterpress books, 205–207
letters, 10. See also alphabet(s)
letters/correspondence. See
    correspondence
lever-arch file, 210–211, 211fig, 216
Lewis, C. S., 167
lexicography, 21. See also dictionary-
    making
Lexicon Technicum, or, An Universal
    Dictionary of the Arts and Sciences
    (Harris), 189

Liber de scriptoribus ecclesiasticis
    (Tritheim), 1
Liber glossarum, 35
Liber interpretationis hebraicorum
    nominum (St. Jerome), 26
Liber scintillarum, 41
libraries
    accession or call numbers in, 97–98,
        165
    catalogs in, 16–17, 29–30, 97–99,
        159–166
    chained, 96
    confiscation of, 166
    Dewey decimal system in, 217–218,
        234
    evolution of, 158–159
    institutional, 43–44
    inventories of, 92
    monastery, 27–29, 91–93, 97–99,
        161n
    mosque, 60
    numbering system in, 172–173
    organization within, xxiv
    palace, 29–30
    private, 30–31, 43–44, 60, 93, 212
    shelf lists in, 165
    shelfmarks in, 97–98, 165
    subscription, 212
    synagogue, 51
    union catalogs and, 94–95
    university, 96, 212–213, 215–217
Library Hub Discover, 94
Library of Alexandria, 15–18
Libri quattuor sententiarum (Lombard),
    59, 72–74, 76, 77, 84, 85
Library of Congress, 185n
Linnaeus, Carl, 122, 198, 233, 234
Lisān al-Arab (Ibn Manẓūr), 62
"List of Taxed Lands, Slaves, and
    other Possessions" (Washington),
    200–201
lists, ordering of, 13

literacy, 27, 56, 124–125
Lloyd's of London, 214–215
Local Terms (Callimachus), 18
Locke, John, 181–184, 183*fig*, 190n, 233
logographic writing, 6–7, 230
Lombard, Peter, Bishop of Paris, *Libri quattuor sententiarum*, 59, 72–74, 76, 77, 84, 85, 120
Louis IX, King of France, 74, 132
Louis XIV, King of France, 143
Lucerne government, 148–149
Lydian kingdom, 8

Magnae derivationes (Hugh of Pisa), 101
Mahberet Menahem, 37
Maimonides (Moses ben Maimon), *Book of Commandments* and *Guide for the Perplexed*, 65–66
Malpighi, Marcello, 175
al-Mamun, Caliph, 60
manicules, 129
Manipulus florum (Thomas of Ireland), 86
Manuel I, King of Portugal, 138
manuscripts
    copying of, 21–22, 23–24, 83–84, 93, 123
    division of, 61–62, 76–77
    indexes for, 69, 74–76, 83
    revisions of, 69–70
    rubrication in, 62, 232
Manutius, Aldus, 119n, 233
    Hypnerotomachia Poliphili, 110
Manzolli, Pier Angelo, *Zodiacus vitae*,113n
Margarita poetica (Eyb), 125–126
marginal abbreviations/notations, 54–56, 55*fig*, 75–76, 129
Marlowe, Christopher, *Dr. Faustus*, 184–185

Marsh, Adam, 75–76
Martial (poet), 112
Martin of Poland, *Tabula Martiniana/ Margarita decretalium*, 54
Martius, Jeremias, 160–161
Masoretes, Masoretic texts, 79
matrix (for printing), 106–107
Maunsell, Andrew, *Catalogue of English Printed Books*, 119–121
Maximilian I, Holy Roman Emperor, 147–148
Mayan glyphs, 7
Mazarin, Cardinal Jules, 162
medical dictionaries, 88–89
medicine/medical writing, 21, 34, 63, 88, 115
memorandum books, 136, 143, 201
memory
    alphabetization for, 23–24
    decreased emphasis on, 181, 195–196
    legal span of, 48
    library inventories and, 93, 164
    non-alphabetical order for, 26
    as primary tool of scholarship, 61–62
Menahem Ibn Saruq, 37
mendicant preaching orders, 71–73
Merovingian law codes, 45
Meydenbach, Jakob, *Ortus [Hortus] sanitates*, 116
military records, 138, 218–219
Mishnah, 214
Mi Shu Sheng, 50
molds, for movable type, 106–107
Molière, *Le Bourgeois Gentilhomme*, 234
monasteries/monastery libraries, 27–28, 43–44, 53, 70, 91–93, 97–99, 161n
money/currencies, 8, 47, 106
Montaigne, Michel de, 156n

Montfort, Amaury de, 81

Moréri, Louis, *Grand dictionaire historique*, 186–187, 233

Moser, Johann Jakob, 179

mosque libraries, 60

Mouseion, 16

movable type, 106–107

Mozart, Wolfgang Amadeus
"Alphabet Song"/"Ah, vous direz-je, Maman", 214n
"Catalogue Aria", *Don Giovanni*, 171n

Mukhaṣṣaṣ (Ibn Sīda), 62

multilingual dictionaries, 102

Nabataean kingdom, 10

Nathan ben Jehiel, *Sefer ha'Aruhkh*, 62–63

Natural History (Pliny the Elder), 20

Naudé, Gabriel, *Advis pour dresser une bibliothèque*, 162–163

Neckam, Alexander, *De naturis rerum*, 66–67

Nelson's Perpetual Loose-leaf Encyclopedia, 222–223

New England Telephone and Telegraph Company, 225–226

newspapers, xix

New York Times, 205*fig*

Nicander of Colophon, 20

Nichomachean Ethics (Aristotle), 126

Nimrud ivories, 12

Nominale sive verbale in Gallicis cum expositione eiusdem in Anglicis, 37

Nomina multarum rerum anglice, 37

non-alphabetical cultures/scripts, xxi, 22–23, 227–231. *See also individual cultures and scripts*

North Semitic script, 8–9

Notary in His Office, A (Berckheyde), 145

notebooks
ledgers, 51–52, 136, 141, 204–205, 206*fig*, 219
paper books, 132, 175
ring binders, 210–211
tabbed, 175, 200

numbers, symbolism of, 32

numerals, Arabic, 65, 65*fig*; roman, 111, 112, 134

Nuremberg Chronicle, The, 114

octavo, 118n

Officina (Workshop; Textor), 128–129

Ogham script, 64

Old Hebrew script, 9

Old South Arabic script, 10

Old Testament, 9, 20, 65

Omne bonum, 187

Onomasticon (Eusebius), 25–26

Onomasticon (Julius Pollux), 24, 39

On the Place Names in the Holy Scriptures (Eusebius), 25–26

On the Properties of Food (Galen), 21

Oporinus, Johannes, 118

oracle bones, 6

Orbis sensualium pictus (Comenius), 179–181

Ortelius, Abraham
Theatrum orbis terrarum, 114–115
Thesaurus geographicus, 144, 144*fig*

Ortus [Hortus] sanitatis (Meydenbach), 116

Ostrogothic kingdom, 28

Otlet, Paul, 221–222

Oxford University, 57, 77, 96, 159–160, 161

Oxyrhynchus Papyri, 18, 22, 24

Pacioli, Luca, *De computis et scripturis*, 135–137

page numbers, development, 75, 111–113

Pamphilus of Alexandria, 89

Panckoucke, Charles-Joseph, *Encyclopédie méthodique, ou par ordre des matières*, 193

Pandechion epistemonicon (Aldrovandi), 145–146

Pandectae (Gesner), 121–122, 164, 169

Pandects (Roman law digest), 44

Panizzi, Antonio, 213

Papal Chancery, 131

papal records, 46, 48–49

paper
  cost of, 132
  development of, 25
  impact of, 51–52
  increased reliance on, 197–198
  quires, 111, 132
  in Sicily, 50, 51
  slips of, 144, 145–146, 159, 164, 168–170, 177, 198–199, 178*fig*

paper books, 132, 175

paper pouches, 200

paperwork. *See* documents

Papias the Lombard, *Elementarium doctrinae rudimentum*, 38–39, 45, 102

papyri/papyrus scrolls, 5, 13–14, 18

paragraph marks, 110

parchment, 14, 25, 51, 54, 78, 132, 141, 168

Paris, Matthew, 55–56

Paris, Université de, 56–57, 66, 67, 82–84, 85. *See also* Sorbonne

Paul IV, Pope, 156

Paul the Deacon, 22

Peacock, Thomas Love, *Headlong Hall*, 195

pecia (piece) manuscript-copying system, 84, 93

pencils, development of 133

Pepys, Samuel, 133, 139–140, 141, 142, 143

Pères de l'Oratoire library, 169–170

Perotti, Niccolò, *Cornu Copiae*, 112

Peter of St. Fleur, 89

Petra, 10, 13

Petrarch, 117

Philip II, King of France, 49

Philip III, King of France 49

Philip IV, King of France, 49

Philip II, King of Spain, 141

Philitas of Cos, *Rare Words in No Particular Order*, 15

Philo of Alexandria, 41

Phoenicia/Phoenicians, 9, 12

phone books, xxiii, 223–227, 233

pictographs, 1, 4, 10

pigeonholes, 182, 207, 208–209, 208*fig*

Pinakes (Tables), 16–17, 18

pinyin and computers, 231

Pinyin Chinese–English Dictionary, The, 231

Placcius, Vincentius, 176–177
  The Art of Excerpting, 178*fig*

Plautus, 20

playing cards, sorting, indexing with, 171–173

Pliny the Elder, *Natural History*, 20–21

Politics (Aristotle), 14

Pollux, Julius, *Onomasticon*, 24, 39

Ponte, Lorenzo da, "Catalogue Aria", *Don Giovanni*, 171n

Pope, Alexander, 40

population, increase in, 46, 197

Portrait of a Tax-collector (Gossart), 140–141

portable writing desks, 149, 207

post office directories, 223

pouches, paper, 200

preachers, mendicant, 71–73

primers, children's, 179–181
printers' broadsides, 109–110, 117
printing
  binding process, 111–112
  block-printing, 105–106
  colophons, 107–108
  copper plates, 106
  diple, 110–111
  folios and signatures, 111–112,
    118n
  footnotes, precursors to, 56
  form (for typesetting), 107
  formats, 118n
  impact of, 104, 117
  italic typefaces, 110, 119, 129
  manicules, 129
  matrix, 106–107
  molds for, and movable type,
    106–107
  page numbering, pagination, 75,
    111–113
  paragraphs, 110
  printing press, 106–108
  punch tool, 106
  quotation mark, development of,
    110–111
  running heads, 76
  symbols used in printed texts,
    110–111
  tables, 16
  tables of contents, 31, 46, 69, 154
  type cases, 107, 173, 174*fig*
  typographical elements,
    distinguishing elements with,
    110, 119, 129, 187, 188*fig*
provenance, principles of, 202n
Prytaneion, 13
Psalms, Book of, 9, 20
Ptolemaic Egypt, 14–15, 19
Ptolemy, Claudius, 63
  Geographia, 114

Ptolemy I of Egypt, 15
Ptolemy II Philadelphus of Egypt, 15
punch (tool), 106

quadrivium, 31, 57, 68, 216
quarto, 118n
Quintilian, *Institutio Oratoria*, 40
quires, 111, 132
quotation mark, development of,
  110–111
Qur'an, 60

radicals, 23, 230, 231
Rare Words (Zenodotus), 18
Rare Words in No Particular Order
  (Philitas of Cos), 15
al-Rashid, Harun, Caliph, 60
Rasis (Muhammad ibn Zakariya al-
  Razi), 115
Rastell, William, *Collection of All the
  Statutes*, 153
Raymond of Toledo, Archbishop, 63
reading
  in monasteries, 28
  nonlinear, xxvi, 25
  purpose of, 82
  Rule of St. Benedict on, 43
  teaching, 125, 179–181
  technologies for, 24–25
  types of, xxvi–xxvii
real concordances, 81
rebus, 2, 4, 4*fig*, 6
recto, 112
reference works
  cross-referencing, 61, 87, 154, 163,
    190–191
  development of, 25–26
  first, 74
  legal, 153
  *See also individual types of reference
    works and individual titles*

Reger, Johann, 114
Registrum librorum angliae, 94–95, 98
Res rusticae (Varro), 20
Revelation, Book of, 235
Rheticus, Georg Joachim, 144
rhyming dictionaries, 37
Richard I, King of England, 48, 49
Richard of Stavensby, 80
Richard of Wallingford, 90
Richelieu, Cardinal Armand du Plessis, Duc de, 124n
ring binders, 210–211
Ringelberg, Joachim Sterck van, *Chaos*, 173–174
rock paintings, 1, 2
Roget's Thesaurus, 229
Rolle, Sir Henry, *Abridgment des plusieurs cases et resolutions del Common Ley*, 152–153
rolltop desk, 207–209
rōmaji (Japanese roman script), 230
Roman Empire, 10, 19–20, 27
Rostgaard, Frederik, 162n
"round robin" letters, 2, 3*fig*
Royal Court Library (Vienna), 170
Rozier, Abbé François, 170–172
rubrication, 62, 232
running heads, 76

Sacra parallela (John of Damascus), 41
Salamanca, University of, 57
Salesbury, William, 100n
Schedario Garampi, 202
Schöffer, Peter, 107, 113, 116
Scholasticism, 57–58, 65, 66
School of Wisdom, Basra, 60
Schwenter, Daniel, 215–216
scribes, 22, 35, 39, 48, 65, 75, 82, 84, 85, 92, 123
scrolls, 5, 15–18, 24–25

Second Sex, The (Beauvoir), 156n
Second World War, 222
Sefer ha'Aruhkh (ben Jehiel), 62–63
Sefer ha-Shoham (Hanessiah), 102
Sentences (Sextus), 23–24
sermons, 71–73, 86. *See also distinctiones*
Sextus the Pythagorean, 23–24
Shakespeare, William, *As You Like It*, 113n
Shannon Company, 210, 211*fig*
shelf lists, 165
shelfmarks, 97–98, 165
Shirley, James, 162n
Shuō wén jiě zì, 23
Sic et non (Abelard), 58–59, 84
signatures, 111–112, 118n
single-author volumes, 117
Sir Gawain and the Green Knight, 160
slates, writing tools, 174n
slips of paper, 144, 145–146, 159, 164, 168–170, 177, 198–199, 1787*fig*
Smithsonian Institution, 215
social status, organization by, xxii–xxiii, 214
Solander, David, 198–199
solander box, 199*fig*, 199n, 209–210
Sorbonne, 57, 81, 87, 93–94, 96, 156. *See also* Paris, Université de
sorting furniture, 175–179, 178*fig*
sorting systems, non-alphabetical
 a capite ad calcem or head-to-heel, 88, 115, 116
 chronological, 131
 by donor, 161n
 genealogical, 13
 geographical, 13
 by grades/grading, 213–214
 hierarchical (*see* hierarchical order)
 by social status, xxii–xxiii, 214
 by sound group, 62
 by subject, 45, 53–54, 60–61, 62

theologically based, 33–34
by *topoi*, 39–40, 41–42, 126–130,
190
Speculum maius (Vincent of Beauvais)
Speculum doctrinale, 67–68
Speculum historiale, 67–69, 86
Speculum naturale, 67–68
Speculum vitae (Zamora), 113–114
spelling, not standardized, 39
spindle/spike, 204, 205*fig*, 206*fig*, 210
street guides, 223
subscription libraries, 212
Suda, 34–35, 76
Sumeria, 2–3, 5, 11–12
Sumerian cuneiform, 2–3
Summa, or *Expositiones difficilorum
verborum de Biblia* (Brito), 101
Summa confessorum (John of Freiburg),
79
*Summa grammaticalis quae vocatur
catholicon* (Balbi), 102, 103–104,
107, 122, 168
Summa theologica (Aquinas), 58, 59,
66, 126
supermarkets, xix–xx
surnames, alphabetization by, 120, 162
switchboards, telephone, 224–226
syllabaries, 228, 230
symbols used in printed texts,
110–111
Synopsis basilicorum maior, 45

tabbed cards/dividers, 215–216
tabbed notebooks, 175, 200
Table Alphabeticall, A (Cawdrey),
100–101n
*Table Generall del Common Ley
Dengleter &c.* (Ashe), 154
tables, 16
tables of contents, 31, 46, 69, 154
*Tables of Men Illustrious in Every Field of
Learning and of Their Writing*, 17

*Tabula Martiniana/Margarita
decretalium*, 54
*Tabula notabilium gestorum quae in hoc
libro continentur per alphabetum
reducta*, 46
*Tabula septem custodiarum super
bibliam*, 95
Tabulating Machine Company, 218
Taejong, King of Korea, 106
Tale of the National Library, A
(Cheng Ju), 50
Tanach, 37
tax records, 18–19, 46–47
telephone directories, 223–227, 233
telephone exchanges, 223–226
Terence (Roman playwright), 128
Termes de la ley, 153
Textor, Johannes Ravisius, *Officina*,
128–129
Theatrum orbis terrarum (Ortelius),
114–115
theologically based sorting method,
33–34
Thesaurus geographicus (Ortelius),
144*fig*
Thomas of Ireland, *Manipulus florum*,
86–87
Threepenny Novel (Brecht), 193n
time
as abstraction, 90
divisions of, 32
relative dating and, 52
topoi, 39–40, 41–42, 126–130, 190
Torah, 65
translations of classical works, 63–64
Trefler, Florian, 159
Tritheim, Johann, *Catalogus illustrium
virorum Germaniae* and *Liber de
scriptoribus ecclesiasticis*, 119
trivium, 31, 57, 68, 216
Trumbull, Sir William, 175
Turri, Pellegrino, 211n

two-hole punch, 210
type cases, 107, 173, 174*fig*
typewriters, 211–212, 229–230
typographical desk, 179, 180*fig*
typographical elements, distinguishing
    elements with, 110, 119, 129,
    187, 188*fig*

Über die Manipulation bey der
    Einrichtung einer Bibliothek
    und der Verfertigung der
    Bücherverzeichnisse (Kayser),
    165–166
union catalogs, 94–95
Universal Bibliography (Otlet), 222
universities, early, 56–57. *See also*
    individual universities
university libraries, 96, 212–213,
    215–217
urbanization, 2, 71, 124
Urra=hubullu, 11–12

Varro, *Res rusticate*, 20
Vatican library, 100
Vatican Secret Archive, 201–202
Venetian Chancery, 145
verbal concordances, 79–81
verso, 112
vertical file, 219–220
Vertuose Boke of Distyllacyon, The,
    117
Villiers, Édouard de, 199
Vincent of Beauvais, 67–69, 74, 86
    Speculum maius: Part I, Speculum
        naturale; Part II, Speculum
        doctrinale; Part III, Speculum
        historiale; Part IV, Speculum
        morale, 67–69, 86
Virgil, *The Aeneid*, 21
Vitruvius, *De architectura*, 115

Vives, Jan Ludovicus, 126,
    181–182
Vocabolario degli accademici della
    Crusca, 123–124
vocabulary tablets, 11–12
Voltaire, 156n

Wadi el-Ḥôl, 8–9
Waldensians, 72
Walsingham, Sir Francis, 142–143
Wanley, Humfrey, 164
War Department, US, 218
Washington, George, "List of Taxed
    Lands, Slaves, and other
    Possessions", 200–201
waste books, 136, 145
Watts, Isaac, 184
wax tablets, 12, 132, 134
Wedgwood, Ralph, 211n
Western Desert, Egypt, 8–9
White Pages, 226, 233
Wikipedia, 233
William of Nottingham, 75
William the Breton, 101
William the Conqueror, King of
    England, xxi–xxii, 49
Wolfenbüttel library, 163–164
Wonders of Nature, The (Vincent),
    158*fig*
woodblocks, 105–106
Wooton Company, 207–209
word lists, 11–12, 18, 22
WorldCat bibliographic database, 94
World War II, 222
World Wide Web Consortium (W3C),
    230
writing
    alphabetic and syllabic, xviii
    control of knowledge of, 7
    of grammatical elements, 2
    history of, 1–26

ideographic, ideograms, xviii, 1, 5–6,
7, 231
importance of, xviii–xix
invention of, 6
linear systems for, 2
origins of, xvii–xviii
See also alphabet(s); nonalphabetical cultures/scripts;
individual cultures/scripts
writing mediums, 12, 13–14
writing tables, 133–134,
141
Wu, Jinrong, *The Pinyin Chinese–
English Dictionary*, 231

Wunderkammer, 156–158, 157*fig*

Yale College, 212, 214
Yellow Pages, 226

Zamora, Rodrigo de, *Speculum vitae*,
113–114
Zenodotus, 15, 16
Rare Words, 18
Zheng Quia, *Jiao Chou Luo*, 50
Zodiacus vitae, as *The Zodyake of Life*,
113

Clive Barda

Judith Flanders is a social historian. Her works include the bestselling *The Invention of Murder, Inside the Victorian Home*, and *The Victorian City*. She is senior research fellow at the University of Buckingham, as well as a frequent contributor to the *Times Literary Supplement* and the *Wall Street Journal*.